"Loren Weisman has "nailed it!" with his new book. What an insight to the "Business of Music!"...Every up and coming Artist should read this book. It is THE guide to follow in this ever changing world of the Music business."

"JC" Johnny Conga - Gloria Gaynor, Jackson 5, Gloria Estefan, Mongo Santamaria and Volcano Percussion Artist.

"Loren has proven over many years he is adept at both the business side of the music world, as well as the hands-on creative side. Beyond simple me-to ventures and solutions, he is always trying new things as the industry and technology changes. This wide-reaching approach to the business of music always results in interesting things happening to those he mentors, those he works with, and those with whom he shares wisdom with or absorbs advice from. He listens, he learns, he does. His extra mile is often another mile beyond what most do. An artist at any point in his or her journey can't help but learn from Weisman's treatise on success."

Christopher Laird Simmons
CEO, Neotrope(R) Entertainment

"Bands could spend years learning industry protocol the hard way. I read through Loren's work and can't find anything I disagree with. Very realistic and grounded."

B.King, Goldtone Artist Development/Management.

"Loren Weisman is the Anthony Bourdain of Music."

Marie Mersinger, Mersinger Theatrical Services

"Loren has some of the bravest ideas going in this tough industry."

Trey Gunn, King Crimson

"This book is jam-packed with GREAT tips ... some very 'common sense' stuff and lots of things that would only be known by one who has been there. Nothing can absolutely guarantee success ... in music or anything else ... but Loren has provided an excellent roadmap that can surely improve the odds!"

Pat Brown, Director of Sales Worldwide and
former Director of Artist Relations Pro-Mark Corporation

"Loren Weisman has written a musician's guide to our galaxy with humor and blushworthy familiarity. He mixes sober advice with a cocktail of experience. If you can put the book down, you will think "I'd love to meet that guy.""

Patti Rothberg

"This comprehensive guide gives musicians a leg up in tackling the many obstacles along the road to music industry success. Loren's practical advice comes from his own real-life experiences, and in *The Artist's Guide to Success in the Music Business* he generously shares his ideas and opinions to help artists think outside the norm."

Steve Beck - Online Rock

"Weisman calls it the way he sees it. This book is full of practical, no-nonsense advice from start to finish. It is definitely a good guide for anyone venturing into the wilderness that is today's music business."

Max Cohen

"Loren Weisman cares enough about your career in music to be honest, truthful and straight up with you. This book will not only provide you with ideas to grow as a professional musician, but as a mature adult as well."

Dave Hayes

"Loren Weisman's book is, in a word, comprehensive. It is an impressive book chock full of practical advice for musicians interested in being successful in the music business. His book, *The Artist's Guide to Success in the Music Business*, covers every aspect of what emerging artists need to know. Although it pertains to younger musicians primarily, older musicians can benefit from the information and frank discussions in this book.

Every chapter has practical and theoretical advice with checklists for daily actions to take. Loren Weisman stresses the need for marketing, networking and promotion without ignoring musical issues like practicing songwriting, recording, set lists, playing gigs, personal presentation etc. He emphasizes personal responsibility, interpersonal skills and being respectful in the pursuit of career goals.

Organization, orderliness and efficiency of action are emphasized in the book. Creative artists are not necessarily the most organized and motivated people and this book gives strong directions about how to accomplish tasks. Mr. Weisman also gives advice about avoiding self-defeating behaviors and identifying bad advice. To his great credit he also does not hesitate to recommend other resources to the reader.

Loren Weisman speaks from experience and with authority. In his own business he practices what he preaches. He's had a fair amount of success in the music business himself and with this book he is liable to have more. My own experiences with him in the recording studio have been completely positive because of his respectful, good attitude and his organizational and musical skills. He is a true professional and is capable of helping others along in their careers."

Murl Allen Sanders - Chuck Berry, Etta James, Lee Oskar,
Leslie Gore, Glenn Yarbrough.

THE ARTIST'S GUIDE TO SUCCESS IN THE MUSIC BUSINESS

Loren Weisman

BOOK PUBLISHERS NETWORK

Book Publishers Network
P.O. Box 2256
Bothell • WA • 98041
PH • 425-483-3040
www.bookpublishersnetwork.com

Author's Note: Some of the events described happened as related; others were changed. Some of the individuals/companies portrayed are composites of more than one person or music organization, and many names and identifying characteristics have been altered or removed.

Printed in the United States of America
First Edition: March 2010
10 9 8 7 6 5 4 3 2 1
For information, address Jenée Arthur at Rellihan Satterlee
3511 SW Henderson Street, Seattle, Washington 98126

www.rellihansatterlee.com
www.artistsguide.net
www.braingrenademusic.com

LCCN 2010903762
ISBN10 1-935359-33-9
ISBN13 978-1-935359-33-3

Copy editor: Julie Scandora
Typographer: Stephanie Martindale

In Memory of Arnie and Jeanne Weisman

For Alicia

It is going to be a harder road than you thought, and short-cutting, half-assing, and second-guessing will only hurt your career in the end.

Step Out,

Step Up,

and Step Forward.

If you can't take those three steps, you don't belong in today's music business.

- Loren Weisman

CONTENTS

FOREWORD

Music! Yes, music… that entity that can calm the heart of the savage beast, or calm the psyche of a sixth grade teacher before the arrival of his students. *Spyro Gyra, Roy Ayers, Earth Wind and Fire, Modern Jazz Quartet or* a host of others were all a part of my preschool ritual that included preparing for the day's lessons. Watering the plants, duplicating student activities, and setting up the class weather station were also a part of the ritual as well. There was and is to this day a blessing in being able to listen to music allowing it to integrate its fortifying nature to strengthen a classroom warrior!

Enter one student, Loren Weisman, a quiet introspective young sixth grader who came before school with his cello. Carrying a cello onto a school bus is not recommended. So, Loren has arrived early. He immediately connected, or at least tried to make the connection, with whatever music came out of the cassette player. (That was a long time ago.) Sorry, Loren! We began as a student and teacher learning about music and all the academic rigors a sixth grader needed. We have become friends whose love of music was just one of the binding factors of the relationship! Loren would sit a listen and ask many questions about the history of the music. He would begin to comment on the nuances of the music. All forms of music were the basis for these conversations. There was a serious tone that told me that Loren was doing some kind of research.

Subsequent years were marked by visits to school and to my home where the conversations would eventually turn to music. Loren put down the cello and began his work as a drummer. He was more than a drummer. His conversations would always turn to his love of music and the desire to help the "sound reach everyone who cared to listen". Music was truly a driving force and a way of life for him. Experiences in recording studios, on the road, with famous and not so famous musicians somehow helped him galvanize his vision. Whether they were good or bad experiences Loren managed to find the "silver lining".

He shared his hopes and dreams all born from his love of "the music". The diversity and depth of his ideas have always fascinated me. He never wanted to take the journey alone. In sharing these ideas, Loren wanted a community of "music lovers" to be a part of his adventure. He saw himself as an aide to get the music to the people. He was talking about many facets of the industry. Loren's road has not always been smooth, yet his passion and love for the music and the people who make the music have always seemed to sustain him!

The book represents his vision and pragmatic ways to help others create, produce and share their creativity and passion for music. I applaud the effort, his knowledge, and the willingness to share in such a useful way. Such is the way with music. A song should be sung and then shared with all who want to be touched by it (whether they know it or not). Loren has my admiration and hope for his continuing vision.

Roger Wallace
Loren's 6th Grade Teacher
Fort River Elementary School

ACKNOWLEDGEMENTS/ THANKS

Scott Ross, Peter Fernandez, Kurt Hilborn, Chris Dee, Julie Scandora, Sheryn Hara, Laura Zandstra, Marian Li-Pino, Peter, Kelleher, Jenée Arthur, Alicia McBarron, Bean, Corrine Bonneau, Dave Stoup, Jana Pelinga, Hank Hollman, Darlin Gray, Eliza Grinnell, Mike Sinkula, Cherie Becker Cormier, Alyssa Horn, Christine Constantini, Tony Ober, Trey Gunn, Jaisen Buccellato, John Ramsay, Melinda Shaw, Richard Gordon, Rosemary Caine, Roger Wallace, Andrew Larson, Pat Brown, Marilyn Tomlin, Peter Levy ...

Pam & Peter Hoagland, Roger Weisman, Rodney Kunath, Jeanne & Arnie Weisman, Terry, Karen and the McBarron and Crowder families ...

Christopher Simmons, Rusty Annis, Mark Alan Miller, Max Cohen, Dea Shandera, John Moroney, Jason Atteberry, Rich Gantner, Steve Wilkes, Dave Weigert, Dony Wynn, Gary Chaffee, Jerry Marotta, Chris Sweet, Emery Smith, Dave Hayes, Marcus Tellefson, Pat Boltz, Justin Nisly, Dan Magden, Melissa Unger, Glenn Huntoon, Mareatha Bowen, Dainis Kaulenas, Billy Ward, Café Ladro, El Diablo Coffee Company, The Five Spot, Sully's, and Sport ...

Thank you all,

LW

Note to the Reader from Loren

The main intention behind my work is to get you, the musician, to recognize that you must become a synergistic mix of artist and businessperson.

It is crucial that you blend your creativity and art with the hunger and discipline of a businessperson. Your willingness to learn these new methods of achieving success within this ever-changing and developing industry will determine whether you will have a sustainable career or one of failure that mirrors far too many musicians in today's industry. That is simply the truth.

I will show you the most effective steps to success in both large and small ways. You will create your music, build your business, and understand the organizational and marketing skills required to succeed.

It is one of my greatest pleasures to provide my insight and industry experience to musicians of all genres. I am confident that my full-spectrum approach and the unique avenues I share with you will contribute phenomenally to your success. My best wishes to you on your journey.

Loren

INTRODUCTION

This is not the end-all-be-all answer book for success in music. It's not the secret to the music industry. I have not paved the yellow brick road to success in the music business.

But this book *is* a map, a set of blueprints, a layout, a business plan.

The Artist's Guide to Success in the Music Business is a detailed analysis of the subjects that all musicians should understand and apply in order to pursue a successful and sustainable career in music. Full of ideas and practical advice, this book provides comprehensive detail on how to optimize success and achieve sustainability and self-empowerment in today's music business. From production and performance to marketing and career-building, this book instructs artists on how to take the hard-earned lessons of a fellow musician and put them to work in their own careers.

Few books currently provide both the spectrum of information needed by someone just starting out in the music business as well as a window onto the complex facets of the industry faced by seasoned professionals.

My advice is both inside and outside the box. It's not an ego-driven rant, but a delivery system of information and insight gathered throughout my career, which has spanned almost two decades of unprecedented change in the music industry. It is the kind of book that will be found in practice spaces, in instrument cases, in recording studios, and on the bedside table. This is not a reference book to be read on rare occasions but a guide to be constantly consulted. Every miniscule detail is not addressed, but the broad spectrum of ideas, applications, and methods is laid out in a solid blueprint form.

It delivers ideas on how to communicate with everyone from your band mates to people in the industry. It will make you consider whose advice you are listening to and what you can take away from every person you come across and every book you read, as well as what you should leave behind. It will make you question what you want, what you *can* do and what you need to do today, next week, next month, and next year.

That said, the book does not draw or create an exact approach because there is no one exact approach to success in the music business. What rings true for you in these pages? What bad habits can you get rid of, and what good ones can you build on? It's the artists' responsibility to learn and analyze the industry and, from there, to organize the ideas presented here into a plan that they will execute on their own for themselves.

This book will be a reference point. It won't carry you. It's not the answer to success in the music business. But it will guide you to the explosive ideas, methods, and applications for artist production, empowerment, and sustainability in today's music industry, and how you can make them work for you and your career.

In the end, it's up to you.

THE INDUSTRY AND YOU

The misconceptions about the music industry and how to make it in music are loud and constant. The industry itself assists in generating rumors of that one artist who breaks through and has an amazing career from out of the blue.

From what is said on reality shows, in interviews, and stories, the road to success is a fairy tale. Unfortunately a very, very small percentage of artists gets to experience that fairy tale path, and those who do very often come to realize the illusion that fairy tale truly represents.

Think of a band you know that was playing small rooms, with each member holding a basic day job and living check to check. They practiced, recorded, struggled, and played everywhere they could. All of a sudden they come out on this amazing album. Then you start to see them in nicer cars and spending more money. That should raise a couple of red flags. When a larger scale record company spends a fortune on the recording of an album and gives the band new things, such as cars, clothes, and money, it is doing it as incentive. What the bands don't recognize is that the record company wants all that money back, and with interest. The record labels are a business, and they use artists' dreams as a way to lock musicians into deals that have crazy percentages. All the bands see is the light at the end of the tunnel. They see the ability to quit jobs, play all the time, and live the superstar lifestyle. What they don't see is that the light can often be a train coming at them with a terrible contract that will own and control their choices for years to come.

Many of these artists sign the dotted line and do not read the contract. They hear the hype, and it blinds them from the reality and length of the contract. Words and phrases buried in these contracts can restrict the artist from making choices that everyone would assume would be theirs to make. Examples include what you can and cannot say on camera, what you can and cannot do, where you can and cannot go. Some of these contracts put artists into servitude, if not basic slavery. Those cool new logos, the bios, and the merchandise are created by other people, and sometimes, basic merchandise profits are not given to the band. Artists on all levels can be badly hurt by the deals they sign. The reason it doesn't seem like it with the larger artists is because even the small percentages that go to the artist are more than most could imagine. Regardless, they are often stuffed with requirements to record a certain number of albums, do a certain number of performances, and be under binding agreements for years and years.

Even deals that the smaller labels make can hurt the artists. Sometimes bands are signed into deals that will make them less attractive to larger labels and managers. Many small labels will incorporate percentages into contracts beyond the work that they do. This can include long-term publishing deals, royalties, and other percentages. The goal for these labels is to continue to get a piece of the artists if they go big, but many of these artists will not get better or larger deals because larger labels and managers don't want to deal with the hassle.

All this information, along with everything else that's happening in the industry, is why I push so hard for artists to look to a business side of things as they go ahead into the creative world. Learn the industry. Work to understand the loopholes, and if it seems too good to be true, especially in the music industry, you can pretty much bet that it is.

I'm not saying to turn down every deal but read the contracts and take the time to learn what you don't know. If something is unclear, don't ask the guy trying to get you to sign. Get a lawyer to review and explain it for you. Talk to a disinterested third party, someone who is not tied to the contract in any way. Don't ask for a lawyer from the label or manager that's handing you the contract.

Look to a realistic career and not just number-one hits and playing for thousands of people. Think about the spectrum of sales that are possible.

Look to creating as much as you can by yourself so you can bring more to the table and not have to have labels, managers, and agents take away from what is yours and take you in a direction you don't want to go.

Look to the possibilities of licensing your songs to movies, television, commercials, video games, corporate videos, and news reels.

Look to how you can license your songs to other performers, or even hire performers in other countries to sing your song in other languages.

Look with a set of eyes that can believe in the fairy tales, but aim for the real dreams that can happen—the dreams where you can achieve self-sustaining, long-term success and give away as little in percentages to others as you can.

Make that light at the end of the tunnel a real light and not an oncoming train carrying awful deals, long-term percentage loss and commitments that bind you for years to come.

If It Were Easy ...

I'm not sure how many musicians out there have noticed that working in the music industry is not easy. You know, all that practicing, creation of music, then playing it out. But that's the fun stuff, right? That's all you want to do. That's what it's all about, right?

Wrong.

All the marketing, promoting, attention to detail, the problem solving, the failures, the losses, the pain, the strife ... Damn, I sound like a Cure song.

You get the point. It's challenging. It's even more challenging when you are closed-minded or stubborn and don't do the things that you have to. I wish it were all about the music. I wish there didn't have to be any business in the middle of it. I would love it if you didn't have to deal with the politics and outside issues that take time away from your art, but it's a part of the equation of your success.

It's hard. It's hard as hell. If it were easy, everyone would do it.

The point is to stop looking for the easy way out. It's going to be challenging. It will take a longer time to do it if you're doing it the right way, and—you'll love this—even when you *are* doing it the right way, it's still going to be a real bitch and a lot of hard work.

So, what's the secret? There isn't one. The bands you've heard about that just magically made it or were seen by the right person and signed all have their horror stories as well. They're just not publicized. I'm not trying to be a conspiracy theorist, but the industry as a whole wants to have musicians believe all you have to do is buy the right gear, play out, and you'll be seen and taken care of.

Many companies thrive off musicians failing more so than they do on ones succeeding. I know someone's going to give me crap about that statement, but when you look at patterns and sales, it kind of rings true.

So, back to the answer …

You're not going to want to hear it, but here it is: If you want the dream, it's obtainable, but you have to work your ass off to get it. It means taking stock of the time you spend each day and how effectively you're spending it.

Can you cut back thirty minutes on your video games to do thirty more minutes of marketing? Can you miss a TV show and spend those thirty minutes practicing? Can you find five minutes here and there to pop up a blog, market your band online, or work on finding a new venue or another band to work with?

The point is that sometimes doing a little each day will get a lot more done over a longer period of time. The consistency, especially in advertising, marketing, or promotion, of small daily segments, can actually be more effective than just a one-time numerous-hours blast. Then when the days come, in which you do have hours to put into a given project, you'll be even more productive and see continuity as well as growth.

The little elements can work for you just as much as the big ones can. Mostly, though, the Secret, if there was one, is continuity, commitment, learning, and patience. Stay true to your dream, but go out and learn all the elements of what you're doing and what you have to do. Take the steps each day and don't short cut. It will be the hardest thing you ever do, but if you do it—all of it, every element and every step—you will find success.

If you haven't found that success, take stock and analyze what you're doing and what you aren't doing, and alter the game plan. More often than not, something is not being done. I talk to so many musicians who say they're doing everything they are supposed to be doing, and then when I bring up a laundry list of approaches, they haven't touched one of them.

The industry is in a new place. There are countless avenues and possible approaches that can help artists find self-sustainable and self-sufficient success. I'm not talking about becoming a millionaire; I'm talking about paying the bills, taking care of basic needs, having basic insurance, and maybe even having a little left to put away. That's a realistic approach to the industry, considering the magnitude of changes that have occurred in the past twenty years.

Today a musician has to learn to be the businessman or woman as well. It's crucial to have an understanding of marketing because these days it's necessary to put in as much time promoting your songs and your band as you do practicing your music. Anything short of this, more than likely, is not going to work.

The labels are still out there, and people do get signed to deals. Even the super marketing dogs that get picked up by either a label or management can get the opportunity to get back to a place where it's all about the music, or at least as far as you can see. It's a common misunderstanding that if you get picked up you will have marketing people and promotion people and agents to do that busy work for you. While it's half-true that many of the larger scale acts get promotional teams with large budgets, the artists are still promoting.

Go ask someone like Jason Mraz. You know the guy who had that hit with Remedy back in 2002. He's on a major label and touring non-stop, playing to large audiences all over the world. Rumor is Jason spends three-quarters of his day on phone interviews, magazine interviews, radio or TV promos, and all sorts of other marketing-type events so that he can play for, at max, an hour or two a day. Even the large-scale, higher echelon artists have to market and promote. It can't be all about the music all the time. The only difference is that a team is there to set up each marketing or promotional event that Jason has, while the independent artist needs to search out each marketing and promotional opportunity every day.

I'm not trying to say put the music second—no way. The music, of course, is first. You need to craft the tunes, practice the tunes, prepare the tunes, and make sure that you write new tunes as you continue to mold the old ones. The music, in the end, is the final result, but the thing that artists need to be much, much, much, much (did I say much?) more aware of is that it's the marketing and promoting that will bring your audience to the music.

There's no way around it right now; whether you score the deal or not, you're going to have to be assertive, you're going to have to work harder than you might have thought, and you're going to have to take a lot of punches along the way. Is it worth it to you? If it is, then make it happen.

It is this way in life. When you talk to someone, whether it's a manager, a club owner, a band member, a potential label, or whoever, speak real. So many people don't say what they are thinking these days, and it drives me insane. Be assertive. You don't have to be an asshole, but you can be confident and stand by your opinion. Be open to hearing someone else's, but step up and stand up.

If you need to say no, say no. If you need to say stop, say stop. If you need to address an issue, then bring it up. Stop being passive, stop complaining, stop holding onto things, and start stepping up. Use that negative energy to fuel your dream and bring you to where you want to be instead of bitching about why you aren't there.

If you know you should be doing something ... DO IT!!!! One of the things that blows my mind the most is when I work with clients and they learn an element and apply it while I am working with them, then after they're done with a production or consult, they revert back to the ways that were not working before and then they find themselves being ineffective. I'm not saying don't adapt, embellish, and make things your own as you learn, but if something is working, why stop?

By the same token, if something isn't working, don't keep doing it over and over and over again. Take tabs of where you're at. Have you been playing the same room to the same crowd size for over a year? That's not forward motion. Take the problem-solving approach to continue to move forward in all aspects of your career. Are sales stagnant?

What steps should you take to increase them? Figure out what you were doing when your sales were better. Where can you look for new fans, and how can you find new markets in which to sell?

It takes an assertive set of ideals to be truly successful, and it takes humility to realize when things have to change. Apply those aspects, step up, and achieve the dream. If you say you're going to do something, do it. If you say you're going to call someone, call the person. If you want to try a different approach and you have new ideas, test them. Take the steps in music, and in life, to be true to yourself, to others, and to your dreams. It's either step up or shut up.

I hope you choose the former.

The Drive to Succeed

Inside all the elements that lead to success, from the considerations of the music to marketing, promotion, and networking, you have to have drive. That drive has to be constant; it's something you cannot give up on. You have to maintain it through the periods of your greatest doubt. When things are going slowly or not the way you want them to, you need to persevere and continue on towards your goal. When things are looking up and moving in the direction you want, you still need to keep that same level of drive. It's not an option; it's a requirement if you want to make it in this business or any other business.

I'm very proud of the FSRP system. The Freedom Solutions Recording Plan that I've set up, with the help of colleagues and my own life experiences, has allowed me to outline a game plan for artists. It includes every step from the pre-production and the funding to the release, marketing, and solicitation. The FSRP covers it all, except for one part—the drive, the desire, the determination, the persistence, and the attention to detail. These are the true core elements to your success. Period. These pieces apply to every element of what you have to do to achieve what you want.

The FSRP, or for that matter, any plan that's implemented to bring an artist to success, requires that these elements be brought to the table by the artist. They must be used in all the stages with the same intensity. The most common mistakes happen when the artists lighten up. They've worked really hard to get their dream recording and all the materials in place; then the "sit back and wait" mentality begins to creep in. What the artists need to do is take the exact same work ethic that helped them create the recording and bring it to all the other elements of post-production, marketing, and branding. If artists apply the same efforts to every stage, they will succeed.

You can succeed. I'm not talking about some type of self-help, inspirational book or tape. I'm talking about what's inside you and knowing how badly you want it.

When you were little and you decided you wanted to walk, you didn't jump out of the crib and all of a sudden start walking. You stumbled, made mistakes, grew stronger, learned what worked and what didn't. Each day you got a little further. You were able to do things you weren't able to do the day before, and you were proud of your achievements.

One of the amazing things about us when young is that we don't know failure. We could dream of achieving anything and everything we set our hearts on. It was all possible. Over time we learned limits and boundaries, and a lot of them were smart ones. I learned very quickly and painfully that the stove was hot and I should not touch it. Other elements—failure, fear of failure, fear of trying—were instilled later. Sometimes I think these elements of failure mix us up inside, and maybe that's where fear of success comes from.

The persistence and the ongoing effort are what can define your success and your path toward your dream. Deciding that one thing is less important than another can hurt the final result. So take the drive that's inside, that maybe you've forgotten about, and apply it. Get out of your comfort zone. If you have a hard time fundraising, getting the investors or working on elements of pre-production, take the small daily steps in marketing and promotion on the backside. Push yourself.

Push toward the dream and push toward the goal. Don't make room for failure. Take the steps needed, both small and large, with every element and in every stage, and you will achieve success. You might not become a millionaire, you might not play to fifty-thousand people or sell two million copies, but you will find success.

Take away your fear of failure, take away your fear of success, and jump into that uncomfortable place—that place where you stumbled as a baby when you first learned how to walk or where you fell over when you first learned to ride a bike. It's exactly the same thing.

The drive. The desire. The determination. The persistence. The attention to detail.

These elements will bring you through the challenges and uncomfortable places on your way to your dream. Bring the same effort to each aspect and every benchmark no matter how hard, no matter how you fail at first, and no matter how you might doubt yourself.

If you do this, you will succeed.

Do You Think You're Worth the Investment?

For some very strange and unexplained reason, it seems that bands still have this mindset—or maybe it should be called a pipe dream—that as soon as they're heard by the right person, they'll win the record deal and move onward and upward to million-dollar success, fame and fortune. Of course those inexpensive demos will showcase the amazing ability of these artists and automatically make labels and investors want to lay down tons of cash for this new act that will be going worldwide in an instant.

In a perfect universe, maybe there's a chance, but in the real world the likelihood grows slimmer each day. Labels are going bankrupt or combining forces with other labels, and there are fewer investments more risky than backing a musical act. Industry people know: Money doesn't automatically mean success, but it can be a big part of its foundation. So why are you worth a label's cash?

I hate to be rude, but your sound is not new, you are not about to change the face of music, and you are not going to see a million dollars in the next month. Those who tell you that have to make sure they tailor their cuffs extra wide since they'll have a lot of problems up their sleeves, which they'll take out on you.

Tens of thousands of bands filled with delusions of grandeur are out there soliciting to labels with substandard demos, no marketing, no promotion plans, and piss-poor organization. These artists seem to hold the expectation that they're worth all the money they expect to receive or have invested in them, and yet those very few who get the money and services needed get pissy about having to pay back all the money *with* the percentage and can't seem to understand why it's taking so long for them to see any profit.

With the economy where it stands, the record deals are much fewer and further between. It's no longer about finding a label that will support and stand by you with a large investment. It's about how you can be worth the investment to a label.

First off, forget the studio recording. Don't try to shop half-ass demos or poorly recorded songs. You may be showcasing your song and your talent, but you're also showcasing that it's going to take a greater investment to record the song or songs the right way. The studio is a major expense with all the line items around the room, the engineer, the producer, the food, rental gear, travel, lodging, and so on. The studio recording is also a risky investment for a label: It's money that has to be budgeted for a project in which many of the other elements are not in place. This album that they are potentially funding might never be released. So why should they take a chance?

Now as the artist, the band, or the talent, if you come to a record label with an industry-standard recording, you take away a great deal of fear as well as a great deal of necessary funding. Work to find the right studio with the right engineer and the right producer. Record the album with the consideration of submitting not a demo but a finished product that's ready for the industry. Don't short cut; if it takes a little longer to get together the money to record it the right way, then take the time that's needed. Apply that same time to the mix and the mastering. Do everything you can to make it the best product possible that's up to the industry standards.

Then, when you take your package to a label with an album that's ready to go and at the necessary level of quality, you're going to jump ahead of many other artists bringing in half-ass demos because you have something that's going to save the label money. And not only that: The more prepared you are for the industry when you bring your package and product to a label, the sooner money can be made for all parties. Remember to ask yourself how you're helping the label. Don't just sit in the mindset of what the label will do for you.

Now on that same line, if you have your logo, your basic branding, your image, and all the secondary elements that cover your marketing and promotion in place, it makes you all the more appealing to labels, managers, and agents. If you have worked to create a complete press package in which everything is uniform in appearance and content, as well as sharp and professional looking, you have just saved the label more money and brought them closer to making profit from you and with you.

Think again of all the bands that don't have the right product or quality recordings. Think of all the bands that don't have a font, a logo, or the tools to brand themselves. Think of the bands that don't have a tight bio, stage plots, and other artist-contract materials together. Think of the bands that haven't set up a strong fan base on their own or have little Web presence. These are all things that are absolutely necessary for the successful launch of a group that's looking to make money. If any of these elements are falling short, they need to be made up in both time and investment so that the group can be a financially viable entity. In other words, if you don't have any of these elements in place, you're going to need money, time, and a development period to get them to where they need to be. If you're expecting any label right now to invest money and time into such a band without either taking a very large percentage or being very hesitant, you are well mistaken.

If you come to a label with everything in place, then you can approach it in a very strong, original way by showcasing that you have everything in place to make money for the label and yourself sooner than most. If a label just has to invest in advertising, distribution, and tour support, then it's putting money into things that can see returns much faster. If it has to invest in development, recording, promotional layouts, logos, and branding, then it's investing in something that's further from profit and a lot more chancy.

Make it easier for yourself to be distributed, to be put on the road, and to move product and merchandise. In turn, you become less of a risk in a business that's taking fewer and fewer risks every day. If you want representation, a label, or to be signed, get your product and your package up to par and beyond; then go to the managers, the labels, and agents with the professional and prepared package that will make it fast and easy for them to get you out to the world.

I Have Serious Label Interest

This is not something you want to advertise even if it's true. Label interest is nothing to write home about or brag about on Facebook, MySpace, or your social networking sites, especially to people you want to impress or potential producers with whom you might be looking to work.

Most of the time when I hear or read that line, I move on. In the world of way too many labels and so many small labels that aren't working with the right people, it's better to say nothing until you actually have serious label interest.

Even larger labels are victims of liars and people who claim to work with them when they actually do not. I've heard artists tell me about how they're signing with Warner Brothers with a contact that has nothing to do with Warner or any of its affiliates.

Many of the scouts who are real or work with certain labels don't have the rights or the jurisdiction to sign or promise anything. It comes down to a deal that's on paper. Anything before a signed contract is only talk, and those who talk too much end up looking suspect and fake.

It doesn't look any better when artists are talking about their serious label interest from a number of labels and don't have anything together, or when they're asking for help beyond a proposal or final solicitation package for representation, management, or label signing.

The point is to display with actions, not words. Even if you have label interest and are on the cusp of signing a deal, keep your mouth shut. It looks classier, more professional, and a lot more impressive when things you say happen and continue to go in the direction of productive growth.

Impress with your actions. Keep the lips zipped and talk about the stuff that is locked in place because the rest of it is always up in the air, especially in the entertainment fields.

Opinions on Opinions: Who to Listen To

In the music business there are a lot of avenues that offer advice, consulting, counseling, ideas, expertise, and everything in between. It's always good to research where you are getting the "help" from, but it's also important to define what you're looking for and if you're receiving information that's relevant to those questions that you have.

Just because someone had a record deal doesn't mean that he or she fully understands the industry, though that person will likely be able to give you a wealth of knowledge about that record company. Today in the world of so many different blogs (yes, I am guilty of adding yet another music blog to the mix,) magazines, books, and Web sites, it's very important to know from whom you are getting your information.

A very common issue with a lot of music business courses, and some music consulting firms, is that the information you're getting is dated and not as applicable as it once was. It's not to say that these people weren't pros in the field at some point, but just as a lawyer has to keep up with laws that constantly change and adapt, so do those in music. The past couple of years alone have brought major changes in the industry.

When you talk to people, especially if you're going to pay them, find out as much as you can about them. What's their current and past experience? How varied is it? Many people talk about being around the industry but have never actually been a part of it. This is not to say that you can't study the industry and subsequently have a good sense of it, but personally, I would rather collect my information from someone who has been knee-deep in it.

What were some of the successes and the failures of this person? Remember, someone who has had nothing but success, which is a rarity, may have had some really good deals and an impressive résumé but may not have the understanding or problem-solving skills to help you through rough patches. Those who have failed as much as they have succeeded will often have a much wider view, which can be incredibly helpful.

Watch out for "promises" or phrases like "trust me." Be wary when you're given guarantees or you're told how big you'll be and how far you'll go.

When people give you their opinion or their information, ask them what it's based on. Make sure your questions are answered and that you have a clear understanding of what was said. This will help you a lot.

I always tell artists I produce that I make no promises or guarantees. I don't tell people to trust me; actions and repetitive experiences between the client and me show that trust can be created. I was never with a single label or company as either a drummer or producer. I was a hired gun, and I jumped around quite a bit. I took the experiences of my work and have come up with the information that I share based on that—both the failures and the things I did wrong in my career, as well as the successes that I've had.

Remember, it's not about trying to find one person, one book, or one site. You can find numerous people to help you, and there are many places to find solid information. Just be picky. Find out who is saying it or writing it, where the person comes from, and what his or her beliefs and approaches are. This will help you build a much stronger resource list.

Anyone can tell you anything, and it's great to reflect on what you hear and always be respectful to someone offering advice. However, it takes a mature and patient mind to navigate through the information that's given and find the best road possible.

It's You Vs. the Industry

Go to any musician's hangout, whether it's a practice building, a bar, a club, or a music store, give it a little time, and you'll eventually hear a rant about the music industry. People will inevitably start to talk about why they aren't where they want to be. They have every reason for how the clubs, labels, booking agents, or some facet of the industry has messed up their career. They use this as justification for where they are at.

I don't mean this to be a dig—well, in a way, maybe I do—but you can blame all you want, you can fault the RIAA (Recording Industry Association of America), you can fault managers for shady deals, agents for screwing you over, publishing companies for not getting you your royalties, or the big names for taking away your deserved popularity. I have heard so much whining and moaning, and it's completely useless.

Complaining is a negative thing that gets you nowhere. Actions beget actions. The ones who bitch the most are the ones who will often stay in this pathetic holding pattern and go nowhere. These are the people who feel they deserve something from the music industry and are waiting for it to come up and knock on their door. Oftentimes these are the people who rip on other musicians and do a solid job of burning bridges in the process.

Let me tell you something: The music industry doesn't owe you anything; it was here long before you were. Publishing and licensing deals date back to the days when musicians were hired to write for kings and queens in the Middle Ages, and where do you fit into that? Nowhere. You want success, you want opportunity, you want to make money? Then make it happen through actions, not bitching.

The music industry is one of the hardest and dirtiest industries out there. Hell, at one point it was run by the mob. Doesn't that set quite the precedent?

One of my favorite quotes to sum up the industry is by Hunter Thompson:

> *The music business is a cruel and shallow trench, a long plastic hallway where thieves and pimps run free, and good men lie like dogs. There is also a negative side.*

This is so true. So Earth to the negative people, Earth to the bitchers, whiners, complainers, and blamers … that is what it is, but it's also one of the most incredible industries in the world.

I've been a part of numerous tours, recordings, bands, sessions, substitutions, and productions. I've cried, I've practically killed myself from exhaustion and overworking, and I've had the time of my life. I love music. I love what I do and do what I love. There is a terrible and very broken aspect to things, but I've never let it deter me or move me from being a musician. I've wanted to quit, but I couldn't. I know what it's like to live the five-star tours just as I know what it's like to be shoved into a very small van with five very large people for a very long time. I wouldn't trade any of it for the world. I've made a great deals of money and lost a fortune as well. I've played for thousands upon thousands and played for a single pissed-off bartender who wanted us just to go home. It's been a spectrum of love and hate, anger and joy, frustration and pure fun.

I will say it again: I love what I do and do what I love regardless of the pain at times. I would take the pain to get the joy I have received.

That being said, and this is not a bitch fest, but it's true, the music industry is pretty messed up. There are some really screwy, fraudulent things that happen to artists every single day. Some labels do sign artists to awful deals. Some managers do rip off artists. Some publishers do take way too much from artists. Some producers do wrong by their clients, and some booking agents do take advantage of bands. But for all you can bitch about, there are also labels, managers, agents, and bookers that are doing it right and taking care of the artists. These are the people who take action and move things forward instead putting out a stagnant, go-nowhere attitude.

When you bitch, complain, and whine about it—well, it actually doesn't do anything. Being negative doesn't make change in the industry nor does it help you or your career. Make a difference; educate yourself. Read the contracts that you get, and have a professional read them as well so you don't sign a deal that will allow someone to take advantage of you. Learn about the problems in the industry and how some people ran into them so you don't make that same mistakes yourself.

Advocate change by effecting change. I was annoyed with how independent artists were being messed with and screwed over. They were not being protected, so I created my first music production company. That was my action to try to make a change in the industry.

No single one of us can change the industry alone, but each of us can take small steps, which together, can amount to big ones. So shut up with the whining or—honestly—give up. The music industry is not for you. It's hard, and a lot is stacked against you. Working your tail off to take the right steps, learning from your own and other people's mistakes, and working together to give yourself and others a fighting chance is the best forward motion you can take.

Next time you are ready to complain, move that energy and effort to fire you up to make change, take action, and push yourself even harder to succeed. Keep whatever you were about to complain about what it should be: a small speed bump. That attitude has worked for me and many others. It's OK to be pissed off with how elements of the music industry treat musicians, but if you harness that energy into positive actions, you will create positive reactions.

One of my inspirations once told me when I wanted to quit....
"Buck up, Binky; it's worth it, and it's a hell of a ride."
And you know what? ... He was right.

Take It with a Grain of Salt

We all wish that everyone would love, appreciate, and understand our art, our ideas, and basically, us. It would be so much easier if each could just "get it." And there's no reason at all for people to cruelly bash others or go on the attack, and yet it happens all the time. Every day someone deals a harsh word, a negative opinion, an insult. Now, it's true that opinions differ and no one is going to like everyone and everything. Still, for some reason, while each of us can have very strong opinions about others, we often get hurt or offended when someone has strong opinions about us.

First, Grow a Pair

You have to learn to take it. You have to learn to brush it off but also see when it might actually be constructive criticism or have a seed of actual honesty. When we hear bad things about ourselves, especially relating to things we feel good about, the natural reaction is to go on the defensive. But take a step back and take a breath. Before you go on a counter-offensive, take a look at what has been said or written and see if it is something you should consider.

On the other hand, there are people who are just going to be brutal. They are going to tear into you, and really, do the reasons matter? Why justify it as jealousy or a personal grudge? It doesn't really matter. Let go of it.

I have been writing a blog for almost two years. At least once a week, I post an entry that contains the ideas and approaches I've developed from firsthand experience in the music business. Without a doubt, my opinions are different from others, but I don't think I've ever been completely off in any of the articles I've written. Ask some of my readers, however, who have both publicly and privately sent scathing comments, harsh e-mails, and called me every name in the book, and you would get a different story. They accuse me of being a hack, a scam artist, and someone who doesn't have a clue about the music industry. Hell, I got one guy who says my writing pisses him off more and more each week. (Side note: *Stop reading.* I don't intentionally want to upset people, but I'm not going to stop, and I'm not going to cater to you, so skip my blog. Easy enough right?) But for all the rude comments, I get many more that are kind and wonderfully supportive, so I keep on trucking. It can hurt sometimes, but when it's more good than bad, it's better just to let the bad go.

I was walking downtown in Seattle, and a guy actually shouted from across the street that my articles are retarded. I kind of felt like a rock star in that moment. He hates my stuff so much yet continues to read it and even knows what I look like. It didn't phase me at all. And instead of giving him the reaction he might have been looking for, I bowed, thanked him, and said the next article would be out Monday morning. But the point is take a moment to consider. If it isn't something constructive and it isn't something you want to change, whether it's your writing, your music, or anything else, then take it with a grain of salt and let it go.

Literally let it go. I know I've repeated that a few times, but it needs to be done. Don't get into the habit of responding to these people. If you're getting genuine questions, that's one thing, but if someone says you suck, your song sucks, your picture sucks or whatever, let it be. I used to erase the negative comments, but now, more often than not, I just leave them up. They are others' opinions, and it's their right to say what they want. Responding is only going to light a fire for them to attack you more. The more you react, the more you set them up to bother you more. You let them under your skin, and by responding, you just give them the power to crawl around more.

Every time I have responded to someone being negative, the person has only become more of a jerk. When I don't waste the time or the effort, he or she usually goes away or bothers me less frequently.

Wasted Energy

Regardless of your job, what you create, and what you want, people are a little more tired these days. Energy levels are down, and we need to be at 100 percent to get what we want and have the endurance and energy to continue to go after it. Worrying about the people who are being negative or giving you crap takes away from the effort you can put toward what you want and bringing it to the people who are actually appreciative of it. Don't waste your energy on the negative few.

And though I hate to say it, it may only get worse as you gain popularity. The more reads I get on my blog, the more kind comments have come my way, but at the same time, the number of rude and harsh ones has jumped as well. The more you play out, the more you are heard, the more you get your music out there, your writings, your image, and yourself, the more people there will be to tear you a new one. The more people who will give you crap, the more people who will mock you, tease you, attack you, and all around try to piss you off.

Take it with a grain of salt; let it roll off your back. Move forward in confidence and assertiveness and create what you want to create. That power will allow you to reach many more people than playing scared, responding to every bad comment, or getting into it with every person who doesn't like you. Don't waste the time trying to turn a hater into a supporter. Spend your time going after as many people as you can to build a strong fan base that supports you.

Stay sensitive to your art but become less sensitive to criticism, or it will eat you alive. If you can't handle the scrutiny, you are going to have a rough go in any art or entertainment related business.

YOUR BAND

Many solo artists and bands don't think much beyond the music, and of course, the music alone can easily take up all their time. They think about the styles, the technical approach, songwriting, and the influences of everyone involved. Unfortunately, because these are often the primary points that are looked at, many bands and musicians get into numerous fights and arguments over just about anything and everything.

Finding those other musicians that are a musically strong and relatable fit is the first step, but what about the variance in personalities, communication, problem-solving, and sharing? These are elements that have to work just as well to keep a group running smoothly.

When you first connect with other artists, of course you'll find out about the musical elements—heck, that's what you're there for. But there's a lot more to the story. Way more. Consider your personality:

Are you the type that would do better in a band that is more of a dictatorship, i.e. a group that has a leader or two that run the show? A dictatorship is not always a bad thing. Some people feel more comfortable in bands where the major decisions are made by one person.

Or, maybe you prefer a democracy where all members of the band are even across the board. This takes a good core and good understanding between people and a lot of communication. This is also the harder route to go. Disagreements will come up more often when you have

21

numerous people whose opinions have equal weight. When it comes to a democracy, having band meetings where you discuss things as they happen are crucial. Planning and making decisions in advance about future moves, such as how you may go after a manager or label, record an album, or take any other action, can make things much easier as you are faced with those decisions.

You also need to think about the size of the band and the involvement of each member. Talk about the decisions, the votes, and the options of each member. Sometimes horn sections are a hired-gun part of a democratic band, while other bands decide to have everyone as an equal member. There is no template that is right or wrong; this really comes down to personality and what works best for the artist or group as a whole. Size matters—whether you are a trio or a fifteen-piece band with horns, you need to clarify what is going on and how you will work together in order to have a positive, productive, and effective group.

Now, what if you don't want to be in a democratic band and want the control of a band without sharing in small ways? Maybe you would be better suited as a solo artist. There is nothing wrong with being in a band *or* being a solo artist. There are pretty much the same number of pros and cons to both. If you really want the songs to be a certain way, if you really have a vision that you don't want to alter, solo may be the best way to go for you.

There are many options available. If you want to be more of a hired gun that doesn't take part in the major decisions, being the sideman might be for you. I worked as a hired gun and session player for many years and loved it. I didn't have to deal with band politics, artists' emotions, and annoying situations; I was just flat-out the drummer for hire. There are many that will call that whoring yourself out, or having commitment issues, but if it is what works for you, why not do it? I did not want to be involved as directly with artists, and by taking the hired-gun approach, it allowed me to be happiest in what I wanted to do and how I wanted to do it.

If you decide you want to be in a band, take the steps to clarify and communicate. Make sure that everyone is on the same page, and even as things may change or ideas may alter, make sure everyone is clear on what is going on. The better the communication and understanding, the less chance you will have of blow-ups on stage, group-ending disputes, and people not talking to each other as they are stuck on a long tour. Trust me; I have watched all of the above happen. All of the incidents that I watched through my career, or was involved in myself, came down to lack of clarification, misunderstandings, different expectations, and different desires. The music was often the only thing that was agreed on, though in many other situations, even that isn't agreed on. Being in a band is like being in a relationship with more than one person. Hell, being in a decent relationship with one person is hard enough; then add in your art and your passion mixed with opinions, egos, and stubbornness, and you can have a regular World War Three on your hands. Take the steps to find out the commonalities—as well as the differences—between people to be assured that your band can survive and thrive beyond the music. In the end, you will spend more time working on things such as marketing, traveling, eating, and going over business than you will working on the music, so you really need to know you can work and deal with these people outside of the music.

Putting the Band Together and Defining Your Dream

I have met a lot of artists and bands that have worked together for months, even years, and when I ask certain questions like, "Do you want to tour?" or "Would you prefer to stay local?" you would be surprised at how many different answers are given. You'd be even more surprised at the shock within the band when members look at each other in disbelief of each other's answers.

Just because you have a dream of what you want and how you want it to go, it does not mean that it is the same dream as others you are playing with. It is a smart and very helpful idea to have a band meeting or a talk about what everyone wants and what everyone is expecting. These meetings also should happen over and over again as time passes.

Where one member might have had a similar vision with you six months ago, it doesn't mean he or she does now. A girlfriend, job, kid on the way, house, or just burning out might switch that place where he or she was. So right off the bat, check in with everyone, see where people's heads are at, and make sure you are all on the same page. Sometimes when a band has been together for a long time, a deal falls through, or even when nothing seems to be on the horizon, attitudes and ideas can change. Staying on top of that will make life in the group, and life in general, much easier and help to avoid surprises and member changes.

Coming back to you, the individual … whether you are the solo artist, a member of a band, or the leader of a band, what is your dream and what do you want?

It seems like a simple question, and most people make assumptions even when it comes to themselves or the band as a whole, so take a step back and ask yourself: What do you want?

There are so many avenues and opportunities in music today, and the market is still growing. The chance to make a solid and self-sustainable living is better than ever. When I say solid and self-sustainable, I'm not talking about being a rock star, making millions, or for that matter, even playing in front of millions. I'm talking about all the different avenues out there that will allow you to do what you want on a realistic and financially secure level.

Do you want to tour? How long do you want to tour? Do you have a timeframe for how long you would like to be on the road? Would you rather teach? Do you hate traveling and prefer to play only locally? Would you rather do sessions? Would you rather run a studio? Do you really love songwriting, and if so, would you prefer to write songs, jingles, maybe soundtracks? If you think you will do it only for a while before calling it quits, how much time do you want to put in?

All these questions can help you find the answers that will help get you where you dream to be. It doesn't start with understanding the music business; it starts with understanding yourself. The clearer you are on your dreams, your goals, and your aspirations, from the best-case scenarios to just getting by, the better you'll understand what you have to learn and what direction you have to take.

Each step you take toward your own clarity will define the opportunities and approaches that you will need to take. These steps to your personal clarity may also help you know what to look for in other musicians beyond their playing. Take the time to figure out exactly what you want so you can find the direction, knowledge, and approach to go after it with nothing else in the way.

Hiring Musicians

Whether you are forming a band yourself, replacing someone, or adding a member, the first step in finding the right musician for your group, after the musicianship of course, is to make sure you all have a clear understanding of what you are looking for and what your expectations are. As you are looking for the right players, you have to make sure you are getting the right personalities as well. Are you a good fit? Do you have things in common outside of the music? Remember, even successful bands usually spend more time together at marketing events, on a bus or in a van, doing music business, marketing, and promotion. You will be stuck in hotels, back stage, and playing a lot of the waiting game very often. The thing you will actually do the least of in a given day with the other members when you are on the road is play music.

It's all about the music in the end, but if you can only play together and otherwise can't stand each other, then either it will be a short-lived relationship, or you will be hating life pretty quickly. Of course you are going to want to have a great feeling of playing together and jibe well in the creative, improvisational, and technical aspects, but you really are going to want to like the guys or girls you are playing with. These are people who should be like friends or coworkers who you have no problem living with. Make sure the dynamic is there.

Now on the music side of things—let's say you have the right personal traits and a good team, and you have a good vibe and sense of each other. If you are compatible in ability levels and have similar influences and skill set, you will be in good shape. If you are looking more to hire someone, you can up the bar, as you should. You want to have the strongest players possible supporting you and complementing your music to be able to bring it to the best level it can be.

Across the board, I would say go for a people who are well trained and well versed in styles. The more styles they know, the better they can supplement your sound with what you are looking for or maybe even better. Whether it is a bassist, a pianist, a horn player, a guitarist, any other instrumentalist, or a singer, make sure the person has good timing and can play to a click. Players that can read music can be incredibly helpful, allowing you to get ideas recorded faster and with the precision you are looking for. Musicians who can read and have a good sense of time, with the ability to play with a click, make for quality takes in the studio, getting you what you are looking for much faster You may pay a little more, but it will save you money in the end.

Make sure the professionalism is there apart from the instrument that they play. Players who are on time, not drunk when they play, call if they're going to be late, and are well organized make the difference and stand out above the rest.

If you are looking for a solid keyboardist, make sure the person knows piano too. Make sure he or she has both classical and jazz training. The classical background comes through in technique and theory, while those trained in jazz have a solid sense of improvisation and a better sense of how to voice chords.

This can ring true for bass players, guitarists, and singers as well. Depending on your style, it is not essential that everyone you hire be able to read note for note on a chart, but having the foundation and the background as well as the experience in different genres, styles, and ensemble or band types will make a big difference and add a lot of versatility to what you can musically accomplish.

Having the right gear is also important. Make sure they take care of the instruments that they play and come with their gear in the best shape, maintained to a professional standard. You can have the greatest keyboard player in the world, but if he is playing on an old broken-down Casio, it's not going to sound as good. The keyboardist should have a quality keyboard with the ability and sounds to give you a wide number of sound options. Make sure the drummer has an array of cymbals and snare drums. The bass player should have a fretted electric, a fretless, and a nice upright. Musicians should also have backup gear and the skills or tools to repair things. I used to say as a session drummer and hired gun I was not paid to record; I was paid to be able to solve any problem that could arise.

Anyone you hire should be top notch and have the skills, the knowledge, background, education, gear, and professionalism to bring to your project exactly what it needs. It may cost a little more, but it will both save you down the line and be worth it in the end.

A Bit about Drummers

I want to go into a little extra detail about drummers, and not just because I am one. A good drummer can really make the band, regardless of the style, and a bad drummer can really hurt the band. Settling for less can end up costing you more in the end. A drummer should have solid time, as in being able not to rush or drag too much, and feel comfortable with a click track. When you have a drummer that can keep the band in time and stay solid, it helps the foundation of the music. It will also make things go worlds faster in the studio. Often when I am producing a record on a serious time budget, the first problem we run into is a drummer who is not able to be solid with the click, and that person is the first to be replaced in the studio.

When you put up an ad or you talk to a drummer, explain what you are looking for and where you are at. While you might not be able to afford a session drummer, if you display yourself, your music, and your career as something that could be going somewhere in a realistic fashion, you might find a drummer who will dedicate time without charging you for rehearsals or too much for shows.

It might sound crazy to some, but drummers should have drums that sound good. They do not need to have some brand-new, top-of-the-line kit, but their gear should be well maintained and sounding great. The drums should be in tune, and the drummer should know how to tune them. It sounds obvious, but a lot of drummers do not know how to tune their drums.

Dynamics are another big key. You are going to want to find someone who can support you not only with energy and excitement but also with the ability to be quiet sometimes. When I have helped artists audition a drummer for a tour or for a band, I've asked them to play a really deep, in-the-pocket, hard-rock feel that is at a higher tempo and then seen if they can play with the same feeling, emotion, and energy at half the volume. This is a great way to see how the drummer can handle dynamics.

Something you are also going to want to look for is consistency, patience, and taste. Can the drummer lie back, sit on the groove, and not embellish at all? Can he or she just play the groove and fill only when it is needed and not when he or she feels like it? A lot of drummers that have the chops and the technique will display both at the wrong times, so pull out a stopwatch and ask a drummer to play a simple beat. Use a beat that has a repeating bass-drum pattern, simple two and four on the snare, and a basic eighth note pattern on the hi-hat. Now here's the trick: Have them play this for three minutes. Can the drummer play a solid groove with no extra dynamics, no fills, and no changes? This is a great test of the basic abilities of a good drummer. It sounds simple, but I have seen many drummers who have not been able to do it.

Lastly, even though there are a million other elements to look at with drummers, it is good to look at their understanding of different styles. When you have a drummer who has a solid foundation in many styles, it can help you find the pattern or beats that you are looking for. It's crucial not to settle for lower quality and to find what you are looking for. Sometimes the pickings might be slim, but it's key to search out the players that you need to make the music you want. Cutting corners on players' abilities can cut your chances with different opportunities that may arise.

You have worked so hard to create and write your music. Make sure you find the right people to perform and record it, to get it across the way you envisioned. You may not always be able to find the perfect drummer or be able to afford to pay the drummer you want, but try to make sure you have the drummer you need on the big shows and on the recordings. It might sound a little harsh, but it really can change how you are seen and how you are heard as well as open up the opportunities that can come from a good recording and a good show.

Band Names

Picking band names is a pain in the ass. There. Done. I mean, it really is a pain, and there is no simple way to get to a name. There are stories of bands that have actually gotten into fights, physical fights, over a name. Come on. I mean what's in a name?

These days there is a lot in a name, and when you are coming up with one, of course, you want to see if it has already been taken. Sometimes just searching online to see if there is another band is not always the answer. Certain bands do not have great optimization, so you might want to look through some of the band name registries, copyrights, and trademarks. Make sure to review the legal rights. If a name is trademarked, don't use it. The hope is to get popular, isn't it? While people might not catch you at first, if you have to change a name later after you have been building a career and marketing with it, it can be a tremendous setback. On that same note, don't settle for a name until you decide on one you like. As soon as you start a Web site, your social networking sites, and then performing, that should be the beginning of your branding and marketing. Toad the Wet Sprocket started with that thought and went so far with that name it ended up sticking. So work to find the name that you want.

Remember, as you're coming up with the name, think from a marketing and branding standpoint. Is it easy to spell? Will people be able to remember it? Is it too long to make an effective logo? Is it available as a domain name? Does it work in the font you have already been thinking about? When you take the wider approach and take into account all the different elements that should be considered, it will be easier to weed through and figure which name will suit you best.

Often I tell members of a band that is in its early stages to separate and, on their own, come up with keywords or even just words that they like. Find books from their favorite authors, chapter names, characters, whatever they enjoy or like. Is there a theme, a story, something they want to tie into the name? Think about these things separately and then together as a group. Come back with lists and go over everyone's words. This is not necessarily the place where they will find the name, but they will find commonalities.

You do the same. Break up your lists. If you have some initial names or off-the-cuff things, they are on one list. Your keywords are on another. Lastly create a list with your themes, ideas, or other bits of information that you might want to use. The better the communication and organization, the less frustrating it will be to find the name. When you get to the place where you know your theme and have begun to find words that seem to work, take those words and ideas and step away again. See what you come up with separately for the next time you meet up.

Also keep a pen and pad on you or near you, not just for band names. I always have a pad by my bed so I can write down ideas that come to me while I'm sleeping. I always keep a couple of extra blank cards in my wallet for ideas, lyrics, or things I want to jot down. I know you can go all technical if you have your phone, but I prefer to write things down and then look at them later to see what I still think.

Sitting down and knocking out all your keywords in one sitting is not the most effective way to a name. Spread out the words over time and see what is working for you. As you meet again with the group, on your cut-down list of words you like, begin to find the band name. Work on the idea of a series of names. When you are working on a couple of thoughts, you may be more creative than trying to be perfect and get it all done at once.

As you collectively weed out what you don't like and hold on to what you do like, you can usually find a name that will work for everybody. Take your time finding your name. Work on ideas, together and separately, and think about every issue associated with the name, from the name itself to branding and marketing and even the way it will look with a logo. When you take these steps, as you try to figure out a name, it can make things a lot easier and a lot less stressful.

Practice

Whether you are preparing for a show, getting ready to go in the studio, or just looking to tighten up a new song in rehearsals, it's important to take a professional approach to practice. There are a lot of details that can be overlooked or that could get in the way of making the most of precious musical rehearsal time. It's not about how much time you practice. To tell you the truth, I am never all that impressed when people tell me they practice for five hours a day. You can waste lots of time practicing or rehearsing if you are not making use of the time as effectively as possible. I am more impressed when the bands I produce put together game plans for rehearsing and preparing materials.

To sit in a room and just go over songs is pretty pointless. It only reviews the song. If you work on different elements inside the song and switch things up, you can really develop the strength of the tune, the performance, the approach, and the creativity toward the song. Also, preparing the songs for performance will give your live show an extra edge. It will give you that little something that people will not be able to define but will be registered as something special and a little different.

Here is the top-ten list that I give to musicians for effective practice in preparing for the studio, live shows, and working on new and old materials in rehearsals.

1. **Tempo Alteration**

    a. Practice with a click. Make sure the tune is where you want it to be. Especially when it comes to the studio, you are going to want to have that song dead to click but also comfortable so you don't give it a robotic feel with a robotic sound.

    b. Try the song faster and slower. Create the pocket of the song. Take the tune up ten beats per minute and work through it faster on one day; then the next day practice it ten beats slower. This can help you feel exactly where the tune's tempo should lie and give you a new sense of what it feels like when the song is beginning to rush or drag.

    c. Make a dramatic tempo change. Play the song as slowly as possible. Set the click radically slower than what you are used to and what the tempo of the song actually is. This method will really help each person feel his or her part and define the parts that are being played. This helps a lot with the development of solo sections, time-keeping, and an awareness of the little intricacies that are lost when it's at the faster normal tempo.

2. **Song Section Loops**

    Anyone can practice song after song. Most will work and count in the tune from the beginning and take it to the end. Not surprisingly, many songs, especially new ones, really sound great in the beginning but then as the song progresses become weaker. By starting the song in different places, you can work the sections to a point where they become a lot stronger.

    a. Start the song from a different place. For instance, play the last verse out and then loop it back to the beginning and up to the start point.

    b. Play a verse, chorus, or section over and over again. As you come to the end of it, just loop it and repeat it.

c. Try transitions that don't exist. Play the bridge into the intro and loop that a couple times. It may not occur in the song, but you are familiarizing yourself with the different sections and increasing your understanding of each transition.

d. Play it backwards. Literally, play each section from the end to the beginning. This will also help you feel transitions in a stronger way.

After playing through these variations, play the song straight through. You will feel a greater control of the form of the song.

3. **Song Transitions**

Test the waters between songs. Have a rehearsal that is just about song transitions. This can help you decide on the best -set orders sequence for live shows, or the song order of songs on an eventual CD. Take the last twenty-five seconds of a song and the first twenty-five of the next song and play through a set of just beginnings and endings. Take five seconds from the end of the tune that you have started, and then launch into the beginning. Be aware of the tempos, the keys, the feels, and the relative levels of energy of the song you are coming from and then heading into. Spending the time on this will really help to mold different sets that have different effects, making your show that much tighter and stronger.

4. **Other Keys and Modulations**

You're comfortable in a certain key for certain tunes, and that's fine, but why not test the waters in other keys? Try the song in a number of different keys. This can help your voicing, phrasing, and understanding of the song. You may even discover that there is a better key for the song than the original due to guitar voicings or your singer's range. By modulating and using different modes, you can also open up ideas for different types of solos and additional creative approaches for the song.

5. Staging, Locations, and Setup

Bring in the video camera or a normal camera for this. How do you look on stage? What kind of setup works best to help the band members communicate with each other? What bad habits or silly faces occur and on what songs? By watching yourself in rehearsal, you can help format the stage show that you want to give. Does the guitar player always look down? Does the drummer play with his mouth open on certain songs? By watching your own rehearsals, you can go for a more natural approach or any approach that better suits your music. Having an idea of what you look like and how you are delivering your music in the visual sense can take your show to another level. You can also address how you get on and off the stage and even how quickly you set up and break down. All these elements will show a higher level of professionalism and raise the bar for your performances.

6. Set Alterations and Tracking

Whether you are in a rehearsal or in a live show, write it all down!!! Write down every set for every show. Write down every set for every rehearsal. Cover what felt good about it and what felt bad. In reference to the song transitions above, think about overall set transitions. What seems to work the best, and what doesn't?

Having someone in the rehearsal or an extra person at a show taking note of the crowd reaction can help to define what songs and what part of the sets seemed to be the most effective and the most exciting. This person can also note when people seemed bored or when they seemed to be waiting for a song to end. Make the effort to do the research. Compile the data and figure out what works best and what doesn't. It will make a difference.

7. Worst-Case Scenario Arrangements

Rehearse for problems that might occur live, and the show will move along better when those unexpected scenarios happen. Whether the drummer breaks a stick, a guitarist breaks a string, the monitors go out, the vocal microphone shorts, a pedal breaks, an amp shorts out—you get the idea—you can have a back-up plan.

Practice some plans to keep your songs going or to do something to get out of the tune without showing that everything just went wrong. Have a joke ready and secondary arrangements or solos ready to enable a quick recovery. Have a cue for each person so anyone can alert other band members that he or she is having a problem and that a back-up plan needs to take place. Things go wrong—they always will—but when you handle an unexpected problem without showing that there even was a problem, you will raise the level of your performance significantly, and even when things do screw up, nobody will care. Instead, your audience will be impressed with your professionalism and skill.

8. **Time Signature Alterations**

This is a great practice tool that will make you think about your songs in a different light. It will also really help define songs in their original time signature. Switch it for a practice. Play a song that is in four, in three instead. Try adding a beat or a two; then try subtracting a beat or a two. This will help you sense the form and the chords that you use when it is in the normal time signature. It's a great exercise, and it will play with your head a bit.

9. **Style Alterations**

Try altering the style and the feel of the song. Try taking a tune that is jazzy and play it with a hard-rock feel. Then take a quieter tune with soft dynamics and play it in a style that is really loud and brash. This can help you feel the dynamic and approach differences to the tune, as well as make you more aware of the foundation of the song.

10. **Minus One Rehearsing**

Sometimes as musicians, we clue in to certain instruments and find ourselves not listening to or not as aware of others in a song. Do some rehearsing without any vocals at all. Make sure the group knows the changes without the vocal cues. Rehearse without the bass, without the drums, without the guitar, and so on and so forth. This will help each player feel the songs in a different light and become more aware of the structure and more aware of instruments that he or she might not have been paying attention to before. It also may help bring to light wrong notes or chords that one instrument is playing that were hidden among all the other instruments.

Of course, last but not least, run the sets straight through as you would perform them. Can't forget that one.

Try applying some or all of these techniques to different rehearsals. They can really help to tighten up your songs and, at the same time, make rehearsing more effective and more fun. Some of these techniques may even find their way into sets. Maybe certain nights you can take a song and switch the time signature or the feel to add a different approach for an evening. Practice and preparation are not about the amount of time you put in but the way you spend that time and how effectively you use it.

Internal Contracts, Copyrights, and Publishing

There are great books on the legal details of internal contracts, copyrighting music, and publishing, as well as setting up your own publishing companies. The problem is that these books are often overlooked or avoided because they come off as intimidating or a little intense. The Business of Music, Tenth Edition, Legal Aspects of the Music Industry by Richard Schulenberg and Making Music Make Money: An Insider's Guide to Becoming Your Own Music Publisher by Eric Beall are some great books. I highly recommend that you dig into the details of publishing and contracts.

The point is, you have to take that step. Not only think about it, but act on it. You need to take your music to the next level beyond the old put-the-music-in-the-mail-and-send-it-to-yourself. Just as you hit all the other details with all the attention needed, you absolutely, hands-down need to take care of the logistics in the professional and correct manner.

It can be a pain in the ass and you may have to go over things with a lawyer or a consultant to make sure you have everything you need and want correctly written and organized, but it will make your life easier—much easier—especially when the problems arise.

The books listed above, as well as information on the ASCAP, SESAC, and BMI sites (if you are an American, those are the organizations you will be affiliated with), will walk you through the steps. Now, personally, I believe you should not only copyright but also set up one or more publishing companies yourself, but there are others who might tell you to publish your music through other companies. That comes down to your personal choice, but make sure you understand all the exacts and details of the contract if you choose to publish with another company.

Pay attention to the details, read these books thoroughly, and if you do not understand something, find the right person with the knowledge to clarify it. You need to take the active approach and execute the minute details. You also need to make sure you do this in consideration of where you stand when you are happy and content with the members of your group (if you are in a band), but also write these contracts and organize as if you are broken up and never speaking to each other again.

When it comes to the copyrights, make sure you register who wrote what and do not just share in the creation of the songs. Avoiding this registration can cause major problems down the line if you break up and begin to argue about who the song belongs to. How you copyright it is how it stands. The same goes with publishing, so you better be damn sure that you list every party how you want it listed, as the friends or partners you may be at the moment may not last; give consideration to how the chips may fall should you hate each other and never talk to each other again.

Everyone says it will never happen. No problems will ever arise, and if you fight, everything will be made up. Friends forever, Care-Bear power and all that cheesy stuff. Wrong answer. Plan as if things are going to go to hell so you will be set and organized under all circumstances.

Take the steps and the time to discuss what will happen if someone chooses to leave, dies, quits, or any other possible scenario arises. Discuss the rights to continue to use the music or not use the music. Figure out how people will continue to be compensated or not. The more you can put on paper from copyrights to publishing, performing to breaking up, people leaving, starting other formations of the band,

and so on, the better. Does someone have rights to the band name? The logo? Do you have an agreement stating the dirty laundry can't be discussed publicly? Does someone have rights to license the music, and does that person get a cut for getting the deal before royalties and payments are split?

Have a brainstorm session and think of every issue that could possibly come up. Then do some research on problems that either broke bands up or gave artists serious problems or hassles. Lay out everything clearly, professionally, and legally. Make sure you are protected and the group as a whole has a crystal-clear understanding of how things stand legally. You will be much happier in the end, regardless of best- and worst-case scenario band endings.

Keeping the Band Together

Communication

Communication is an essential part of being in a romantic relationship, in a friendship, and even in a band. A lot of the problems that often occur personally, and inside a band, are based around misunderstandings, miscommunications, and assumptions. Such issues can cause anger and frustration and become a huge debacle if you don't feel as if you are being heard. Just make sure you are listening as well.

Have meetings with your band. Talk about the songs, the gigs, the expectations, and the direction. Talk about things in a positive manner, and try not to be defensive when you hear something you don't agree with or feel differently about. Communication can be difficult, and outside influences can make it worse. If you let long hours and rising emotions mix into the situation, you can have a recipe for disaster. Take the time to communicate, try not to assume, and listen as well as you can.

The Passive-Aggressive Condition

Music is a hard career in which to make it and stay successful. That's a simple fact. You have to have a hard shell; you have to be prepared to run into uncomfortable situations. You need to be prepared to develop problem-solving approaches, to get past internal issues as well as issues you may have with producers, managers, labels, booking agents, venues, and most everyone else you come in contact with.

I live in Seattle, Washington. The word passive, or for that matter passive-aggressive, is very evident in this city, more so than what I've seen in any other city, and I believe it's one reason many who have the dreams do not make them realities here.

Passive actions and passive-aggressive approaches can be a leading part of why problems continue to resurface. Many people use a passive approach to keep things stable and non-confrontational. Yet, this can make things more and more problematic and overwhelming, as issues will continue to occur every time something similar to the initial problem comes up.

Taking a more assertive approach to issues or disagreements can help solve the issue at hand more quickly and can also build the foundation for better communication between two parties, along with a greater understanding of expectations and how to address a particular person in the most effective manner.

How Do You Listen?

Take a few steps back from the normal day-to-day things you do, from writing and practicing songs to marketing online and postering for upcoming shows, and think about how you listen, how you learn, and how you communicate.

Anyone can read a book or listen to someone speak. It takes a special effort to learn the materials and apply them to your life, your career, and your dreams. It also takes humility and maturity to look at the larger picture and decide who you take information from and how you apply it directly to what you are trying to achieve.

Listen with ears that want to understand no matter how hard and confusing things may sound. Learn with a desire to retain and keep the information. And apply all the concepts to reach your goals and achieve your dreams. Leaving anything out will just be a weight that will drag you down and hold you back.

Arguing

Any interaction that consists of two or more people with strong views, opinions, and personalities is going to involve disagreements. It's human nature, and sometimes that human nature just *sucks*. You're going to have confrontations. You're going to have disagreements. You're going to get frustrated and upset. So why not work to learn the best ways to communicate, as well as the best ways to argue, so these problems can be a little more easy to deal with and a little less stressful?

Patterns

Look at patterns that emerge when you argue. What are things that set you off? What are things that set the other person or people off? It's very common to find that many arguments reoccur not based on the item or issue but based on how people are communicating and approaching that issue.

If you are saying or constantly hearing "We always have this fight" or "It always goes here," then maybe it's time to look at the patterns of communication and make a dual effort to work out the issue being brought up as well as to identify the traits and tendencies that get you to the bad place you may commonly go.

First off, it comes down to trust and respect. Can you and your business partners, your band members, or your spouse establish a trust and a promise that no one is trying to belittle anyone else? Set a foundation of trust by securing the fact that both parties will not attack and are aiming for solution, not just a fight. Add to that the promise that everyone will do his or her best not to become defensive, jump the gun, overreact, or assume. Make an agreement to trust that the other person is not intentionally trying to hurt the other. Make the agreement to build trust around knowing that everyone is looking for resolution. This will help communication during tense moments as well as day-to-day conversation.

Watch yourself for patterns just as you're watching others. Get away from telling people what they're doing and why they're doing it. You don't know everything, and that approach can come off as condescending and assumptive, which will almost inevitably anger the other person. Identify things together, but listen to each other. You may have a conclusion as to why so and so always does this or that. You may have identified some patterns, but what if there is more to it? Don't claim to know everything. It will only bring the tension to a higher level.

A Couple of Fighting Tactics ... Keep Your Fists High.

Some dos ...

1. **Listen**

   Listen to what the other person is saying. Don't start planning your response as the other person is speaking. That's being defensive, and it will pull your attention away from what the person is saying. Put the ego away and listen to the other side instead of preparing your response. Prepare it after they're done.

2. **Stay calm**

   Do your best to breathe, stay calm, hold back on your volume and erratic behavior. Try not to wave your arms around or make frantic movements that will only add more stress to the situation.

3. **Eye contact**

   It can be hard when you're upset, but try to stay connected by eye contact. Demonstrate that you truly want resolution. Although at the same time, for some people, eye contact is interpreted as an aggressive maneuver. It totally depends on the person. This is why it's good to know the person you're arguing with.

4. **Work to understand the other point of view**

   Just because you see things one way doesn't mean another vantage point isn't equally valid. Just because you have resolution and feel content doesn't mean the issue is resolved. Get out of the selfish mindsets of solution for one and look for solution for everyone involved. You don't have to agree with the other opinion, but if you can work to understand it, you're meeting halfway, and together you can get to a resolution faster. It's not about agreeing with the other party's point of view. It's about understanding it so you can all move forward together.

   If you feel slighted, give the other the benefit of the doubt, or ask the person why he or she did whatever it was that upset you. If the other says he or she didn't intend to upset you, explain how it hurt you as you work to understand that the intentions you imagined were not the true intentions of the actions. It's called trust, and you have to apply it.

5. **Keep the goal of solution, resolution, and problem solving in mind**

Remember that you're trying to fix an issue while learning to communicate better at the forefront. Don't forget that arguments will occur again, so make the next one a little better. Keep your attention on finding methods together to solve and resolve.

6. **Trust the person in what he or she is saying**

Trust that the other person wants to solve this and is not trying to pick a fight or be difficult. You may be angry, and you may see it another way, but if the other is coming at you honestly and you don't believe the person, your problems run a lot deeper.

Some don'ts ...

1. **Do not assume**

If you don't know for sure, then don't claim it to be. Tell someone what the situation feels like for you. Explain what you're seeing. Telling others what they're doing, especially if they might not be doing that particular thing at all, can only add fuel to an already tense situation. If you're unsure about something, then ask. Of course, others have the right to their feelings, their views, and their opinions, but if you ask them or tell them it feels like this, you're taking a better step to solution. Still, you have to be prepared at that point to hear the reason why they see it in a different way.

2. **Do not interrupt**

Allow the other person to speak. Try not to interrupt. Give the person the respect that you want when you are speaking as well.

3. **Do not go on the offensive**

When others are addressing an issue they are concerned about, listen and try to respond to that issue without bringing up any concerns or accusations that you might have. It may be something you'll bring up later, but take one thing at a time. Respond to the issue at hand instead of changing the topic or trying to re-point fingers. This, again, will only add stress to an already stressful situation.

4. Do not go on the attack

Do not start attacking. Again, go after the issue at hand with the idea of better communication. When you start attacking or trying to hurt the other party, the argument is taking a number of steps backwards. It can make people shut down and not want to listen. They begin to concentrate on what they want to say back, and that can often be why you don't feel like you are being heard. You have used a form of communication that is viewed as an attack, and now the defenses are up, and the ears are down. Hurting someone is only going to build walls. When walls go up, your point, opinion, and view are going to become harder to hear.

5. Do not state the redundant or make rude comments that will not help at all

Saying sarcastic things that you know aren't true is not going to help get you any faster to resolution. When you're asked a question and then go right to "It seems like we fight all the time," how does that help resolve the issue? It may be a fact, but it's a fact that is probably known by all parties and really doesn't need to be stated. It makes more sense to be productive than to reiterate all the issues that everyone knows are present. It will only cause frustration. Work to use only problem-solving questions and statements.

When it comes down to discussing issues, cite examples and patterns. Don't go for the exaggerations. Stop saying things like, "You do this all the time" and, instead, replace it with examples and patterns of why you believe something is a certain way. So instead of yelling, "You always use too much distortion at the end of every damn song," try to cite the exact songs in which you feel you might be hearing too much distortion and offer an alternative as well. Keep the creative process going by bringing in creativity. Instead of shooting something down and having it all negative, bring up some ideas of what might be better or something different to put into a song.

6. **Watch for selfish traits**

Look at yourself and watch for where you may be a little stubborn, and work to find ways to meet the other party halfway. Avoid the blame game. It doesn't matter whose fault it is. It's about the resolve. If others refuse to acknowledge that, then get out of that relationship, business, or group.

It's a Challenge

Communication doesn't always work between certain types of people. People can be stubborn or have a certain way of seeing things or a specific way of communicating. If you're in a band with someone you cannot communicate with, it's a recipe for disaster in the long run. Of course things feel great early on when you're playing music, not unlike the infatuation of a new romance, but it's the rough times you have to think about. Being in the back of the van for five hours, someone getting on your nerves, or simmering issues finally being brought up is where things can explode.

We all have baggage that comes up now and then. Whatever fear it is, sometimes a person can put that out in a way he or she doesn't intend to. Get to know your other band mates. Knowing about their past can help you learn the best ways to approach them without triggering things that have nothing to do with the subject at hand.

Read the stories about Sting and Stewart Copeland from the Police, or even more recently, the Dave Matthews band. A few years back everyone was on a separate tour bus and not talking except when on stage. As crazy as it might sound, sometimes having a therapist or a third-party mediator can help vent smaller problems before they become destructive. Other times, taking a break and creating some space can help mend things. Most of all, be proactive and productive instead of defensive and small-minded. It takes an open mind and a big heart not only to say what you feel but also to listen to what people say without feeling attacked.

Relationships of all types are a challenge. You have to decide if the one you're in is worth it. Your communication and arguments will not go away overnight or, for that matter, get better in a week. Still, small steps can be taken. If you really care and really want to make it work, then make it work, and don't half-ass it. That will only cause the same fights to repeat themselves. It's going to take 100 percent of your efforts to meet a person halfway and work together to find resolution for whatever the problem may be at that time, as well as making communication stronger.

Stay the Course. It's a Long Track.

Work on communication—it's an ongoing skill to learn and grow with. This, like any instrument, is something you will never truly master but should practice every day. I am still having my issues with it. Any artist I have done a full album or long-term project with has gone around the ring with me in a couple of verbal bouts. The difference is that the artist and I both realize the argument is about the long-term resolution and the success of whatever is being worked on and usually turn the issue into a productive conversation.

Look for small victories, small aspects of communication growing stronger, better, and more effective. Things will not change overnight, but if all parties give an honest effort, the relationship can work. Take a break if you need to and think about what you want and what you're willing to give. Research options and look into having a mediator or counselor help if you hit a wall and need a third party. The best relationships, the greatest loves, the most wonderful connections take work and effort. Recognize, compromise, and truly work on the small steps to better communication. At the same time, recognize the efforts of the other person. Move forward together, learn together, grow together, and then experience the benefits of all that work *together*.

Dividing the Workload

Whether you are a single artist or a complete band, the work that has to be done to keep things moving onward and upward can be intimidating and overwhelming.

The problem that I see occur is that an artist or members in a group look at everything they have to do as this big, massive, single item that just seems unobtainable or impossible to get done, so they shove the work under the rug, then work on the scraps or the small things that seem doable All this happens while core elements that are being ignored become more and more problematic and harder to solve.

Of course if you are a band, you can divide up the workload among members. The question comes down to who does what and when. For right now, I am going to discuss dividing the workload over time and days as a single artist.

You are not going to sit down for three hours on one day and be able to knock out all the things you want to. Most people cannot commit that kind of time. With day jobs, rehearsals, girlfriends, and boyfriends, a lot of artists can't pull that out of a day. But sitting down for half an hour is something that can be scheduled into a day and actually happen. We all have the best intentions and want to put the most time that we can into a project and our careers, yet too often life gets in the way.

The key point is to work smarter and more effectively over a series of days instead of trying to knock out everything in a single day.

Let's look at the basic list that artists should be covering in a given week …

- **Marketing**
- **Promoting**
- **Booking**
- **Rehearsing**
- **Maintaining equipment and gear**
- **Networking**
- **Advertising**
- **Administrative**

And the list goes on. But above we have the basic core, and now we can begin breaking those elements down …

- Marketing online via Web site, Facebook, and other sites to draw new friends and fans to you.

- Promoting for shows, promoting your recording or latest merchandise, promoting sales and keeping content new with blogs, picture updates, and schedules. Printing up the posters, ordering, and keeping stock of your music and merchandise for sale.

- Booking shows, preparing tours, organizing press packs, soliciting and submitting to festivals, concert promoters, managers, and venues, as well as talent buyers.

- Rehearsing your old material, writing new material, working out arrangements, getting songs ready for recording or stage.

- Taking care of the gear that takes care of you. Allotting the time to maintain, clean, repair, or just check your gear to make sure you don't run into problems on stage or in the studio.

- Networking by reaching out to the companies of the gear that you use to begin to build relationships for endorsements, meeting other bands, and connecting with groups you could share a bill with. Finding ways to market and connect with people and media in places where you are playing to find different avenues of exposure. Talking with management groups and record labels or agents that you may want to be involved with, so that in turn ... You don't have to do all this stuff and someone else will!

- Advertising your group, getting the group up on different sites, getting reviewers to do stories about you, postering, organizing, and stickering around the country and world. Buying ads in different markets and different media channels.

- Administrative details include tracking your receipts, your spending, your profits and making sure your taxes, bank accounts, and other finances and contracts are in order; double-checking about shows, making sure the hotels are booked for the overnight shows; dealing with everybody's schedules and personal issues or calendar issues; keeping the paperwork organized and up to date.

And you just wanted to play music????

Well, unless or until you are part of a label, management group, or agency, you are going to be responsible for all these elements.

I personally prefer to see artists stay independent, but when things mount up and get busier, you will need help. It's a great thing to spend some time early on handling these elements, though. By doing so, you will not only get a full sense of the inner workings, but you will also gain an understanding of what needs to be done and what to ask of a rep, manager, agent or label. You will also have an idea of how hard people are working for you or, for that matter, how hard a manager or label should be working for you.

Back to the dividing up of this massive amount of work. Like in any situation, the first step is to know what you have to do and then clearly set in the game plan to get it done.

The next step is to designate each section to a day or the allotted time needs. For example, when I was drumming, I would spend fifteen minutes a week just going over my kit with a rag, oiling the pedals if they needed it, making sure all the lugs were in place, and looking for any kind of problems. Once a month, I would take a half hour to really clean the kit and go over everything with a fine-tooth comb. Then, every six months, I would plan for a couple hours where I would strip the kit, take off all the heads, check the edges of the drums, and really give the kit a day at the spa, as some would say.

Approach any of the items you have to address in the same way as above. What can you do for five minutes a day? Take the list again, pulling the equipment and gear upkeep as well as the rehearsing out of the daily mix, since the upkeep is more of a weekly thing and the rehearsing—well, that depends on the artist or band.

It may feel like a beast of work, but step back and allot five minutes per item six days a week. It totals out to three hours of solid work a week across the spectrum of things that need to be done. What most bands don't really think about is that five minutes of work, while it may feel like it is not enough, amounts to a half hour of work if you do it for six days. After a month, it equals two hours of work on whatever you have designated that time to.

So now the list, but in five-minute intervals for the single artist in a single day amounting to only a half hour …

>Marketing—five minutes. Go add a new friend or connection on one of your social networking sites; post info about a show in a new forum or message board or a site related to the topic. Link a new band or a new company to your site and then send an artist, a fan, or a venue a quick e-mail just to check in.

>**That's five minutes down.**

>Promoting—five minutes. Find three social networking sites where you can advertise a scheduled show, maybe a few sites that are local to the area you are playing, and just add in the info of the show and your basic info.

>**Boom, another five down and still effective in a short amount of time.**

>Booking—five minutes. Research a new venue or booking group. Copy down the info and save the info for either the networking of that day or another day, or send out an electric kit to a new agent, venue, or festival.

>**Fifteen minutes in and you are grooving.**

>Networking—five minutes. Research and make a new contact every day. One contact—what are they about, what can they do for you, what can you do for them?—and pop out a basic e-mail. One contact attempt a day, that's all.

>**Twenty minutes …**

>Advertising—five minutes. If you have the money, buy an ad once a month in some kind of media outlet, newspaper, Web site, radio station, anywhere. Add your banner to a new Web site, join a new Web group or contact a new postering group for a city you play that is too far away for you to poster yourself so you have that outlet for when you are playing there.

>**Twenty-five minutes and almost done for the day!**

Administrative—five minutes. Lastly, update your files with some of the info you collected that day. Make sure it is organized and saved in the right databases. Set the calendar for the next day's plans and the things coming up.

Thirty minutes!

It might seem oversimplified, but it really isn't. Being effective for short spurts of time on a regular basis brings results.

As you do small amounts of work each day, it adds up. Your databases for venues, contacts, and all sorts of information will tally up, and it is all in a reasonable amount of time. On certain days if you have more time to commit, then do so, but don't neglect any element.

Leggo My Ego

Ever heard this one? How many guitar players does it take to screw in a light bulb?

The answer is one hundred—one to actually do it and ninety-nine to say how they could have done it so much better.

There are a dozen jokes like that representing the egos and competitive elements of musicians. Words like egomaniac, arrogant, egotistical, and pompous have been used to describe some musicians. Some are based on stereotypes, but a lot can be, way too often, very true.

Musicians that have confidence and healthy egos can go much further than those with egos that are out of control. Music can sound better, communication with band mates can be better, and the individual musician's appearance in the industry as a whole can be much, much better.

A lot of rock artists as well as rap and R&B artists add an excess of ego into the lyrics of their songs and the marketing as a whole. These days, in a larger scale market, the ego has to take a back seat; otherwise you as the artist just become another band with attitude, and there is not much original about that. Come across confident but respectful in the industry, and your attitude will open a lot more doors.

When you are working up your bio, your tagline, and your basic marketing, think humbly. Don't use words or phrases like innovative, new, never been done before, best, greatest, can't be compared to anything else, or anything like that. If you were standing in front of one of your biggest inspirations, one of the guys or girls you have looked up to, how would you describe your sound, your album, or your band? Would you put yourself in the same class as someone who you think is the best? I am guessing most likely not.

Think humble, think honest. Put across an image that is …

- **confident without being cocky**

- **strong without being arrogant**

- **descriptive without going over the top**

- **humble with respect for those around you and those who came before you**

It's not about playing yourself down or being underwhelming as opposed to being overwhelming. It is simply about taking a few steps back and designating your music, your image, and your materials as something that is a little different, a little more respectful and a little more aware.

Don't over embellish, don't talk above what you have done and who you are. Artists become much more impressive when they talk less and show more through their performance. Again, when you reference your sound, your skills, all the people you know, and all the things you have done … make sure that you don't say anything you wouldn't say if those people were standing right in front of you.

Highlight the facts and showcase the talent and the concept. How many downloads you get or how many friends you have on this network site or that network site should not be for the public; these are things that would go on a stat sheet.

Don't make up a label if you don't have one. Don't talk about show-cases for labels and how you are right on the verge of breaking through, just define the simple truths, and that will take you worlds further.

If you're not incorporated or you're not a business, don't claim to be one. People check that stuff out and when they do, you have then made a bad first impression. If you don't have a copyright, go file for one and then post your music. Don't lie about the details—your lies will come back and bite you in the rear.

It's one thing to look professional, but it's quite another to pretend to be. You'll look the fool when people check you out. Humility is the foundation for a greater gain than any wordplay or arrogant statement you will make. Stay humble, it will take you higher and further than that attitude and ego ever will.

Your Résumé—Deflated

I have been reading a good deal of band bios lately, as well as seeing people update their Web sites, their different social networking sites, and what not. The common thing I notice is an inflated résumé with information that is over the top and not particularly beneficial. The idea of tamping down the ego for the sake of professionalism has already been touched on a little earlier. Use the same approach not to come off as over the top. Don't highlight singular events that might make you look unprofessional or inexperienced to the people who really matter when reading your résumé.

Take a minute and think about anything you say and how it could be read, misread, misunderstood or seen as confusing. Ask other people outside of the group and ask how it is viewed. A common mistake I often see is an overly embellished résumé or bio that can look really good to friends but carries a bad tone for booking agents, managers, labels, and other industry professionals. I told one artist to tell the girl he wants to impress about the big show he played, but make the bio and the Web site impress the industry people who will do the booking and promoting.

We won the Battle of the Bands, or we won this competition or that competition. I am really not a big fan of those types of events. They are usually marketing events to fill a room on a slow night and really push the venue or sponsoring organization. I have even been a judge on a few, and these are not major steppingstones or bullet points to add to Web sites.

Sometimes, artists get concerned that they don't have enough to fill up a bio or the promo materials, and they add things like playing a club or winning a battle of the bands. These are not strong marketing points. Try to look at things from an industry stance. Try to decipher what would make someone want to do a story on you.

The other big no-no is about the plays or friends you have on MySpace or Facebook or any of the networking sites. Putting out bulletins or bragging about numbers of MySpace friends, hits, or plays was something that held some kind of prominence and impressiveness when MySpace first came out. Now with the ability to buy friends and plays, it really is no longer something you want to advertise. If anything, by advertising that, you look cheap.

Even if your résumé is small, work to build it off the foundations of what you are doing. Talk about the songs, the group, the shows, and the steps you are taking toward your dreams. As more things come into play, you can add them; just make sure you're adding elements that are going to highlight you in a strong way to the industry and not better used impressing some girl or guy.

It's better to push what you have done and the things that matter than to inflate things that the industry as a whole will not care about or will make you look like an amateur or unprofessional.

The Band House

The wonderful world of living together—or not—as a band is an age-old dilemma and not one that has an easy answer. The band house for some groups can be an amazing experience and a very negative experience for others. This is less about the individual personalities; it really comes down to the collective of the group and how the group can mesh together.

Just because you practice four times a week, play on two or three other occasions, and spend lots of time together in cars, vans, and buses doesn't mean a total living situation is the best option for the group. There are a lot of questions that need to be considered. People are definitely different at home than they are on the road, and some of these "jump the gun" living situations have actually broken up bands that should have stayed together. Keep in mind that not all groups that work well professionally can successfully live together.

Knowing the traits of each member's lifestyle, beyond his or her instrument or role in the band and on stage, is a good start. Also, if you can get out on the road and get a solid tour under your belt, meaning something that is at minimum three weeks long, that can help show you how you live as a group and how you handle yourselves in a tighter, private environment.

Begin by asking yourself questions about the group.
- **What traits do you like about each of the members?**
- **What traits do you dislike?**
- **Do you like each person's friends outside of the band?**
- **Do you have hang-ups about sharing, or do certain members have a more communal sensibility than others?**
- **What rules would you want in place in your living situation, and what rules would other members want you to abide by?**
- **When you have to compromise on different subjects or details—and you will have to compromise—do you feel it is an even compromise, or will it cause animosity amongst you?**
- **What are each of the band members' needs for personal space, and will the house allow for that?**
- **What about other people living in the house with the band? If there are extra rooms and it is a larger house, do you want to rent the other room or rooms to people outside the band, and if so, to whom?**

Remember you are now taking things to a 24/7 level. It is an intense situation to bring a number of creative people into a place where you are all practicing together, playing together, and living together. It really comes down to having a plan and looking at both sides of the coin before committing to something of this scale. A great deal of pros will oftentimes outweigh the cons when it comes to a band living together. Still, even those few simple cons can cause a member to be unhappy or pissed off which can have an effect on the music as well as the future of the band.

Sometimes a couple of members already live together, and too often it is assumed that it will therefore be an easy transition for all to join in. But think about it: Two is easier than four, five, or six. The two who already live together could have something down as band members and friends outside the band. This will not necessarily make it an easier transition. Some bands have even experienced anger or jealousy when a couple of members click in a living situation and spend more time together than with the others. It may sound sappy and stupid, but it happens a great deal.

It would be smart to put together a checklist in advance to review whether it will work or not. Also, decide on the costs and who's paying what.

That said, what about the positive side of bands living together?

- **All the gear goes back to the same place**
- **Big savings on rent, food, electric, gas, and other bills**
- **Creates a center of operations for the band. You will potentially have a band office and a band rehearsal space in the same place.**
- **If your band is a business, it will allot you a great deal of write-offs tax-wise**

You will be able to hold band meetings, have everyone around for practice and be able to problem-solve a number of different issues that are a lot easier to resolve when everyone is under the same roof. This can make it a fun experience. It all comes down to weighing out the options, the people, and the mix that is created by everyone being under the same roof.

Ask questions of each other. Spend time talking about the best roommate and worst roommate experiences that you have had in the past. What was the longest living situation for each member, and why did it work out so well? What was the absolute worst experience, or are there people you don't talk to anymore that you lived with, and what do you feel caused the rift? Each of these questions will help give you a better sense of your band mates, which will not only help you to see if living together is a good idea but also bring you closer together by giving you a better understanding of the people you play with and potentially might be living with.

Good luck, either way; you will need a little of it on your side, especially when it comes to living with others.

Romance

The last couple of relationships I have been in were nothing short of train wrecks. I don't imagine myself as the easiest person to see in a romantic fashion, and I know that I put music first in most cases. I tried very hard in my last situation to put someone else first, but it did not end up how I wanted. I know, for me, communication is paramount, and I cannot stand assumptions, nor can I stand the passive-aggressive, held-back, and held-in stuff. Still, who really wants to hear about my love life?

What I know from the bands I have toured with and the relationships I have witnessed that were most effective is that they were, as I mentioned before, based on clear and concise communication and expectations.

If music is number one to you, then tell that to the person you are seeing. The more that is clarified from the start, the better things can be. Talk with your date or partner about what it means to be with a musician. Talk about your dreams, your goals, and what you have to do. Explain that the hours are awkward and different; that rehearsals are part of your job, and that the weekends will often be packed with shows. The more that's understood up front, the fewer fights down the line.

Now as far as inner-band dating, I've always found it to be a no-no. The line we used to say was, "Don't Fleetwood Mac each other." You are living and breathing music with your group. It can only make things harder if there is a romantic relationship occurring in that dynamic as well. A number of years ago, I was on tour with a band in which two romantically involved band mates did not speak in the van from Chicago to Houston. The only interaction was on stage. Those ten days in the van sucked for all of us. You could cut the tension with a knife, and the worst part was that the rest of us had to deal with that tension as well. We practically killed each other by Oklahoma City. The guitarist who was involved with the keyboardist had packed his bags before the show in New Orleans and planned to quit after that show, by the end of the night, they worked out their differences.

Not that it made it all better: The rest of us then had to deal with lovey-dovey crap until we reached San Diego, when the guitarist and keyboardist started hating each other again, by which point we found the animosity a relief.

Leave the significant others out of the practices and the studio most of the time. Let them visit now and then, but would you go to someone's office and just hang out and watch all day? Don't let that happen here. Also, opinions should be reserved unless asked for. You don't need someone sitting in the middle of your practice and asserting how the music should go and why.

It's challenging enough to date, much less be in a relationship. When you add an artist or a musician to the mix, it can become downright challenging. I'm not trying to be all pessimistic; I know that some inner band relationships have worked and I know that there is hope for those who see musicians. From what I have witnessed, it's all based on communication and trust. If you're not up-front and honest, it can become a real challenge after the initial infatuation is over.

Drinking and Drug Issues

Drinking and drugs can be an issue. This is not any kind of newsflash to anyone. There are extremes in both directions: both those who over consume and people who freak out if you are having a sip in front of them or doing drugs around them.

I'm not going to tell you to do or not do alcohol or drugs. It is not my place.

Personally I've stayed away from drugs. I'm not claiming to be any kind of angel, and I've done my share of pot and even a few times the harder stuff, but I mostly keep it to alcohol, and I stay in control when I do drink.

I was very young when I saw drugs kill two people close to me and two other musicians I admired, which acted as a deterrent, showing me a path I didn't want to end up on. On the other hand, I think people can take it too far in the anti-drugs and the anti-drinking aspects. Every person and situation is different. If a shot of whiskey loosens you up and gives you a better performance, then take the shot. If you need to have a *bottle* of whiskey on stage and then you act belligerent, drunk, and forget words and parts to songs, well, maybe not such a good idea.

It comes down to responsibility. Can you have a whiskey, a glass of wine, a beer, or a shot and not be adversely affected? If so, I don't really see the problem. If you can't function without it, then it's time to take a responsible look at what you are doing.

Is alcohol something you use for fun, or are you trying to mask things, using it as a crutch or a needed supplement that you cannot record, perform, or live without? These are the questions you have to face. Ask yourself as well: When do you find yourself most *need*ing a drink as opposed to just having a drink?

A test I did with myself when I was on the road and drinking very regularly, or let's just say every night, was to stop cold turkey. I checked myself to see if I could just not drink for a week. I stopped the morning after a show in Chicago and told myself I would not have a drink again until we reached Orlando. For me, it was easy. I actually felt I had a little more energy and stamina in the day. I was not as tired, and I found that I was able to warm up before shows a little faster. So I cut back the drinking some, but I did continue to drink.

That's a single experience; it's different for everyone. If you did that test and found yourself needing to drink, then it might be time to address the issue and whatever issues might lie beneath. I'm not going to tell everyone not to drink or not to do drugs. I'd rather tell people to take note of the habits that they and their band members have developed around drinking and drugs.

Prior to touring or even as you're forming your group, if you have strong opinions on drugs, state them up front. I've been on tours where we actually signed a contract stating we would not drink before a show and would not have a drink till we had completed the gig. I had no problem with this. This was how the bandleader wanted it, and I wanted that tour, so I did it.

There are other people who are recovering alcoholics and can't handle alcohol around them. If you like to and want to drink, but are in a situation where someone is going to be on your case if they see you drinking or smell alcohol on your breath, that really isn't something you can change about that person. It might not be the right fit for you. Otherwise you will likely get very upset with each other and want to go for blood. I saw this on one tour, and it wasn't pretty.

My personal beliefs for the studio are to avoid alcohol and drugs. I like people to be at their sharpest and most aware. I like people to have stamina and to be able to maintain a coherent energy level that is productive, effective, and positive. I do not try to draw the lines or figure what is the right amount for a person; that is not my job as a producer. I just usually like to say "none of that" in the studio and leave it at that.

There are exceptions though. I have gotten whiskey for some singers toward the end of a session. I know some vocal coaches that are going to send e-mails about that statement, but that was what we needed to do to get the job done.

In the end it's a very personal thing. Whether you are looking at drinking and drugs and the effect they might have on you or the rest of your band or you are looking at another member and wanting to bring up your concerns, it can be a hard thing to do. It requires a specified and individualized approach. Sometimes when it comes to alcohol and drugs, having a mediator with the group can make discussions easier.

When it comes to you and looking inside to see when too much is too much, ask yourself the different questions. Think about how it affects you in practices, on stage, and on the road in the hotels. Work on the figuring out why you drink and whether it is for fun or out of necessity. I have told a couple of musicians to videotape some of their performances, and then I watched them see just how they looked and sounded on stage when it was played back for them. That was very sobering for two of the guitar players to whom I suggested the idea. They went from feeling that they were on top of their game on stage and just amazing to seeing the footage of themselves playing the songs not as sharply and not looking half as cool as they thought they did.

Take the issues and personalize them. Figure out what you want, what works for you, and how alcohol or drugs affect you. If you need to be in a group that doesn't drink or do drugs at all, then state that right from the get go. At the same time, don't go to the opposite extreme and try to sell your drinking to others. Every person handles alcohol differently, and every person handles drugs differently. You are not the shrink; you are a member of the band. Discuss your thoughts on the matter as your opinion, as your feelings, not as an ultimate authority.

It's like that line from a comedian I forget the name of. He said, "I don't have a problem with Jesus, and I don't have a problem with Elvis ... It's just some of their super fans that piss me the hell off." I think there are a lot of the super freaks around alcohol on both sides of the spectrum, people either stating that alcohol makes you more creative or drugs make you more expressive and free, or that you can't touch a drop or take a hit. There's a middle ground of those elements that doesn't need to be sold to anyone or overly explained; it's where you are personally. So keep it personal; be honest, and be true to yourself and the others you perform with. Be open to talking about issues as they come up and stay away from the soapbox; everyone is different. Accept that.

Members Who Quit or Get Fired

Do you remember the first band you were in? The one you were convinced was going to change the world? Do you remember those rock star fantasies you had when you played in a basement or bedroom? You knew that you were the bunch that was going to go the distance. Mine was a group called Orenda. I still remember all their names: Kurt Hilborn on bass, Jon Zahourek on guitar, Bill Murphy on vocals, and myself on drums.

It's interesting what we remember and what we forget. I have played with tons of people and tons of bands over the years. I have forgotten a number of those band names and especially the members, but I don't think I will ever forget Orenda or those guys.

We were not good. I mean ... we were really bad. We had no original songs, only covers; yet we were going to rock those covers harder than any one else in the world, or at least that's what we thought at the time.

We seemed to have more band issues than we did good music. We replaced the bass player and fought about the direction of the music ... Again folks, keep in mind that we played covers, not even original music. Then we got rid of the vocalist, and the band imploded. Yet for some reason, I still often think about Orenda.

I remember standing on the porch one day with a musician who had been, in a way, a mentor to me for some time. He told me that I should plan on being a part of many bands in my lifetime. He reminded me that I was only fourteen and if I was going to make music my career, I should plan on breaking up with just as many bands as I form or join. I have not spoken with him in years, but watching and learning from him helped me out a great deal, and his advice to me that day was no exception.

The point of this rant is to prepare you for those scenarios in which a band member quits or you have to fire a member. As much as you think it will never happen, it inevitably will. It's an extreme rarity for bands formed with musicians who have never been in other bands actually to stay together.

So before the honeymoon is over, plan the divorce

I know it's kind of morbid, but it's something you should be prepared for. Whether you are firing a member or a member leaves, it's crucial to have a game plan as to how the situation will be handled. You don't need to have a specific contract or template. You can set it up yourselves, a pre-nuptial agreement of sorts, but it would be smart to have a lawyer or someone with a legal background review the contract for the sake of wording. To set up a game plan for each member leaving the group by choice or by force (request) will make life a great deal easier if and when it does occur.

As awful as it may be to think about, it's also a good idea to make provisions for the worst-case scenario: death. What happens if a member dies? Handling it like a will can help address issues such as royalties, ownership, and who has rights to what.

Again, what it comes down to is that this attention to detail and planning for those worst-case scenarios will allow you to be better prepared should things go wrong. Just think about it like natural disaster insurance. It will make things much easier should something happen and provide the reassurance of a backup plan if you're one of the few bands that can keep the same crew together.

Here is a checklist of items to address for total band agreement as well as individual members. The details should be decided by the band, and the specifics are always different.

- **Songs, Copyrights, Publishing. Who has the rights to which songs, and what happens if someone leaves?**

- **Are you paying group fees for management or solicitations, such as press packs, that you have already purchased? Will you give a percentage back to the exiting player? Are all monies nonrefundable?**

- What issues surround the label if you are on one? What happens on the business side if you are involved with a label?
- Band Gear. The band bought it, so how do you want this to go down? Buyouts? Do you want to give the gear in question back to the exiting member or pay them a depreciated rate for their share of the purchase?
- Merchandise and Sales. What percentage should the exiting member get and for how long? Should there be a flat buyout of monies invested in product?
- How long should the artist have to play before a replacement is found, and what kind of notice needs to be given if someone is leaving?

These are some of the key elements to think about. It gets a lot more detailed as you sit down to make the decisions that will create the contracts, but having a plan will make a potential ending for any member a much easier transition. It can also help in the total breakup or dissolving of a band. If you incorporate as a business, you can lay these out as bylaws. Just make sure everyone is on the same page and put these agreements in place.

Remember, being part of a band is like being in a relationship, just with more than one other person. It takes effort to make it work. Plan wisely and major hassles, fights, and lawsuits can be avoided.

New Blood in the Band

Way too many bands make the mistake of bringing someone into a band as a full member too quickly. It's not about distrusting the new guy or girl; it's about developing over time the kind of trust that is needed. You wouldn't move in with someone after just a week of dating, right? So why do so many bands audition and bring in a new member that quickly?

Auditions

When you list for auditioning a new artist …

- Be detailed.
- List your influences and your approach.

- Explain the plan or concept of the band.
- Be clear about what is expected regarding rehearsing, investing, writing, recording, and time commitment.
- Find out about the person's social life. Does he or she see this as a hobby? Does the musician have a controlling partner or spouse who could make things difficult?
- Does the performer have a job that will not allow the time to tour? Does he or she have a criminal record that may make it difficult to get a visa to play out of the country?
- What is the credit situation of the potential member? If you bring the person into the band and into the business side of things, will it affect the band in a negative way?
- Is this person committed to any other projects that might get in the way? Is he or she just out of a band and might try to get back with it? Are you sure you would keep this person if the old member wanted back in?

Men and women are attracted to certain people with specific qualities; so why not look at it like a personal ad instead of a music ad. It will inevitably come down to how your personalities mix anyway, and by taking the proper steps to get to know your new member and also letting the person get to know you, you will have a better chance of building a long-term partnership that can be successful.

Trial Period

Letting someone become a part of a band with a few guys who are starting at ground zero is one thing, but if you have merchandise, recordings, bookings, and other tangible assets and structures, it's a good idea to think about setting up a trial period. This is the time when you observe the following: Does the new member come to practice on time? Perform well on stage? Come prepared? Does his or her part? What are some of the core issues for you as a group? Is the band vegan? Political? Is there some other social or moral viewpoint that is very important to the group?

Certain things that may be important to you or may be already agreed upon by the band might not come up early on, so bring them up. They don't have to make sense, but they should be brought up with a new member. Being clear and fair is the best way to go.

Allow yourself the time to review and observe before committing to a new member. The same can go with a producer, a booking agent, management, or any partner you are going to be involved with. See how things go. See how you feel working with that person. Watch for warning signs and red flags and address them immediately if they come up.

Lastly, decide where you are able to compromise and where you will stand firm. If there are elements that you can bend on, define them, just as you should define the elements that you will not bend on.

Taking the time and building trust will make adding a new person to an already established group an easier transition and, in turn, will not overburden you with the normal stresses of the new blood syndrome.

Individual Musicianship

It's an important element to practice as a band. Of course you want to be tight. You want to have the songs as strong as possible, both in the sense of performing live and being able to record in the studio. It's key to know the beginnings, endings, changes, and transitional sections of a song.

Bands need to be aware of each other and how each player brings his or her piece to the song. Even the untrained ear knows when a band is sounding really good together. Practicing builds the strength of the songs, but also helps develop the communication needed to play songs the right way. This same communication skill set will also help you be able to cover mistakes, problem-solve any issues that can arise on stage, and make on-the-spot changes without an audience even noticing.

Still, musicians often forget to work on their personal musicianship, ability, and technique. It's stereotypical for a guitar player to set up his gear and go into a chop frenzy during sound check, showing off riffs he or she already knows and could never really use in a song. The same can go for the drummers; I know I've been guilty of setting up and starting to see how fast I could move around the kit.

Some say this is warming up, stretching out, or even practicing. It really isn't. Just as you need to exercise to stay in shape physically, it's key to keep your technique, ability, musicianship, and improvisational and creative knowledge in shape as well.

I used to keep a very steady practice routine, always keeping up on the basics while mixing in new styles and different techniques. Practicing with the band is not enough. It will help the band and help you some, but you need to continue to grow. If you are not growing, you are shrinking in skill sets, abilities, and knowledge.

Take the time to go through the technical exercises that give you the rudimental skills that you need *for* the band but also *beyond* the band. Practice styles that you find challenging or create your own challenge; working out of your comfort zone will make you grow. Work with metronomes; take lessons. Just because you're in a band doesn't mean you shouldn't take lessons, and just because you're on the road doesn't mean you can't connect with a local teacher and work on different methods and approaches.

Listen to a new song in a style that you aren't used to and one that might not be your favorite. With iTunes, YouTube, MySpace, and all the other sites, you can find music easier than ever. You can also find music that is very different or that, years ago, would've been impossible to search out and get a hold of. Expose yourself to new sounds and styles even if it's only for ten minutes a day. This can really broaden your ears and your musicianship. Hearing how another player in another genre might approach something in a different way can really affect you and inspire new conceptual ideas. Now, don't go over the top: If you hear some kind of riff that's way out there, you don't have to learn it and add it in to a song that really doesn't call for it. Still, it can become a source of reference for new and different ideas and approaches.

Work on your reading. If you don't know how to read music, learn to read music. Use the time you have and the musicians around you to gain knowledge in areas in which you are not as proficient.

Learn and work on another instrument. Let someone in the band teach you one of the songs you know so well on another instrument. You already know the song front to back, and starting on a different instrument with the foundation of your knowledge of the tune may make it a little easier.

Buy different books on music; rent documentaries or educational DVDs. Read magazines that interview your favorite musicians or influences. Bring more to the table as a complete artist who is working on his or her own craft to enhance the band as a whole. Talk to the band about *all members* taking the initiative to better themselves for individual purposes as well as the benefit of the group.

There are players, and there are bands that have players. There are musicians, and groups that have musicians, too. My favorite artists and bands are composed of musicians who continue to work on their craft and develop their voice individually while being a supplementing voice and player for the other artists they play with.

Grow, learn, develop, study, and aim to be better than you.

Supplemental Income

So you can't quite support yourself on the music alone yet, and although it would be much easier to donate 100 percent of your time to your craft and your dream, there is that whole thing about paying for the roof over your head, keeping the heat on and the water running, buying food, making car payments, and doing all those other adult things that demand fiscal responsibility. So you have to either continue what you're doing for a day job or find the right job to counterbalance your craft and your sanity.

It's not just about having a job and making the money you need until you can cross over to the full-time status of musician. It's about finding the right type of job that will enable you to perform both in what you have to do for the job at hand and allow you the energy and the stamina then to spend another day's worth of work on your craft.

First you have to make the decision about the job at hand. Is your goal to leave your job and become a full-time musician? It may seem like a stupid question, but the answer for many musicians is no. There are a number of people out there who are too scared of the concept and will continue to maintain the "day" job.

There is a checklist of items you have to go over when deciding what the best job is for you. Are you a morning person? Can you get going on little sleep? Does an early afternoon nap give you enough stamina to get moving for the rest of the day? If so, early morning jobs like a barista, a packer, or other early manual gigs can be a good idea. These are often shifts that get done early in the day and give you the rest of the day and evening to practice, play, and work on your music. These types of jobs can also allow for certain days off and being able to take small chunks of time off.

Whatever the job, be upfront during the interview. Explain what you are doing and how you are looking to work until you're able fully to support yourself musically. While some people want to hide this from bosses and potential employers, it can sometimes actually work in your favor. It shows you have drive and desire and that can be very attractive to a potential employer. Ask the employer about time off. Mention that you may be doing some short or long tours, and find out if the job will allow you to leave early on a Thursday and come back late on a Monday. They are out there; you just need to do a little more research to find them.

From there, work to figure out the finances and decide whether you have to go full time or part time. Do you have the option of a part-time job, and will it give you enough to get by? Or if it is a part-time job and hourly, can you work somewhere where you can put in a surge of hours on one day and work less on another?

Watch out for later-day jobs or evening jobs. Those tend to be the most problematic with bands. Though jobs such as being a bartender can bring in fast cash, you can run into scheduling issues on nights that you might need off to play. Which brings up the point that if you're in a band, try to create or have the same basic working schedule. If everyone is working mornings, then it will be a lot easier to practice, play, and work.

Now, as helpful as it may be to have the same schedule, you might not want to have the same jobs as other band members. As much hassle as a job can be, it can also serve as a little downtime from the band. I really advise against artists working together or working the same job. I know it's OK for some people, but I really find that having time apart from the group can be helpful. Stresses at work can come home and into the band dynamic, which is something you don't need. Even worse is when a band member of an equally divided group is working for another band member. This can create incredible frictions internally and affect the band as a whole.

So add a couple more questions and thoughts into the mix when you're figuring out what job will be best for you. Remember: It's not just a job to pay the bills. It's a transitional job that you can do to make the money you need while allowing you to be as productive and effective for your music as well. That's the best-case scenario and will help move things faster towards getting you out of that day job and achieving the goal of making music your full-time job.

A Life Outside of Music

When I was first starting out, I was practicing an obscene amount of hours. I got into a zone and knew I wanted to be a drummer. I would practice every day for anywhere between five and eight hours a day. I traveled two hours east, once a week, to study with my teacher Gary Chaffee for drum lessons, and I was also playing with four groups at the time.

I was living and breathing drums, and it was my dream. I wanted to keep getting better, and I wanted to learn all I could. My car was filled with albums that were very drummer oriented, and I was renting or buying every drum video that I could. I did grow during this time as a drummer, but at the same time, I was stagnant in other ways. I was living the life I dreamed of, but I had no life outside of it.

Then I began to notice that certain things I was working on weren't getting any better past a certain point. I found myself becoming more mechanical than I wanted to be. I felt my approach was becoming stifled while my technique and awareness still grew. I was obsessed with being as good as I could be and with being as prepared as I could be for my lessons. I was not thinking of the outside elements that supplement music. Even my main teacher told me to pull back some on the practicing. Then I got to do a session with an amazing saxophone player who I had looked up to for many years, and we had dinner after the session. I was in awe of his performance and thrilled to be hanging out with him.

The first question he asked me was, "What are your hobbies?" As I was going to answer him, I realized everything I was about to answer with were either things I wanted to do or things I had done in the past. I didn't have any hobbies. I didn't have any life. I didn't do anything outside of music. It was eye opening. Then he asked me what I would like to do, what could I do that would relax me, outside of music?

As this guy explained his hobbies and talked about how they affect his playing and his music, I began to think about ways to make some time for things I enjoyed. I got back to exercising, which was fun for me. I got back into the Red Sox, my favorite team, and I got back to comedy. I'm not funny, but I love comedians and comedy clubs.

The funniest part about all of it was that when I started practicing less, the practice time became more effective. I was growing again, both in my technique as well as conceptually. I was also finding a life outside of music, which brought more verve to my music and my playing.

The point is: It's crucial to experience life, to experience relationships and feelings outside of music, and bring them to the music in the best way possible. Don't use it as an excuse not to practice and not to work on your craft; use it as a supplement to expand your craft. This especially applies in songwriting. If you are only practicing and writing music around music, it may be hard to write songs that have more diverse and extensive topics.

For example, I can't stand the song "Wanted Dead or Alive." To me it's an example of a group that was writing while they were touring and produced a song that not even 1 percent of the population can relate to. Now, I know people write for themselves, but that particular song has always rubbed me the wrong way and just seems like an ego boost.

Either way, I prefer to see artists, musicians, and producers who not only work to hone their skills but also have a life outside of their work. I've gone back and forth at times, but I have found that when I can get away for a while, even for a few hours, I'm much more effective in the studio. Oftentimes at the end of a full session, I'll pop out to a bar to get away from all things music or just to get together with people who have nothing to do with the industry, to recharge some.

I also love catching Red Sox games, walking, and people-watching downtown. I've gotten back into swimming, hiking in some of the mountains around Washington, meeting people, and making new friends outside of music. I am reading again, even books not related to music.

The point is, even in the flurry of living the lifestyle I love, I'm taking the time to live outside of it. Hobbies help me relax, clear my head, and make me better at my work. Make sure you take the time to balance your life. You won't regret it.

Depression

Music, and any other field in the arts, can bring the most pleasure and, at the same time, the most pain. The despair that artists and musicians have faced over the years has been revealed both privately and publicly and now more than ever with the paparazzi capturing every move. In the past six months you couldn't turn on a TV or read a newspaper without seeing something about an entertainer who had either taken—or tried to take—his or her life, gone too deep into drugs and alcohol, or been viewed as "losing it" or going nuts.

Tours and shows have been cancelled as well as millions of dollars lost. Yes, the alcohol, the drugs, and the lifestyle contribute to the problem, but the root more often than not is depression, anxiety, and despair. It's that low, that worry, that has a very high rate of turning musicians to drugs, to alcohol, to gambling, to violence, to seclusion.

Depression occurs at all levels, whether it's the stress and strain of popularity and fame for those who are higher up in the industry or the stress and hopelessness of musicians who have been trying and can never seem to catch a break. It appears everywhere in between as well. The stress of recording, being fired from a group, having to fire someone, losing a deal, abrupt highs and lows in sales and attendance, feeling like the dream is never going to happen, internal arguments, the strain of relationships outside of the music, and tons more.

It's a lifestyle that's amazing, but at the same time it's loaded with challenges. To me, the challenges make it all worth it in the end. I'm not trying to be too blunt or harsh here, but if you think you're a little weak of heart, weak of mind, or weak of soul, the music industry is not for you, nor is any other entertainment field. If you cannot accept or prepare for terrible depressions, ongoing doubts, fears and disappointments ... again, you're in the wrong field.

Even planning and awareness will not prevent the emotional roller coaster of the music business. Regardless of how much you prepare, you will go through it; it's part of the deal, period. If you can take the right steps, you can make it easier and a little less painful, but I promise it will still hurt.

Think about the root of it all. Take just one element, like performing on stage for a show. Earlier in the day, you may have the anticipation, but you have to do other things, whether you are on tour and waiting to pull into the city or you're working your day job till you can get home to load out and get to the club. After you get to the venue, you set up and get to play for a few minutes during sound check; then there's the waiting game, which can last for hours. Finally, you get to your performance, and it can be amazing, but it only lasts so long, and after the spike of the music and the crowd energy, you're loading out your gear to either go home and work the next day, or you're going to a strange room in a strange bed in a city you might not know all that well.

That kind of shifting and swinging of energies can really do a once-over on your general mood. The wild high followed by the cut-off to the lowest low is a hard thing to take. I remember after playing one of my best shows as a drummer—you know the ones—the stage was amazing, the crowd was packed in and screaming, the lights, the sound, everything was just perfect. I got such a high off it, and then it was over. I was in the hotel room in a strange city that night alone, and I remember feeling like I just wanted to die because I was so sad, and I couldn't figure out why. I was in the middle of an amazing tour, I was having a blast, and yet the lows were so excruciating that they tore me apart.

I did my share of drinking, and I did my share of partying. For that matter, I did my share and a couple other people's shares as well. I found that by drinking and partying as well as sleeping, I could close the gaps between the lows and stay on this constant high. This was not the healthiest approach. The answer eventually came from a balance and from understanding myself and the way the moods and feelings would swing based on what was around me.

When I controlled the high of the stage, it in turn controlled the countering low later at night. I was not enjoying the stage experience any less or taking away any of the energy; I just didn't let myself get lost in the high, and it balanced out the low. I also paid more attention to my diet. I made sure to eat the right foods that would energize, always making dinner a lighter meal that would not make me crash after a show.

The better the balance during the performance, the better the balance was on the front and backside of the show. It can make a difference, and just because you control how high you allow yourself to go, it doesn't mean you won't be able to have as much fun. Think of it, in a way, like controlling the dynamic of an effect or the volume of your instrument. It's not any less powerful; it's just the way you're approaching that part of a song.

Being Stubborn

I run across a lot of stubborn artists. It's a big part of the reason I have potential artists that I produce or clients that work with Brain Grenade Entertainment fill out our initial client question form. It's a long, six-page form that has repetitive types of questions that help us get an initial view of the artist. Anyone that fills it out gets a free consultation, but even the length weeds out a great number of people, and if the attention to detail is not there, they are definitely not an artist that BGE or I would take on.

A couple of the questions hit toward the ideas of how hard a client wants to work and how open a potential client is to learning new ways or updating old ways that aren't working into new ways that do. If a client is coming to us or wanting to work with me as a producer, it's usually because what he or she has done so far has not worked effectively or the person wants to learn and take things further.

The problem that we sometimes run into, after the fact, is the stubborn artist. Artists in general tend to have strong egos, strong opinions, strong feelings, aggressiveness, and an all-around obstinate persona about them. I know this not just from those I have seen; I carry those traits as well.

A stubborn artist, who has a set of beliefs or views that cannot be adapted or altered, is an artist who is going to fail. Adapting, changing, learning, researching, and reviewing different ideas and ways to execute are fundamental to success.

If you're not prepared to bring those attributes into play, then keep the day job, period. A great number of artists find approaches on

TV, or read them in books, magazines, and interviews. Many of the elements are good, yet oftentimes they can transition to bad execution plans when the artist does not look at the entire scope.

Every element, every approach, is different and has to be individualized for the specific artist, and from there, it must be catered to for the style, sound, and plan. This is where the shortcuts occur and the failure ensues. A parallel concept is seen, or a parallel opportunity presents itself, and the artist follows a path that may at first seem to allot for the same style of success or fruition, and then they find that it can lead to more work, more effort, and greater costs to get it done.

Whether it's recording, production, advertising, touring, marketing, branding, fundraising, practicing, or anything in between, it takes a plan that can be the roots of something else or that has been effective for others. But then it must be carefully specialized for the specific client. Just because you sit through a ninety-minute lecture or clinic from an artist that made it big doesn't mean that you shouldn't further research and analyze the points that he gives you.

A good example is Band A. I am using the name Band A to protect the innocent. Sounds very Perry Mason, doesn't it? Anyway, one of the members of Band A, a successful platinum-selling group with videos, tours, groupies, the whole bit, was on a music panel that I spoke on three months ago. The event was put on to talk to independent artists about the best approaches and plans to succeed in the industry. As I sat next to this guy, I listened to his story, which was really pretty interesting. I learned about how the band actually formed and its road to success. I knew a fair amount about the band because of its popularity and the assisting producer is a friend of mine from San Francisco, but it was cool to hear the information right from one of the members. As the question section of the event began, I had to continually drink my coffee and cover my mouth to keep from screaming out – REALLY??!!!!! You actually are telling musicians to do that???????

Note: Band A is one of the .0007 percent groups. It was seen at a show and quickly signed to a manager. The thing that is left out is that the manager owned a major percentage of this band, and still does. When he brought the members to the label they are on right now, he penned the deal with the label since he had exclusive bargaining rights, a little thing the band signed away to him in the small print of the managing contract. He cut the deal, giving himself, the label, and the new touring agent, which became a part of the deal, the upper percentage and long-term rights to the band as a whole.

Now, some people don't mind this concept and would take it in an instant for the fame, immediate money, and success, but this band is going to end up in debt to the label for at least three more years. Although they are making money and they have fame, they are owned by this same label for five more albums and seven years with no "out" in their contract.

The advice that the member from Band A was giving could not have been more wrong. What he was telling the audience was what he had seen and what he was doing. He wasn't even aware of the promotions, marketing teams, and foundations being built around him and the rest of his group. He was not aware that their initial promotional roll-out was a $45,000 campaign that had interns galore working on it.

Then I took a few questions and explained some elements along the same lines. I carefully explained how another band actually did it the way I mentioned above, being careful not to say, "Dude, that was how it worked with your band, and you had no freaking idea?" He immediately chirped up and said, "No, that's not how the music industry works." This is where his approach switched from unaware to stubborn. A guy that was in five local bands who was picked up and controlled by management, a label, a touring agent, and a public relations firm, with one album under his belt was telling me, a person who has worlds more industry experience, **"This is not how it works."**

I'm not trying to pump up my own ego, but experience in a spectrum of groups, positions, labels, and albums that ranged from platinum to never-even-released, outweighs the single album and single experience of playing with one group. Afterwards, he signed the autographs, but to his surprise, people came over to talk to me and three others on the panel who were a lot more versed in the industry and the realistic approaches. **Let me be clear: I do not claim to know everything, but I've learned a great deal through the experiences I've had.** I'm also the first to admit when I don't know something and am always looking to learn new ways and new approaches that will work.

Talking with him in the car on the way back to the airport, he continued to explain to me how the industry works and how his band made it. As we were now in private, I asked him about his producer and the teams that worked with him, from the label to the PR people. He waved them off, saying that it was the shows that brought them to where they were. This was a conversation that I knew was going nowhere, so I changed the topic to sports. I am a Boston Red Sox fan, and he is from New York and a Yankees fan. I had a much more enjoyable argument with him talking about how I hate the Yankees and he hates the Sox.

The point of this story is that stubbornness can hurt you. To avoid it, look at all the facts. Even if something looks like a good thing, don't be impulsive.

Go through a checklist first …

- **How will it help in the short term and the long term?**
- **Who has it helped so far?**
- **When is the best time to execute this contact or opportunity?**
- **Do I need to have other elements in place to make this work?**
- **Am I working with a producer or creating a plan that is in motion?**
- **Have I consulted to see if this is good or when it would be best to apply?**

It doesn't matter if you have a studio that offers you all the time in the world. How good is the engineer, and what are the costs? Also, just because you might get into an amazing, famous studio, will it come with a great engineer or an intern just starting out? That doesn't help in making the industry standard recording, even if it is an industry standard studio.

What if you get a Web designer who gives you an amazing price but doesn't set up the site to allot you the most options and opportunities on the Web? Even if you have a service or a person who is more than up-to-snuff with what he or she can do and has done, does the person understand the details of the project you are creating? Is this a service or person you should back-pocket until he or she can be of maximum use, or is this person someone to use right out of the gate?

Don't be stubborn about these elements and facts, and don't claim to know what you don't. That mixes stubbornness with arrogance, which is a recipe for disaster and will hurt the sustainability of your project. It could also make more work, causing the service or person who is helping to end up either being wasted as a contact or not being used to the most effective potential. If you are working with someone who is guiding your project, talk to that person and tell what you have found. Communicate. Explain what you have and see how it can most effectively fit into the plan. Work together as opposed to separately. It will change the outcome of the project and bring the pieces together so much better.

Look to those with the wider array of experience over the one-shot or high profiles because often those people don't have a clue about the details of what got them there or they have a linear success that usually included tens of thousands of dollars that you don't have.

In the end, it's about patience and awareness. It's about educating yourself and learning from others while looking deeper and researching the extent of anything that is coming at you and anything you are going after. Not to knock anyone down a few pegs, but if you are so right in your approach, then why aren't you already where you want to be?

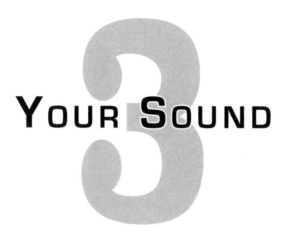

YOUR SOUND

The Hit Song

What makes a hit song is a question I've heard many people answer. I've read some articles that address the question and give downright embarrassing answers. I think what makes a hit song can be measured more by opinion than an actual formula, and even if you complete a formula, what kind of hit song are you creating?

Some say success lies in the melody, some point to lyrics, others point to hooks and turn-rounds. In my opinion they're all right. The hit song can be based in any one area of a song or it can be based in a meshing of different sections. I think it's a bad idea to sit down and take the approach that you're going to write a hit song. Many times the contrived mindset of this approach can make a song go down the tubes. For every time someone can tell you his or her approach on how to make a hit song, there are hit songs that break all the rules.

I highly advise reading up on your favorite songwriters and their approaches to your favorite songs by them, but learn the structure and the ideas and don't set any particular artists' formulas or methods in stone. Many who do end up sounding just like the artist they studied. Using their formulas as a writing exercise can be a good tool to understanding their particular approach. Don't forget, however, to mix the inspiration with the improvisation and creativity that you have, in order to achieve the songs that mean something to you and belong to you.

A hit song can be viewed as something that is a commercial success, but the root of it is a mixture of ideas and formulas. There are basic rules in the theory of music, but when it comes to creating that hit song, the guidelines are few and far between. In a sense that's why it can be so hard.

When I am producing an artist or the client's songs, I try to pay attention to the song as a whole, making sure that each section is clearly defined and developed. Along with the definition of a hook, the clarity of motion in each section is also important. Most imperative of all is the way the pieces fit together. Just as if you were cooking, you want to make sure you have all the right ingredients separately. They should all be the best they can be and not spoiled or rotten. Sometimes songs have verses that might be better if they were the root of another song.

I think this is the same recipe for creating the foundation of a song: Make sure you add the right ingredients at the right time in the right amount and in the right way. Make sure you create a song that not only works in each section by itself but also clearly transitions from one section to another. Sometimes small nuances that repeat throughout the song can tie sections together. Sometimes certain rhythmic or melodic fills can tie elements together.

But consider a different angle: What do you mean when you say "hit song"? Are you looking for a chart-topping million-dollar masterpiece that will play to the point of nausea? Maybe you mean a key track that helps you sell your album but also gets decent airplay or gets licensed to a soundtrack or used in a commercial. It's interesting how artists pore over what song will be their hit track and then spend all their time trying to push it to the charts, usually with no results.

It's good to remember the alternatives. A single song could be sold as a download or as part of a full album. It could be licensed to a movie, a TV show, a commercial, a video game, or perhaps to someone overseas who will sing it in another language. In such a scenario, even if the song doesn't go to number one or, for that matter, even hit the chart, you'll be seeing some solid royalties as you get exposure and make fans you would never have made if you didn't have the song playing in these channels. Using many channels is the most productive way not only to get your music out there but also to make money from royalties and placements instead of just sales off your album and downloads.

Push every song to its utmost potential in order to receive exposure and accrue payments. Maybe it will cross over to a hit song. I believe, though, that if you create a song, you can either go after the large-scale fame of a hit song, or you can make it a hit by taking all the smaller steps and soliciting the song into every avenue into which it might fit. Imagine if you were bringing in royalties and percentages or even a flat one-time payout. This makes the song a hit. It's a success. It's generated revenue and established one more notch in the résumé.

Transitions and Motions of a Song

Even the smallest part of a song can be a big part of its flow, structure, and foundation. Many people, when they write, put most of the emphasis on the intro, the outro, the verses, the choruses, and even the bridges. Often forgotten are the mini-bridges or the transitions between each of these larger sections.

Just like a bridge, but a lot shorter, these transitions can be for a couple of beats, less than a bar, or even an accent. The transitions don't have to be a separate part; they can be the very end of the section before. When I listen to an album, I listen for the song and the sections, but I pay a lot of attention to the flow, the way the song moves as a whole from beginning to end, and how each section moves from one to the next.

Here are a few points I always address as a producer when talking to songwriters:

- Is the ear being carried through the changes, or is it abrupt? Sometimes you might want it abrupt, but that can be the transition, and there is a way to lead it in a strong musical sense.

- Keep the foundation established. Reminding the listener about the foundation of the piece dates back to early classical music. Listen to the music for Bach's Goldberg Variations. He takes very interesting movements while reinforcing the core theme. You can be in a totally different key and a totally different section but still hint at the foundation of the tune.

- Solidify and clearly identify each section. Is the motion of the song from chords to instrumentation to lyrics defined in each section? Does it move forward? Again, it's not about being boring or obvious; it's about defining the tune as the writer.

- Establish the transitional leads as their own hooks to the previous and leading sections. If you have a clear transition from the bridge to the chorus, use it again, or maybe have that rhythm or note set played on another instrument when that section comes around again. Think themes and approaches.

- Identify the active dominant voice of the transition. Which voice is it coming from, and which voice it is leading to? For example, if the transition is a drum fill and it opens up into a chorus where a female is singing a high note, make sure the final hit of the fill does not conflict with the first note of the voice. High notes from females and males can get washed in cymbal crashes. It's not about changing things too much; it's about being aware of the qualities.

Don't get too wrapped up in the mathematics of it.

You want to keep yourself in a creative field. What I recommend to artists is to look at a song in a couple of different ways as they play it. Listen one time for the form, listen another time for the transitions, and listen a third time for another element. Study the art you have created from a number of different perspectives, and you will create a well-rounded piece of work.

Developing Your Songs for the Studio

Below are ten of my favorite approaches that I suggest to artists who want to develop their songs a little further in pre-production and that I apply in the studio with bands.

10. Chord inversions where fifth becomes the root of the transitional chord.

Sometimes inverting a chord where the fifth is in the bottom and the transition allows it to become the root can make for a smooth movement. This is a simpler, more open technique, but it can give a nice easy exchange without complex movement.

9. **Single note voice transitions.**

    If you are transitioning through a single line or note, doing a transition from one instrument to another can be very cool. On the album *Nothing Like the Sun* from Sting, he does a cover of Jimi Hendrix's "Little Wing." At the end of the guitar solo, a note is held and taken over from the soprano sax. It is a smooth and slick transition into the turnaround of the solo before the repeat.

    You can use a number of instruments and mix them into one another. You can use voices as well.

8. **Rhythmic pattern or rhythmic theme in another instrument or voice.**

    If a certain rhythm is used as an ostinato or repeated phrase by one instrument or even the whole band hitting the accents, you can bring a sense of that section back without the accents by having a single instrument repeat the rhythmic phrase in a different section of the song or as an intro to the accents that will be hit by everyone.

7. **Pannings and fades.**

    Panning across different instruments or fading certain voices and instruments up and down can bring a very ethereal change that is not as noticeable or as in the forefront but is definitely felt.

6. **Drum/bass/percussion/guitar/etc. fills.**

    Basic fills from any given instrument or mix of instruments is a common transition. A fill, perhaps played by the guitar into the first chorus, could be played by the bass into the next, keeping the same notes and form while bringing a different sound into play. The drums can do the same pattern as well.

5. **Silence/obscure removals of instruments and voices.**

    Dropping out the bass and the drums, killing the percussion, or bringing out a guitar in a transition can create an abrupt yet smooth change. Changing up the tones and the microphones of the instruments into a different section can help with this as well.

Even something as simple as killing the bass drum and the bass or going to only room microphones on the drum set can create a motion for the ear that will draw the listener in even more.

4. **Added pads of other instruments—brass, strings, backing vocals, etc.**

Fading in and out basic pads in the transitions can add a supplemental element to a song, even if it's just for the transition. It can add another layer and hint at something coming or going in the tune.

3. **Dynamics**

The most obvious and simple yet the most effective and used way to transition a song is to pump up the volume of the band or bring the band way down. You can also bring up or down the dynamics of a couple of instruments. Another way to play with dynamics is to have one instrument get softer or louder.

2. **Doubling with secondary voices and other instruments.**

Almost like padding, you can double an existing voice or instrument with itself or with another instrument to bring a richer texture. If a guitar line is doing a descend into the chorus, maybe add a horn or an acoustic guitar, even a vibraphone, to join and complement the run down into the chorus.

1. **Reverse effect on existing voices/instruments or additional samples or instruments.**

Flip it around. Try reversing any sound from a snare drum to a cymbal to a guitar hit to anything. In certain places, a reverse lead-in can bring a cool dynamic tension into a new section. Sometimes piggybacking can really emphasize it. By turning a cymbal around and then leading it into the original crash you can really open up a section and offer a different type of transition.

Play around and have fun. You don't have to use every trick in the book. Think of these as embellishments to play with, not requirements. Don't go too over the top in the same song with these, or you will run into the world of overproduction and make it a song that will be impossible to re-create live.

There are tons of ideas and a lot more than just these. Play with concepts yourself and read up on how others approach production and songwriting for even more ideas.

These are just a few I think of when I listen to songs I am working on that might need something more. Sometimes the writers exert so much concentration on the chorus, the verse, the bridge, or the hook that they don't think about the leading and transitions in each of the sections.

As a writer, review the changes of your tunes. Listen to other writers—not just the sections but also the transitions. Study and learn about other producers and their ideas. Listen to other styles of music and how the sections transition. It can really help you in your own writing.

Play with Your Food

Many artists strive to get the best gear, the top equipment, and the most stuff that they can possibly cram onto stage or into the studio. Whether it's that drum or this toy or that additional instrument, many musicians today have too much stuff, and most of them don't even know how to use half of what they have. So play with your toys. Mess around with buttons, sounds, tunings, setups, etc. You may know the basic sounds, but what else can you do to find out even more about your gear?

In some ways, when you purchase a certain effect or instrument, it's as if you have purchased a kitchen's worth of supplies and food. When you only use a certain configuration or a certain setup, it's the same as using only one kind of food from that kitchen. I have a favorite food, but I also like variety, and I like to know what all my options are before I prepare or order what I want to eat. Why not apply the same ideas to your gear? Change the settings, do the unusual to get out of the usual mode. You never know what you may discover. Take a little time to experiment each day with your gear and/or instrument to find out what might inspire something new and different.

Missing a String or Not Missing It at All

This goes for tuning, setting up, and practicing. Guitarists, have you ever worked on your songs with one string missing? How would you rephrase the chord or substitute for that chord if you were missing a string? How does it make you approach your soloing in a different way? Do you find yourself creating or finding new licks from having that string missing?

Why not try it over a period of six weeks where each week you remove a different string? Run through your tunes, your practicing, and improvisation to see what happens. You may find you're more prepared and able to continue playing during performances even if you break a string.

Write It Down

Don't spend time worrying about losing your settings and the ones you like the most. Write them down. List where you have knobs turned to or settings placed at. You can take pictures if that helps. Then write down the different settings you discover while playing with your toys. Keep a diary of different settings and their effects, what you like, what you don't like. It will help you learn how to find and remember the sounds you like as well as help you learn what you don't like and how not to avoid it.

Don't just settle for the sounds you know. Take chances, take time, and add some effort to learn the full array of the gear you have. Understand how you can change sounds and how those sounds can change your playing. From turning knobs, to taking away a string, to removing a drum to anything and everything in between, research, listen and think of different ways you can express yourself. You already invested the money in the gear. Invest the time to know it inside and out.

Odd Time Approaches

Having a good sense of time is a great tool in practice. Odd times can be fun and can give a feel to a song such that, when people hear it, they can't quite put their finger on what's different, but they know something is. It's a strange phenomenon, but most Americans feel a comfort in three or four but not many other time signatures. In different countries around the world, feeling time signatures like 11/8, 15/8, and 9/8 are commonplace, yet the average American pulses on the down beat and needs to hear some kind of up beat that's even as well.

Many progressive rock and fusion artists take a very purposeful approach to writing in odd meters as well as bringing sections of songs through a number of different time signature changes. Yet in the mainstream, the mass buying population is all about hearing things in four or three time. Peter Gabriel, with his song "Solsbury Hill," is one of only a handful of artists to chart a tune in 7/4 in the billboard top 20.

Now of course if you ask most drummers, they will reference Neil Peart and Rush, as well as many other groups that are a little more progressive and often a little more open with time signatures. They talk about great feels in odd times, but often when I hear a lot of groups trying to work in odd meters, it ends up feeling very contrived. I believe the best approach to working in odd meters is to be comfortable: Treat the odd meter as if it's a normal meter. Record yourself, especially the drummers!!! Do you notice that you are over-accentuating the one? Would you do that in normal even meters? If not, work to find that comfort zone.

There's no special secret to odd time and meters. It's all about being able to execute comfortably and being able to play phrases with a full awareness of where the beat is in the bar. In a normal bar of four, most people easily feel the one as they land on the beat—when it's about to come around and when they're leaving from it to the two. This comfort zone allows the drums, or for that matter, any instrument, not to need to accentuate the one on every bar or turnaround. Younger artists or artists who are not as comfortable with odd times will punch the one on every bar, sometimes every other bar, but it's much more prevalent and in your face than those same parts being played in a normal four or three bar measure.

Much of the time, these grooves in an odd time signature lock up and become stale or dry. Sometimes, with the lack of prowess or comfort in an odd meter, the drummer, especially, will become robotic.

The best approach to succeed at these odd times is to subdivide. When I was drumming in five, I actually never counted to five. I would count in my head 1-2-3-1-2. So I would combine a three-beat and two-beat pattern in my head. This helped me feel a pocket a little more. It also allowed me to work on developing phrases that were not based on landing solely on the one. I also would phrase it as 1-2-1-2-1 to create a more bouncy feel in the middle of the phrase. To get a more full, staccato phrase I would count out 1-2-3-4-1.

Different techniques work for different people. I really recommend looking up and reading articles about your favorite musicians to see how they approach odd times. It may help you have a greater understanding of their approach.

Try taking songs that are in even time, stretch them out to odd times and see what could be added, or take a song in four, drop it to three, and see what could be taken away. The more you play with moving phrases, melodies, and time around, the more comfortable you will find yourself in odd meters.

Listen closely when you are playing in the times you are most comfortable with. Listen to how you phrase, how you accent, and how you move across the bar. This is a great exercise in both technical practice and in gaining a greater understanding of your personal approaches to writing or performing.

The goal, then, is to work in the odd meters to achieve those same results. When you can feel the pulse of eleven, fifteen, nine, or seven in the same way you can feel four, you will be able to execute a much more solid feel and groove in those odd times. This will also give you additional strength in the even times.

Odd times are tricky, but add them to your regimen of practice and writing. Work to phrase in the meter you are attempting, and try to avoid the biggest pitfall of phrasing an even meter idea with beats either subtracted or added.

I started working on the odd meters of five, seven, and nine when I first started exploring meters, and slowly, I became more comfortable with the ideas of time that stray from the usual. Test the waters with five, and for the drummers … do not crash or accent too hard on the one every time.

Lastly, go back through things you have written, maybe something you have tossed or thrown away … something that just didn't seem to fit for the song or section you were working on. If it had an extra few beats, or if you took away a beat or two, could it work? It could be a song or section that you have already phrased to work in an odd time, and you didn't even know it.

Play around; expand your time vocabulary, both as a performer and a writer. Perhaps the bridge of a song that's in an even time isn't working because you have it phrased in something that would work better in an odd time. You don't have to start right out of the gate writing full songs in odd time. Maybe sections, like bridges or codas, could be in an odd time. Even just dropping a bar at the end of each chorus can give the tune an interesting friction that pushes and transitions it well into the next verse.

Have fun, mess around with the possibilities, test the waters. Sometimes going odd can be pretty normal.

Samples

Samples are still a prevalent part of the music industry today. You can go online and buy beats, loops, grooves, effects, sounds, parts, and even sections of songs. You can also go and steal them, which is becoming too common these days.

I'm not a real big fan of taking samples from other people. I don't like when artists download samples, whether purchased or stolen; it's something I ask artists to avoid at all costs. I much prefer that artists create their own loops and samples.

If you hear something funny or a sound that you like, try to recreate it. If you want that car-start sound, let's go out with a microphone and sampler or recording mobile rig and grab the sample ourselves. I find it better for the music as a whole, both musically and from a marketing standpoint. I would rather see artists be able to say truthfully that they recorded the album—all the tracks and all the samples—themselves as opposed to pulling this sample from here, stealing this sample from there, and buying this sample from somewhere else.

Often, musicians are influenced by a certain song, which then has an effect on a tune they're writing. You take the inspiration and then add your own touch, which makes it yours. Taking a sample directly from somewhere else, on the other hand, feels like a shortcut to me, and what happens if it's stolen and then you start to get sales and are caught?

Then the fit hits the shan (ahem).

The lawsuits over samples are common and extremely expensive. These suits can grab percentages of what you have already sold, in addition to fees and costs associated with stealing property. Don't do it! Don't steal samples. I push artists to own their own music and skip covers for recordings, and I think of samples in the same way. Adding a sample to a song, whether legally or illegally, is like adding a cover to your album. Even if it's part of the song, it's something you didn't create. It's ironic how musicians who use such heavy numbers of samples brag so much about what they've created.

Plan for the best possible success on any recording and make it yours. I'm much more drawn to sample-heavy albums, such as R&B and hip-hop, which list on the back cover that all samples are the creation and property of that artist. It's one more marketing element to make you stand out and show what you're made of.

Take a number of days outside of the studio to think about why you want a sample and the sample you like from something that already exists. How can you record to get that sound or effect or loop? Take the steps to make it yours. Just as you write and produce the music that's yours, do the same for the samples.

As a drummer, I did a number of sampling sessions for different hip-hop artists. I would set up, we would get the microphones up on the drum kit, and I would play a number of four and eight bar phrases with some different feels and ideas. Then those artists and their producers would add the effects and the mix tones to my drums to create the drum loops or samples they wanted to use. I was not there for more than an hour, and they had tons to work with.

Even just going for a walk—what sounds do you hear? How would you capture them? How would you make a normal musical instrument sound a little different or give it a touch that would sample well and create something that's yours?

This is how a lot of artists thought when samples were new, and it's a great mindset to keep. We have had harmonica players play into toilet bowls to get a different sound. Even Paul Simon sampled a snare drum in an elevator shaft to add that powerful explosion sound in the choruses of "The Boxer." Try flanging the sounds of footsteps, playing on trashcans, or doing anything you can think up. Anyone can go online and grab samples and loops that enhance a song. Take the road that's a little harder: Create your own. Make them yours.

I know there are producers out there who will disagree with me on this. I do respect the use of samples and have many albums that have many samples on them. I just believe that when you are creating your own music, you should also create your own samples.

I believe it's much more rewarding musically and a great marketing bullet point to add in post-production that you are the author of the music, the samples, and the album as a whole. It will help make you stand out in a world in which artists steal, grab, buy up, and—in all honesty—cut corners to create tracks that could be so much better if they'd just taken a couple more days to brainstorm and figure out how to enhance a song by making the samples themselves.

Yes, you may use session players and others—musicians, a producer, an engineer, other members of your group—to assist you, but these are all people directly involved in your songs and your work, who help you get them to where you want them to be. Take that extra time to create your own specialized embellishments and supplemental sounds. They are your songs, so keep them that way, from each instrument, to each voice, to each sample.

What Are You Listening To?

What music did you listen to today? Was it one of your favorite songs, albums, or compilations? Was it something you listen to often? Once you've got that figured out, ask yourself a few more questions. Beyond practicing your instrument, writing your music, and managing the business side of things, how are you nurturing your ears and your inspirations? Just as you needed books in school to provide you with a vocabulary that would allow you to write, you need to listen to music in the same way. It's about connecting with what you like but also listening to where it comes from.

In some ways, it's like vitamins—musical supplements. While you might prefer big band jazz, it can be educational to listen to other styles, like pop, country, and Latin, to name a few. Even crooners like Frank Sinatra listened to and even covered artists like the Beatles. It's about understanding what inspires you but also about being a student of music, which means listening to as much as you can, even the stuff you don't like.

While you might not enjoy this style or that genre, it can be beneficial to consume it, just like your vegetables when you were a kid. They didn't taste that good, but they were brain food, and they helped you grow big and strong—you know the old hype. In the same way, listening to something you don't particularly enjoy is brain food. It can give you a better understanding of its successful elements as well as clarity in why you don't like it. Personal knowledge along these lines will make you a stronger musician, writer, and communicator when you're asking someone to play something a certain way or even describing it yourself.

With YouTube, iTunes, and countless artist Web sites, it's easier than ever before to listen to and find music. From samples to full albums, there's a pretty good chance it's on the Internet or possible to get a hold of. Researching music is much easier as well. Since it's literally at your fingertips, why not commit at least ten to fifteen minutes a day to finding, learning about, and listening to both new and old music?

It's true: Everyone has favorites, and I know there are times when I can put on an old album and just listen to it a few times in a row. In many ways that's the joy of music. That can also be educational. Still—add the learning, the exploring, and the searching to your day. Find out about the past. Figure out the influences of your favorite bands and check them out. Hell, find out the influences of their influences and dig back even further. You might be surprised at what you learn and also what you like. As they say, try it before you say you hate it. Some of you probably didn't mind the cauliflower after all—once you finally ate it.

Scott Ross, one of my favorite engineers and owner of Elliott Bay Recording Company in Seattle, sums it up perfectly: "If you are going to be in the music industry, you have to know some damn music history. You don't have to like Elvis, but you better know who he is. If you are a drummer you better know who Gene Krupa is. If you are a bass player, you better know who Abe Laboriel is. If you are a trumpet player, you better know who Maynard Ferguson is. If you don't know who these people are, how can you connect yourself with the history of your instrument to know where it came from yesterday and where you are bringing your sound, approach, or ideas to today?"

It's crucial to know the past. There are many different opinions on what drummer was the most talented and who was the best bass player and so on and so forth. It really doesn't matter. It's not about learning who was the best, the most famous, the most this or that, or spending too much time absorbing an entire catalog of music, though you might find an artist or musician who inspires such a pursuit. The point is to become familiar with these artists and to have a basic understanding that allows you a broader view as a whole and will make you a better musician, listener, and student of music.

It's interesting how many people out there claim they're doing something that has never been done before. Maybe they talk about how they can't be compared to anyone at all and they are totally original. I have talked to way too many artists who claim they sound like no one else, and once I turn them on to a track or an album from some band they never knew about, even they can hear the similarities. This can go for bands, artists, and even individual musicians.

I remember about eighteen years back when drummers were going nuts over Carter Beauford. Now don't get me wrong, the guy burns, but there was all this hype from drummers claiming he was reinventing the drums and doing things that had never been done before. I'm not taking anything away from Carter. He's a badass drummer, but if you study drums, you can hear the influence of Tony Williams and Buddy Rich ring very clearly. Papa Joe Jones is another influence you can hear in his playing. When I checked out Carter for the first time, I was not surprised to find him state that those were three of his biggest influences.

By learning about the past as well as musicians you've never heard of, you'll be able to compare, contrast, and explain where you're coming from, what you sound like, and what you're looking for when connecting with other musicians. The same information can help you develop your promotional materials. I know everyone wants to be original, but we all take from other places. If you can pinpoint influences or specify that you sound a little like this or that artist, it can potentially draw a new fan to you. If you have an array of artists, the mix might inspire someone to check you out who might otherwise not have.

On the harsher and briefer side of it, if you truly think you are recreating the freaking wheel, you don't know history. It was probably done thirty-some years ago. Maybe not with the same effects, but no, you didn't invent it. Same goes for the lack of ability to compare yourself to anyone else. If you can't, you don't know your music history, or you listen to a very limited amount of music.

It's not that there aren't innovators, people who are creating new things, but a completely new thing really hasn't been done in a very long time, and since there are only so many beats in a bar, so many notes in a scale, and so many alterations of a chord, there is a pretty decent chance that, while it may not be exact, you are in the ballpark of someone who came before you.

Find out all you can about as much music as you can. Use the Internet, use your friends' collections. Try listening to something old or new everyday. Give it your attention and see what you love or hate about it. It doesn't mean you have to own the entire catalog. It doesn't mean you have to spend hours upon hours studying the others, but get familiar with as much as you can. It will broaden your horizons and help you in more ways than you know. There's no right way or wrong way to do it; just expand your horizon, your vocabulary, and your ears. You might even enjoy it and find all sorts of things you never knew were out there to inspire you.

GIGGING

Whether it is one show, a weekend worth of shows, or a tour, gigging is a core part of the dream that reaches way back to the beginning of that desire to be a musician. To be out there live in front of an audience, performing your songs and playing for the crowds, is a big part of what it's all about for a lot of musicians. Many of the failures related to music can often be due to the gig or the live show, as well. Sometimes that's all musicians are about, and they don't want to deal with any other part of the business involved in the music industry. But even if they do, there's a whole separate mess of business surrounding gigs and tours. Many people would think that's obvious: There's a lot that goes into a show and even more for a series of them, but just how much they may not realize.

Organization, planning, and attention to detail have to be given to every element in order to make a gig successful. From the marketing to the contracts with venues or booking agents, set lists to loading in and the etiquette considerations for the stage, the back stage and everywhere else, you want to be as professional and effective as you can be.

The better the performances, the more you will be asked to play. Basically, the more crowds you draw, the longer you can stay out on the road and the larger number of people will hear about your band. It's not about driving into town ten minutes before you go on stage, having a couple of shots and a beer, and slowly letting the night get sloppier and sloppier. Today, to find that sustainable level of success, which will allow you to gig more and more as well as tour and sell your music and merchandise, you must take a new approach to the gig itself.

It's still all about fun, creativity, improvisation, and doing what you love. While there are aspects of the business in marketing and Web work that are always going to suck, live stage work will always be incredible. For this reason, it should be given time and planning to make it the best show from an organizational and business savvy standpoint.

The gig should not be viewed as a linear one-time event or just a show. Every show should be seen as the part of your career that you love the most, and you need to remember that love of playing and project that, whether you are playing for ten thousand people or just ten. Then take into account that you need to fill the seats or the standing room and move product so you can continue to play more and more shows. After that, make sure you have figured out all the logistical elements to make sure the show will be a success and you will be taken care of, and don't forget: Even while you're on stage performing, you need to make sure you're adding in all the elements of marketing and promoting your band, the name of your band, your products, and other merchandise as well as bringing more fans to your fan base. When you're playing a gig or a number of gigs and take all these elements into consideration, you're being the most productive and effective you can possibly be, which will allow you to play more gigs and tour longer.

The more you can organize and plan in advance, as well as set in place the templates to allow you the best level of success for every facet of a gig, the less you'll have to worry about come show time and the more you can enjoy performing. Gigging, touring, and performing are the best parts of being a musician. If you take into consideration all the details—the checklist of everything that should be done before, during, and after the show—you will find every show will help you grow larger audiences, lead to better shows, and allow you to enjoy the best part of being a musician that much more.

Gig Essentials

Here are some good rules to live by when you are playing a show. If you are professional and give off a strong presence on and off the stage, you will be invited back. Many of these ideas are simple, and you have probably thought of them, but applying them will ensure your popularity with both the audience and the venue.

1. **Confirm the date with the venue two weeks in advance**

   Call the venue's booking agent or management group to confirm the show and double-check arrival times. Find out if there are any last minute changes that you should be aware of. This highlights your professionalism, and it gives reassurance that you and your band will be there. There are many times when a club double-books by accident or a band doesn't show up. Confirming the date will ease your mind as well as the venue's.

   Add a column in your show spreadsheet for confirmation, and check it off as you call each venue.

2. **Tip the soundman**

   Tip the sound guy or girl. This is the person handling your sound, and he or she has the ears at the front of the house. Take care of this person, and he or she will remember you. When I was on the road, we often gave a ten or twenty to the soundman, and any time we came back, the soundman took extra special care of us.

3. **Be early, be prepared**

   Know the room and know where you are playing. Know the potential traffic problems of the area. Get there early and make sure to double check that you have all your equipment, your merchandise, and your contracts (if required). Print out the directions and contact information so you can call the venue if there are problems. Know when load-in time is, and make sure you are there and ready to go. These small details will make all the difference.

4. **Do a last minute poster run of the area**

   Grab some posters during the downtime and hit the vicinity of the club. Do some last minute promotion, hand out some leaflets, and see if you can book a radio interview between the load-in and the performance. There is so much wasted time between sound check and the actual show that can be filled up with effective marketing.

5. **Be nice and be aware**

Show respect to the venue, the staff, and the other artists. Some nights may not have the nicest rooms, the best stage, or the best shows. Still, showing respect is paramount. Don't talk trash about the room, other bands, or anyone for that matter. If someone is talking trash about you, take the higher road and keep your mouth shut. Venues, managers, agents, and staff will see it and, in turn, will want to work more with acts like you.

If you have problems with your monitors, your agreement, or with anything that's wrong, address it in a respectful manner. There is no need to go "diva," and it doesn't make anyone want to help you. When you come at someone with respect, most of the time you will get it in return.

6. **Organize yourself and your gear**

Make sure all the gear is top notch. As you unload, get your cases out of the way. Find out where the green room is or where you are supposed to store things, and try to consolidate and pack your stuff tightly. If it's a shady place, bring the cases back to the cars. Count up your merch; make sure to track everything you need to go over. Talk to the soundman about issues or important things that he or she might not be aware of. If you are bringing certain sound equipment, make sure it is well marked and not easily mistaken for the venue's gear. Same goes with cords and power supplies. It will make your life a lot easier.

7. **Get on and off the stage quickly**

If you're doing a load-on during the set, organize your gear to the side of the stage. Figure out an order for the gear and find the fastest way to get it up on the stage and ready to go. Ask if the band before you needs help loading off. Too often people waste time standing around, which backs up the sets and ends up either cutting bands' sets or making delays that don't need to be there.

Load off quickly as well. If there's a band coming up, move pieces off the stage right after you are done. Don't take a cymbal off its stand on stage; take the stand with the cymbal on it off the stage. Unplug and move. Show respect to the venue and the next band. People remember things like that. Don't go have a conversation, get a drink, or hang out. Clear the stage first, and then be social.

8. **Market on stage**

Have a great show and have a good time with your audience, but don't forget to market while you're on stage. Mention the band name numerous times. Get it into the audience's head. Bring up the Web site, the primary social network you use; tell them the name of the album or merchandise that you have. Tell the audience where you are from. Brand your sound and your name to your crowd so they'll know how to find you after the show.

9. **Market the show well in advance**

Promote and market your shows well in advance. Promotion brings people out, and even if you do not have a budget to market, you can still go grassroots and make things effective. Using press releases, craigslist, social network sites, local radio, and local Web sites where the venue is based can help. Start promotion six weeks out with releases. This will allow the time to get stories done about the show and the band.

10. **Have fun, or at least look as if you are enjoying yourself**

Whether there are five, fifty, or five hundred people, play the same show. Showcase what you're about by displaying that, regardless of how many people are there, you're having fun, having a great performance, and making the most out of whatever situation you're in. Connect with the audience no matter how large or small, and you'll continue to build a fan base. Every show is as important as the next one: Act that way and you'll see results.

Lastly, work the eye contact. I can't stress that enough. Look at the audience and connect with them. This is where you're going to build the reputation, and it's where the buzz about your shows and performances gets started. If you make them walk away wanting more, they'll come back and then some the next time you play.

I Spy ... Myself on Stage

When was the last time you videotaped or digitally recorded yourself on stage? When was the last time you watched yourself perform, scrutinizing the playback for performance issues, pros, cons, or just an overall review of your stage presence? Most people never have. Or, if they have recorded themselves, the footage was taken by fans or friends from a terrible vantage point, or the cameras were directly on stage for music video footage.

Videoing yourself and your band can be much more than just a marketing and promotional tool for YouTube segments or anything else that shows off you or the band. Self-videoing can be an instructional tool to help you refine your stage presence, tighten your musical technique, even straighten your slumped-over, emo posture.

For the sake of how you appear, how you play, how you stand, and how you act, interact and react on stage, get in front of the lens and record yourself. Learn about your stage show, including all the stage habits you have—good and bad. This awareness and study of yourself on stage can help you present a better show as well as point out problems that may be occurring that you don't even realize until you see them for yourself. Approach watching the video playback the same way you approach your recorded audio playback. Watch, analyze, learn. It will help you in more ways than you could ever imagine.

Lights, Camera, Action?

For starters, you have to set up cameras in places where there are unobstructed views. Sometimes having a camera on a tall stand that's above the mixing board or somewhere close to someone who will keep people from stealing it will help you greatly. Having others shoot you can work well, but make sure they understand that they're shooting for your benefit and not the master genius behind some music video. It's also a good idea to have a couple of cameras if you can, or if you only have a single camera, concentrate on different people for each show so you can see all the different elements that are occurring.

Talk to the venue to try to have enough lighting, or for that matter, shoot in rooms that have good lighting so that you can clearly see and review the video instead of squinting at a dark mash up of the stage and some shadowy figures on it.

Basically, use your head. You are recording yourself so you can review your performance. Take into consideration all the aspects of lighting, placements, and most important, make sure you or someone is turning on and off the cameras. It sounds stupid, but bad communication and lack of preparation can mean you have some great cameras angled that aren't even turned on. Oh yeah, take off the lens caps, too.

Man, I look good, but what else am I looking out for?

Okay, get over that little ego flare of watching yourself on stage—especially you guitarists. Yes, guitarists, I'm picking on you. Stereotypes are based on truth, and this one's no exception. Okay, end of guitarist rant. After you get over the fun of watching yourself perform, it's time to get down to watching for the core elements that can help you develop the best show possible.

1st Review—Technique, Posture, and Exhaustion

This is probably one of the best things to be aware of and review. How are you performing with your body and your instrument? How is it affecting your abilities and your performance? Look for signs of bad posture that might indicate early fatigue. Are you moving around like a wild person for the first half of the set and then pretty much stationary for the second half? Then maybe you should spread out how often you are moving or how active you are to be able to have the best level of endurance for the show.

Watch for the technical aspects of whatever instrument you're playing as well. If you're a drummer, how's the posture of your drumming? Are you finding that you are tiring out too fast or can barely finish the set? Maybe your posture or certain flourishes are actually detrimental and extra exhausting when you're playing live. Reviewing from this perspective can help you with your performance, your technique, and your endurance. Whether you're holding your bass too low or jerking your neck while singing, this first review can help clean up such undesirable mannerisms.

2nd Review—Appearance, Interactions, and Reactions

How do you look on stage to each other? How do you look on stage to the audience? Do you look as if you're having fun? Do you look as if you're interacting with the members of the band and the members of the audience? Is the stage balanced? Is the main action centered? Does every part of the stage get played throughout the performance?

Sometimes having a camera pointed from behind the drum set and out to the audience can help you gauge how the audience is reacting to your performance. Watch for when they are most connected, and try to figure out why. What songs are getting the best reaction? Which ones are getting the worst? When as a whole does the audience look disinterested, and when are they hanging on every note?

Watching the audience can help you design better set lists or become a little more aware of when things are moving too slowly. Remember, you want to keep the audience involved and connected. Videos will help you dial into these specifics.

3rd Review—Eye Contact, Reoccurring Technical Issues, Marketing, and Other Miscellaneous Things

In this last review, watch for both good habits and bad habits that might be occurring from eye contact to marketing. Watch where you're looking. Are you connecting with the other members and the audience? Are you always looking down, closing your eyes, or staring in one particular direction? Watch for technical issues as well. What constant or common problems have to be addressed with your equipment or your setup on stage? What can be streamlined, adjusted, or taken care of before a show to keep those time wasters down to a minimum. Again, this is a great time to watch for and identify such issues.

And what about marketing? Are you saying the name of the band? Are you promoting while you're on stage? Are you keeping it short and sweet and keeping the motion of the show moving? Do people know where to buy merchandise or where to sign up for a mailing list? Make sure you're not talking too much or for too long. Watch for moments that slow down or hasten the pace of the show. Analyze them thoroughly. Again, this can help refine your performance and keep an audience connected with you from start to finish.

Just as you review your audio to ensure you're delivering the right sound, review the video so you can make sure you're delivering the right performance. Most artists perform a great deal more than they record, so it's absolutely necessary to review all aspects of your stage presence. Lights, camera, action—then review. Increase your awareness of what's happening on-stage and use that knowledge to heighten and tighten your show and deliver the best possible performance.

Set Times and Song Plans

Set lists are often altered by bands, depending on the time they have on any given night at any given show. If you have to fill up a couple of hours, you're looking to stretch things sometimes or add extra songs you don't usually do. On the opposite end, if you only have twenty-five minutes, you have to trim the set and decide what you're going to cut out and what you're going to keep in. It's really important to set up song plans logically, creatively, and effectively or to set lists that are not only going to showcase the songs but also going to present them in the best order and with consideration for the time you're allotted to play.

Now on the long side, if you have a full night to fill up, deliver more rather than less, especially if you're playing to new people and building a fan base. Some of the jam bands that spend twenty-five minutes on a song can really bore people. Fans as a whole have attention deficit disorder, especially when it comes to new things. Keep a set moving with new songs and mood changes to keep the attention of the crowd. Pay attention to the keys and tempos. Though a song that's in the same key and close in tempo may seem so different to you, it might seem as if it's still the same song to someone not paying close attention. Spread out the songs that are in the same keys and same tempos.

Keep the show moving; keep the songs moving. If you need to add a couple of extra cover songs, then spread them out. If you're playing a really long night, such as three or four sets, you can bring back some of the songs from the first set. Also, as you start a set, make sure you give the punch, the kick to say, "Hey, here we are, now listen!" On the same note, as you finish a set, give a nice solid ending to the last song. Make sure it's a clear-as-day finale, and make sure to tell the audience you'll be back and where your merchandise is being sold during the break.

On those long nights, keep the breaks limited to exactly what you say they are. If you're taking a fifteen-minute break, stick to it. So many bands will disappear for way too long, which can lose audience members and piss off the venue owners or management. If you say fifteen minutes, make it fifteen minutes. Tell them what time you'll be backup on stage. I know some bands in New York that will actually put up a little back in fifteen sign with the times on it hung on the microphone. I thought that was cute and actually pretty effective.

Playing more songs in a long set is more effective than stretching songs, as far as the attention span of the audience goes. As you build up your audience and fan base and want to explore things further, I would advise stretching things later. The more you give people, the more they can take in and feel as if they're getting new things thrown at them.

I'm not saying don't take solos, but unless you're doing jazz or fusion or music that's based on soloists and solo interaction, keep to a single solo or two short solos for two people per song. If you don't have the material, learn covers to spread across the set. It's worlds better to add covers than to introduce your songs to crowds when you're stretching them out to fill a set. You might be able to fill the set time, but you also might not grab any new fans or people interested in purchasing your music.

For newer artists and bands just laying the foundation to build a fan base, make sure to identify the originals as well as the covers. If you're mixing them up, certain covers everyone will know, but make sure that they know it's yours when you're playing an original. Every gig you play is about marketing your music to the audience, so make sure they know it's your song, the name of the song, and the name of the band. Promote and market even on stage. You can make it a little funny too. Maybe say something like, "That was 'Peg' by Steely Dan, and right now we're going to switch gears to a tune we wrote called 'Stuck in a Moment' by the Acme Band. Oh, by the way, we are the Acme Band—just in case you hadn't heard."

Throughout the night, talk to the audience, and show the CD you're selling or any merchandise you have.

This should be part of your set and is very important!!!!

Write it into the set list where you hold up a disc and then a couple of songs later hold up a sticker, a tee shirt, or whatever. You have their attention; they're all looking up your way—at least you hope they are. When you display the products, you're giving them visuals, and that will help a great deal. So showcase your stuff. Put it in the set list in between songs to remind you. It should be part of the show. If you have a sexy tank top for girls with your band name and logo, have someone wearing it, maybe a cute girl, and have her come up on stage at the end of a certain song and cross the stage. It sounds hokey, but it's effective.

That about covers the long sets or many set shows. You have a plan to fill things up and make the motion of the sets strong as well as effective while including breaks that are planned and promoting your product and merchandise. Now you also have to prepare for the opposite side of things. What about when you have a single set or very short set in a showcase or numerous-band performance setting?

The most common mistake is picking a couple of songs and then just tossing them into an order. If you're given a very tight window, such as twenty-five minutes, or in some cases even less, you have to be time effective. The first step is to make the plan and time the set. Make sure you figure in for getting onto the stage and off the stage as well as a brief couple of seconds for some clapping. Give them as much as you can in the amount of time you have. Don't look at it as if you only have time to do five songs; look at it in the way of how you may be able to cut a solo or shrink a section. Maybe cut off an intro or outro. Consider losing a verse. Doing all these things will allow you to fit more music into the set and thereby present more about your group in a shorter amount of time.

In addition, try to stay away from the songs that are really slow in those short sets. Make sure you say the name of the band in between each song. A lot of times those short sets happen when you're playing with a number of other bands, so make sure they know who you are as well. Allow the audience to clap, but get right into the next song. Try to have very little silence between the songs, and if you have a short intro that you can talk over, do it. It may not be the perfect scenario but it is the most effective and productive. Make sure you mention the Web site, your social network sites, where they can talk to you after you get off the stage, and where your merchandise is. It's a lot like those speed-dating events. You have a certain amount of time to make an impression on someone, and then after the bell rings, you move on. So in a sense you're at a speed-dating event with potential new fans.

Of course you want time with an audience, and you want to share the music the way you wrote it to be delivered, but if you take advantage and adapt to the situation at hand, you'll have a much better chance of bringing new fans to see you in a place where the performance isn't rushed.

Whether you have ten minutes or two hours, prepare accordingly. Time your sets, write into set lists what you will discuss or promote between songs. Figure out the orders that work best, and keep the audience attentive. Work on the set lists; work on your songs and how you can alter and adapt them for different gigs. The more versatile and open you are to arranging and organizing your shows to the time and situations you're given, the more fans you will be able to attract and keep.

The Artist Contract

As you start to play better shows, higher paying shows, and shows with greater exposure, it's important to take your professionalism and organization up a level. Many times when you play a show, it's low-key, with verbal agreements or very crudely drawn-up contracts in the bodies of e-mails. While these work fine for some of the shows you have played, it's crucial to have an artist contract available to maintain the professionalism and organization you need as a group and also to secure information, promises, and dates in a top-notch manner.

I strongly advise using an artist contract for all shows and, for larger shows, the next step: a full technical rider.

The Artist Contract basically secures the show between the artist and the venue or booking agent who has scheduled the show. Having a contract makes things a little cleaner all around. It means both parties are legally responsible to make the show work. How many times have you been in the back of a club and heard the story change about what you are getting paid? How often have you been surprised and disappointed when you thought you had things taken care of but found out that there was a misunderstanding or the club, booking agent, or promoter downright lied?

If you have an Artist Contract, all of these things are clear and in writing, and if something suddenly changes without your awareness, there would be consequences for the side that changes the contract. Now, some clubs and agents will not sign contracts. That should be a red flag, right from the start, that things could get dicey. Some booking agents and clubs will sign very oversimplified contracts, which allow for complex problems to occur and nothing to protect you.

I recommend a basic Artist Contract that you can present to a venue, agency, booking agent, or promoter. Present your contact with a well-organized document that's up for discussion. It's not about being a diva or asking for things that are unrealistic or over the top; it's about having a basic contract that covers all the core issues. From there, you can make mutual edits and agreed changes with whoever is booking you to find a happy medium. If you present the contract as a piece of paper that's not yet written in stone and show that you are open to changes, there is a better chance that you will not intimidate a smaller venue or booker, while still securing core elements, so you can trust that what is agreed upon is what will happen.

Just as in the stage plot, the input list, the sound and light require- ments sheet, and the backline sheet, you should list all the details, embel- lishments, and nuances that make up your group and its needs; then take away as needed. It's a lot easier than adding on down the line.

Talk to a lawyer who specializes in music law and create a per- sonalized Artist Contract or download one from the Internet. There are many Artist Contracts that you can get a hold of and use until you can spend the money to set up a legal document that fits you to a tee. You want to make sure it's properly worded and will stand up legally in the courts should a problem arise. Often when inexperienced bands put together a contract, they end up using wording that does not actually say what they really had intended to say. I tell ya … &*%^ing Lawyers!!!!! Unfortunately, you need them to write the contracts correctly.

These are the basic points that I make sure to include in an Artist Contract. While some seem obvious, it's still good to get that informa- tion, and get it in writing

First, the gig itself:

DATE

VENUE

VENUE/BOOKING POINT OF CONTACT

VENUE ADDRESS

VENUE PHONE #

VENUE FAX #

VENUE WEB SITE

VENUE SOCIAL NETWORKING SITE (if it has one)

OPENING FOR/OPENING ACT(S)

INFO ON OTHER ARTISTS OR VENUE

LOAD-IN TIME

SET TIME(S)

PAYMENT/FEE AGREED

METHOD/TIME OF PAYMENT

ADDITIONAL PERCENTAGES OF PROFIT

LODGING/AMENITIES

ADDITIONAL INFORMATION

Setting up these basics right out of the gate, putting them in a contract, and confirming them will make life a lot easier.

While the venue's social networking site is not something crucial, it's an element that can advertise to its friends and fans. This will help you with the marketing and promotions for the show.

Next, cover your agreements surrounding cancellations. What happens if you have to cancel? What happens if the venue cancels? What does the contract stipulate if a cancellation happens last minute as opposed to a month out? This section should cover these elements.

The next section would cover how you would handle inclement weather as well as something called *force majeure*, also known as an Act of God. What do you do if there's a tornado or blizzard? Do you have a plan or agreement in place? These are the details that would involve things you wouldn't ever expect but should be prepared for.

The terms and conditions portion of the contract is next, giving a basic overview of the agreement as a whole. This is followed by signatures, which complete the contract. You now know what's planned because it's all on paper with signatures. This may seem oversimplified, or over the top, but organizing your performances with an Artist Contract can make your life a lot easier. Now these go both ways. As you're securing your rights and what you want, you have to make sure to secure the rights and desires of the club or venue as well.

While the Artist Contract will not guarantee the end to all disputes and problems, it will move things along faster and make things easier on all parties involved. Again, just think back to every time something has gone wrong or been misunderstood, every time you felt ripped off, screwed over, underpaid, or taken advantage of. In most of those cases, if you had what you thought you were supposed to get in writing, you would be a great deal happier, and things would've probably gone a lot smoother for everyone involved.

Cancellations and Rescheduling

So the show got cancelled. Whether it was your fault, the venue's fault, the manager's fault, or the weather's fault, it really doesn't matter. It's strange to me that when something goes wrong, people seem more concerned about figuring out who did something wrong and assigning blame than problem solving and doing what they can to make the best out of the situation.

Mistakes happen. Gigs are going to get cancelled or rescheduled. There will be times when you're going to be double-booked. You can take the steps to organize and track things the best you can, but problems occur, and sometimes they just can't be helped. I've heard bands scream and moan about this booking agent or that manager messing up. Then I've seen the online postings where bands blast venues and then the venues blast the bands. This really doesn't solve a single thing, and it takes up time you could use to reschedule, install preventative techniques, and reach out to your fans and people who were going to come to the show.

First off and most important, it's about the fans and not your bruised egos and placing blame. Get the word out once you know there's a problem that can't be solved so you can be in communication with every fan possible—hopefully before they come out to the show.

Some bands have text mailers, others have e-mailing lists, others have network sites, and many have all of the above. Use these the moment you know a show has been cancelled. Get the information out to your street teams if you have them. The show may be cancelled, but don't see the cancellation as taking you off the hook. Make that time useful in reaching out to the fan base that's coming out to see you. Ask the venue to post the cancellation on its Web site, and visit any sites that are pertinent music and entertainment sites in the area to get the word out that you're not playing there.

Be respectful and diplomatic in these efforts. Explain that the show has been cancelled and will be rescheduled to that venue or to another location. Don't bad-mouth the venue, manager, booking agent, or whoever is to blame. Be the bigger person. Just explain what's happened without attacking or coming off rude. It doesn't even matter if you're completely right and the other party is completely wrong; be the more respectful person.

Try to spin the cancellation in a strong marketing way. If people bought tickets, tell them to bring the tickets to the next show and maybe see if you can get a discount for them at the door or some piece of inexpensive merchandise. Maybe create a raffle drawing for people to bring their tickets and win some of your more expensive items. This will show you care about your audience and may draw people to come out to see you again.

Remember, cancellations do not just mean you can assign blame and end the night on a bad note. Make a cancellation work for you in the best and most effective way possible. Reach out to every person you can through every media source. Get on the Internet, on the phone, and in the streets to get out the information. Even the smallest thing—like a big magic marker that you buy to hit some of the posters in the area of the venue, stating that the show was cancelled and more information is available on your Web site—is a simple and smart idea.

Take the steps to ensure the mistakes don't happen again, but put your focus on your audience, and you will see them return the next time and the time after that. Think effectively, execute expediently, and communicate clearly to keep everyone in the know and display that you care about the people coming out to see you. It will set you a notch above: Most bands just pack up and go right home.

Load-In and Load-Out

Loading in and out of a show, your rehearsal spot, a house, or wherever is just about the worst part of being a musician, especially if you're the drummer. I used to joke with a band that I was in, telling them that I practice for free, perform for free, and record for free; what I get paid for is carrying all this crap in and out of all these places.

I played in a group with a keyboardist who played on a Rhodes piano. Basically, it was the two-person load instrument. The bass player had to have his double stack amp, and at the time I was all about this drum kit that I did not have any reason to carry around. Yet there I was, lugging it in and out, up and down, and all around.

The first time I got a roadie, I remember thinking it would be hard to go back to carrying my own stuff. During one particular tour, I continuously increased the number of drums, cymbals, electronics, and other miscellaneous toys I used. It was ironic how much smaller my kit became and how much less I needed when I got off that tour and was with a band in which I had to carry my stuff by myself.

There's no way to get around the loading in and out, barring that you get the roadies to do it for you. Some of you have those faithful few who come to every show and will carry your things for a few beers, but most everyone in the low, mid, and even basic pro levels is trucking his or her own stuff.

There's got to be an easier and more effective way, especially when you go from weekend warrior to playing four to seven shows a week. Not to mention when you perform in a radio station or on a TV show during the day and then have a show that night ... the dreaded quadruple load!!!!!!! And that doesn't even include what you brought into the hotel, or wherever you were staying that night, to protect the gear.

Solo artists, this is not really for you. Most of you are only lugging a solo setup that's not too bad. This is geared toward the bands and the groups that are lugging guitars, keyboards, amps, drums, basses, merchandise, and whatever else. The key point to making loading in and loading out bearable is to get the damn singer actually to *HELP*!!!!! Ok, maybe not, but I know that a truckload of you know exactly what I'm talking about. I know it's a stereotype that singers don't often help with the loads, but it's a stereotype based on common occurrences. It definitely happened a lot with some of the people I played with!!!!

Feeling better … got that rant out. Ok, seriously now. The key points to getting through the hell that is loading in and loading out are the following:

- **Simplify the job**
- **Maximize the loads**
- **Work as a team**
- **Practice the plan**

I know that sounds silly in some ways, but trust me; I've watched and been a part of bands that got this down to a science, and it made life so much easier for everybody. Think of the job as loading for THE BAND and not the individual. When you're only thinking of you and your stuff, it doesn't help the process go faster for the group. If you're in a band, you need to realize that you play together as a band, so you should load in and out as a band.

First: Simplify

Figure out what you're loading, not just your equipment but the band's gear as a whole. Ask a few simple questions to simplify the job for the group.

What takes the longest to set up? Are you working with your own PA? Who has the most gear, and is it brought in a van, a truck, or a number of different vehicles? What's the heaviest, or what requires two people to load as opposed to one person? How do you set up on stage?

When you answer each of these questions, you can come up with the most efficient way to load in certain gear first. For example, bringing in the monitors or frontline items and placing them on the stage first is a bad idea if you have to load in the backline of drums and amps that go beyond them.

Second: Maximize

Once you figure out the venue setup and what needs to load in first, pack the transport vehicles accordingly. Do you have to load in on a street corner where only one vehicle can be? Then load in one car at a time as another person finds parking; then other members unload the next vehicle and so on.

Some places work better to chain in the gear for security purposes. In other places, you might all have to grab a load, lock the vehicle, and then return to it. In still other venues, you might want to have a loading team, someone at the vehicle, and someone to begin unpacking and placing for setup. Be ready to work the variables.

Third: Teamwork

This goes back to thinking of the load-in as a band thing and not a "my gear" thing. Numbering the cases and listing points where they go can help with the organization of how stuff is loaded into vehicles and back out again. You can also add simple stage terminology on the boxes like the big boys do, such as U.S.C., which is the acronym for upstage center, where the drums most commonly go. This can help to tell people exactly where something should go when you have an extra hand or two assisting. Having the boxes numbered and coded can also help you keep track of your items when you're not loading right onto a stage or when you are playing a venue with a series of other bands.

Having distinguishing markings on your cases can help as well. Luggage tags are always a good idea as well as numbers, but adding some extra item that identifies them as yours can really do you good—a large logo of the band or even a red stripe, something that would distinguish your cases from others. Think of the luggage collection at the airport. Have you ever noticed those bags that look like everyone else's but have some distinguishing tag or band around them? Notice how they stand out?

Finally: Practice the Plan

Practice a load-in and load-out from your rehearsal space to the car and back in. Figure out what system works the best and the quickest for you. I know it sounds stupid, but the more organized you are with load-ins and load-outs the more professional you will appear.

Work on your setup and getting yourself ready as quickly as possible. Especially on the nights where there are a number of bands, the faster you are up and down, the more you'll be noticed by the club or the promoter. Trust me, this is an area in which you'll want to impress beyond the music. Club owners, booking agents, and other bands will take notice. If you're moving fast and keeping things on schedule, you're going to be asked back faster than a band that is screwing up the schedule because of disorganization.

This is one of the space elements that can make the big things flow easier. Work on your load-in and load-out. Think about investing in cases that will make your life easier *and* protect your equipment. Organize and create the plans for how you get into the room where you have to wait to set up, how you load into rooms where you get to load right to the stage, and how you load into back areas.

The tighter, faster, and easier the load-in and load-out becomes, the less of a hassle it will be and the more professional you will look. Plus, best of all, you can get it done and over with, because even after all this—the right plan, the professional appearance, and the faster results—it still sucks.

Stage Setup and Clear

Most bands get into the groove when it comes to setting up and tearing down off stage. The more you practice your music, the better it gets, and the same is true of stage setup and breakdown. But what about those items on stage that are more, let's say, perishable?

Again, the simple things make perfect sense, but many people skip them. You bring drinks on stage. You break a string or a drumstick, drop it on the stage, and get back to the songs. You have a set list taped up somewhere and leave it behind. You leave a fair mess in the backstage or the loading areas. Maybe you have a bad cable, quickly replace it, and abandon it on the stage. All these things and whatever else you might leave behind can make the stage a mess.

Just as you're loading off your gear, load off your trash. It might be one more trip to and from the stage, but it's a trip that will give you a better reputation with the venue, the soundman, the stage crew, and the other bands that might be playing with you that night.

Do as Mom Says: Clean Up after Yourself

Most don't, so when you do, you'll be remembered. Of course a venue wants to pack a house, but a venue also wants to have bands that are easy to work with, respectful, and not selfish or over the top with the egos. Unless you're sporting stagehands and roadies, pick up your mess. Leave the stage as you found it.

On that note, if you're playing with a number of other bands and some of the gear is either backline or you're using someone else's gear, take care to leave things as you found them.

Sometimes headlining drummers will lend a kit to the opener so they can have things in place for a faster transition. If you have to make adjustments, make small ones. Try not to mess with the kit or the setup too much. If you raise a stool or a seat, drop it back to the height it was originally when you're done. Try to put things where they were before you moved them. If you're borrowing an amp and make adjustments, try to get it back to the ballpark of where it was before.

These are the little things that will be remembered when a band is looking for another band to play with or a venue is looking for a band to fill a slot or a date where they want good music but also need the utmost professionalism. Thus, it's more important than ever not only to deliver the best music to the audience but also to take care of business before and after the show as well. Step up, clean up, and get out of the selfish mindset. Be aware of the other bands, the venue, and the employees who work there. The extra effort and respect will be returned tenfold in most cases since so many musicians skip on these little extras.

Backline Sheets

The Backline Sheet is usually reserved for large-scale acts and musicians who fly to shows with limited to no gear. This sheet covers all the needs in detail, down to the bare bones of what is required. Many Backline Sheets are part of supplemental attachments to riders and Artist Contracts. Having a Backline Sheet available for download off your Web site displays your organization to others, and, for that matter, will help you know exactly what you need for a show.

You may also find that having a Backline Sheet as well as the other contracts readily available may get you bookings that you may not have gotten otherwise, such as certain festivals and corporate shows that have a budget and can supply backline or afford to fill a backline order.

Don't get cocky or overzealous when creating a Backline Sheet for your group. Make sure it has what you play on and what you actually need. It's also a good idea to mention in the sheet that you are open to making adjustments and changes upon request.

This document can also make for a nice supplement to a potential endorsement package, showing that you use certain gear exclusively, if that's the case, and that it's a part of your rig regardless of where you play and where you travel.

As with your press kit and other promotional, marketing, or logistical materials, make sure that the document stands on its own, meaning you should make sure it is properly labeled with every piece of contact information including addresses, phones, e-mails, Web sites, fax number, point of contact, and your logo.

Lastly, if you list all your gear in a clear document, as well as taking pictures, it can help with certain insurance issues.

Drummer Rant (yes, I threw a rant into the book)

Below I have the information from my personal Backline Sheet that I used when doing sessions and sub drumming gigs to which I was either flown or connected with when I was not going to be bringing my own kit. I requested, in detail, the drums I wanted by size, the heads I wanted on them, and the miscellaneous notes and items that would allow me to do my best and be most comfortable.

Seventy-five percent of the time, it was filled to the tee. I would show up and find the gear that I'd requested, was able to add my cymbals, which I traveled with, and get ready very quickly. The other 25 percent of the time, I would be contacted and asked if certain existing backline drums would be a problem, which I never minded, but I would always initially ask for the kit I was most comfortable with and the setup I used on my own.

This is the rig for the fusion and funk things I did. I never used this for jazz and usually play a kit based on the music. I found this layout could handle any type of style and every need, so to the drummers who are about to scrutinize me for the size of the kit, go suck it. This is the complete rig and all the stuff I would ever need for any situation. I'm plenty happy on a four piece, too.

But if you want to give me crap, go look at (well, we are going to leave his name out of this book, but go search for a drum set where the drummer has two seats!) latest setup. You will know him if you search him online. No one knows what the guy looks like since he's behind a small city of freaking drums. Don't get me wrong—I still think he burns—but, really, dude???? Warning to drummers, if it takes you longer to set up and strike your kit than the time you're playing on stage during the show, cut down on the gear. This guy's kit is so big ... how big, you ask???? Like I said before, he has two thrones (drum seats), that's how big the kit is.

Hey, man? Do you bring that rig out if you don't have a drum tech or three?

I'll admit it, when I didn't have a tech, my kit was kick, snare, rack, floor, three cymbals, and hats.

So again to the minimalists who are going to feed me crap for the list below, suck it. It's fun to rant for no good reason sometimes, isn't it? And the kit wasn't that big.

Anyway, here's the text for my old Backline Sheet.

LOREN WEISMAN BACKLINE SHEET

FOR FLYING AND TRAVEL DATES WITHOUT PERSONAL
    CARTAGE

DRUMS AND HARDWARE

1 - 20" X 18" KICK DRUM DOUBLE HEADED W/MIC HOLE IN
    FRONT HEAD
    (Remo Powerstroke 3 heads both sides preferred)

1 – 12" X 9" RACK TOM – DOUBLE HEADED
    (Remo Coated Amb. on top, Clear Amb. on bottom preferred)

1 - 10" X 8" RACK TOM – DOUBLE HEADED
(Remo Coated Amb. on top, Clear Amb. on bottom preferred)

1 - 14" X 14" FLOOR TOM – DOUBLE HEADED
(Remo Coated Amb. on top, Clear Amb. on bottom preferred)

1 - 16" X 14" FLOOR TOM – DOUBLE HEADED (2nd floor tom optional)
(Remo Coated Amb. on top, Clear Amb. on bottom preferred)

1 - 14" X 5.5" SNARE DRUM WOOD SHELL (MAPLE PREFERRED)
(Remo Coated Amb. on top, Clear Diplomat on bottom preferred)

1 - 12" X 6" SNARE DRUM WOOD SHELL (BIRCH PREFERRED)
(Remo Coated Amb. on top, Clear Diplomat on bottom preferred)

1 – DBL TOM STAND FOR RACK TOMS OR (2) TOM HOLDER CLAMPS FOR C. STAND

5 - CYMBAL BOOM STANDS WITH FIVE ARMS FOR CYMBALS – HEAVY DUTY

1 – HIGH-HAT STAND – HEAVY DUTY

2 - SNARE DRUM STANDS – HEAVY DUTY

1 - DW5000 BASS DRUM PEDAL – CHAIN DRIVEN OR EQUIV.

1 - ROC-N-SOC THRONE OR HI QUALITY DRUM SEAT – LOW BASE

1 - FLOOR CARPET TO BE PLACED UNDER THE DRUM KIT

1 - MEINL COWBELL OR EQUIV. AND ATTACHMENT TO CYMBAL STAND

MISCELLANEOUS

- Please make sure all cymbal stands have felts for above and below the cymbals.
- Gretsch or Taye drums preferred. Remo Drum Heads preferred.
- Please make sure all drum heads are new.
- Drummer travels with cymbals and sticks. No cymbals or sticks are needed.
- Please supply duct tape, a Phillips screwdriver, flat-head screwdriver, and WD-40 oil.
- Supply one towel for the stage as well as a fan.
- Hiring party or persons are responsible for the pick up and the returning of all gear.

As you can see, items are covered across the board. For a band's Backline Sheet, just add the list for each player and the needs of each. As I mentioned before, don't get cocky: Ask for the things you need, and most of the time, listing what you already have is a good idea. For the items you own that are custom or outrageously expensive and hard to find, ask for either equivalents or realistic alternatives. Also realize if you're playing a smaller market or a smaller city, they may not have all the gear you need. Be flexible.

A Backline Sheet serves many purposes; create one for your band or even yourself. It may help you know exactly what you need and get you some cool shows that are booked by large-scale companies. You've seen those bands at different events, I'm sure, and wondered why they got that gig and not you. They had all their logistics in order.

Many times larger organizations want to make the booking process as easy as possible. If you have your stage plot, riders, contracts, and even a backline sheet in order, you have made booking your band a great deal easier. The easier you make it on a booking agent or talent-buying agency, the more you will play and the better many of those shows will be.

For an example of a full band backline sheet, visit www.theartistsguide.net

Stage Plot, Input Lists, and Sound and Light Sheets

A stage plot and input list should be part of any promotional and booking package that you have, as an artist or band. The stage plot and input list are almost like blueprints for what your technical layout is on stage. While not all venues expect you to have them, it makes life a lot easier for front of house engineers as well as monitor engineers. It also puts you and your group in a more organized, professional light. Some places like input lists; others prefer stage plots; some will ask for both. I also advise, as a supplement, to have a sound and light requirements sheet as well. Though they are not as commonly asked for, it is a preference for some.

When you walk into a venue with a stage plot and input list, you make the life of the engineer worlds easier. It makes it simpler to put up microphones and set up the stage and monitors and will get you to sound check faster. Some of the better rooms will ask for these materials in advance. I recommend that you not only walk into a room you are playing with a couple of printouts of your stage plot and input list but also have them easily accessible online for instant download. Then, if people request either of the documents, you can send them a direct link to a downloadable PDF, JPEG, or protected word document. (PDF is the best way to go.) Even if you have sonic bids or any other booking assistance site, make sure you have easy access to downloadable PDFs.

When you know what you're bringing, what you need as well as the basic aspects of technical, setup and sound issues, you become a band that's easier to work with and, in turn, a band that the venue or booking agent will want to have back. Think of it from another angle: So many venues have to deal with so many bands that may be good musically but can make life difficult technically. The groups that are easier to work with are the ones that have the supplemental materials, such as stage plots, input lists, and even sound and light requirement sheets. This will open up more doors for you. The music, of course, is the staple and the foundation, but with the proper documents, just like with the proper promotional and marketing materials, you may be able to open more doors and more opportunities faster.

The Stage Plot

The stage plot is the most commonly requested document. This shows your stage layout to whoever is doing sound. It also helps define the space and the equipment locations. There are a lot of different versions of how you can set up a stage plot. I find the style explained here to be the most effective, professional, and informative.

For starters, have the stage plot, or any document for that matter, on your own letterhead. It doesn't take that much time to set up a basic header with your name, tagline, and Web addresses and a footer with contact information: contact point, address, e-mail, phone, fax, and contact Web sites.

Next, the clear header: "Stage Plot." Yes, that's obvious, but many people often don't take the simple steps. From there, a clear, concise layout with the basic descriptions of each instrument. Also include a numbering of the microphones needed. For the drums, show the drums and basic placements so the soundman or engineer can prepare the microphone setup before you even arrive, as well as the monitors and basic sound layout.

Side note: Getting a stage plot to the engineer or producer who you are recording with, in advance of a session, can also make the drum miking go easier.

Make sure to designate the picture in a simple, clear, and size-proportionate way. Take some time with it and get it right so that it will be an easier document for people to use and understand. Next, I advise adding a small box—you can create it on Excel or a similar spreadsheet program—to show the different channels, the instrument list, and the microphone preference. Oftentimes you will get what they have, but the more you know and learn about your live sound and the microphones that work best for you, the better chance a soundman who doesn't know you can get your sound right.

I always tell artists to repeat the basic contact information right in the middle of the stage plot document for redundancy reasons. Better safe than sorry if they need to touch base with you in advance of the show. Finally, have a notes section where you can add your requests or core preferences, such as separate monitor mixes or specific sound requests. Don't go over the top and don't be surprised if you don't get every microphone you're looking for or every wish you put in writing, but it never hurts to ask for the basic needs.

For an example of a full band stage plot, visit www.theartists-guide.net

Input List

The input list is more of an informational document than it is a picture or diagram. Again, in a spreadsheet format much like the stage plot, you're going to want to have the basic channel number and the instrument and microphone preference. However, the input list goes further in depth, adding a column for microphone stand preferences, insert or effect preferences, a comment section, and a symbol that can be used by the engineer very easily. Many front-of-house engineers prefer the input list for a reference point, while oftentimes a monitor engineer or the stage technicians will want the stage plot.

In place of the diagram, having a column that designates location of the microphones is a good idea too. There are easy three-letter designations such as USL, which stands for upstage left, or DSC, which is for downstage center. This will allow the engineer to be able to reference the location of each channel to its microphone and be able to solve problems much faster should they occur.

I also advise adding REAL # and MNTR # columns, which can be used by the engineer to list the channel that the specific instrument is in. Just because you're using eighteen channels doesn't mean that the lead vocal will always be a certain channel number on every board. Some engineers who have larger boards will reassign channels, and others will use a different channel altogether. Either way, adding a REAL # column and a MNTR # column will let the engineer designate the correct channels for your gear as well as for your monitors.

Like the stage plot, I recommend putting the input list on the band's letterhead with a clearly defined header of "Input List." I also recommend having a definitions table on the bottom to make sure that your definitions for your particular acronyms are understood, as well as a notes section to put in core details that you want the engineer to know.

That's the basic input list that I believe is the most effective to have. You can also add a column for names and instruments so that when the front of house is calling out to you, he or she can call you by name.

For an example of a full band input list, visit www.theartists guide.net

Sound and Light Requirements Sheet

This sheet is the least commonly used in the set, but many, if not most, higher-level touring bands have this in their performance contracts or supplements. This is laid out as more of a listing of the minimum requirements that are asked for by artists. It's usually broken up into the following five sections: Minimum Lighting, Minimum Monitoring, Minimum Front of House, Miscellaneous, and Microphone Setup. This document is often part of a full touring rider or a supplemental form for the stage plot and input list.

Again, putting it on a letterhead document with a clear header is always a good idea.

For an example of a full band sound and light requirement sheet, visit www.theartistsguide.nett

The stage plot, the input list, and the sound and light requirement sheets are three simple documents that you can put together to make your life and the lives of the venues, the people who book you, and the crew that helps you worlds easier. They can potentially help you get a better sound, a faster setup, and a greater understanding between you and the room you are playing. Don't go for the brass ring, go for the basics that you need, and always mention that you are open to adjustments and alterations. If you're an artist that performs with different size bands, make these documents for the largest scale group you would play with; then just edit out who is or isn't going to be there for the specific shows.

Having these documents available shows a greater professionalism and, as I mentioned before, may open up opportunities to perform in shows and festivals that you might otherwise not have the opportunity to play in. When larger festivals and shows are booked, many of these talent buyers are looking for the easiest bands to put in front of a headlining act. They don't care if you're the best or worst, they just want to know they can get you up, performing and off the stage in the best and most expedient manner. Your professionalism and organization may be the difference that will get your band in front of a whole new set of ears.

Make life easier on yourself, prove that your group is well organized, and show the venues, talent buyers, and booking agents that you are ready to play, from the smallest club with no PA, to a top of the line sound system, and you will see the results of your efforts come through. When you handle the details in advance and make life easier for the venue and all those involved in your show, you will find that more and more opportunities appear.

First Aid Box for the Stage

What do you bring on stage with you? What do you keep in your case? Most people have the gear they need and occasionally some backup stuff, but many don't keep the essentials needed for worst-case scenarios.

Now, unless you have a roadie who's sitting side stage with a tool belt and his little handy box, you should be prepared like a roadie for the problems that can occur on stage. Having that first aid kit in arm's reach can help things go smoothly and keep the flow of the show going in the face of any problems that can and often do arise.

Yes, it's one more item to load in and load out, however it's an item that can be just as important as the gear you use since it will keep your gear happy and operational.

Go through a mental checklist of your gear. Come up with a list of items you'll need to fix anything and everything. Now it's true, if your amp blows up, you can't always carry a second amp around, so this box won't be backup for every catastrophe, but it will be the first responder, first aid, mend-the-scratch, and cover-the-cut kind of box.

Every person's needs are different, and every box should be individualized to that player and his or her needs. It should contain the things that will keep the artist and his or her gear happy. I also recommend that it be the color black, since black can fade away in to the background of any given stage.

Here are the contents of my first aid for the stage box (for drums) when I was on the road a number of years back without a tech.

1. **Backup Stuff**
   - Backup beater (1)
   - Backup drum lugs (5)
   - Backup kick drum lugs (3)
   - Backup kick pedal springs (2)
   - Backup cymbals felts (4)
   - Backup hi-hat clutch (2)
   - Backup drum-tuning key (1)

Most of these were the physical backups of items I needed. If a head broke, I usually had a second snare with the kit, and that switch was easy. Yet, I still wanted to problem-solve and usually had heads in the bottoms of my drum cases or in the bus. If a head broke on a tom, I just wouldn't use that tom. I never really was the head-breaking type, but you never know when something will break.

I kept this other stuff in reach of the kit at all times as backup for the small items that can easily get lost.

2. **Mr. Fixit Stuff**
   - WD-40 oil (for the pedals)
   - Phillips screwdriver (loose drum nuts, or bolts)
   - Flat-head screwdriver (same as above)
   - Wrench (hardware repairs)
   - Pliers (hardware repairs)
   - Allen wrench set (drum or hardware repairs)
   - Duct tape (to fix a hole, mute a drum, and keep a drum together)
   Love the Duct Tape always!!!
   - Small towel (for spills on gear)

- Rope (if you're on a slippery stage or missing a rug, roping your kick around your throne can keep it from running away from you)

3. **Personal Stuff**
   - Flashlight (if the stage is dark or it's hard to see, a small Maglite will help you see what you are doing)
   - Band-Aids (if you cut yourself)
   - Advil (I have taken this on stage plenty of times)

Items for other players can include batteries, extra tuners, extra cords, strings, and a backup microphone.

You may think having a list and a box like this is over the top, yet I know many musicians that not only do this but continue to build and add to their boxes. These boxes can also be useful on off days as you do maintenance on your gear.

Each problem you can solve quickly under pressure will showcase your skills as a musician who can keep the show going regardless of setbacks.

Be your own roadie when you need to be. Plan ahead for potential problems, and you will solve them more quickly, often with an audience none the wiser.

The ability to problem-solve is so important in many aspects of the music industry. When you have a little box of fun to make certain problems get solved faster, you will be a step ahead of the rest.

Safety

The safety of people and gear is often overlooked by musicians and is only addressed once something bad happens. Playing on the club circuit, the theatre circuit, and even the arena circuit all involve hazards surrounding the people who come to the shows, the people in the neighborhood, and the time of day or night.

Most shows occur at night, and these shows don't get out until late, so the band inevitably gets out even later. Loading out can be dangerous and downright frightening in some of these neighborhoods. People get attacked, things get stolen: anything and everything can go wrong.

It doesn't matter whether you're female or male, big or small, incidents happen. Most of the time they occur when you aren't paying attention and are taking things for granted. I walk a very normal route most evenings when I visit a bar in Seattle. The neighborhood I walk through is fairly well lit, and I've never had any kind of trouble before. But not long ago, I was walking home late one night and got jumped by two guys. Now here's the kicker for those of you that don't know me: I stand 6'4" and weigh about 255 pounds. I'm broad shouldered and generally not someone that gets messed with.

Anyhow, one guy grabbed my bag. The only problem for him was that I never let go, so the other guy smacked me with some kind of stick. It happened really fast, but the next thing I knew, they were running across the street and I still had my bag, my wallet, and an adrenaline rush like no other. I think these guys were on drugs and pretty amped up. I'm not a tough guy, but no one takes my bag. It contains, on any given day, production notes from sessions, backups from sessions, my laptop with everything I write and everything else, and though I was told I was stupid for hanging on to it, it was my bag and no one takes my bag … period.

The point of the story is that things happen when you least expect it. Things can go from usual to unusual in a split second. The corners that we cut to save time and effort are the same corners that can cut us in an instant and when we least expect it. So think first and foremost; then act

Think about the things you take for granted in the loading-in and loading-out process, you know—when the van or truck is unlocked and you'll be right back out. Come on, everyone's done it!!! Or when you're loading out from the venue and everyone is taking a load-out, leaving a ton of gear sitting inside. What about when you're storing cases with a ton of other bands' cases or gear? Or when the merch boxes are sitting somewhere unwatched while you're doing sound check? What about leaving clothes hung in an unwatched backstage area? Or when you run down the street late at night to grab a coffee or go into a convenience store after a gig and leave the van running or carry the cash from the gig on you? These are all common things that occur and don't faze you till something goes wrong.

There's nothing earth-shattering or revolutionary here. It's just the simple, stupid things that will keep things from getting simply stupid.

Leave someone with the van as you are loading in and loading out and leave another person with the gear inside. It's the safest way to go. Whether one person stays out there or you rotate, keep someone with the gear at all times.

Make sure you double check the locks on your doors and chain your hitch if you have a trailer. Save up for a security system and to keep your merch and other expensive items locked up.

Take pictures, get serial numbers, and inventory your gear. Make sure that if something happens to it, there's defined information or markings that show it belongs to you.

Watch your back, and in the bad cities and neighborhoods, travel in twos. It may not stop everything, but it will reduce the chances.

Have a clear system of knowing everything you have loaded in and everything you have loaded out from a venue. Track your stuff; otherwise someone else might.

Find out if you have a place that's guaranteed to be secure in the venue or not. Look at your contract and see what it promises. If you don't have a secure area or security guarantee, be prepared to watch your own stuff. If it isn't in writing, it isn't secure.

Keep your wallet with you. Keep your personal items with you. I know artists who will actually bring personal items on stage and store them in amp racks and by the drummer. It may seem over the top, but when something happens to your personal items, you might change your mind.

The overall idea is to problem-solve before the problems occur and avoid common short cuts in security. These initial measures can help prevent the negative situations that many run into.

Shows and Appearance Redundancy

Have you ever picked up one of those weekly magazines you'll find in any given city and seen all of the bands listed for performances? You sometimes see them listed as playing three nights in a row in a radius of less than fifteen miles, and then they wonder why they have such a bad draw on the last night and a mediocre draw on all of the nights.

It comes down to getting out of your backyard. This is the where the difference kicks in between how many gigs should be booked and how best to draw a crowd. I heavily recommend that bands think about playing shows from the perspective of the audience members.

If you play every weekend in Seattle, as many Seattle bands do, you'll end up over-saturating that market, creating a lax fan base. When people begin to see you constantly listed in the local papers and always playing, then you no longer become the must-see band; you become the "Hey, I can catch them whenever" band.

Over-saturation of the playing market occurs in every city with thousands of bands. They look from the angle of "the more gigs the better," even if it's in a consolidated radius. This is a bad move.

The best way to market to an audience in any city or club is to be the artist or band that's a must see. Spreading out your appearances will make you more desirable and more of a must see since you're not available every weekend in the same town. You create the tease, which is effective. You'll create a base of fans that will move things around in their schedules to make sure to see you because, if they don't catch you on a given night, they won't be able to see you for a long time.

This approach can also make booking much easier. It will make clubs and booking agents want to bring you into better-paying shows and larger rooms. When you present from a business perspective that you are appearing for the first time in, let's say, eight weeks, the club, manger or agent is going to be given the sense that the market will want to see since you didn't just play down the street the night or the weekend before.

In presenting to a club or venue that you have not played in a certain radius in more than a six-week period, you will show that you have a better chance to pull a larger crowd. Certain venues even have it written into their show agreements that you're not suppose to play for a certain number of weeks or even months before and after your booked night. This is written in specifically to prevent the negative effects of over-saturating a market.

The number of weeks can vary between shows. I've found the bands that draw the most and have the best responses are those that play in a given twenty-five mile radius no more than every eight to nine weeks.

So you think I'm crazy, but a nine-week spread really is the best for constant promotion as well as the greatest chance to get the rooms you play packed up. Think of it from a marketing angle: Doing a press release five weeks out from a show is the best time line; then at the two week point, get the posters out and the hype building up; then the show.

After that you disappear for a month. It's the best tease possible. You had a great show, tore up the room, and gave 110 percent, and people are going to want more. They don't hear a thing for four weeks, and then on week five, the press release comes out about the show; then at week eight, the posters go up. Between the release and the posters, you're grabbing people to make sure that they come and see you at the end of week nine.

It's a strong and effective formula that works the marketing concept of people *needing* to see you when they can, as opposed to having the opportunity to see you every weekend. I still believe a month is too close. A month doesn't really allow for the best marketing and preparation for a show either. This is why the nine-week window works well.

So where to play on those other weeks? Venture further out. I was based in western Massachusetts for a number of years and was surprised that bands would play every damn weekend in the smallest radius. I remember seeing a posting in the *Valley Advocate*, a great local arts and entertainment magazine for western Mass., of a band that was booked on a Thursday not two blocks up the street from where they were playing on Friday. Then I overheard them complaining in a local music store in Northampton about the lack of crowds at both places. Foolish, that's all I can say. Nothing more: just foolish. Especially when western Mass. is so close to a variety of music towns.

Anyway, in western Massachusetts, you're twenty-five minutes from Springfield, two hours from Boston, an hour and fifteen from Albany, three hours from Portland, two from Providence, four from the Big Apple, five hours from Montreal, four from Stowe, Vermont, and forty-five minutes from Hartford, Connecticut.

So you've got nine playing markets right there over a nine-week period:

- Springfield, Massachusetts
- Boston, Massachusetts

- Stowe, Vermont

- Providence, Rhode Island

- Hartford, Connecticut

- Albany, New York

- Portland, Maine

- New York City, New York

- Montreal, Ontario

Even if you didn't want to journey out of a five-hour-driving radius, you could still play every weekend in nine different markets without even considering the smaller markets you could play the night before or after the larger markets. This technique would allow you to increase the strength and numbers of your fan base since you're are not returning to the same rooms night after night and week after week. You'll create new fans that will need to see you because you don't come around as often, which makes the times you do appear a date that people are going to want to put in their calendar.

Think about it: If they were planning to see another band and you're showing up in town and they see that the other band is playing all the time, that other group becomes the "I can catch them whenever" group and you become the "must see" for that night. That is performance marketing in lieu of over-saturating a market.

Tease them, but stand your ground. Play and go away for a while. When you come back, the fans will too, and your base will grow stronger and stronger.

The Danger of the Regular Gig

The Paragon is a great Seattle restaurant that has live music on the weekends and a few days during the week. Oftentimes they have a series of a couple of bands that rotate over different weeks. Now for a place like the Paragon, that can be a great thing. As a restaurant and venue, they have a solid, consistent set of acts that people are expecting. That's a good business move and benefits the restaurant. They're not paying these groups a large fee, but at the same time, the restaurant is supplying the stage, the marketing, the consistency, and the regular crowd. The bands, of course, are supplying the entertainment, but this is where things cross over to the idea of general business as opposed to a band working toward its greater career or future.

There's nothing wrong with general business gigs, and if you prefer more stable shows, there are many avenues to approach, such as cruise ship work, casino gigs, weekly performances, open mic hosting, and the coveted hotel band. There needs to be a clear understanding, though: In many cases, it's one or the other. These are two levels of performance that don't mix well.

Think about it. If you're playing every week at a restaurant or bar, listed as this group that can be seen at any time, then when you try to play somewhere else or do a larger show, why should anyone come? They can see you every week. That takes away from the effect of your performance that you want people to come hear.

So you still want to do the weekly gig? One thing that effective bands do when it comes to making the money for a weekly gig while working up their own group is to play the weekly gig under another name. Work it from a different angle. Keep the promotion about your band separate.

Overall, if you're trying to become a sustainable band that tours and draws larger crowds, I discourage the weekly gig. It's too redundant, and while most feel they're building a following by doing so, it's usually a very small and localized following that doesn't add up as you want it to. Different members can play shows, or you can add the occasional acoustic show or even a band hosting an open mic-style show, but the constant playing in a local venue will end up keeping you local with a niche-following that won't come out when you're playing at the club where you really want them to see you, especially if there's a cover charge and they know where to see you for free.

In the end, weekly gigs are not going to take you where you want to go; they'll just keep you playing in circles for the same circle of people.

The Post-Show Follow-Up

The show rocked. You just got off stage after playing a great set. The audience loved you, and everything that was supposed to happen actually happened. You load out, get paid, and are either on your way home or to the hotel to sleep before the next show. However, there's one more step that will close out the show, but it doesn't take place till a few days later. This is the "post-show follow-up," and it will not only help you stand out but also help solidify your contacts and connections for future shows to come at that venue or with that booking agent.

Remember when your Mom or Dad had you write thank-you notes after your birthday and holidays? You wrote those notes and even sent them out to people who gave you the crappy socks or sweaters or things you wouldn't want in a million years. It was the good thing to do. It was the right thing to do, and it's something you should do after any gig, especially those shows and venues to which you'd like to return. Thus far, I've discussed how professionalism in your marketing, load-ins, load-outs, and stage performances will make you stand out. By adding the post-production follow-up, you will have put the cherry on top.

Write an e-mail and thank the club, the booking agent, the soundman, and whoever else was there. Use your letterhead for the note and try to remember names. Take some of the names and specifics down when you play. This will bring the professionalism to a more personalized level, as well as show the detail and care you're committed to. Even if things go wrong—sometimes it's not the booking agent's or the venue's fault—don't use this letter to gripe or sound like a princess.

If the club was bad, the people were awful, and you have no intention of playing there again, just skip the note all together. *Don't* go sending letters scolding clubs and venues, giving them a piece of your mind. As much as it may be true, you don't want it in the hands of people who might spread it around and make you look like divas. I was at a club recently where the owner blew me away. He really has his stuff together and has built a nice room. The sound, however, was awful and the soundman did a piss-poor job. If I do shows there in the future, I will simply ask if I can bring my own sound people or if he has other people on staff. If he inquires further, I will explain verbally, but I'm not going to write a note about the lack of professionalism and quality. I'm not going to blast names in letters. That said, sending a nice letter is the kind of stuff you want to be known for.

Thank them for whatever was good. If there were problems, try to address them in a positive and considerate way by saying how you would like to make things better for both the venue and the band. Say that you want to return and maybe add a picture of the band taken at that venue. Mention that you did a blog about the show and on your Web site and that you've linked the venue to your Web site. By the way, doing all these things is great for making connections as well.

So, basically you're setting up a thank-you letter, but hey, we have the Internet now, and you can send them by e-mail. These notes can make the difference in the long run. For larger shows, make the effort to send out a letter along with the e-mail. For the smaller ones, you can stick to e-mails. Thank them for the night and talk about how you would like to return. You will stand out because very few acts do this, and it will make you more memorable. I usually recommend sending out a note to arrive on the Monday or Tuesday a week after you played, if you can time the postal service. More things are reviewed and more mail is opened on those days as opposed to show days or busier nights late in the week or on the weekend.

The follow-up can help foster a stronger connection with that venue or that agent and get you back in there again or maybe on a better bill or with better stipulations around your show. So, as Mom said: be nice and send a thank you note. Stay in the mindset that every gig starts at the booking and ends with the follow-up.

TOURING

Touring is a good thing. That is a simple fact. You want to be out on the road, supporting your product and all secondary products as well as establishing marketing and branding your name. Touring with the purpose of playing the music to keep your band and your business operating is a smart way to approach things.

Of course, from the start you wanted to tour and be out in front of those audiences, but to tour and perform while being able to pay the bills is where the business comes in. Remember: touring is expensive.

Think about all the costs that are associated with it. You need gas, which is a killer; you have lodging, food, and instrument upkeep. You have to spend on basic toiletries and hygiene items, clothing, vehicles, as well as vehicle upkeep, like oil changes and maintenance. There are tolls on certain highways; you'll need Internet access, and many times you'll have to pay for city parking since free parking isn't always available. From there, don't forget about laundry; you're going to have to keep you clothes clean. Printing up flyers and posters at copy shops. Postage fees to send things home or have things sent from home to wherever you are. Don't forget about ordering products to be shipped to you so you can keep selling it. Then add in the fact that you still have your usual bills for rent, electric, water, cable, credit cards, phone, insurance, medical, and whatever else, like student loans or other monthly debts. Lastly, what about those little morale elements like going out to a movie, going to a bar, or visiting a touristy or historical place that might cost you a little cash?

Touring suddenly seems a little more expensive than you may have initially anticipated. There are ways to trim back and prepare, but the point is that you need to make sure you're working on selling your music and your other products to make this a realistic and sustaining venture.

Some nights you'll get a good amount of cash, but there are going to be a lot of nights on which you're barely going to make enough for gas money. It's the reality of the industry. So the answer is to tour *and* market the product. If you're out there pushing people to come, pushing the recording, and taking the steps to market before you arrive in the city *and* once you get there, doing some additional posters or seeing if you can get a couple of CDs in a local store or hand out some download cards, then you might be able to make it work. Plus, find out about the local music rags and newspapers so you can contact them the next time you swing through that particular town.

The more you make every stop as effective as possible, the more the sales will grow, the audiences will grow, and the tour length will get longer since you can sustain yourselves on the profits coming in.

Make sure you're not spending too many hours on the road if you can help it because the more time you're on the road, the less time you have to work the next destination with marketing, flyering, and researching the local TV, radio, newspapers, and magazines, etc. Some bands and booking agents will try to book only larger markets and have you on the road for hours. I remember being on the bus for nine hours straight some days and thinking, "OK. Why can't we play out in three-hour increments?"

Now, it's easier to be on tour and traveling long distances when you're on a nice tour bus, but only a very small percentage of artists have that luxury. For those traveling in smaller vehicles with larger numbers, it's a good idea to be on the road for only short distances. Find small markets you can play. With all the social networks out there, this is easier than ever, and if you're traveling a maximum of three to five hours a day, it can allow you ample time to get in town, do some marketing and research, then hit sound check, and continue to promote the show up until you have to go on.

That also means no sleeping in!!!! Or, if you're going to sleep in, only do it rarely. All these artists who try to live the rock star lifestyle and drink till four in the morning and don't leave till the latest time possible so they can arrive at sound check in the next city, then just sit around or drink until the start of the show, are wasting valuable time which could be used to make every stop a better stop and a better show the next time they return.

Work every city and every town. Pick up all the local rags and enter the information into a spreadsheet about that city. Mark down other clubs or venues. Find out who the hot bands are that fill the houses and then make nice with them by e-mail or through a social networking site. If you find a band that you can open up for that can bring in five hundred people, that gives you a much greater number of people to play to, sell to, and potentially gain as fans, instead of playing a headliner somewhere in front of a room of twenty-five.

Find out about local festivals and larger scale events that occur. As you do future tours, you can book yourself around larger gigs that pay a little better and then fill in the travel days with smaller ones that will bring you to new cities or towns that you can learn about and market to.

Stand out when you go to a new city. I was in a band whose manager would hand us each two CDs, a tee shirt, a hat, and a truckload of stickers after sound check, and we would go out to the local restaurants and bars to talk about the show and hand out a couple of free items. This helped. If you're playing during baseball season in a city that has a baseball game in the afternoon or evening, head down to the ballpark. You don't have to go to the game or pay to get in, but you can hand off a flyer to an excited fan and—you know what they say—if the team wins, people don't want to stop partying and maybe they'll come see you. Ask if the club will give an entry discount for people bringing a game ticket stub. There are tons of ways to play the city you are in before you play the stage.

Make it work for you. When you see touring as a marketing opportunity, a chance to grow your fan base, perform, and sell merchandise *while* learning about these cities, their media, venues, and people in charge, you'll make the next stop even more productive, effective, and lucrative.

Tour Packing

When the opportunity to tour comes up for the first time or even the first ten times, it's a new exciting adventure in many ways. You're stretching out your base and expanding your music to more and more people in more and more cities and towns. The playing is the same as the local shows you do, the loading in and loading out is the same, but the rest can be worlds different.

Before going further, I'd like to give my definition for what is and isn't a tour. Anyone can, and many do, play a series of shows, but if you're playing Wednesday through Saturday night, you're not on a tour. If you're going home every night after the shows, you're not on a tour. If you're playing within a fifty-mile radius of your home base, you're not on a damn tour. As far as I'm concerned a tour is, at minimum, two weeks out on the road, a good number of different cities and states, as well as a constant run that does not take you home. A decent tour in my mind is a four-month block of this. A successful tour is a six- or nine-month run that moves you around the country and maybe even into other countries as well. Now I know different people have different definitions, and I'm not knocking those, but from my experience, that's my definition.

Let's look at the middle of the road. A month out on tour, which is a more realistic run for a lot of aspiring bands, is a tour in which everyone cashes in vacation time from the day jobs, maybe even taking a bite in pay for a few weeks, to do a full four-week stretch. You probably have been playing for a good while and have the load-in, load–out, and packing down, but what about clothes and supplies and backup needs since you won't be home for a bit?

Before packing equipment and personal items, consider the order in which you pack to make unloading and loading a lot easier. If you're in a bad neighborhood and are not able to check into your hotel before the show, bring your personal bags in. Trust me: Don't wait for that day when someone steals all your personal items and clothes.

If you're in a van or even a van with a trailer attachment, I always advise groups to have two packing methods down pat. The first is for when you know that you're going to the hotel room first if it's not a night-traveling day. When you're loading up in the morning to leave and you know you're checking in before the show, make sure all your personal bags are closest to the door so you can take them out easily and quickly. I know, it sounds stupid and incredibly simple, but it will save you time and grief in the parking lot when you're trying to dump your personal stuff and get on to the show.

If you're doing a show before you load your personal stuff into your hotel room, or if you're doing a radio promo on which you're playing early in the day, load the personal items and the clothes in back of the van or the trailer. This whole process will avoid the unpacking and repacking that happens way too often and can take way too long.

It sounds silly, but color coordinate for memory.

Things often get lost in the transitions of loading in and loading out. So, just as you add better cases with numbers on them to make the load-ins and load-outs easier, you can also do the same for personal items. If you have a band with four members, assign a main bag and a backpack or side bag for each person, each with a different color, like red, black, blue, and white. This way, regardless of who's loading the van, you know that all the personal gear is packed and accounted for. If everyone knows every item that's supposed to be in the transport vehicle, it's more likely that it will be there or at least asked about if it's not seen before you leave any city. This can also go for your gear.

Suck it up.

Bringing those vacuum seal bags on tour can also be great to consolidate clothes or pack dirty laundry. You can get one of the little mini sealers, so you don't need a full vacuum. This way, you can store dirty clothes with your clean clothes without spreading the odors, and more important, after a good run of days and the sweating from stage, the van will not stink!!!!!! It will also compact things. They have smaller vacuum bags that can pack and consolidate, giving you more space in a bag that would probably be bursting at the seams.

Keep it clean.

One of our old tour managers took us to Costco the night before we left for a tour and bought us an industrial size laundry detergent and shoved it in one of the backs of the wheel wells in the van, then gave us a hundred dollars in quarters that were shoved in the glove compartment for small city tolls, parking, and laundry. Whenever we had to do laundry, we had the quarters, we had the detergent; we saved a lot of time and a small fortune. You say quarter machines are always at Laundromats or hotels? Ask any musician how much trouble they've had trying to find quarters when they're on the road.

What to pack?

When you play that one-shot gig or that local bar, you don't pack a suitcase. Well—I don't know about that. I've seen some pretty high maintenance glam band types that actually do, but that's another story. You know how to pack the van or the cars with gear for gigs and short runs, but how do you pack for a tour that is four weeks or more? Think of where you are going and pack light. I was, by far, not the lightest packer for most tours. I brought way more than I should have, and in most cases the room was allotted for it, and often others were carrying it. I got spoiled some, but in early tours I would bring as little as possible.

Plan to do laundry once a week if not more than that to keep the basics clean. If you do it more, you can bring fewer clothes. You're hitting numerous cities, so you don't have to worry about being seen in clothes you wore two days ago, so get over that. Think about what you want to perform in and then what is comfortable to travel in. I know you all want to look the part on stage, but remember to pack for the majority of your day, which is traveling. You're going to be on the road, in the van or bus, setting up and tearing down, and in hotel rooms, diners, and truck stops.

Pack and dress for that; it's the bulk of your tour.

Packing a cooler can be a good use of space and a great way to save money. Buy an Igloo, and when you're at a supermarket, pick up the essentials for snacks and basic road eats. It will save you from spending too much in the truck stops and fast food joints. When you're picking up the detergent at Costco, grab large packs of energy bars, vitamin mixes for water, and so on. This keeps more money in your pocket!!!!!

Set aside an extra bag that contains all the stuff you don't need in the hotel room or for the gig, like the extra drumsticks, boxes of guitar strings and the wires, cables, and backup repair items. Even better, these things can be put in small tight bags and shoved under seats so they can be accessed when needed but out of the way in the meantime.

Lastly, use the postal service. If there are items you don't need or you amass purchases, mail them home. Save the space and save the loads going in and out of the hotel rooms. If you head to a warmer climate and don't need your colder weather clothes for the rest of the tour, consolidate them, pack them, and mail them off. The longer the tour, the smaller the bus will become. The more room you can make or keep, the better for everyone.

Plan for the tour, think about what you need and what you don't, and keep in mind that the tour is, unfortunately, more parts road time than stage time. The better you prepare for the realities of the road, the better the tour will be.

The Show Sheet

They go under a number of different names and have been referred to as itinerary sheets, schedule sheets, day sheets, and probably a dozen other names. I'm going to stay with Show Sheets. It's one of those stupid simple ideas that just makes sense yet is used by so few bands. It's basically a sheet that's passed out to each individual, most often by the manager or managing member of the band, to give everyone the information needed about a tour or specific show. It's an adaptation of the itinerary or schedule sheets and is sometimes slid under the door of the hotel room to keep everyone informed about the day's agenda. It helps facilitate communication within the group and keeps everyone on the same page, no pun intended. A lot of things happen within a band when it comes to booking, and the confusion around the details of the shows can lead to problems, misunderstandings, and arguments among members.

As with most elements of relationships, the best answer to keeping problems at bay is communication. When you book a gig, a show or even tours, consider using a Show Sheet for the date or dates. It's a great way to make sure every *i* is dotted and every *t* is crossed. It will also answer any questions that the group might have and allow you to spend time on more important things instead of going over and over information that simply has not been put out correctly. Here are the different fields on the sheet.

DATE OF SHOW: This is obvious, but at the same time, every member that has a sheet knows he or she has to block off the date. I'm sure you've experienced issues with dates or confusion around schedules. This helps.

VENUE: Captain Obvious flies again.

ADDRESS: The location.

CITY: The city it's located in.

STATE: And the state. Yes it's obvious, but trust me; the details help.

HEAD LINING/OPENING/PLAYING ORDER: Who is playing before you, after you, or around you? This can be a chance to figure out some cross-marketing opportunities among the bands playing in order to get more people to the show.

CONTACT POINT: Who booked the show? This is something that gets lost in the mix way too often. People lose the contact or one with others, which can lead to problems around the show. This is a good field to fill.

PHONE: The phone contact for the person who booked you.

E-MAIL: The e-mail contact for the person who booked you.

WEB SITE: If the venue or the booking agency has a Web site, this is nice way to double check things.

SOCIAL NETWORK You know you have at least one, hell, everyone does these days. Find the booking agent's or venue's network sites, too, and put it here.

CONTRACT SECURED/RIDER DETAILS: Is the show confirmed? Do you have a rider, artist contract, or any kind of basic agreement that confirms the show? Place that here.

DATE SECURED: When it was confirmed, and who it was confirmed by.

LOAD-IN: The time for load-in. If you have a number of different shows booked, it's good to know in advance when to schedule your load-outs and driving time around when you are suppose to load in.

SOUND CHECK: What time is sound check? This will help you determine how much time you might have to do a last poster around the location where you are playing, to check into a hotel, or to take a moment of free time.

PERFORMANCE TIME: Sounds simple, sounds stupid, but isn't it best to know what time you are supposed to go on stage?

GREEN ROOM/BACKSTAGE: Do you have a green room or backstage? Is there food being supplied, or do you have to fend for yourself? Do you get drink tickets and, if so, how many? Is the room secured, or will there be security around it? Do you have your own area, or is it shared with other artists?

DIRECTIONS: OK, Captain Obvious flies yet again, but isn't it ideal to know how to get to the show? Remember, there's always MapQuest, and it seems as if everyone has GPS on a phone or in the van.

ESTIMATED DRIVE TIME: Having a good idea of how long it is going to take to get from point A to point B is helpful. Check on the roads; see if there is construction or other issues that might cause a delay.

STAGING POINT/TIMES: Where are you going to meet? Are you loading out together? Are certain members not going to be able to be there for load-out, or will certain members have to get to the venue a little later? Figure out where everyone is, where everyone will meet, and who might be late or delayed.

FINI: Adding fini or finish to the bottom of the sheet shows where the sheet is finished. Sometimes notes or items get moved to another page. Adding fini, finished, end, or just done, finishes the document. This lets the reader know there is no more.

Again, it comes down to attention to detail and the simple, stupid minutiae that make life easier. Take the steps on the front side to set up the best communication and organization to make the backside, the gig, or gigs much easier and smoother. The basic steps of solid organization will make everything else much more relaxed and fun.

Hotel Etiquette Rules for Touring

Gone are the days of destroying hotels. The stories-turned-fables of debauchery that had Led Zeppelin fishing for sharks out the window of a Seattle hotel are long gone.

I was a good respectful boy in my touring days, but I can't say that for others I was with. I will not name names, but I knew many musicians that used to steal various items from each room they stayed at, in an almost competitive way. These guys created collections of towels, ashtrays, alarm clocks, glassware, and many other items. They never really destroyed anything, although one time an unnamed bass player and guitarist of an unnamed touring group took everything in the hotel room and stacked it on top of the bed. I mean everything. The hotel couldn't trace the band because the room was paid for in cash under a fake name.

You can't pull off those kinds of things anymore, or well, you really shouldn't. And now it's a lot easier to get busted. With advances in the Internet and communication amongst hotels, it will catch up with you. Beyond that, it's now a good idea to incorporate a few elements of hotel etiquette into your routine when you're on the road. Just as a hotel will report a person, a band, or a group for doing bad things, they will also note the good stuff you do as well.

When you book a room, don't book each night separately. On a few tours I was a part of, where we were staying in midrange hotels and motels, management would book through Choice Hotels International for most US dates. The Web site is www.choicehotels.com.

Choice Hotels International books Comfort Inns, Comfort Suites, Quality Inn, Sleep Inn, Clarion, Cambria Suites, Mainstay Suites, Suburban, Econo Lodge, and Rodeway Inn. Booking rooms in advance for a number of nights through a chain, affiliate, or Affinity group will save you a fortune. I mean a FORTUNE. You can also join rewards programs or find other deals and reductions with some research. Think smarter, think about the whole tour and not just each night, and you'll come up with incredible savings.

Keeping a good relationship with a chain or hotel group is key as well. If you're a good frequent client, you will be more likely to get the hook ups and the perks. An old road manager once gave us a very strict but good list to follow, and in turn, some nights we were upgraded to top-notch suites for nothing. We received free meals, we even got free nights and beyond, all because we followed some simple rules of etiquette for both the hotel and the band.

Here is the top ten list of hotel etiquette that I strongly recommend.

10. Be Quiet.

You're obviously going to be coming in late at night. Leave the party in the bars and try to keep it quiet in the hotel rooms. An old manager used to request the rooms by the stairwell or the rooms that were the most separated from the rest of the hotel. Bands have stereotypes about being loud late at night and partying till all hours, waking the other guests. Many hotels will report on this. At the same time, when you're quiet and respectful, that is reported too.

9. Park your vehicles in locations with the most lighting.

Whether you have a van, cars, or a bus, try to park in a well-lit and more public area. Thieves are less likely to try to steal from vehicles that are easily visible. If you can get parking in front of a hotel or somewhere with good visibility, that's best.

8. Strip the bed and towels.

It sounds crazy, but when you leave, strip the sheets and put them in a pile on the floor with the towels and the trash. Hotels notice this, and the maid service will love you. We used to get a lot of our perks because we did this. It takes two seconds, and it's a good thing to do.

7. **Bring the sensitive gear into the rooms.**

   Don't leave the really small and expensive stuff outside. Bring it inside and inventory it, just as you inventory when you load it out. Think of it as a show. This will also enable you to rest easier.

6. **Bring your own pillow.**

   This is one of my tricks. You sleep in a truckload of different hotels, different beds, different rooms, different cities. Give yourself some continuity and bring your own pillow. It really can make a difference.

5. **Avoid room service, pay channels, and the charge food in the refrigerator.**

   Make money on the tour. Avoid going through the pay food stash that's in the rooms. You can easily go to a supermarket and buy cookies for five nights instead of opening the cookie pack in your room and paying five dollars for it. When you avoid additional charges, it will also allow for faster check out the next day.

4. **Leave a tip.**

   If you are in a room for more than a night, leave a tip for the maid service. Again, this can make a difference, and you will be better taken care of. Even a few dollars or a five spot is a really solid idea.

3. **Bring and split air mattresses for the floor.**

   If you are a four-person group, book a single room and rotate people from the floor to the beds on different nights. If you are trying to stay out longer on a tight budget, bring a couple of air mattresses. It will save you a small fortune.

2. **On the off days, give alone time in the room to each person for sanity's sake.**

   It may sound crazy, but on tour, you will be in a van, a single room, on stage, in restaurants, at gas stations—pretty much everywhere, together. If you're not on a tour that allows for individual rooms, sanity can drain quickly and easily. Walking in a strange city alone is great and all, but to be able to have some time alone, whether it's in the shower or just sitting in solitude, can be a very helpful and healthy thing.

Schedule times for everyone else to be out of the room so each member has a little time to take a shower, take a nap, make a call, anything, for an hour or so. The tour and your group's mental health will be a lot better.

1. **Leave a recording, merchandise, or swag products with the management.**

   For the cities that you do best in and in places where you begin to establish a good audience and good relationship with a venue, do the same for the hotel. Drop the management a CD, a tee shirt, some kind of merchandise or item. It will set a good tone and help you develop a relationship with that hotel for the returning trips.

As you leave the hotel, take down the name of some of the staff just as you would with the venue agents or the local media. People forgo collecting information about the places they stay in, but it's one of the most expensive costs on any given day of a tour, so pay it the attention it deserves.

Every step you take toward addressing even the smallest issues will give you the best results. It's all about the music. Don't get me wrong, but you are only on stage for an average of an hour or so every day on tour. The rest of the time you spend dealing with other elements. Think, research, and plan around those other elements, and you will find that a greater amount of success is possible.

Wellness on the Road

Just as you oil your pedals, change your strings, or tune a piano, you also need to do the same maintenance for your body. A musician's life can wear on the body. Long hours followed by sleepless nights of driving, alcohol, fast food, smoke in the air … the list goes on, all of which can have very detrimental effects on the body. As much fun as the road is, it can become draining and even depressing at times. You can change that and make the experience more exciting and even invigorating by taking small steps to stay healthier while you are out there.

First off, make the right food choices to maintain and improve your body. This involves accepting what is around you and balancing what your body needs. I mean, let's look at the perfect scenario. What if you could get everything your body needed anytime you needed it, at no additional cost, and it was all fresh and tasted great? OK, so that's not going to happen, especially on the road, unless you're working with one of those wild riders where you can request a bowl of all green M &Ms and get sushi every other night. (I have done the sushi but never asked for the M&Ms.) But there's an in-between. You can find the right foods in certain places and bring them with you. I used to keep a lot of my per diems (daily or weekly allowances) and go to a supermarket or Whole Foods store to stock up. You can easily buy a cooler and bring essentials with you as needed. For example: Why eat those crappy road-side fries and donuts when you could have a healthy snack of carrots, broccoli, hummus, or peanut butter? I also love those Cliff bars. I buy them by the box to have around for shows and the road.

It doesn't always have to be about cutting things out; it can be about replacing or having things ready so better choices can be made. When your body is being fueled by the right foods, it will handle the stress of the road much better than if you are eating fast food every night.

Sleep … everyone needs a good night's rest, and on the road it can be erratic at best. As I've said, pack your pillow. I also recommend bringing along a basic toiletry bag with the items you like the most. Sometimes having your favorite soap or shampoo just makes things easier. The smallest things really can make the biggest difference.

As everyone says, exercise is crucial, but finding a gym can be hard on the road. Fortunately, there are things you can do in your hotel room to get exercise. Try to work out when you can. Stretch every morning and night. It's good for you and for your body. I found that a mix of yoga and Pilates worked wonders for me, and when I was somewhere where there was good gym equipment, I would jump on a treadmill or do a solid work out. If there wasn't, I would try to get out for a good walk, just to get the cardio going and to see the city or town I was in. If you do go for a walk, though, make sure you know where you are and how to get back. I've screwed that up now and then and gotten lost. (Oops!)

The point is to take care of yourself on the road and at home. Look at your life and see how you can improve it from a wellness standpoint. A great tour, a record contract, or an amazing gig is not going to mean that much if you are slowly hurting yourself and damaging your body. Find a way to get cardio into your daily routine, not just when you are on the stage. Look at the labels and what you're eating. Try to stay away from soda, hydrogenated oils, corn syrup, refined white sugar, refined white flour, and fatty fried things. Skip the fast food places when you can. They may not always be avoidable when you're on the road, but you can keep eating at them to a bare minimum. Also, stay hydrated!!!! Make sure you drink plenty of water on stage, on the road, and while you are just sitting around. If you're going to drink alcohol, do it with moderation and make sure to stay hydrated with water to make the next day easier.

Following these steps will make the road an easier place to be. You will have more energy and more stamina. When you treat your body like your instrument (assuming you care for your instrument), you will be able to maintain a healthier body and demeanor. When I cut the crap out of my diet and added exercise, I noticed I was warming up much faster, I was less tired after a show, and I was sleeping better at night. The cases felt lighter as I carried them to and from the venues, and I was a happier person all around, for myself and for others. Think about the changes you can make. They don't have to be all at once, but taking small steps can bring you a new awareness of your body and how much better you can feel everyday, whether on the road or at home. Don't see it as a daunting task; see it as caring for your craft, caring for yourself, and attending to what your body really needs. Put down the Snickers bar and reach for a Cliff bar. Drop the soda and have some water. Experience the difference in how you feel. The changes come fast, and then it will become easier and easier to adapt to a healthier lifestyle both on and off the road.

As you can see, touring comes down to much more than the shows and the traveling. Prepare for the broad spectrum of all the different elements that are included, and you will find yourself in a much better and productive space creatively, musically, and financially.

YOUR PRODUCT

When you think about your product, how do you define it? How do you define its avenues of profit, and how do you create, control, track, and decide on the right product? When it comes down to it, your product is much more than just your songs or recordings. It's a strange but common mistake: People concentrate heavily on the primary product—music—and then skip on all the secondary products that would actually support, sell, and market that primary product.

It's important to have a solid production plan at all phases of recording: before you go into the studio, in the studio itself, and then afterwards in post-production. If you're organized enough to have a plan and a producer, you'll be able to create the best product possible, that being the music on your album and the downloads that people will be able to purchase. This product will then allow you to license music to commercials, movies, corporate videos, video games, TV shows, and other places where your songs can be inserted and bring in revenue.

That's only one step, though. Your product is also the CD itself, the CD cover, your press and promotional package, as well as every item in it. Your product is your logo, your tagline, your font and your secondary merchandise, such as clothing, stickers, posters, novelty items, and whatever else you create to brand, market, promote, and make profit from. Your product goes way beyond just the music; it's every aspect, every sheet, every item that will either directly bring you revenue or will contribute to the marketing, promoting, or recognition that in turn sells any of your physical or digital products.

Your product or products as a whole have to be organized and created with the attention to detail that you used when you were working on the music. You need to design the right plan as well as the right budget. You also need to track your product from cost to profit to know what's working and what isn't. These days you need to spend more time, money, and energy on your products as a whole in order to move the CD or music that you want to concentrate on.

Avenues of Profit

There are many avenues for profit and sustainability when it comes to having a recording that is well made and prepared for the most options. Follow the steps in pre-production, production, and post-production, and have all the marketing, promotional, branding, and solicitation items in place. That done, this is the order I believe is the most effective avenue for profits.

1. **Digital download sales**

2. **Physical CD sales**

3. **Shows and touring**

4. **Physical and digital sales on compilation recordings (Make sure the compilation is legit!!!!)**

5. **Basic merchandise—hats, shirts, etc.**

6. **Secondary marketing merchandise—posters, stickers, etc.**

7. **Specialized marketing merchandise—coffee, beer, wine, obscure products, etc.**

8. **No-vocal versions of songs for licensing**

9. **Licensing to radio**

10. **Licensing to video games**

11. **Licensing to television**

12. **Licensing to movies**

13. **Licensing to corporate or educational videos**

14. **Licensing to sports teams, complexes, and organizations**

15. **Speaking for educational organizations, schools, and after-school music programs**

16. **Ring tones**

17. **Backing band work for other artists coming through your city**

There are a number of other ways to derive profit with your music, but I believe these seventeen are the most beneficial and realistic. That said, make sure you have samples of your music ready. Make sure you have a mastered-down no-vocal version of your recording (I'll explain this in detail soon). Prepare yourself for as many avenues of revenue as possible, and you will find the opportunities and the chances for your success to grow and grow.

The Business Plan Approach to Recording Budgets

Budgets are a key element in the success of a project. The two problems that show up the most often are either a group that does not budget at all or a band that plans an unrealistic budget and rushes, cutting corners. But be warned: Every time you cut a corner or ignore an element, you're bringing the viability, sustainability, potential longevity, and success rate down.

The larger labels put together budgets and spending caps and designate where funds will go. These budgets are made up by accountants and producers who charge a small fortune to create them. The pre-production budgeting is one of the most popular services that we provide for artists at Brain Grenade Entertainment, and for worlds cheaper. I will always begin working with the artist on a budget that he or she can apply to a recording, whether the person works with me as a producer, through Brain Grenade Entertainment, or through an already existing label or producer. We budget for artists, labels, and managers to help them either designate and clearly define the money that has to be raised or justify the money that is going to be spent, down to the last penny.

Just as in any other business that needs to be funded, it's important to create a business plan that elaborates on each cost, explains why the money is needed for that item, and describes why using that item, person or studio is good for the project. When I create budgets for recordings under the Freedom Solutions Recording Plan, I work with the artist over a series of weeks to discuss the exact details of not only the recording itself but the project as a whole.

Most people would not invest into recording a CD alone. This is not considered a very safe investment. However, displaying recording as part of a full project and explaining how the project will go from start to finish adds reassurance. As post-production, marketing, promotion, branding, and release considerations are added, this creates a plan that shows a realistic and attainable chance for success.

It's a good idea to stay clear of talking about how the album will "change music," "become legendary," "be the best thing released this year," and anything else that is arrogant and, frankly, ridiculous. Explaining how realistic approaches will allow the artist to achieve obtainable goals and self-sufficient success highlights a mature and professional approach that will be taken much more seriously.

Show the process from front to back and discuss the marketing encapsulation of you as an artist and the recording as a whole. This will allow the donor or investor to see the vision in a detailed way that will create a sense of confidence and, in turn, will bring funding of some type. Having details about the people with whom you are working can also help to justify funding. Having the right engineer, the right studio, and the right producer is important; if you're attempting to put out something that is going to stand on its own in the industry, you're going to have to use the right team.

Explaining in detail why certain items are going to be used is important. In the Freedom Solutions Recording Plan budgets, Brain Grenade Entertainment includes the layout and blueprint with an appendix section that incorporates:

The Studio Expectations Sheet – This document explains the expectations we have for an artist in the studio in order to save time and money and to run the session at the highest level of efficiency.

The Communication Document – The Communication Document explains the communication we expect from an artist to make sure everyone is on the same page so things can move forward clearly and concisely.

The Production Approach Plan – This is a step-by-step overview of what will occur in each phase of the production.

The Mastering Document – This is a detailed description of the importance of mastering and why it is a crucial part of the project.

The Producer Sheet/Job Description – This document covers the job description of the producer and the roll that he or she plays during the process.

The Artist Responsibilities – This is what BGE and Loren expect from the artists.

The Legal Jargon – This is a short description of some of the legal elements of the process, highlighting and protecting the artist and his or her music in lawful terms.

Line Item Layout – This is a spreadsheet of every cost, the industry comparison cost, and the percentage differences.

Line Item Justification Glossary – This is the glossary of each item and the justified reasoning for it.

All of these documents help the potential donor or investor have a greater understanding of the project, the level or professionalism, the approach that is being taken, as well as the attention to detail that is being implemented.

The introduction to the plan describes the band in detail, along with a mission statement of sorts, and the goals clearly defined. All of this should be well thought out: Invest some time on the wording and the way you define your group and your project. Keep it uniform throughout the plan, pre-production, production, post-production, and release.

The body of the plan consists of all of the numbers and details of the plan from start to finish. I use eighteen categories that are broken down into subsets. This explains, to the penny, each step from the creation of the business plan to the day the album is released, as well as the assisting support of marketing, branding, and promotion that will supplement the recording for best-case-scenario achievements.

The artist does not have to apply every item from every category. A plan is always tailored specifically to the individual artist. The artist works with us to create exactly what is needed. We do explain in detail why we feel certain items are crucial and when others can be cut. In the end, however, it is the artist's choice.

Note: *Cutting certain elements such as primary post-production items can be detrimental to the funding of a record. If you take out elements that will take away from the album achieving a higher level of exposure, it can hurt your financial backing and support.*

The numbers are also compared to industry standards in New York and Los Angeles, which can often show the savings comparisons and instill more confidence. It shows that you are being smart with the budget while still paying close attention to detail.

These are the sections that detail the costs and explain what is covered in them.

1. **Pre-Production** – This cost covers the formation of the business plan, the basic layout plan of the recording, and the initial outline and blueprint of the project.

2. **Fundraising Plan/Investment Costs** – This covers the elements around the fundraising plan or investing plan, including the consults and the steps to acquire the funding.

3. **Producer Costs** – This covers the cost for the producer

4. **Recording Dates/Engineer & Studio Costs** – This shows the layout for the recording plan as well as the costs of the studio and engineer who is chosen for the project.

5. **Mastering Costs** – These are the mastering fees around the recording.

6. **Miscellaneous Studio Costs** – These cover the miscellaneous studio costs that are often missed or skipped over.

7. **Food and Nourishment Costs** – The preplanned food budget.

8. **Musician & Crew Costs: Core** – The core crew and musicians who are hired for the project.

9. **Musician & Crew Costs: Overdubs and Additions** – This is the budget for the additional musicians and crew who may be required for the recording.

10. **Wellness Costs** – For artists who want to add in massage or per diems to their budgets, as well as chiropractic or acupuncture.

11. **Travel** – These costs are derived from gas, parking, and other travel as needed, such as hotels or flights for artists who are flying.

12. **Rentals/Rehearsals** – Gear rental for the sessions, booking some of the session players for rehearsals in advance of the recording session.

13. **Graphic Costs** – Graphic design is a key part of branding and exposing the band in different media. This cost is just as important as any of the others.

14. **Promotion and Marketing Costs** – These are the costs surrounding the promotion and marketing of the project. This includes the press kits, the promo items, and the campaign to gain exposure for the recording and the artist.

15. **Web site/Social Network Setup** – The Web site design or Web overhaul to have a top-notch site or sites.

16. **Pre-Release Cost** – This includes duplication and the plan implemented to prepare for a release.

17. **Release Cost** – This includes the press release and the other costs surrounding a successful release and launch of a product.

18. **Post-Release Costs** – This section is more optional. These numbers and items include tour planning, ongoing advertising plans and additional marketing.

This is a basic overview of what our business plan covers. It goes into more detail on each subject and line item. A business plan that is formatted this way can not only help to acquire funding but also become a blueprint for the artist to follow and understand through the whole process. When you organize a solid plan that touches on every base, covers every detail, and addresses most questions, you come off looking much more professional and much more prepared.

In the end, by sharing your dreams and goals through a plan that has the proper foundation and attention to detail to become a viable and successful reality, you showcase that your plan can truly succeed.

Production Approach Plan

Below are the ten phases to recording a well-planned and prepared album, EP, or song. By making sure each phase is addressed and executed properly, you will find that you will save time, money, and hassle.

Phase 1 – Pre-Production

Keys

Tempo

Beginnings

Lyrics Charts

Endings

Instrumentation

Arrangements

Tracking Charts

Solo Choices

Primary Effect Plans

Music Charts

Phase 2 – Basic Tracking

Click Tracks (Optional but highly recommended)

Instrument Tracking

Solo Overdubs

Back/Harm. Vocals

Basic Quantizing (Optional)

Basic Mix

Lead Vocals

Additional Overdubs

Phase 3 – Post Pro Initial

Sounds

Basic Effect Processing

Noise and Clip Removal

Track Consolidations

Arrangement Adjustments

Technical Mix

Phase 4 – Post Pro Mid

Mix

Pitch Adjustments (Optional)

Vocal Edits/Overdubs/Copies

Review 1

Final Effects

Intro/Outro Fixes

Phase 5 – Post Pro Adv.

Final Equalizations

Final Volumes

Spot Checks

Phase 6 – Final Listen Session

Double Checks

Last Thoughts/Notes

Final Mix

Phase 7 – Post Pro Final

Spot Edits and Volumes

Fade Decisions

Send to Master

Phase 8 – Master

Master

Setup Industry Master Layout

Burn Master Copies

Phase 9 – Edit/ Double Check

Double Check Final Master

Double Check Album Layout

Double Check Budget

Phase 10 – Duplication

Send for Duplication

DONE

Artist Responsibilities

This project demands significant involvement by the artist and band. Ultimate success is highly dependent on your individual efforts. To help achieve a smooth and successful implementation, it will be your responsibility to perform the following:

Weekly meetings (at minimum): at least one thirty-minute meeting a week with the producer for three weeks prior to the beginning of the recording.

Information Purge: Compile, attain, and write requested documents such as bios, legal copyright documents, songs, lyrics, and recordings.

Accounting: Create the statement formats desired by the producer for the balance sheet, income statement, and other financial reports meant to keep the artist's budget on track.

Pre-Production: Work to enhance skills through in-depth rehearsing and practicing with the artist, vocal and instrument instructors, and hired studio musicians.

Equipment & Infrastructure: Acquiring needed programs, gear, documents, and contracts to ensure the success and forward motion of the artist to attain his or her goals.

Documentation: Preparation of all required documents and templates to be filled out by time lines advised.

Fundraising and investing: It is your responsibility to achieve the goal of funding. Please put your efforts into this section as best you can.

You are saving, on average, over 75 percent of what it would cost to do this in Los Angeles or New York, but in turn, you need to put in the effort to make it happen. This project forms a team between the artist, the producer and the other musicians and crew brought in. It is the artist's responsibility to deliver 110 percent, or the project will not achieve the fullest fruition.

Industry Pro Sheet

The Industry Pro Sheet is an extra item I tell most bands to have ready for their press packs. This sheet does not go into every single packet sent out, but having it available for specific packages as well as for download off a Web site is a strong element to have and a good idea all around. It shows an extra touch of professionalism and can allow for other opportunities and shows because the artist is prepared for them.

The Industry Pro Sheet is a layout page that shows the organization of different samples of the recordings that an artist has. It lists each of these samples in different sections and how they can be used and acquired.

The first section is a list of basic twenty-five- to thirty-five-second samples of the songs from a given recording. Each song can have one to two samples, which will show industry professionals that you are sending them a disc that will allow them to get through your album quickly, with the chance to hear as much as possible in as little time as possible. Setting up a disc that goes in order with the Industry Pro Sheet is a good idea, as is having a page on your Web site that does the same.

These samples, properly mixed and cut with fade-ins and fade-outs during the mastering phase, will also give the artist a number of good sample tracks to put up on MySpace and any other Web site where samples are used. Having the sample fade in professionally and fade out the same way, perhaps right before the change of a section of the song, will make the listener's ear want to hear more.

These samples also could be used as ring tones. Having this first section of the Industry Pro Sheet allows listeners you are soliciting to get a fast idea of what you sound like. This is better than just sending your disc. A number of people are sending off their discs, but by having this sheet as well as an accompanying demo disc, you show respect to those to whom you are sending it, and it will allow them to hear the scope of what you have. Make sure to list the name of the song, the fact that it is a sample, and the length of the sample. When listeners see that the tracks are short, you have a better chance of getting those listeners to hear all the samples. You also come out of the gate showing that you have music prepared for other avenues of revenue, which will make people listen that much more.

The second section is the no-vocals section. This consists of a cut of each of your songs with no vocals and no backing vocals. So in the list for the sheet, if you have ten tunes on your album and you have decided to do one sample per song, the track order of the Industry Pro Sheet would show tracks 1-10 samples, then tracks 11–20 no-vocals versions.

The mastered down no-vocals versions create opportunities for your music to be used in TV, movies, commercials, radio, video games, and other areas where music is desired with no vocals. Already having something ready for use shows a professionalism and preparation that exceeds most. A no-vocal version could even be sent to another country for another singer to sing in a different language. I always master down a version of every album I produce with no vocals. It's a smart thing to do, and it allots for more opportunities and faster ones, should someone want to move on a song immediately.

The third and fourth sections depend on the style of music. For a solo artist who may not always have a backing band or may be looking to do certain TV and sing-along appearances (these days called karaoke tracks), having a version without lead vocals and only with backup vocals and instrumentation can allow for the artist to be able to do performances without a group, or perform certain songs on different TV shows.

The fourth section is the samples and loops section. Some add this and others don't. This is where samples or loops are taken from songs on the album and set into a loop format for potential use in other genres and fields of music. A potential record company, or even another artist or talent buyer, might want to purchase a loop or a number of loops for a new song.

That's the basic layout of the Industry Pro Sheet. It displays the spectrum of opportunities possible for a song or album but also shows whoever reads your materials, listens to your music, or sees your group that you possess the attention to detail, the preparation, and the extra pieces that go above and beyond most.

The Demo

When you're recording a demo, make sure you know what the demo is for. Earlier we talked about the idea of a pre-production demo to really get a sense of where you're at for an upcoming recording session and to lay down ideas for songwriting. Sometimes booking a single day at a nicer recording studio where you can get a very rough mix, but at the same time have decent sounds and simple isolation, can help you when you're using it to come up with ideas for songs or arrangements of songs.

Recording demos, though, often turn into songs that are released and which then represent you poorly. You may get some music out there quickly, but it can turn off potential opportunities down the road.

If you really need to get some samples and music up and all you have are demos, then list them as such. Let people know that what they're hearing is a demo and that better recordings are coming next. There are a great many artists out there who put up substandard recordings and begin to give off the sense that those songs represent their best. Simply add the word demo to the song name so that people know exactly what it is.

Demos can serve as a great tool for the artist and band. They can also serve as basic samples, but know where you don't want to push too far with a demo. A demo is a demonstration recording and should be used for that specific purpose. Be careful with the cutting of corners, where people try to remix demos and make them into more. If you're going to go that route, at least record the demo in a better studio with better microphones and rooms so that the demo could easily transition with additional mixing and overdubs. That can be an option, but if you're recording in a bad room with poor microphones and a lot of bleed, you're going to make any advanced use of that demo a big challenge.

Figure out what you're doing when it comes to demos, and make sure that if you want to use basic tracks later, you record them in the right way so you have made the demo as effective as possible.

The Information on Your CD

I'm pretty amazed with the information that is put on CDs these days, and even more so, by the information that is missing. I have long been a big advocate of making sure you have the right information on your CD. I'm not really concerned as much with the cover. I think covers are pretty standard. Go artsy, have fun, do your thing. Just make sure you use the font of your band logo in a legible size on the front side along with the album name.

As for the rest of the front cover, it's all yours, and I'm not going to step on anyone's vision or artistic approach. The same goes for the inside of a disc. If you want to go for a pamphlet that has fourteen pages, every single lyric, thank yous to the guy who delivered pizza on the second day of the session, that is totally your choice. I really don't care because, in some ways, if someone is looking at the inside of your disc, that person has probably already bought it and is listening to it. To me, the two most important parts of the CD and its design are the compact disc itself and the backside of the case.

First, in reference to the disc ... People often lose the covers or the inserts, and for those who still have CDs, they're putting them in those travel cases with a hundred other discs. As for the CD back, if someone is looking at a CD in a store—yes folks, there are still people who buy CDs—it likely has a plastic wrap or cover film around it. This doesn't allow the potential buyer to sift through your small book inside. The only information that is given to them is what can be seen on the back. So combine the two: For that person going through a friend's disc case or the guy or gal in the store looking at a plastic covered disc ... wouldn't it make complete sense to use those two areas, the disc back side and the disc itself, to properly advertise, market, and promote your group and the recording?

Think about it another way. Someone you're soliciting your CD to is probably already getting hundred of CDs a day, oftentimes, shoving a number of discs (which may or may not include yours) into a multiple disc player where those discs are separated from their covers, which can be lost easily in these offices. If the listener likes you, wouldn't you want to have all the information needed to get in touch with you made easily accessible? It makes the most sense, but most artists don't think of it and end up with minimal to no info on their discs. Bad idea. Trust me.

Now, I'm no Sony, and I'm not William Morris. I have a small, very independent production and consulting company, yet we still receive close to a hundred solicitations a month. Now think about those larger groups—the labels, the management firms, and the touring agencies. They receive thousands of CDs and solicitations a week.

Stand out!!!!! What if your package and cover are lost when they put your disc in????? How are they going to put together your disc with your package????

Take the smart approach. Make sure you pay attention to details. Make the disc a promo package in itself. Yes, it's a lot of information, and yes, it takes away from the art you might put on the disc, but you make the decision: Would you rather have an artsy disc or a disc that gives out the information needed to be a promo pack in itself?

I would go for option number two.

Here's the layout I give to artists for the most effective discs. Again, lots of info, but it's all good information, and if they don't have a CD cover or a package, they still have everything they need. Each element listed below shows your organization, your professionalism, and your attention to detail. This is smart effective marketing for anyone you want to see your disc, including labels, booking agents, venues, talent buyers, management agencies, licensing groups, TV and movie music supervisors, reps, and more.

Below are the elements you are going to want to have on the disc as well as on the back of the disc cover:

- Name of Artist in the Artist's Font
- Name of Album
- Song Titles and Times
- Writing Credits
- Copyright Credits
- Publishing Credits
- Produced By
- Recorded At
- Engineered By
- Mastered By
- Album Short Description – Single Sentence Summary
- FBI Warning:

  Warning: The unauthorized reproduction or distribution of this copyrighted work is illegal. Criminal copyright infringement, including infringement without monetary gain, is investigated by the FBI and is punishable by up to 8 years in federal prison and a fine of $250,000.

- Compact Disc Graphic

- Representation/Contact Name
- Rep Address
- Rep Phone
- Rep E-mail
- Rep Web site
- Band Logo with Tagline
- Band Web site

On the back of the disc cover, I advise all the above, as well as:

- Barcode Number
- Extended Bio on the Disc or Band

I know it's a lot. It's a lot of information. It does take away from the art element.

It does give a very business look to your disc.

But ...

Isn't that what you want? Isn't that what you need in the beginning? You can still be artistic. There are ways to lay out the information in an organized way, and a great deal of the information can be in a small font. You are a new artist trying to launch into a world with millions of bands. Open the door for every opportunity by making your package, including your CD, the easiest, most organized, and most professionally prepared materials possible.

Take serious steps so you'll be taken seriously.

Releasing in Other Languages

So you're going to print with your CD, posters, and other promotional materials. You're making sure all your content is uniform, organized, and properly laid out; well, at least you should make sure. Either way, once you have that promo pack all together and the information laid out on the site, the disc, and in print, you're ready to go, right?

Most of the time, yes. Still, you're not covering every option and every opportunity for revenue and success. Sometimes the obvious things are right in front of us, and we don't realize them. It's important to take a step back and look at everything you are doing for your career and the different approaches you can act on.

One approach many don't take is doing their release in another language. Do you know someone who can translate your information to another language?

Why not save some money from your first run in English and do a small run in another language and market to another country a few months after your first release? It doesn't mean that you have to re-record the whole album, but if you have a member who can sing in another language, why not have a song or two from the album recorded and put up digitally in another language as well?

This takes a couple of steps:

1. **Pick a language first that is tied to the heritage of a member or a language where your style of music is very popular.**

2. **Look for someone who can properly translate your information and then double check it.**

   While it's a great marketing tool and it shows you as a more respectful artist, it is key to take the steps to make sure you are spelling or wording the information correctly. Simple translation mistakes can make you look foolish. There have been many marketing blunders made by Coca Cola and Pepsi due to bad translations. The original Chinese translations of Coca Cola translated as "Female Horse Stuffed with Wax." The Pepsi campaign in Taiwan that they thought would say "Come Alive with the Pepsi Generation" ended up being read as "Pepsi will bring your ancestors back from the dead" in Taiwanese. Again, check and double-check your translations.

3. **Make a basic distribution connection with a distributor or sales group from that country.**

   Come from the angle of an American band that wants to promote in another country and show respect by doing it in that country's language, and you will find a lot of doors open up to you that might otherwise not be offered.

4. **Add a front-page link that can have your site be seen in another language.**

    This comes down to copying the information and making sure someone translates it correctly. Do not use those automated translators. You will look a lot more respectful if you're respecting the language and the culture you are trying to reach.

5. **Put up a second MySpace/social networking site in that other language and invite friends from that country alone.**

6. **Do a promo pack of your information in that other language and send it to key magazines, TV stations, newspapers, and other media of that country or countries.**

    On top of your normal marketing, you are now adding the element of an artist or band showing respect to another culture and not expecting everyone to read just English. This can go much further than you realize and open up a number of opportunities that you would not have if you just sent over your music in your normal package. This can also open up doors for potential licensing of your music into commercials, movies, and other insertion opportunities for that country or countries. Since you have all your promo materials in that language on the disc and in the supplemental documents, you will be easy to reach, and the only issue you may have is the need to find that translator again to cut you a deal of some type.

Maybe think about doing a different language every three months. Look at the larger international sites for examples. In the upper corner or even in the middle of the front pages, you find an option of languages. It's not that you have to have ten different languages all at once, but it's one more project and one more action you can take to reach a wider audience. You can then market the fact that you are the respectful English-speaking group that is taking the effort to reach out beyond the language barrier. You may also find some additional marketing back here at home for having a release that can be purchased in a couple of different languages, so remember to look at all your options. It can create more avenues to success, sustainability, and revenue.

Remember, your product is one of the key factors that will connect you with the media and the public. It is crucial to make sure this product represents you musically, creatively, and professionally while at the same time serving as a promotional and contact device to give you more opportunities.

THE STUDIO

The studio is the center of everything that will allow you to do all the things you want. ,This is where you create the product that will be the base of your career. The root of your marketing is your music. It's the foundational element that will push you out to the most revenue streams possible. You will build tours around your recordings and press packs to get your recordings out to the world and media. You will use the recording to assist you with your promotion, your shows, your branding and your sound.

Since the recording is so important and the root of what you're about as an artist, it's not a place to half-ass. Taking the steps to pre-produce is the foundation of it all: Prepare your charting, your pre-production, your lyrics, your arrangements, your writing, and basic decisions before you go into the studio. In so doing, you'll be able to save time and money for things that need to happen during recording sessions.

Of course things will change when you get in there and ideas can come about that are not what you initially planned, but if you have a game plan to work from, you'll be much more effective than if you go in and have to deal with a lot on the fly.

That said, there are questions to answer. What kind of studio do I need? What is a producer? What should be set up in advance musically? What should be set up financially? Is a session player required?

These and many other aspects are covered next to prepare you for the most crucial stage and make it much more fun and affordable while still being able to deliver the best product possible.

The Producer

One of the most important elements of successful artists or bands is getting their sound "right" and into the hands of the appropriate fans. With today's recording equipment and techniques, there are a lot of tools at hand to help you with your sound. However, digital boards and Pro Tools are not a substitute for talent, experience, and overall good sound judgment.

To do this right, you need a solid process. It's much more than walking into a studio, plopping down a few bucks for studio time, and winging it. Any local garage band can achieve that goal. But if you want a professional sound, planning, practice, guidance, and judgment are paramount.

The first step is to utilize a seasoned producer who will take responsibility for every step of your recording process, from pre-production to recording, post-production to distribution. It is crucial to find someone that understands your sound, strengths, weaknesses, and overall goals and can weave them into a final product that will help position you with fans, media works, and future agents and handlers.

Please review the following to help familiarize yourself with what is in store to create a "killer" sound. Remember that the scope of these services can be divided among numerous individuals, but this is the standard and you should expect nothing less from a professional. Below is the full scope of services the producer should provide during stages of pre-production, recording, post-production, and overall organization.

Scope of Services: Your Producer/Producer Job Description

Pre-Production and Recording

Accountant – Designating the funds for a recording based on information given by the artist and making sure the money stays on track. Setting up your budget in pre-production should be included as well.

Hires for the Project – Session players help to fill in and enhance any artist or band. Your producer will assist you in finding, accessing, and hiring additional artists to help round out your sound. Players suggested by the artist or band will be reviewed, but final choices will be the responsibility of your producer.

Creative Force – Will add ideas, arrangements, lyrics, and alternate and additional parts to preexisting songs to make them flow better, if needed.

Time Manager – Runs the schedule for recording and calls the session when point of no return is reached.

Diplomacy/Peacemaker – Recording is emotionally and physically draining! The producer's job is to encourage the artist, manage conflicts and emotions, and keep the tensions to a minimum. The Producer is also the middleman between investors, other parties involved, and the artist.

An Objective Listener – Hearing the sound from a pragmatic point of view. Being unaffected by a single instrument, idea, or style. This separation allows the producer to see the songs and album as a whole instead of dwelling on individual aspects that often can send a song in a direction it should not go.

Quality Control – Your producer will listen for the intricate lines and pitches and will also make decisions on the best takes an individual can give. This is an area that needs to be discussed in advance.

If you're looking for perfection you must have the planning, practice, and budget to back it up. Your producer will work with you to achieve the best possible product in all areas while staying on time line and on a pre-arranged budget.

Director/Boss/Mr. Big/Head Honcho – This role can be adjusted and discussed, but when it's set into place, it's locked down.

Visitors can only come on certain tracking days. The Control Room is where it happens. If you or your producer is distracted or bothered by people in the room, they will be asked to leave.

Vocal performance – The vocals are the top layer and usually are the tracks that are worked the hardest. Vocals should be worked with both technically and physically to create the best sounds.

Mixer – The producer will take all the sounds and find the right mix and levels with the artist. Post-production is also a very important aspect of the job.

Assisting Engineer – The producer will work hand-in-hand with the engineer to get the sounds the artist is looking for. It's a good idea to spend the time to get strong sounds right from the start.

Post Recording

Marketing, Promotion, & Distribution – Recommend steps required to successfully gain a higher market and promotional share in the music industry and develop the marketing channels to further this process.

Assist in planning and assembling data for the above groups for use by the artist without assistance from management.

Prepare time-line goals and project plans.

Establish specific databases and media contact groups for press releases, media hits, and Internet viability that will also include keyword and search optimization programs.

Performance – Prepare the artist for proper stage presence, volume levels, and performance skills needed to supplement the music through live shows. Write contracts; create stage plots, sound and light requirements, and riders that will suit the artist's and venues' needs.

Temporary Management & Consulting – Assist in the artist's "next steps" as he or she is being approached by labels and other promotional companies.

Benefits

When the project is complete, the right producer will have successfully set the artist or band in place as a well-oiled, professional touring machine ready to take any venue. They will also have a top-notch product that can be shared with confidence.

The artist or band will have control of the database networks and a complete filing system in order to manage and maintain security on all pertinent information. This will increase their viability as an act that should be signed. It will also control documents that allow the artist to retain all rights and will make sure that the artist will understand all information placed in front of him or her regarding contracts.

Regardless of whether you are working with a particular producer or combining producers, you'll need to make sure that the above items are dealt with, understood, and designated to make a project run like clockwork while saving the most money and time. This strong start to a career in music shows professionalism and drive uncommon for a start-up talent, and this programmed approach to the overall project is sure to benefit the artist's or band's music and success for years to come.

In the end, a lot of people call themselves producers that are not even in the ballpark of doing half these things. At the same time, there are other producers that focus only on certain areas. Either way, make sure you have all these items handled.

Pre-Production

Pre-Production Sheets

I'm a big fan of Pre-Production Sheets. There are a million ways to set them up and many producers and engineers have their favorite ways. For the albums that I produce, I prefer a great deal of pre-production before going into the studio. It's a balance of having ideas in place so that things can move at the best pace while still being creative. I don't try to create the album in a very strict format; rather, I set the blueprints in place to allow plenty of time to create and find inspiration in the studio while working in a smart and time-effective environment.

I like to break up each song or potential song for the record into a series of four sheets.

Pre-Production Sheet

Tracking Sheet

Lyric Sheet

Chord Chart

The Pre-Production Sheet is usually the first one I start on with an artist. I go after the obvious at first.

Pre-Production Sheet

Artist Name - (so as to not mix it up with other sheets)

Song Title – Name of the song, kind of obvious.

Time Signature – Again, kind of obvious.

Key – Still hanging in the world of obvious.

Tempo – Where do they currently have it tempo-wise, and what have they been playing around with for tempos?

Time – How long is the song in its current form?

Songwriter/Copyright Info (if they have it) – It's really smart to make sure to copyright your works prior to doing a full recording. There are producers out there that steal. Write on the sheet so it clearly shows: This song belongs to someone.

I then go to the …

Description and Inspiration of the Song - I like the artists and the bands to talk about where the song came from, who it's about, and what it's about, almost like a bio for the song itself. This helps me see where they have taken it and where it might go while still keeping the essence of what the artist is looking for. This helps me bring up ideas and create thoughts around what could be removed, added, embellished, or complemented. It's a way to step away from the song and attack it from another angle.

The next thing I have the artist fill out is STYLE. I find it interesting to ask bands or artists the style of a song or where they see the song, as a single linear element, being placed. It might be a hard rock band, but if it's a slow ballad Latin-ish Bossa Nova that they have in mind, I would rather get that wording out of them. Then I'm able to attack the idea and the layout of how we can bring the song to the best place musically and production-wise.

Songs this Sounds Similar To – What songs do the artists hear in their mind that would come close to this song? It might not even be the song itself but more of the idea of a guitar solo that sounds like this song or a drum sound like the drums from that song. This helps me and other producers get a little more into the heads of artists and find what they're hearing that they might not be able to explain. This really helps in post-production and finding the mix that the artists really want.

Keywords for the Song – My pre-production ideas feed off the keywords for the song. This allows artists to use words they feel instead of thinking musically or technically. Artists oftentimes talk about not being able to say what is in their heads. These two sections really help to get some of that out. It also allows me to bring the end product closer to their vision and what they had imagined.

One band I worked with kept referencing the word "revving" for a song. They wanted this one section to be revving, like an engine. We had a little fun with the idea, and I ended up putting a microphone on a Jeep and capturing its rev up. Later, the engineer and I added a slow fade auto-tune to the sample, which made the rev slowly come into the root note pitch of the next chord. Then we added a delayed guitar a little backed up, and in the end we had what sounded like a car starting and morphing into a guitar. The section literally revved up.

I may have come up with the idea and the technical plan, but the band had the vision and the concept of what they wanted. Since they filled out the Pre-Production Sheets in detail, I was able to be more effective for them, even if they weren't sure exactly what they were looking for or how to ask for it.

Instrumentation – What instruments do the artist or the band have in mind, and what instruments would they potentially like to try or add, and why? This gives me a tonal idea about what people are thinking, what they would like to hear, and where they want to hear it. It also gives me a better sense of what ideas I might be able to bring to the table that they might like.

Special Notes – I leave this section very open. It really allows the artist to say anything they are thinking. Some random thoughts about the song, about a section of the song, about how a single instrument should sound, can give me a deeper view of where the artist is coming from.

Specific Vision or Ideas – This is sometimes what I see as a continuation of the first section, but for certain bands and artists that feel a song has a very direct vision, they are able to describe it here. They can bring to light any last thoughts or ideas, and it has always proved to be very helpful to me in approaching the song.

Once the artist has filled out this sheet, we go over every section and every idea in the pre-production meetings. This helps the communication, the understanding, and the creative flow as well as better connects me to the artist and the song.

Having sheets like these to use with your producer or engineer can put you on the same page with him or her. It can facilitate a much greater understanding of the artist's vision and allow the producer and engineer to help bring that vision to a reality in the final mix of the song.

Tracking Sheets

In addition to having a pre-production sheet for each song, I like bands to go into the studio with a Tracking Sheet for each song as well. Just like the Pre-Production Sheet, you can have a lot of different formats and go after different information. This is the layout that I use with artists that I produce who are in pre-production for a Freedom Solutions Recording Plan album.

Tracking sheets lay out the song in an easy-to-follow recording format by showing how many tracks you have for that song and what each track is. By having a Tracking Sheet laid out and even e-mailed or mailed to the studio and the engineer in advance of the session, you can save time and money.

The Tracking Sheet can become a blueprint for the engineer to know the following:

- How many tracks to set up for each song and for the session as a whole.
- The basic information, such as song name, tempo, key, and time signature.
- How many microphones and which microphones to have ready.
- What kind of effects to plan for.
- How to place musicians in the studio for the recording.

And plenty more details.

The Tracking Sheet I use is broken down into six sections. Again, there are many ways to set up a Tracking Sheet in different basic categories. This is the one I use because, in my opinion, I feel it gives the most options and the most information.

Section 1 – T# – The actual track number. This is kind of obvious, but it's good for review to know just how many tracks there are on the song.

Section 2 – Track – Each individual track is listed and named in this section. To reiterate, this is each individual track, so you want to list drums as a track, but at the same time you don't want to list every drum and every cymbal. You want to list the microphones here and what they are miking. If the track is prerecorded, use the file name that has been previously cut.

Side Note: Name the track on the Tracking Sheet the same name as you have it on the prerecorded tracks to avoid confusion or problems that can arise from one item being named ten different things. This is a problem I've seen more often than I care to say. For example, if you record a keyboard sample in advance of the session and the engineer is importing that in on a track, make sure it has the same name on the import file as it does on the Tracking Sheet. This will make things move smoother and faster. All too often, the engineer or producer has to look up and ask what file 34543-dub is. **Name your tracks and organize them, ALWAYS!!!!!!**

Section 3 – Microphone Type or Specified Sound – If you have a certain microphone you'd like to have used on this particular track, this is where it can be added. The same goes for a specific type of sound. Listing different words here, even if they're not technical, can give the producer and engineer ideas on how to capture the sound you're looking for on that specific track. If it is a sample or an already existing track, this is the place to note what you are thinking of for it in the production sense.

More often than not, this section is left mostly blank, but those small details can help you get the sounds you desire.

Lastly, you can fill out a copy of the tracking while you're in the studio as part of a studio diary. You can take down what kinds of microphones were used and what kinds of effects were added. It also can be interesting to see just how many tracks were recorded and what tracks were later removed from the mix.

Section 4 – Tracked – This is a checklist to make sure you recorded everything you had originally planned on laying down. Each section that was marked off and tracks that were added during recording need to be noted. This Tracking Sheet is as much for you as it is for the engineer and producer. It will often change, with additions and subtractions, during your recording. By tracking what has been recorded, you'll have an easier time when you reach mixing since you can look down at the sheet and see everything that was done. I know it's up on the monitor, but having that paper right in front of you can make a real difference.

Section 5 – Mix Notes – As the track is being laid, this is the place to make specific mix notes for later. Also, listening to technical mixes and making notes on the Tracking Sheet can help communication during mixing flow a lot faster and smoother.

Section 6 – Issues – This is for any additional thoughts, or if you need more room beyond mix notes. You can list what you don't like about a track that you are on the fence about keeping, or mention the repairs that you feel need to be done on a specific part of a track.

Section 7 – Basic Info – On the top of the Tracking Sheet, list:

- Band Name

- Song Name

- Time Signature

- Key

- Tempo

- Song Length (if you know it)

- Intro

- Outro

Knowing all of the above information will be helpful if it's a fade-in or fade-out. If a certain instrument starts the song, knowing what key the tune is in will be helpful so that if auto-tuning is needed, it's a simple add. You should know what tempo to set the click track at and the most basic element—the name of the song.

That's the layout that I use for my Tracking Sheets. It's that whole attention-to-detail thing, down to the single microphone or single track. The Tracking Sheet will help the engineer, the producer, and you as the artist be able to keep track of all the details that sometimes slip by the wayside. The more aware you are of the sounds that you're creating and the more you can reference them, the better the mix will be for you in the end, and the easier it will be to identify and correct issues along the way. Think of it as a road map to lead your song all the way to final mix; you can edit all you want while being able to recognize and remember each part along the way.

Lyric Sheet and Chord Chart

The last two sheets that we ask our clients to have prepared for the studio in pre-production are the Lyric Sheets and Chord Chart. I don't care if the entire band knows the song or if you're a hip-hop artist who has a non-chord based song that's mostly a simple loop. Having the Chord Chart will allow you to make sure that the band, the engineer, and the producer are on the same page as well as the same chord. It will also allow for easier changes. If you've been playing a song one way for a very long time and decide in the studio to do a light change or adapt something in a different way, it can be much easier to mark a Chord Chart and have that reminder right in front of you for reference. For instance, if you do not have a sax player or backup singers and you decide on the fly that you want to add them, you have a chart that will be easy to read and professional to boot. This will also make the eventual mixing much easier.

The same goes for Lyric Sheets. Being able to mark a word or phrase where you might want to add a harmony, re-cut, or edit can make listening back to the mixes a lot more productive than having to listen over and over to catch all your notes.

With all the changes that can happen to a song in the studio, having the foundation of the Chord Chart and the Lyric Sheet will give you the basic blueprint to be able to track, edit, subtract or add and keep everyone on the same page—literally.

Make both the chord and Lyric Sheets easy to follow. Make sure they are clearly printed in a large bold font or clearly written, so that anyone can catch on to your form and any musicians you bring in will have a shot at getting it on the first pass instead of sitting with a pen and clarifying or fixing errors.

With the lyrics, printing them out double spaced and a little larger, in phrases of how the singing melody goes, will make it easier to change words. Also, if you have a new singer coming in and can clearly see the words, he or she can concentrate more on the notes instead of trying to decipher the horrible handwriting that many of us have. These formats will also make it easy to edit; as you cross out a line or word and change it for another, you will have the room to do so. Some artists will make some dramatic lyrical changes in the studio, and though they may be small notes, they can clutter up a page and throw off the singer, the engineer, the producer, and the rest of the band. By having the large font and the double space, you have the room to cross out and replace without having to draw arrows or chicken scratching around a sheet that was printed too small with no concept of the fact that things could change.

To recap: The Song Production Packet I use includes the Pre-Production Sheet, the Tracking Sheet, the Lyric Sheet, and the Chord Chart. I've been told I'm anal retentive about asking for these four items for every song early on, but it becomes very apparent in the studio that by covering all the bases, you can be much more time-effective and creative and end up with the best studio recording possible.

Beyond that, filling out all these sheets and laying them in front of you, or even pinning them up on the wall, can give you four more views of the song you already know and have been so close to, which can lead to new ideas and creative elements that might not have been there before. It may also make you think about where there might be too many similarities between certain songs and differences you might not like between others.

Production sheets can also serve as marketing items. You can give away or even post online the history of the song to show your fans how it was laid out. It can add another facet, letting your fans see your music from another side.

Even if you're a skeptic, try it with your next song and see how it goes.

Studio Expectations Document

It is key to be organized in the studio and make sure that things are running smoothly. Brain Grenade Entertainment has set up this sheet of expectations for both the artists and players on a session. These are strict requirements that allow us to keep the hours down and the work level up. I advise anyone with a studio to have a basic set of requirements for the artists that come into the studio. I also recommend to artists to talk as a group about how you are going to make the most out of your studio time and be organized beforehand to waste as little time as possible and get as much bang for your buck.

Lastly, these are just good rules to follow to make the most out of your sessions.

Arrive on Time and When Your Call Time Is Set – Allow for sufficient time to get to the studio, find parking, and begin to load in at the designated time. If the call time is noon, you should be parked and ready to start loading in through the studio doors at noon.

Cell Phones Off – Not on buzz and not turned down. You are working this session and do not want interruptions or additional sounds on the takes.

Yakkity Yak … Aware of the Talkback – If the engineer or producer is talking over the talkback to one of the musicians, the other musicians should remain quiet and not play their instruments.

Have Your Gear Ready and in Top-Notch Condition – Make sure to have your instruments ready upon arrival. Change strings and drum heads at least two days before the session. Bring extra batteries, strings, and cables, just in case. Make sure your instrument is properly intonated.

Physically and Mentally Prepared – Be in the state of mind to work. Do not be drunk or hung-over for the session date. Do not bring any alcohol or drugs to the session.

When Concentrating on a Sound, Don't Add Others – If the engineer is moving a mic around the kick drum or a loud amp, that's not the time to do the drum solo to In-A-Gadda-Da-Vida or your Eddie Van Halen tribute!

Bring in Samples – If there's a specific sound the band is going for, bring some CDs in to show what you like. This works for tracking and mixing. No sense going for a John Bonham drum sound when the band likes Steely Dan!

Drums First – Drummers, have your drums ready for the session. Make sure you have either removed your front head for the session or have a hole in your bass drum dead center of the head. Make sure you have the sticks you need and a backup snare head and duct tape with you.

No Guests – Try to bring only yourself. If you have assistance for loading in, ask them to come back at the end of the session. This allows for the control room and environment to be as conducive to working as possible. This also keeps people working on the music and not trying to impress guys, girls, family, and whomever else.

Respect the Engineer and the Studio – Watch for cords and do not step on them. If a take is playing and the engineer and producer are listening, remain quiet and do not interrupt. If you have thoughts or ideas for the mix or things you feel should be mentioned, note them and deliver them when the take has stopped.

Shhhhhh – Don't talk, play, or move for a count of eight after you finish a take. Wait for the last notes to die away completely. Use your volume knob to fade out at the end of a song. Don't jam or play between takes or songs. Either tune up or sit quietly. Goofing off just wastes time.

Open to Change – You may have to change your normal amp settings to get a better sound on tape. Sometimes your stage settings don't work in the studio, and the studio may have to experiment to get your sound back—even to the point of switching amps or going directly into the board.

Never Start with a Ballad – For energy levels, for sound levels, for everything on all levels, plan on the first song being something up-tempo or mid-tempo and something that showcases the higher side of the dynamics in order to make things goes easier and faster.

Watch Where You Are – Never walk into a room without seeing if recording is going on inside of it. It sounds stupid, but oftentimes people walk right into an isolation room where someone is tracking.

Lose the Extra Percussion – Take off any clingy or noisy jewelry that could affect a take. This goes for everybody.

Stink with Consideration – The studio is a small and closed-in environment. Avoid heavy colognes and perfumes during session days. Also, bathe and do not have an excess of body odor.

Enjoy yourself; make the experience a fun one. The more prepared you are, the more work that can be done and the more money that can be saved in the process. Applying these simple steps can make everything move smoother as well as keeping the endurance and confidence levels of everyone high. It is about the music, but it is also about the mental state when it comes to recording. If you can keep the vibe in the best place, you can bring the best results.

Session Players

Session players can really help make an album sound its best possible. When you're a solo artist, or even a band that's bringing in a session musician to play an extra part or an overdub, that professionalism and skill will support the song, and the playing will be executed in a fast and top-notch manner.

"But my friend is really good …" I've heard this hundreds of times. I understand people want to bring their friends in to play on their recordings. Oftentimes I hear, "It will save money because Billy will play the horn part for free!" Does Billy have a professional tone? Does Billy know how to perform in the studio? Can Billy adapt or adjust things very easily or quickly be able to change a part or improvise a section?

Usually when friends come in to play, it becomes much more expensive. Even though our imaginary trumpet player Billy is playing for free, with his lack of studio experience, he adds a lot more time in the studio. That's time you're paying the studio, the engineer, and the producer. Every take that Billy doesn't get adds to the end price tag. I'm not trying to be rude about your friends, but if you're on a budget and a time line, it's best to bring in a top-notch studio player to deliver the part you are looking for quickly and professionally. Studio and session players may cost more than friends, but they will deliver and deliver fast.

Decide in pre-production what you're going to need beyond the core of the band, and book your session players early. The really good players are often booked well in advance. If you've followed my format, you can send these players a Chord Chart, Lyric Sheet, Pre-Production Sheet, and scratch demo on CD or by MP3. This will give the player more than enough information to be able to come in and knock out exactly what you need.

Be realistic about your abilities to execute parts in the studio as opposed to hiring session players who can really keep the quality at its best. For instance, you may have a great drummer. He grooves well and is solid with the click; he has great feel and hits the drums right. However, he or she might not be a percussionist. Yes, there really is a difference between a drummer and a percussionist. Amazing drumming on the recording could be pulled down by uneven shaker patterns or very beginner conga playing.

A lot of times I'll hear a drummer and make sure he or she has strong percussion ability, enough not to take away from the drumming or the song. If not, I'll advise the group to bring in a percussionist to play the parts. It may sound silly or as if it's an insignificant difference, but listen to albums where there are top-level percussionists. Even the small things like the tambourines and shakers are placed just right and played with continuity and accuracy.

The idea is not to replace you or your members as secondary part players. If you've already made the decision that your group will play all the instruments, that's fine, but for songs that have the best and most opportunities for success, you want to have all the instruments sound as if they're being played just the way they should. If you play guitar for the group and your guitar part is top notch and you want to add a part with an instrument that you play at a beginner level, bring in that session artist to play that part or instrument while you play the guitar. This will keep the ability and the sound at its best.

Session players for one of your players???

This is a topic that is talked about in small and careful circles. The idea of replacing certain band members with session players on certain songs in order to get them done quickly or up to snuff is a hard one for some people to swallow but a reality in the industry in certain circumstances.

Ghost players have been on the recording scene for a long time. Very often they're the drummers and bass players who will come in and fix or play a part and be paid a little extra not to take the credit. I've spent a great part of my session career doing ghosting sessions. I enjoyed it, and it was fulfilling even though I didn't get the credit directly. I've had people ask me how to build a résumé doing that, and the answer is the same way as if you're hired as a session player who gets credit. The album might not have your name in the credits, but the studios, the producers, the engineers, and the labels know who did what and that it was you.

Which leads to the last part of hiring a session player. What if you're in a situation where something is not happening in the studio with a core member? There are three choices at this point, and they all have pluses and minuses.

One – Keep trying to get the track with the band as is, or cut the session and go practice the crap out of the song, and then come back and try to nail it. Now this can waste time in the studio as well as add another day or extra time for which you might not be budgeted. If you're under a contract with a larger scale label, the producer will often make the call at that point to pull in the session player to finish it. This happens, and frequently. Don't kid yourself; it's a daily occurrence in the majors and even high-level independents.

Two – Call in the session player. It can be something of a blow to the ego, but it will get the track done and the player being replaced can work to get that part down afterwards. Good session players will not play far above the skill set of the player they're replacing. Many times they'll listen to what the replaced player sounds like and play a part that works, is solid, and is something that, with brief practice, the replaced player could quickly achieve. Anytime I replaced a drummer, I tried to bring his flavor into the track or tracks I was brought in for. I would reproduce any signature fills or consistencies, and then I would just tighten up what was not working.

Three – Call in the ghost session player. If you want to bring in a guy or girl to play the part, but leave it as the band member's name for continuity, ego, or whatever, call for a ghost player. The way it most commonly works is the label, producer, and management will contact a session player that is familiar with and has done ghost sessions, after which a payment will be arranged as well as a non-disclosure agreement. The Non-Disclosure Agreement or NDA will be a contract with the ghost player to keep this session a secret. You'll be paying a little more to hire someone who's not going to be receiving direct credit, so be prepared for the pricing difference.

When it comes to session players to back you up, or session or ghost players potentially to replace parts on songs or even full tracks, it can be a hard decision. Look at all the angles and make the decision based on what's best for the band and the recording, but also be careful to read recording contracts if you've signed one. Inside many larger scale contracts, there are already stipulations that allow the label or producer to make that decision for you.

The best approach is to be prepared. Practice, practice, and practice, and hopefully the only session players you will need are those who will embellish the band and the sound if the tune calls for it.

What Is a Session Player, Anyway?

There's a wide-scale definition of what a session musician is today compared to what it used to be, and in all honesty I find the new definition disappointing, as do many true session players. Session players, by my definition, and what I look for when I hire a session player or studio musician, are as follows:

- Musicians who truly have professional, technical, and tasteful control, skill, and prowess on their instruments with the ability to execute in numerous genres, time signatures, keys, feels, and improvisational concepts.

- Musicians who know their keys, their modes, the best way to draw the best sounds from their instruments, and are able to listen briefly to a song and know what should be played to fit the song.

- Musicians who can take direction and criticism and who possesses the ability to alter and change parts easily and without hassle.

- Musicians who have the best sounding gear and a spectrum of options for different sounds, tones, and embellishments. They keep their instruments studio-ready and in top shape.

- Musicians who can get through Chord Charts. I prefer players who can sight read, but if you have all the elements listed above and you are not the fastest sight-reader note by note when it comes to certain genres, it's fine.

- Musicians who are always on time and ready to work until the job gets done, players who have the endurance to go a full day without a problem.

- Musicians who show up with everything they need and all the problem-solving tools for any issues that might rear their ugly heads later on. They should be ready with extra strings, sticks, backup whatever, oil, clamps, duct tape, whatever might be required of their instruments.

- Lastly, musicians who have hundreds to thousands of hours of studio experience working in studios of all sizes, and knowledge of how to play to a room, to the microphone, and for the song. A player with at least twenty-five recording credits, bare minimum, scaling from top echelon studios to smaller independent studios and everything in between, as well as references from other engineers, producers, labels and studios.

This in my mind is the definition of what true session players or studio players are and should be. I'm not knocking those players who are building up their résumés and working toward becoming session players, but I have a really hard time when I see people call themselves studio players who do not encompass the above list. Don't make yourself out to be more than you are. It doesn't take away from your growing and learning, but remember, if you sell yourself too high as a player and get fired from a session, you're starting your reputation with a bad taste in the mouth of the producer, engineer, or studio.

When I record in a new city or in a place where I don't know the local players, I often have to ask who the session players are. Many people will talk the talk but then will not be able to walk the walk. If you're honest about where you're at, you will more likely land a job with a producer who understands where you are, as opposed to selling yourself well above your level and not being able to cut it.

If someone is honest and just can't cut it but has the right raw elements and want experience, that's someone I would consider in the future for projects he or she can handle. If I have to fire someone because the person lied about the level of experience and ability, then he or she is not going to be hired by me again, ever. I'm not the only person who works this way; there are many. So set a precedent, be honest, and be truthful because bad reputations get around just as fast, if not faster, than good ones.

Again, even if you're a great player, be totally honest about your playing. Your humility will be your ticket to growing the résumé that will give you the right to call yourself a session player. My first ten albums on drums I did for free. I put up posters around four studios in Boston and the Berklee College of Music studios. The poster simply said, "New drummer looking for studio experience. I WILL PLAY FOR FREE!!!!! Use me and abuse me. I have a great drum kit, no ego, and I will give you the best I've got."

That got me a truckload of sessions and ten albums. I was recording almost every other day. Some were just demos, some were pre-production tracks, but inside of all the experiences, I got my name on ten albums, too. I also began to build a reputation with the studios around Boston. It was based on truth. I got some very nice compliments. At that time I would hear feedback like, "Not the greatest guy, needs more chops, only fluent in certain styles, but works his ass off, takes criticism well, and doesn't complain."

I was used by them for free, and at the same time I got so many experiences and got to work some amazing guys that helped get me gigs, shows, and experience. Experience that helped me grow as a player and grow into a session player. I remember one session I was fired from: I could not get the track. I was easily the youngest guy there, seventeen at the time. As I kept screwing up take after take, the other players who were worlds above me gave me the evil eye. They had another drummer called in from a session in the studio down the hall. He was in the control room when I was called in and told the news. I knew it: I was fired.

As the other drummer was getting ready to bring his drums in the studio and the engineer was heading out to strip my kit and send me packing, I swallowed my pride and offered my kit to the other drummer. The evil eyes around the room lifted. Everyone was amazed that even after being pretty much ridiculed, I offered up my kit.

The kit was much better than I was. It was tuned up right and already covered with microphones. The drummer sat down and nailed the track that I couldn't get in two takes. That stung. He finished out the other tracks so fast and with such precision. I sat in the corner and watched him with tears welling in the eyes. Yeah, I felt humiliated, but I was trying to save face and trying to learn.

After the session was done, I quietly packed up the kit and loaded out as fast as I could. Just as I got home, I got a phone call from the producer of the session. He offered to take me out to dinner. He told me that what I did was probably the best thing I could have done and that he wanted to work with me on things that he knew I'd be able to handle. He also turned me on to some other styles and a few teachers, but best of all, I got to be a fly on the wall at his sessions. A number of years later, I got to work with him again. It was a kick, we had a flawless session, all the players were top notch, and the session was a blast. Of course, he had to tell that damn story to everyone during a break, but whatever.

The point is you can't just go calling yourself a session or studio player. That's a prestigious term that should only be associated with years of practice and experience. You have to build up the chops, the knowledge, and the experience over time, and it takes time. You don't start karate and then become a black belt overnight. You are honest, you tell people what belt you are and what your experience level is, and you have the belt to prove it. Maybe session players should get a belt like karate.

Either way, sell yourself—and I'm not saying don't—but sell yourself on your current ability and your experiences, not on where you want to be. You can get there, and you can earn that term, but earn it. Study the art of the session musician, because it's an entirely different world than the average musician. Don't put on the black belt if you don't have the experience; otherwise you might be in for an ass-kicking.

Tips for Session Players

For session teams like Funk Brothers to the Wrecking Crew, from the session drummers like Vinnie Colaiuta and Hal Blaine, being a session player is lucrative, but out of the spotlight. These are the guys and girls who have been on more hits than you could ever imagine, but the average person cannot even recognize them on the street. A perfect example is Hal Blaine. This session drummer has been on over 8000 tracks, more number-one hits that any other drummer, and it's often said if you turn on an oldies station, it's hard to go ten minutes without hearing Hal.

But how do you jump in and become a session player? What do you charge? How do you get your name out there and how do you develop a solid sustainable career as a session player or set up a realistic and supplemental career as a session player to balance out touring or live performing that you may already be doing?

Be Versatile, Be Good, and Be Able to Listen

First off, it takes a strong musician. Jumping right into session playing is not realistic. You need to be good. Know your instrument, know how to make it sound good, and have a strong mixture of the technical and the creative when it comes to your instrument. Mixing this with excellent communication skills, a great deal of patience, and the ability to keep the energy, performance, and concentration up, even after a series of takes in which you might have played it the same way four different times but the artist or producer is asking for a fifth.

A good session player is a musician's musician who knows many different styles and is aware of numerous genres, players, and sounds. If the player doesn't, he or she has the drive to find out what needs to be known and do it quickly. A great ear is a crucial element to be a great session player. It also helps when a player can listen for what the song needs and what will work, not just what the player can do. Basically, in a band setting, you might want to play a really wild and full line to showcase your self. As a session player, you want to play whatever will showcase the song.

As the session player, you are the side man, the supplement to the song, the support for tune, and unless the chart or song calls for you to go wild, it's your responsibility to understand what should be played and, even more important, what shouldn't. A good session player is as professional in his chops as he is in the upkeep of his or her gear. He or she shows up for a studio date on time and exemplifies patience and, my favorite as both a former session player and now a producer, the ability to SHUT UP when arrangements are being reviewed in the studio.

It comes down to being more than just a good player. It comes down to an array of skills that make you the go-to guy or girl when a player is needed. That's a true session musician.

Show Me the Money and How Much to Get Paid

Now, even though it's important to discuss how to advertise and how to present and market yourself to get out to the studios, the engineers, the producers, and the labels, the questions I get asked most are, "How much do I charge?" and "How much should I pay for a session player?"

Unfortunately, there's no simple answer. There is a spectrum of possibilities. For a while, it was routine to pay a session player a certain amount plus a performance royalty later. While this can work to your favor on high budget recordings, it really doesn't do you all that much good on smaller recordings, and it can only hurt the artist as more pieces of the pie are being distributed before the album is even done.

My preference as a session player and as a producer that hires session players is an agreed-upon solid fee.

Deciding a fee based on either a full day, by song or by full project can work out well. Make sure that the fee fits the project and that it fits you as a player. My first sessions, I didn't charge at all because I wanted referrals and reviews. As I built a solid reputation with my playing and also my professionalism, attention to detail, and patience, I got more calls, and in turn, the price tag went up.

Find the Balance in the Fee

It's not about doing freebies for every session, but it's not about charging top dollar every session either. Finding a happy medium in marketing yourself as well as taking into consideration what a session could do to get you future work is all part of the equation. Take the concentration off you for a moment. Think about how a studio, a producer, an engineer, or an artist would feel about hiring you. You may know what you're worth or what you think you are worth, but how does it appear to someone else? Building up the résumé with recordings, reviews, and references can help with the initial presentation, but keep in mind: how are you selling yourself to these people you want to work with who more than likely already have a crew they prefer.

The Best Option: Pay per Day or Pay per Song

Make a decision based on the work and time that's going into the session. As a session player, I preferred to be paid for the day. Sometimes if it's a half-day session or even less, I will set a basic minimum so if the session is done fast, it's still worth the time, travel, setup, and so forth.

Try to get a sense of what is being planned for the session. If it's some band that's still in the writing phase and you are recording for hours on the same song, being paid by the song is not the best bet. At the same time, if an artist is running off a truckload of charts for some kind of licensing thing and you are able to make a fortune per song that day and you are recording with some solid players, payment by the song can work.

Some people will talk about being paid X, then being offered performance royalties. These days, with sales drastically down and most recording on a more independent level, I would advise against it. As an artist, you need to maintain as much as you can, so work up the budget to pay the musician. As a session player, being on twenty session dates in a month in which you didn't make all that much and are thus watching what's happening with this album or that song is a pain. These days, especially with both less sales and tracking issues, it's really not the best option.

Amounts

Again, it's about considering the economy and the individual session you're working. Even top names that I have hired in recent years as a producer have asked me what the budget of the recording is and understood that no one is making what he or she used to. Top session cats from L.A. are working in general business and cover bands these days, too. So don't get cocky when setting a price tag or referring to what someone was making a number of years back. The average rates were never that average. The standard doesn't really exist. In my experience in hiring musicians, everyone has a different rate system. I do know that if I'm hiring someone for the first time, he or she is making less than my usual crew so I can get a sense of the player. At the same time, the guys and girls who I know are going to bring everything I need to a session will always get more.

As a session player, think of how you're being viewed by a producer, engineer, studio, or artist. Are you bringing not only your musicianship to the project but also the professionalism, the patience, the ability to change things, and the willingness to adapt? A great deal of great players are not session players. It takes a special mold. For me, I work in the budgets to make sure every player is getting a full day for at least a five-hundred-dollar payment. Of course shorter days pay more, and many of the crew that have worked with me will get paid in the range of seventy to one hundred dollars or more an hour. There are times when I have a smaller budget and ask favors and see if these particular musicians will consider working for less. Since they usually get a good rate, they will often say yes more often than no.

In the end, taking the occasional free session to get involved with a studio, other producers, engineers, or musicians can help build you up even more than word of mouth, but when it comes down to the actual price tag or what you should charge, it should stay open for negotiation until you have truly established yourself. Don't short yourself, but make sure you understand the situation you're going into and charge accordingly. Ask questions, too. Will meals be covered? Is there parking? For drummers or key players, will there be equipment at the studio already? All these elements can make you decide about your costs and what to charge.

In the end, exactly what to charge or what to offer can be tricky when it comes to sessions. Consider all the elements and decide accordingly. Make your decisions reflect the specific situation and be sure to have the ability to compromise to a point.

The Demo Session

When an artist is preparing to record an FSRP album with me, there's often a good amount of time in pre-production and preparation before the recording is made. Even after, there's a lot of work that goes into preparing the release and putting out the album the right way. That doesn't stop the need to continue to book and play in the meantime. You can't just wait until you have the top-notch product. It's key to have something to use for booking and continuing to promote your group. You need to keep making forward motion. Whether you already have a recording, or if you have really bad demos, it's important to have a demo that will represent you well for booking.

On another note, wouldn't it be great to have a hint of the studio you are going to be recording in before you do the full album? Familiarize yourself with the feel of the room, the engineer, the producer. Getting in a pre-session to get more comfortable with the room and the people, as well as to generate some inspiration to get into the studio to record the album, can really get an artist or band pumped up about the project.

This is why I recommend what I call the Speedy Gonzales session, or demo session, for recording the best demo. The artist comes into the studio where he or she is eventually going to record the full album and spends a day recording a demo. It's a fast-paced day and not for the weary. Most, if not all, of the tracks are recorded live with the setup time and recording taking a little less than half a day. You leave the other half of the day for a quick mix down, giving the engineer and producer half a day to speed out a solid mix. You'll leave with a really solid demo that you can use for booking shows, putting up new samples, or playing for people who will donate or invest in the full project. You'll also have an excitement about what's to come for the full-album session. You'll have a greater sense of the studio, the personnel, and how things will go when you record the full length as well as a greater level of comfort once recordings begin.

Remember, you're going in to record a demo. It's a demo. The more time you take to record, the more time is taken away from the mix down. The goal is to split the day in half. Budget your time to do the recording in the first half and the mixing in the second half. It will be a solid rough mix, nothing even close to the full album, but it's crucial to get the best rough mix you can. If you continually try to redo, re-take, or overdub, you're only making it harder to get the best mix possible in the shortest amount of time.

Know your producer and know your engineer. Make sure that they can work at the speed they need to so you can get the quality you should have. In Seattle, I work exclusively with Scott Ross. He's an amazing engineer with a great set of ears, but he also knows how to move and work fast. I can promise artists (and I don't usually promise anything) that if they do a single day run with Scott and have an organized production and recording plan for that day, the artist will leave with a great demo that would be on the level of what some bands would use for an album.

Once the recording is mixed, a basic mastering can be put on it, and you leave with a product that you can be proud of. Using the day for marketing can be smart as well. Bring down a camera, or even a video camera; give people a look at the place where you are going to be recording your full album. This can really help with the fundraising part. Make sure to take notes as you see things that you want to understand better, and make sure to set up a meeting after the session to discuss your questions and your observations.

Doing the speed demo helps in so many different ways. Most of all, though, a great pre-production session can help you save time and money once you reach the actual full-album recording. The more you understand and the more you're comfortable with the environment in which you'll be working intensely for a number of days when it is time to do the full length, the faster and more effective things will go. It may cost a day of studio time, but it could save you a lot more on the back end when you do the full recording.

Food and Nourishment

In the album budgets I apply, we always allot a line budget for food in the studio. Food is one of the most overlooked items in a recording budget and can amount to great costs as well as large amounts of time wasted in people leaving the studio to pick up food. That's not to say that you should be locked in the studio for the entire ten hours with no breaks, but you should take breaks that are breaks and not leaving to do more work, such as picking up food and then eating and having to get right back to work.

Food should be factored into the number of the days you are in the studio and how many people will be in there each day. By planning a basic menu of snacks to be available as well as main courses and meals, you'll know what is needed up front and it will allow you to make a clear plan. Some bands have each member prepare meals each day to bring in. Others will set up a shopping list and go to stores, such as Costco, to pick up bulk supplies at a cheaper rate than it would be to go out and buy these items in convenience stores each day. Items such as bottled water, coffee, soda, and other basic snacks can add up terribly.

It's evident that planning a budget for food is a much better idea when you think about coffee purchases alone. I produced a record at a studio in Los Angeles, which will remain unnamed, for a label that will also remain unnamed. This state-of-the-art facility in Hollywood (gotta tease a little) had all the bells, whistles, and toys you could imagine. Two-inch tape, Pro Tools, isolation rooms galore, and a main room that had a ceiling that was very, very high. Yet with all the incredible toys, gadgets, effects, out board, and plug-ins, it was missing something interesting: a coffee maker.

I remember talking with the engineer who was often hired at this studio and being told that there were five coffee shops in walking distance and any time we needed coffee, one of the interns would go out and fetch it. This was fine with us, because it was not on our tab. Any coffee we wanted would be billed to the budget of the band that we were working with. The problem was that when you started to do the numbers, those simple coffee runs added up.

Play out a simple equation. Let's say a band is in the studio doing a record for ten days. Let's say that there are ten people in the studio between the band and crew:

6-Person band

1 Engineer

1 Producer

1 Assistant

1 Intern

So we have ten people floating around for ten days. Let's then say the sessions are ten hours or more, and using a low average, we will say there are three coffee runs taking place each day. Again, I'm being very sparse here; I remember days of five to six runs easily. Next, let's average out each drink to three dollars. Some will want tea which might be less, some might want the frilly high-maintenance drinks which will be more, some might want a bottled water or Odwalla juice drink, cookie, whatever; any way, three dollars a person per run.

So back to the basic math: three coffee runs a day for ten people at three dollars a drink. Now multiply that by ten days, the length of the session. This is also assuming that the entire crew is in the studio for every day, but you get the idea.

Thirty dollars for every run, not including tips; ninety dollars each day for coffee.

And the Grand Total—Nine hundred dollars for the coffee for the session.

Yes folks, but it gets more expensive, because that nine hundred dollars that was spent on coffee is now owed back to the label or investor with a percentage rate.

This is just one of the places where waste and abuse occurs in the industry. When you plan and organize your budget you can save a fortune on coffee, food or anything else you want or need to have while you're in the studio. Under my budgets, we would look at a ten-day session with ten people and see how we could make it as affordable as possible. One answer I use is to have a coffeemaker in the studio. Elliott Bay Recording Company in Seattle, Washington, has a great coffee maker, by the way. Just let Scott make the coffee if you are in a session with me; I always make it way too strong.

Next, prior to the session, someone goes out and buys a two-and-a-half-pound bag of coffee, filters, sugar, creamer, milk, soy milk, honey, and assorted teas (for you non-coffee people). All of those combined can cost thirty dollars, more or less, depending on your coffee choices or if you need soymilk, rice milk, or whatever your condiment fancy is. So balance it out: nine hundred dollars plus interest to a label, plus waste time on trips to a coffee shop, or spending only thirty dollars. That's a pretty big savings as well as smart budgeting.

That's the basic idea for all the food, regardless of whether it's a snack or a main meal. Say you want sandwiches for three days for ten people; instead of going to Subway, purchase a meat plate and all the condiments. You will save money and have it available anytime someone wants to eat, which makes for an easier and more productive use of everyone's time.

As with most elements surrounding music, organizing and executing a well-formatted plan is the best approach. Think realistically about how many you have to feed, what people eat, and what you would like to have on hand. Also think of effective food to have in the studio. Try to stay away from heavy meals and too much junk food. Have fruit and water available; make sure it's not all candy bars and Doritos. When you eat crap over and over again, it will make you feel like crap and potentially deliver a worse performance in the studio.

It's also OK to plan into the budget a night where everyone eats out. Sometimes at the end of recording or during a mixing day, getting out all together and eating somewhere can be a good stress reliever, and if you plan for it and have a basic budget set for it, it will be something you can realistically do.

Finally, plan what food is going to be picked up and when. If the sessions are on top of each other, this aspect is easier, but if you're booking over a series of a couple of months or longer, remember to figure in the bulk purchases that can be made plus the weekly purchases that will have to be made. Organize the shopping list and make purchases accordingly. If that means that before you lock in the budget you head down to a local Costco or supermarket for standard costs, then do that.

If you're recording a well-budgeted album, the food and nourishment budget is one more additional point that proves just how organized and well thought out every piece is. When everything is prepared for, from recording down to coffee, it can dramatically increase the level of confidence in those potential donors and investors. The less you leave to be questioned about your plan, the more people will believe that what you're planning will actually be done.

Studio Wellness

Wellness in the studio is crucial to ensure the level of performance, endurance, and patience necessary to handle the long hours of a recording session. If you're not well, you're not going to be at your best to represent your music on the recording.

Wellness of the body and the mind makes for the best sessions. When you're not worrying about things and you're feeling relaxed and able to work, you'll get the finest work done. The best plan is preparation and practice. Having all the Pre-Production Sheets available and all the preliminary elements in place is essential, but that is only one part. What about the worries around money and the stress of the studio on your body?

The two main parts of the wellness budget I add to my budgets are per diems and some type of massage.

First, the per diems. When a group is doing a long run in the studio, I like to make sure that the budget includes money for the artists to be able to take that time off from work. It's more effective to have the artists concentrating on the music and not on finances while they're in the studio. It's also not as effective to have a musician put in a full day of work and then come into the studio and have to put in another day's worth of work that night. This is especially problematic when it has to happen many nights in a row.

Preplanning a fair and realistic per diem for the artists allows them to feel less worried about the time that is being taken away from work. I have noticed a drastic difference in the patience, endurance, and energy level of the bands that either raised funds or found the investors to cover this part of the budget. Being able to write a couple of checks to each member of the group before entering the studio gives everyone peace of mind. Everyone can settle basic financial issues before going in for a long run of sessions, so the group can focus on the music and not on the work they might be missing or the money they aren't making. Basically, work to remove all the parameters of outside stress, and the creativity, performance, and abilities will be dramatically better.

Second, the massage ... yes, massage.

In many of my budgets, we offer the outsourced services of a massage therapist, a chiropractor, and even an acupuncturist. I've had a lot of people laugh at this initially and then either add it to the budget or wish that they had. Whether you have ever had a massage, chiropractic adjustment, acupuncture treatment, or not, they can be very helpful. Though they appear to be an added unnecessary expense, they can be a money saver in the end. The basic concept is that you are in the studio and working hard. After a lot of hard takes or long hours, your body can tire out, and energy can be lost. A massage, which is definitely the most popular of the three, can be relaxing, invigorating, and even energizing.

A massage can help tired arms that have been playing for long hours as well as shoulders that are holding up a bass, guitar, or horn straps. In a lot of cases, a massage therapist can come in for a bulk rate and give fifteen-minute massages to each member on a portable table set up in a room not being used for recording. You can also set up a different location before the session to have everyone relaxed as each starts the session for a certain day.

Of course it's an added expense and one you might not want to make, but when you think about sessions in which you get really tired or burned out early, a massage is the thing to keep you playing at the best level possible. That massage might also be the difference between getting a keeper take later in that long day and having to push it off for another expensive day of studio time.

Know your body, know your exhaustion levels. When do you find yourself getting most tired in a day? When during a practice or gig do you start to feel exhaustion set in? What songs are the hardest and bring the most tension?

This might just be the time to bring in a massage therapist, chiropractor, or acupuncturist to give that extra boost of energy, relaxation, or invigoration. Just as you tune your instrument and make sure it's able to sound just right, the same can be said for your body and your mind. Think about how using per diems to relax the mind and body might play a helpful role in the recording. What might seem like additional expenses may end up saving a lot of money later.

Video and Photography in the Studio

When you're recording, there's a lot going on, and your concentration should be on the music, but remember that everything you do to be effective can have a ripple effect. Let's say you're in a recording session and you have a friend, or even a professional photographer or videographer, in the studio to capture some of the recording time for yourself. Keep in mind that this could also be useful for marketing and promoting purposes.

Bring in the cameras at times that are low stress, like while you're setting up. I usually tell people to avoid bringing the video camera during vocals. When the stress is high, having cameras there can be a bad idea, but if you can find someone who can be a fly on the wall, you can capture some great moments that you can use for your Web site, social networking sites, and other marketing materials.

Being able to document, with photos and video, can be a good learning tool as well. How were the drums set up with what microphones? How were the settings on different amps? Sometimes a quick picture of certain setups can help you discover how things might have sounded better on your rig. Also, what if the band as a whole becomes famous or a member goes on to a band that becomes very well known? People pay a lot for video these days. Who knows? The simple footage you take of the guitar player in a local bar band could be footage that you sell in ten years when he is a famous arena-touring player.

This footage could be edited into shorts that you can put up on YouTube, some of your networking sites, or any other video Web site that can help get your music and your band out to more people. These videos can also be the start of a documentary you could do on the band, from being in the studio to doing shows to touring and beyond.

By the same token, the more photographs you can get, the more you can put up online and not only have images around but also have more items to optimize on the Internet. You can start up Flickr accounts, Imagebam, MySpace, Google—anywhere you can post photos. It's great to be found online with your name and your music, but these days the more people can search and find your images, the better.

Think of video and photography in the studio as one more element that can help from the educational, marketing, promotional, and documentary standpoints. Make sure that everyone feels comfortable and is not distracted by someone taking either photos or video. The last thing you need is a distraction that will hurt the music.

Make sure the person taking pictures or video understands the environment of the studio. He or she must understand that you are working and you have to concentrate. Sometimes it can be better to hire a professional photographer who knows how to fade into the background quietly to capture the best shots of the band.

Photography and video in the studio can capture a group in ways that the fans may have great interest in seeing but rarely get to witness. The behind-the-scenes kind of stuff can do well for a group and bring more exposure and marketing to a release. Bring in the cameras, have fun with them, but don't let them distract you. Let them capture another side of you, something to share with your fans, your friends, your family, and the world.

Production

Tracking Day

For me, my favorite days in the studio are right toward the end of mix, when everything is being pulled, nudged, tweaked, and adjusted right to where you want it. This is when you make the song into what it's going to be. I also love the looks on the artists' faces as they hear the final mix. My other favorite day is the first day of tracking. That's when the energy is at its highest for me, when everyone is running around, and when the most is usually being laid down at the same time.

I'm always completely jacked up and on fire on the first day. Running between the control room, the main room, and the isolation booths, answering a billion questions coming from a billion directions—conducting the cacophony that is tracking is what I live for. Don't get me wrong; I enjoy vocal tracking, overdubs, and the other days, but hands down, the first day and the initial tracking days just rock. They can be cacophony in a good way. So much is happening at the same time and in so many different ways, but the chaos can be organized and work to your favor. On the other hand, an unorganized and unprepared one can be downright brutal.

In my Freedom Solutions Recording Plan, we have all artists prepare every song to be tracked with the four Pre-Production Sheets. Walking in on day one with a Tracking Sheet, Lyric Sheet, Chord Chart and Pre-Production Sheet for each song can make your life infinitely easier and will allow for things to move at a faster pace with everyone on the same page.

The schedule and direction sheet are two more elements that we have with the FSRP. Most studios and labels will send them out as well. These act as call sheets, so people know when they're supposed to be there and how to get there. Along the same lines, calling and confirming the crew and the people who are supposed to be there is a small detail that will avoid confusion and stress on that day.

It's almost impossible to schedule the day the way you want, which often leads to no schedule at all, but laying out a ballpark schedule and a checklist of what you are looking to do and time lines you'd like to do it in is an effective approach. Also, bringing people in as you need them on the first day can make things run smoother. It's not always about all coming in at the same time. You're most likely going to be in for a long day on the first tracking day. Why not show up when you're needed and not be there to hang out for longer than you need to be? In my opinion that can keep the energy level higher.

Under most circumstances, at least for me and many people I know, we are going to go after the drums first, so planning for the drummer to load in, get tuned up, miked up, and ready, can be done by the drummer, the engineer, and the producer alone. It comes down to the band and their ability to be as smart as possible with the time they have. If the guitar player wants to set up guitars and doesn't disrupt the drumming setup, then great. If there's going to be the guitarist and a couple of friends who are just in the way and making noise while the drums are being prepped, then none of them need to be there.

If you're the bass player and you show up and sit around while the drums and guitar are getting sounds, if that happens to be the order of the day, then you're just going to be sitting there for some time. Why not come in, start to get ready, settled, and then right to work on getting your sound and setup happening? I find that from an energy standpoint and even a mental standpoint, this approach is much more effective for the majority of musicians.

Next, when you're all getting sounds together, things can move faster if you **obey the engineer**. When the engineer asks for certain sounds or certain instruments, don't embellish with other players or other instruments. Play what you are being asked to play. So much time is wasted at this stage with people screwing around. Listen to the engineer, give what he or she is asking for, and don't play if you are not asked to.

Along the same lines, if the engineer or producer is moving a mic around an amp or, especially, has heads or ears in close proximity to the drums, cymbals, horns, whatever ... **shut up!!!!!!!!!!!!**

One more time ... **shut up!!!!!!!**

Think about it: I know you want to play, but while a microphone is being moved or adjusted to help make you sound better, do you think it's a bright idea to make your engineer and producer deaf? Not smart, not good, so don't.

The tracking days on which the most time is wasted are the ones that find the musicians just screwing around. Cut down on the messing around, or even cut it out all together, and things will move exponentially faster.

Now you're underway, you got the headphone levels, a basic mix that works, and it's time to hit the first song. Make sure it's not a ballad or something that is all-out crazy intense. Find that middle-of-the-road tune, the one to get the energy moving and the band flowing. Pick the tune that is almost like a solid warm up, something where work is getting done and a song is being tracked but it's also loosening you up for the others.

It's all about making every moment as effective as possible to have the best first day of tracking. Ask questions as you have them and be aware of things around you. If you hear something that's off and it's one of the foundational things being tracked, call to stop the take. On the same note, don't stop if you're in a flow and you hear a scratch instrument do something wrong. Most times, unless you're tracking the entire song live, the focus is going to be based around the drums, the bass, and maybe rhythm guitar.

Grab a number of takes of a song before listening. It's also a serious waste of time to listen to a track after every take. Be aware of the energy in the room; if things are really in a flow, just keep tracking.

When the natural live energy is moving and the sound is coming, don't stop. If you have cut three takes of one song and feel as if you have a keeper in there, but you're in the flow to play another song, go right after that other song.

Have fun with the first day; it can be a blast. I find this to be the most exciting day of most records, and if you have all your ducks in a row and everything ready, you will be able to relax more, play better, and have a really great time with it too. The more you are prepared, the easier it can be.

Separate Tracks

Sometimes separation is a good thing, especially when it comes to recording and you're looking to have the chance to make the highest quality and lowest trouble mix. The more you can separate sounds, instruments, and voices, the easier it will be to address each sound, instrument, and voice individually.

I'm all about the idea of recording together and like the vibe and the connections that can occur under these circumstances. If this is something you want and you're prepared to have the mix reflect that, then it's an option. If you're looking to record with fewer microphones and grab a more live feel, recording with instruments in the same room and musicians in close proximity is something you can do. However, if you want to be able to make the most of a mix, in consideration of all its possible incarnations and uses, the more you can separate the sounds, the instruments, and the voices, the more control you will have when you're mixing and the easier it will be to give attention to each element.

Isolation is a key factor. If you can put an amp in one room and a drummer in another, you can avoid the bleeding of sounds into other microphones. This can allow you to track together while separating the sounds at the same time. A second way is to record guitars directly into the board and record the amplified version later in the room where your drummer recorded earlier.

It comes down to the fact that any sound can be picked up in the microphones meant for other instruments, which can make the mix of the specific track different because it's picking up other sounds. This goes for the digital recordings, as well, when recording drum machine patterns, loops, and more complex samples that should be separated to different tracks for the different sounds.

A perfect example: A bass drum is a large, full, round sound whether a sample or a real drum. It's a deeper, darker, and low tone most of the time. It has some resonance and low-frequency hum to it. Of course it can have other tones, but that's the essence of a kick drum or kick sound. Now a snare drum is a smaller, tighter drum with a much higher pitch. It has a resonance that's at a much higher frequency with a crack and sharp sustain. This tone is higher, shorter in resonance, and lighter.

Most of the time when a drum set is recorded, you pick up a little of each in the other's microphone, but it's barely noticeable because usually these two drums are closely miked and do not really get in the way of each other. You can still get a great amount of separation. You have the ability to get the best sounds for both the bass drum and the snare drum. If you have a loud guitar amp in the room, you're now, in some ways, infecting the microphones and may not only pick up the guitar in the drum tracks but much worse: you may pick up the bass drum or the snare drum in the guitar track.

Let's keep going to the worst-case scenario: The drummer was off on a few hits, and you have to move the drums digitally some when it comes to the mix. The problem now arises because you have drums that are off in the background of the guitar track, and it may tie the hands of the engineer or mixer who might want to add this effect or mix a certain way that he or she now can't because it will highlight the drums in the background. What might be a small adjustment to really make the guitar sound exactly as you hoped can't be done because it will highlight an off-beat drum in the background. So now the mix is being adjusted for problem solving instead of creativity.

On the same idea, if a drum loop is recorded, and the snare and bass drums are on the exact same track, which commonly happens, you now have two very different sounds that will have to be mixed the very same way. If you want extra highs on the snare, those same highs are now going to be on the bass drum sound as well. If you add any extra reverb to the snare, it will be heard on the bass as well.

What if the song doesn't sell great on the album but someone wants to license it for a TV show and change the drum mix radically, maybe separate two parts or keep one part and lose the other part of something that is tracked on the same track?. It will make it much more difficult.

The basic point is if you have tracks, use them. Separate the sounds so you can have as much control over them come mix time. Isolate as best you can so you have the most options when it comes to editing. Lastly, keep a well-marked Tracking Sheet so you know what's on every track, including small things that you might forget about otherwise, only to remember them after you have finished the record.

The easier it is to isolate tracks, the easier and faster the mix can go. It will also allow you to mix more creatively and not worry about problem solving and making mixing and effects decisions. The more separation, the easier it will be to remix or make fast changes if requested, so add more tracks and more isolation for less hassles in the end.

Click Tracks

Click tracks and metronomes are hated by a lot of musicians. I remember the scrapes and dents that ended up on my metronome when I used to practice with it for hours on end. It would drive me insane and occasionally it would fly through the air and find its way to the wall at tremendous speeds. Still, they're necessary tools for practicing and learning your instrument. Good timing is crucial and an absolute requirement if you want to work in the studio or with top-notch artists.

Energy levels can fluctuate; tempos can change drastically both live and in the studio. Listen back to some of the songs that were recorded prior to click tracks being used and you can hear it. A really drastic example is "Canary in a Coalmine" by the Police. The intro and outro of the song are drastically different. I am a big Police and Stewart Copeland fan, but Stewart was known to heavily and radically fluctuate tempos. He often wanted it faster, and Sting would want it slower.

Another interesting fact about the Police is that "Every Little Thing She Does Is Magic" started out as a ballad—just another example of how varying opinions on the timing of a song can have a big effect. It was so drastic that when Sting went to make *Dream of Blue Turtles*, he rehearsed the band with a metronome in their practices.

Practicing with a metronome or a click track can help you zero in on the tempo of a song and learn how to play patterns with precision and total rhythmic accuracy. They may drive you crazy, but they'll help your technical and groove abilities.

Some say the click (playing a certain beat per minute) is robotic, but it's more accuracy, the time and speed being played perfectly. It's up to the musician to play and set a feel that's comfortable, locked in, and relaxed while still playing in time.

One of the biggest mistakes that musicians make is thinking that they have to lock right on top of the click. There are more options to groove in time than just sitting on the click. You can play a touch behind it, play a touch ahead of it, or move around it and create all sorts of feels while still being with the click.

In my opinion, I've never thought that the groove was the beat. I always saw the groove as the space between the beats. The space between two beats is where the groove is made. I believe that's where the phrase "In the Pocket" originated. In the same approach, think of the click track as your foundation for the beats while still having the freedom to work with it and create the grooves or the pockets for a tune.

On the production and business side of things, a click is essential these days. If you want a song with the best opportunity for success, it absolutely, hands down, MUST be performed to a click track. This makes songs easier to rearrange since every part of the tune is in the same tempo and locked into a click. If the song needs to be shortened, lengthened, or altered, it will be much easier to make those adjustments.

A song can't just be recorded with the hope it will be a hit anymore. A song that has a chance at being successful needs to be prepared for numerous mediums. When a song is recorded to a click track, it has the chance to be used in TV, movies, commercials, insertions, international licensing, video games, and all other avenues.

The click track can be hard and very frustrating at first, but it can increase the opportunities and avenues for your songs. Working on your songs with a click or metronome will also make your music tighter and stronger as a whole.

On a final note, practice with metronomes if you aren't used to them. Don't make the assumption that because you've been playing a song at a certain tempo you'll be able to lock it right into the click in the studio. Prepare yourself in advance; practice with the click and make it line up. Don't go into the studio only to be surprised that certain sections are rushing or dragging. You'll end up taking up a lot of studio time and wasting a lot of money.

I'm not saying that a click track must be used for every song, but it can make a difference in the possibilities of success for a song in today's industry. Take the time to talk with your band mates or with your producer about using a click. Using the click track gives more options down the line, and more options equals a better chance of success.

Drums and Drum Machine

The last time I wrote about drummers vs. drum machines it was for a magazine a number of years ago. I got bombarded with e-mails about every approach under the sun, hence the reason for this forward. This is my view on the topic of drummers vs. drum machines, when it comes both to the studio and to the productions that I'm a part of. I also want to remind you that I started my career as a studio and touring drummer. It was during that time that I had an eye-opening experience.

I remember getting a call on a session where there was already some drum machine tracks put down on a number of songs. Before I even heard them, I was critically biased, coming from the view that all drums should be played by a real drummer. I had heard a great deal of drum machine and electronic drum sequences that sucked, and I made my stand.

After finishing the few tracks for which I played live drums, the producer asked if I wanted to hear a couple of the other tracks and help with some manual fades that were going into mixing. (Yes, for the younger crew, there were boards where you needed to move the sliders to get the dynamic effects you were looking for.) As I was pushing the faders I was assigned, I heard something I had never heard before: a really cool electronic drum loop. I liked the tones that the producer and engineer had gotten and I liked how it layered into the song. Right then, I became a convert ... with stipulations.

I believe drum machines can be programmed tastefully, and I believe drum loops can work well for a song. At the same time, they can just as easily be poorly used. There are certain tones that I have tried to mimic and even trigger while playing live drums. So yes, I have joined the electronic nation for certain types of tunes. I don't, however, believe in using a drum machine when you want real drummer sounds.

I know that the advances in technology allow for amazing sounds, but a strong ear can hear the difference. If you are using a drum machine, program the loop or sample in a strong and musical format. I prefer to use things that a drummer and percussionist could actually physically do, not some of the crazy mach five-sample loops.

There are many different ways to use electronic drums and drum machines in an exclusive way, but there are also ways of mixing them with live drums and percussion. One option that I like is to add in a live percussionist to play conga, shaker, or tambourine parts over the drum machine track. It can bring a very interesting mix of perfection and human imperfection together. A shaker that is played with a little of a pull on the backside of the beat going over a perfectly timed drum machine loop can deliver a very cool feel. The same can go the other way: Have a live drummer play a solid groove over a percussion bed from a drum machine.

For a lot of years, some drummers were hired to play simple short patterns that were looped, triggering more electronic sounds. I'm suggesting a mix of the real drummer and the machine working together again. I like the creativity. I enjoy the hip-hop and funk techniques of mixing live and electronic voices. For instance, I have cut a drummer playing a groove without a snare drum. He played the hi-hat, the bass drum, and the rest of the kit but stayed off the snare. I kept a solid click going for the drummer and then later laid a snare drum sample from a drum machine. The mixture of the two really embellished the feel.

On the same note, when you're setting up a click track, you can program an interesting pattern or feel with sounds or voices from a drum machine that can serve as a foundational bed underneath the live instruments.

Explore and expand the horizons. There are a lot of options where both the drummer and the drum machine can work together instead of fight. When you can see the drum machines as an additional tool or a supplemental voice, you can create new sounds and arrangements of percussion that can work well together and complement each other.

I am a drummer and I always will be. I love the sound of a live drummer more than anything, but there is a compromise and a creativity that I have found as a drummer and even more so as a producer that has allowed me to see the extent and expansiveness in a situation where the drummer and the drum machine don't fight. They can work together and create even wilder ideas than just one or the other alone.

Percussion

Anyone who has worked with me on a recording knows … I got a thing for percussion. Maybe it's because I'm a drummer. I remember listening to "Rhythm of the Saints" by Paul Simon when I was thirteen and just being blown away by the album because of its percussion. I also started paying attention to Sting and Peter Gabriel, not just for the songs but also for the percussion. I started to listen to more Latin and Cuban music as well as West African and Turkish music. I got really deep into Trilok Gurtu, Airto, Ed Mann, Tito Puente, Lionel Hampton, and other drum-set players who were much more percussion minded. I loved Max Roach's approaches and views on percussion, along with guys like El Negro, Joey Heredia, and so many more. If you're not familiar with some of the names above, go check them out when you can.

I found percussion and drum set, though in the same family, to be two very, very different jobs. Learning about the history of percussion helped my drum-set playing, but in the end, I had a greater understanding that I was a drummer. I have applied many percussion techniques to the drum set, but I'm not a percussionist by far. I've studied basic percussion and can perform basic level percussion in the studio, but, again, I am not a percussionist. In my opinion, a percussionist is a musician with the technical ability, as well as the understanding and education, of numerous percussion instruments. A percussionist has a steady hand and can play the most complex pattern while playing a simple quarter-note pattern on the cowbell for ten minutes without deviation.

A lot of drummers who say they don't need percussionists in the studio because they're drummers find themselves to be very mistaken once the take starts. It really is a different world. To be able to play solid parts, especially in more modern music such as rock, funk, blues, country ad pop, requires top-notch precision that many don't have because they simply aren't trained in it. Studio percussionists like Don Alias, Luis Conte, Jorge Bezerra, Cyro Baptista, Robby Ameen, and many more, have blazing percussion chops but can also sit rock steady in front of a microphone and deliver a precision and groove that is nothing short of amazing.

If you're a great drummer, but not a great percussionist, hire a percussionist. It's not a personal attack, but bad percussion will take away from your drumming as well as the song. Don't take away from what you already have down; let percussion embellish it, and let it be played as well as you played the drums for that track. In the studio you want someone who can get the job done fast and support your songs as much as possible with percussion. That's a big reason why I will try to block a good couple of hours, if not more, for percussion overdubs and percussion time.

It's not about filling the song with too much percussion but going back to the palette concept: Laying a good amount of percussion allows you more options to play with in the mix of the song. Just because you track it doesn't mean you have to keep it. But if you don't track it and then end up wanting it, you have to do it again.

Keep these things in mind when you have a percussionist come in. Think about every possible piece of percussion you have ever thought about having on the given song. Talk to your producer or the engineer about ideas he may have. Talk to people who have more experience and a different set of ears on what might and might not work. Work out in advance what you absolutely know you want and what you may consider and track so you can save time. Again, layer to be able to cut out, as opposed to not laying enough and having to rehire a percussionist on another day, which would add more money to your budget that you don't need to add, not to mention the aggravation.

So now you're in the studio, you have blocked the time for a percussionist, you have a basic idea about a shaker part, and that's all you hear. It leaves you with two options. Is this a simple tune that you don't want anything more on? Or do you want to play? If you're happy, leave it be. If you want to play, then there are a couple of different approaches.

First is the conceptual arrangement concept. This is where you have a concept of how you want to see layers run across each other and how the different parts could work together. This brings up accent ideas and looping-type ideas that you might want to have occur in one voice or across a number of voices. As an example, you could have a single accent occurring on a tambourine in a pattern that lasts two bars and then repeats, or you could have the accent pattern be the same and move across the tambourine, a shaker, a bell, and a bongo.

Second is the bulk concept. If you're only putting tambourine and congas in one section of the song, and if you have the time, add it to the whole tune or add it to the section before and after where you want it so you can play with transitional ideas when it comes to mixing. The more you have, the more you can play with.

Also a really good trick is to go to the end of the track and get a series of samples of each percussion item alone. Have the percussionist either play a basic part or a basic sound to the click after the track, and then if you want to add or play some more in the mixing stage, you have some easy samples to pull from in case you need a little extra piece here or there.

As far as the overdubs are concerned, have fun, be creative. On most tunes, I will usually lay at least a conga, cowbell, shaker, and tambourine part. Again, in a mix, many parts are often ejected or simplified to fit the tune. Sometimes, just like guitar, you can double parts, play around with different percussion instruments phased or panned differently in the mix. Play percussive lines on items that are not always used for percussion, like pipes and tires and other items you would not usually hear.

In the end, as far as percussion is concerned, there is a world of opportunities and options. I have not even scratched the surface with these couple of ideas. Think of where rhythm could supplement or complement a song, or where a layer or pad could be added that would embellish or highlight the song or its motion. Listen closely to some of your favorite albums and pull out the percussion in your head. You'll be surprised by how much you'll hear, even in more contemporary songs. It's there; see if you can find it. Play with some extra percussion while you're tracking, and give yourself an array of sounds and layers to play with and mix around. If you have the time in mix, layer and play with volumes, as well as the tones and sounds of the percussion. Try to create beds of supplemental rhythms to drive some of the songs that need that extra push.

The simplest clave or shaker can bring an extra touch or a little more motion and punch to a song. Not all tunes need percussion, but take a listen, or just think of your tunes from a more percussive standpoint. Could something be added? Maybe it's not another guitar or vocal that it needs; maybe it's percussion. Take some time to listen to and study up on percussion and the possibilities it can offer. You might be surprised at how they could work for you.

Overproduction in Early Tracking

How much is too much when it comes to production? Where do you draw and define the line between supplemental sounds, embellishments, and having way too much going on? Even in the takes or sounds you might not be using, the same questions can be asked. How many vocal takes should you work from? How many solos should be recorded? How many basic tracking takes should you have for each song?

This is an area that's very hard to define and in which many are extremely opinionated. Some view it as a money issue and a time issue. If you have the money and time to do the tracking, why not track the hell out of each song, overdub, and vocal? In response to that approach I would just wonder how bored the musicians might get and how lackluster the takes would become.

There's a fire and an attitude in early takes. There's energy before the monotony sets in. The excitement and newness of a song or a take really can shine through. Even on the largest budget recordings that I was a part of, we would really try to get the tune in no more than six takes. If we were going past five or six and the energy was still there and the vibe was good, I would sometimes continue to try, but most often I would move on to another tune and return to the song later in the session or on another day.

Gauging the sense of an artist or a band can really help to decide what you need to go after and how many takes you might need. What is the mood of the band? What is the mood of the songs that have to be recorded? What songs cause the most problems for the band as a whole or for specific members? Taking all the elements of technique, personality, and confidence into account can help you plan how to approach tracking and overdubs. Who has the short attention span? Who hates to redo things over and over again? This all has to be taken into account.

So again, with the pre-production knowledge of a group and the song or songs that are to be done, I personally feel that if you have to go over six takes, you should step away. I prefer to find that one take to move forward with as opposed to having a number of different keepers, unless it's an album or a song that doesn't have a great deal of overdubs, if any, and we're just trying out different feelings at different times.

A jazz approach I like to take for artists who are not overdubbing is to record the series of songs for a record like a set. Have them run straight through the set a couple of times in a row. Then take a listening break, see if anything stands out or anything needs to be addressed and is constantly showing up in the performances. Then another couple of sets, listen once more, and call it a day. I like to bring back the jazz or non-overdub groups to do the same thing on a second day, but mixing up the order of the sets. Then at the end of day two, send them away for a week with a rough mix to listen to the eight to ten sets they have recorded so they can pull and grab each song from those different sets. I've found it to be a very productive approach.

I don't take this approach with other styles that are going to require mass overdubs. I take the time with the jazz groups or the non-over-dub groups because it will capture a certain energy and those days are covering all of tracking. With the other types I prefer to work a number of takes and search for the foundation and the single keeper take. This makes life easier, and it reduces stress for the players.

Having a producer's set of ears listen to the take while the group is playing can save time and money. I can stop when I see the energy getting low or I know it's the right time to bring in everyone to see if each approve of a take. I was pretty blown away when I read up on the Michael Jackson "Thriller "sessions and how many keeper takes they had to sift through and, even more than that, how they pushed Michael for more than seventy vocal takes.

Which leads me to vocal takes and production, and some people's overproduction of vocals. I really don't think you need to get seventy-plus takes on a single song; I don't care how big your budget is. I find that to be a complete waste of time and money. I personally believe that getting four to five takes of vocal tracks for a song gives you plenty to sift through. I like to try to get a full take or two of the song as well as grab a couple of takes of each section of the tune by going backwards.

For example, if a song has three verses and three choruses, in the best-case scenario, I look for the singer to run the tune front to back, twice straight through. Then I will have him or her do a take or two of each section and then stop for a small break between each verse and chorus. Then for a last take or final couple of takes, I have the singer do the sections backwards to add new energy to the back side of the song and see how that affects the takes.

I look for solid keepers or takes that have great performances that need little to no pitch adjustment. I find that this is an effective approach—without overproduction—to getting a series of vocals to choose from without going over the top or going Michael Jackson style.

When it comes to overdubs and solos I like to capture two to three solos to choose from and also do a take or two where the soloist just does runs and embellishments throughout the entire tune. These might not even be used, but it provides some extra textures to play with in mix and does not take much time to get.

I believe in this approach, and it's worked well for me and artists I have worked with. Occasionally, if I hear a take that's dead to rights, I might go after one more just to have, but I may not go too much further than that. Some people have told me I overproduce in these phases, but I find it to be a fine balance between too little and too much. I would rather have some solid things to choose from, but I also don't want to have someone track a song fifty ways from Saturday where listening back alone takes hours on end. In the end, it's best to decide your plan of attack in pre-production, and remember, if you want to do twenty takes, if you want to do the overproduction, you're going to have to spend the time listening back, and even if you want to listen at home, all these tracks need to be burned to disc in the studio. Basically, the more you track, the more there is to be reviewed and the more time and cost you are adding in the studio. If you designate a plan of attack and go after a preset number of takes and keepers, you will save time and money.

Guitars

Layering guitar in the studio is an art in and of itself. When you listen to tracks—from Pink Floyd and U2 to Led Zeppelin, The Who, and too many more to mention—you can hear amazing guitar tones that just don't compare to anything else. The tone itself blows you away; then add a great guitar player, and you have a real winner.

Yes, you're going to want to have a great guitar tone first and foremost before you go in the studio; then you'll want to take some time to play with microphones, preamps and amp placement to find that perfect tone you want, but what is that last step in the recording that seems to make some guitars stand out and have a richer, broader, and warmer sound? While a lot of that comes directly from the above mentioned, a great deal can also come from guitar layering in production.

It's that place where you decide what and how much you want to put into a given guitar sound. I have no problems with laying a single guitar track for a song, and some songs call for just that, but I do tend to have a great deal of fun when we can play with different layers and tones to bring out something a little different.

The first tool I use is basic; it's just simple secondary layering. The guitarist doubles, or sometimes even quadruples, the part that he or she's played; then you simply spread the guitars across the mix, in a way, opening up the sound and the tone.

A variation of this idea is only to double or quadruple certain sections to beef up a chorus, a transition, or a segue that is felt more spatially than in volume. Sometimes the panning and the fading of sections coming in and out of a primary part can draw an ear to hear something that it might not be able to actually define, only feel.

Move the amps around and change them out, play with microphones, and even play different guitars for the double. For example, if you play one guitar track with an amp in a very large room and the microphones are a little bit backed up, then try the double with the amp baffled tightly and a moving rug over it. This will create a different type of tone and allow for the double to bring a different texture.

Another variation of that concept is to double clean. That is where you're just looking to thicken out the tone and use more of a panning production approach while you go after a double or a quadruple of the exact tones and the exact layering that sounds the same. Mix it up.

I'm also a fan of doing a second run of the original guitar with an acoustic on some songs. This can bring some punchiness and draw some higher tighter tones that can really sound great, depending on the tune. One alteration that I use on this is having the acoustic guitar double cut out for part of a repeating phrase, or only double the acoustic on the lower notes of an electric guitar arpeggio line to beef up the lows but not double on the highs.

A third variation is to double with other instruments buried under the guitar line, like a banjo or a medium to large string instrument. Sometimes running a small horn line such as an oboe, a coronet, or a soprano sax or even defined keyboard sounds can be mixed in to seem like it is the guitar and guitar alone. Sometimes transitioning from a voice into a guitar or a guitar into another voice is a great trick as well. Slowly cross fade one instrument into a guitar taking over, or vice versa.

You can sing as a double too. Double a guitar line, then sing a double part of that guitar line with a voice, then pan the four tracks with the singing a little more buried. This will allow for a breathy foundation for the guitar. Note: You can make some cool sounds, but if you're not making the guitar the primary and mixing the additional tones to supplement the guitar track, it will not sound as if it is part of the guitar.

If you have the time to experiment in the studio or even at home, play with guitar layering. It can help you create a more individualized sound and a different sound presence in the song. Try amps in different rooms with different microphones as well. Take that extra time to experiment and create your own sounds for your songs instead of just plugging in and going. You'll find a much more pleasing result in the end.

Vocals

Vocal production and vocal tracking can often be the toughest part of a session. It is taxing, repetitive, annoying, and exciting all at the same time. Some of those little things that can occasionally get passed over in the tracking of other instruments can stand out like a sore thumb when it comes to vocals. It's an absolute necessity to approach vocals and the production of vocals with the fullest attention to detail and top-notch preparation.

There are many different ways to approach vocal recording. This is the technique I take as a producer and how I work with vocalists and clients using the Freedom Solutions Recording Plan. I like to split up the concepts into "before" and "during." I have found these methods and ideas to be the most effective to get the best vocals and the best performance.

1. Before

So you know you're going to go in to record an album: Be ready!!!! Practice, work on strengthening your voice and your chops to be able to sing the songs, but also work on your endurance. You will need to be able to work for a long time through many takes because it will often take more than you planned.

"I can get these vocals in one run …" I cannot tell you how many times I've heard this from singers and it has never, I repeat, *never* happened. Practice the songs, work on your voice with exercises, and prepare as best you can.

Which leads to the vocal coach or teacher. Think about it: Before you go on a really long trip, you do an overhaul of your vehicle, right? You change the oil, check the tires, and tune up if needed. You do preventative maintenance so that the car will run well and potential problems will not arise. On that same note, take a couple of lessons with an experienced, top-notch vocal coach. Having a vocal coach go over your songs with you will help you be as strong as possible. This person can give you exercises and helpful hints to prepare well in advance, which will make things go much smoother and faster in the studio. Often when I recommend this, singers turn it down, saying it's too expensive or they don't need it. In the end, the time spent on having to go over tracks and lay extra vocals can be more expensive in studio time. Vocal coaching is an investment that will save you money and time on the other side as well as prepare you in a way that is vocally healthy.

Also, take care of your instrument. Maintain it with the right food and activities to help you be the most effective when it comes to recording. Have your body in shape to make sure your lungs are at their most effective. During the sessions or just prior, stay away from phlegm-inducing foods and drinks; go for the teas and water.

Lastly, I prefer to cut vocals in larger rooms. I really don't like the hip-hop boxes or the miniature vocal booths that, to me, deaden the vocals. They are the easiest room setup with which to repair vocals, but if someone can belt, get the fullness and richness of the room's acoustics in there as well, as opposed to only processing the voice with effects and digital enhancers.

2. During

There is a basic checklist of things that can simplify your vocal sessions. Mixing preparation with problem solving will make the workload move fast and flow well.

So first the studio administrative ...

Don't grab the microphone, especially if it's one of those three-thousand-dollar microphones that's on a top-notch microphone stand. It doesn't want to be touched. If it's too high or too low, let the engineer or producer make the adjustment, and most of the time, he or she will want to be the one adjusting heights and angles. You don't want to try to adjust a microphone the wrong way and end up dropping it. This is a surefire way to make things much more expensive for you.

On that note, don't put the headphones down on the microphone stand. That stand is balanced out for the microphone. Don't add weight or throw off the balance; this may send the microphone falling to the floor.

Watch for the cables around your feet and avoid stepping on them. Those are some nice cables, and they don't need shoes—especially high heels—breaking through them.

Navigate your position to the microphone when you sing. Look at your body position to the microphone. You are going to want to keep that same spacing. It's not just the feet. You do want to stand in the same place, but also be aware of your posture and where you're leaning compared to the location of the microphone. Try to find the most consistent position for your body to the microphone. This will help get the best vocal takes, and it will allow for easier overdubs and mixing different parts of different takes together with ease.

Be aware of the dynamics. While you do want to lock your lips and your body in a single, consistent location to the microphone, you'll want to back away at the times when you're hitting louder, heavier dynamics. When you're hitting a dynamically loud word with a very enunciated "T" or "P" or even "K" sound, you may want to lightly turn your head. This will keep the natural performance at its strongest and require less editing on your voice.

Watch your posture. Make sure you're singing and breathing in the best form. Practice this in front of a mirror. When you're slouching, you're constricting airflow. That said, I like to work with certain forced constrictions if artists are having problems. I will try to either open them up or constrict them to get certain notes or phrases—everything from crossing their arms to condensing their chest to holding their hands clasped together behind their back to open up a little extra. Sometimes I use what I call the "hostage position" where the singer puts both hands together clasped behind their head. Try singing troublesome parts while moving your body around in different ways to see what may work and be a quick fix for the studio.

Sometimes when singers are not hitting a pitch or are having trouble going flat or sharp, I'll have them take off one headphone to help them hear themselves in a different way.

Think about where you're singing from. Feel your body, your lungs, and how you're positioned. Wear comfortable shoes and balance your body. This is different than posture; it's allowing the notes to come from you in a strong way. A lot of times if I see that someone's posture is strong, but we are still having problems, I will have the singer lightly bend the knees and concentrate on the chest or stomach to remedy the issue.

Not everyone has to be in the studio staring at the vocalist on the vocal sessions. It can be a great strain in the studio, and it's very different from being on stage. Try to keep the number of people around the control room down during vocal days. I've found that the fewer people, the faster the vocals go.

I like to get many takes with a singer. I try to have four to five solid takes of a tune and then listen to the different phrases, notes, emotions, and performances to be able to put together the fullest and best sounding take. Pro Tools makes this worlds easier, and though I love the idea of a full vocal track in one pass, being able to have a series of takes to work with and choose from can make the song stronger and save money and time.

At times, I'll have the singer start in different sections of the song to get the energy up to where it might have been in the earlier verses, or if the vocalist is feeling especially powerful, I'll have him or her go after the really loud and dynamically challenging sections. I also prefer to get a single song in one day rather than breaking up tunes across a series of days. Voices can change. Temperature, humidity, and a thousand other variables can make small changes in tone and sound. As far as harmonies, those can be done on other days, in my opinion, since they will be a different part, but I still try to capture all harmonies from a single voice in the day they are tracking for that song.

Understand the PONR (point of no return) and respect it when it's called. If your voice is about to reach that point and you're going to be singing the next day, LISTEN when the producer calls the session. Stop singing!!! Small shakes in the voice or the exhaustion of a voice can be heard by a solid producer, and if he or she calls the session, it's not a doubt of your abilities; it's your producer making sure that you will be fresh for the next session. It's all about caring for your voice. Trust the professionals who are there to help you get the best work in the shortest time.

After you're done, take the time to listen to the tracks and the different versions if time allows, but take them home to listen. Don't spend hours and dollars of studio time listening to the different takes and versions unless you want to go right into a vocal production session. If you feel you need to take the time to pick and choose sections and phrases, then ask the engineer to burn the rough mix copy with the different vocal takes, and you can go through them outside the studio where the clock is not running.

If you want to go right to choosing the tracks in the studio, it can be much faster and more effective to go right after the takes. This also allows for small corrections if one of the tracks or sections needs to be redone.

Think and work smarter not harder. Prepare for your session with the mindset of being tuned up but also armed with tricks and skills that give you preventative maintenance for problems that can arise. Do this and you will get the best and most effective takes.

Studio Endurance

A lot of attention is centered around the music and production prep when an artist is heading into the studio. It is a lot to deal with, considering all of the elements of the songs, the budget, the schedule, the overdubs, the time line, and everything else that goes into a solid and successful recording session. Still, something that's often overlooked is studio endurance.

The studio is a different beast than playing live shows, yet bands often approach it as such, only with more repetition. There's a lot more to it than that. Artists need to be physically and mentally prepared just as much as they should have the music prepared. The pre-requisites that I ask of artists I'm producing is to take a day off or at least a light day from work before coming into the studio. Getting a good night's rest the night before is always smart, too. The biggest misconception that people have about the studio is that it's a laid-back environment.

It *can* be laid back, but it can also be a very draining and stressful place if you have to play a high number of takes on a song or if you run into trouble that you didn't anticipate. Listening to a song over and over can be tiring as well, and don't forget that a lot of bands do some pretty high-intensity arguing among themselves in the studio. Realize that the days are going to be tiring and draining, and get the proper rest so that you can be at your most productive.

It's also a good idea to stay away from loud music the night before a session. Your ears can take a beating at a club or a show, and even with earplugs, you're putting your ears in danger for the next day. Keep the day before the session a quiet one and you'll have stronger ears for the session.

Everyone knows the old rule about avoiding dairy before you sing, and it's a good rule to live by. Dairy produces an excess of phlegm. Most people don't go too much further, though, when it comes to food. I heavily advise that you stay away from heavy-smelling foods like garlic. Sometimes you'll be recording in a smaller isolation booth, or you may all be together in the control room, and making the room a more pleasant-smelling environment makes it easier to stay in that room for longer. The same goes for heavy-smelling perfumes or colognes.

These ideas are all designed to make the studio a place you can and will want to stay in for long periods of time. Also, having food, coffee, and magazines around can keep the nourishment level up and the boredom level down. Remember, the goal is to try to get the best results out of each day with few interruptions. What do you feel you could use in the studio? If it's reasonable, then bring it with you.

Wear comfortable clothes. I know it sounds crazy, but wear layers. As you're playing, you might get hot, and then as you're sitting around, you might get cold. For the more active players, bring along a towel and an extra shirt to change into if you're sweating heavily.

Take breaks to give your ears a rest. Oftentimes I will kick everyone out of the control room for ten minutes or send everyone out for air for a few. Sometimes going too long between breaks can kill the effectiveness of the band toward the later part of the day.

Look at it like this: A band that can go four straight hours but begins to slow down and fade after a long break may require more frequent breaks as the day goes on and will eventually be completely ineffective. This does not make for an effective use of your studio time. Breaking for five or ten minutes every hour to hour and a half in addition to a dinner break can keep the effectiveness and endurance of the band up and make the time used much more effective.

Get up at a good hour and be outside for a bit before you go into the studio. You're going to be inside for a lot of hours, and many studios don't have the best lighting, so spend some time outdoors before the session; go for a walk, take in the sun.

Guests in the studio vs. studio endurance: Personally, I don't like guests in the studio all that often, but sometimes, if it brings up confidence or helps an artist, it can be a good idea. If a guest is not talking too much and serves as an energizer for the session or the band, then by all means, get that person in the studio.

Keep the endurance up and plan for the day to be long. Think about what can help you. Think about what you need in order to be at your most productive for the longest amount of time. Ask yourself what helps you maintain endurance in other circumstances. What did you do when you were able to be effective, either playing your instrument, doing your job, or keeping attention to detail. Once you figure it out, apply it.

Of course you want to prepare the music and the work that's going to be done, but paying attention to the details around the working environment as well as preparing physically and mentally will make your time in the studio much more effective. Go the distance at the highest level of quality and you will see results. And, again, it will save you money and it will save you time.

Point of No Return (PONR)

There is a point in the studio where people will hit PONR, as I like to pronounce it ponner, or point of no return. You know what I am talking about: that point where you've been recording for hours and hours on end and the quality is slowly beginning to diminish, as are the technical abilities, the listening abilities, and the overall ability to make decisions and play at the level you want to. Hey, we're all human; everyone hits a wall at some point.

It's a really, *really* good idea actually to recognize this and not push beyond it. I'm not saying don't do your best and don't try to do things a number of times to get them right. I'm just stating that it's important to recognize when PONR is reached and to call it a day at that point. There's a major difference between takes that are worsening to the point of no return and ones where you know that you have the adrenaline to carry you to the take you're looking for. There's also a magic in some takes being done when you're a little fatigued.

A lot of this comes in pre-production. Yes, the song order as well as the overdub order should be considered when you're scheduling so you don't just jump around from song to song. What's the vibe or the difficulty of a song? Which song gives a certain player a lot of confidence that can lead well into doing a harder song that the particular player may not be as sure about? All these pieces can help you or your producer construct a strong recording plan. Again, that doesn't mean, if someone all of a sudden feels the energy to do a specific song, that you shouldn't go track it that very moment; but having the blueprint is going to help you. I promise.

When PONR is reached, it's time to stop for the day. If it's being reached on a specific song earlier in the day, it's time to move on. As a producer, I will *never* let an artist track more than six takes in a row of the same song. I know some of you will argue with me, but this is my rant and my point of view, so there!

It's not an ego thing; it's not about saying that you can't do it. It's about being effective for the track or for the next day. If it's time to move on, MOVE ON! When you hit the point of no return, it's not just that energy and ability are lost; it's that frustration, anger, fatigue, and a pissy negative mood begin to set in, which will hurt the song you're working on. If it's early in the day, it can have an effect on other songs, and if it's at the end of a day, it can actually screw with the next day.

Early Tracking PONR

If a song is just not going right early on or an overdub is not happening early in the day and you're advised to move on, then move on. Move to an easier track and rebuild the energy and confidence to go back and hit the one you're having problems with. Sometimes you may find that doing another song will warm you up or loosen you up to be able to do that problem song and do much better than where you started. When you have the feeling of excitement mixed with achievement, your performance vibe will reflect it. Confidence begets confidence; feeling like you suck can make you suck.

If you need some air, get outside. If you're thirsty, get some water. Think about the different elements that might be making the take go bad. Problem solve as best you can, but once you can't think of any more options, it's time to move on. If you continue to push on that track, the stress and the frustration can hurt the song and haunt you the rest of the day. You may also affect the mood of the other band members, which will make the day as a whole less effective than it could be. Accepting at the right time that it has reached a point of no return will help you return to the track sooner and get it faster without affecting other tracks in a negative way.

End of the day PONR

Some people feel that, if they book a certain number of hours in the studio, they have to be able to perform for all of them. Sometimes when a studio day is booked for ten or eleven hours, a burnout point or PONR can be reached at hour nine. Now, in the smart, effective world of being well, it's time to either call the session, move on to some backups, or maybe have the producer or engineer do some work on basic mixing or preparation of other tunes in order to make use of those hours. That is effective use of time. If an exhaustion point has been reached after a long day and you push to either track or continue to try to overdub, you're going to get more angry and not get the take that night. Not to mention you leave the studio stewing on how crappy the end of the session was, and it can carry over to the next session when you listen back to what you might have thought you got when you reached PONR only to realize with refreshed ears that it's pretty much crap and you have to cut it again. That sets a real good tone for the beginning of a day, doesn't it?

All bands that I've seen go past PONR and continue to track has never gotten that last take as a keeper. They all come back and need and want to fix something. They find they are pissed off since they thought they got that magic take and now with rested ears find out it was not so magically delicious. This inevitably hurts the confidence for the new day.

I discuss with every band I produce that I have the right to call PONR and stop the session or move on. I allow it to be my right and give a ten-minute get-out-of-jail-free card where they can fight once on my call; then if I call it again, the session or that track is over for now. I will bring everyone into the control room and review what has been done that day or play a rough mix that we might have ready or work with the engineer to put a light speed mix on one of the tracks so all can hear the direction of how it's going to sound. I ask if they want to start with that song the next day or if we're going to try another angle and then come back to it.

That makes the next song or the next day feel much better. The end of the session ends on an up note. People leave the studio knowing there is more work to do but are left realizing all the great work that was done that day and not having the focus on the song or the point where the energy fizzled.

If you don't have a producer, look for the signs of PONR and realize sometimes the most effective thing you can do for a song is actually to stop playing it. I always watch out for tones of voice, sighs, change in posture, continued sloppiness, or loss of technique in a performance. I also watch for people not playing together or not playing for the song. For example, if the guitarist was hitting juicy solos all day that transitioned well, padded the form of the tune, and had strong definition from their beginning to end and I hear a total change that's not fitting, that's a real sign.

Also watch for overall energy levels. Do the breaks taken throughout the day have to be longer and longer to get the most effective takes? Is there a plan in place for some of the easiest songs to be laid first if certain members have the ability to go longer? Let's say the drummer hits PONR first. Then you can have the guitarist do his or her guitar overdubs when you call PONR for the tracking for the day. Think of the session from many different angles. It's not just about laying it down; it's about having everyone in the best space mentally, physically, and technically to achieve what you're going after.

My mentor in Massachusetts had scribbled on the upper right corner of his studio, "The later it gets, the better that take sounds." It couldn't be more true as the ears fade and the mind goes as well. Be aware enough to make the PONR call or, when a producer calls it, listen!! Remember it's not about that moment or the very end of that day. It's about making the best recording and the best songs you possibly can. If you need to call the session for the day, call it. Make sure you're not wasting studio time, going well past the point of no return, and only creating a frustrating environment that may carry over into future sessions. When you hit the point of no return, STOP!!!!!!!

Overproduction Revisited

Sometimes the line between solid production and overproduction can be difficult to distinguish. When is too much too much, and when is too little too little? The idea and execution of production is a very individualized thing. Oftentimes, this can be based on what the artist is looking for in a song. Other elements can be based on if the song is being produced for the recording or for the performance. Should this be a song that can be performed live on stage with the basic group, or should it be a richer and fuller production that would take a pretty big stage to allow for a crazy number of instrumentalists?

There are a dozen angles to take when it comes to production, and they are all right in different ways. The one universal approach I like to take towards songs where the artist is open to production ideas is figuring out how best to represent the song. If a song is very deep, heart felt, and has nice melodic flow and harmonic motion, then in my opinion it can go with a simple arrangement, even just a voice and a guitar. In other cases in which the song might not have as strong a motion or arrangement in naked form, such as one with repetitive chord progressions, not the strongest transitions, or simpler melodies, the addition of production and richer arrangements can be a support system for the song.

It's not that the song is bad, but you're trying to move it into a place where it will have the best chance at success. Discussing ideas and ways to layer, whether it's throughout the whole song, only in sections, or just in transitions, will help you designate the arrangement and production of the songs. Are there deeper or lower parts of the song that could be supplemented with some high sounds or voices? Is there a rhythm that could be complemented or supported by being played on another instrument? Take the time to create, feel what could add to the song and what might belong in the song without overwhelming it.

There are a lot of ways to approach production and to define that line where it becomes too much. The more time you can take to create, experiment, and test out ideas, the better you can decide what belongs where and how. Also, listen to your favorite music with a producer's ears. Listen to the way things are layered and see what stands out to you.

On the more sparse side of production, is there a way to dress up a chord or make some simple changes that will make the song flow better, even when it's a simpler production? It doesn't always have to be the usual instruments. Think about the sounds, tones, and textures that will highlight what you want in your song. Play around and take chances. Lastly, as you track, track all your ideas to the fullest extent and then take away when you're mixing. It's a lot easier to subtract in mix than it is to add.

Post-Production

Give the Engineer Some Leeway

Artists, engineers, producers, and everyone in between often argue about the time it should take to mix a project, and they all have a different opinion. The key element for many musicians is money. The band or artist has tracked for a series of days and has added all the overdubs, vocals, and whatever else. Now comes the point where no one put together the budget correctly and the money left for mixing is minimal. The engineer at this point is often asked to mix down a ton of songs with only a few hours. You have now taken the song and the track that you worked so hard to lay down and are finalizing it with a shortcut mix that's not going to allow the engineer or person mixing to take the right amount of time to address the mix in the best way possible.

Basically it comes down to thinking about what you're doing before you do it. If you have a song that's going to have a lot of overdubs, horn parts, vocals, or backing vocals, then budget for the engineer to have the time to really address the mix the right way. Don't just budget a certain amount of time for each song. Figure out what you're tracking or looking to track. The more instruments, overdubs, and vocals, the more time you'll need in the mixing phase whereas tunes that are just vocals and guitar are going to take less time.

Other factors to consider are the basic edits as well as auto-tuning if needed. Those edits of cleaning up fades as well as lining up certain notes and doing cross fades between different takes or fixes are all things that need to be checked as well.

In some ways, you'll hurt the work you've already done by forcing it to be mixed too fast. There are some amazing engineers out there who can mix very fast and still deliver an amazing product, but they all have their methods and the way they like to pull different sounds together. Ask the engineer or producer you're working with how much time he or she will need to mix the song or songs to the best of his or her abilities. Discuss in advance what you're thinking about doing when it comes to overdubs and additional tracks for each song too. You're taking the time and the effort and spending the money to get the right take, so make sure you're getting the right mix to present the work you've done in the best way possible.

How Many Mixes for a Song?

The band is coming around the corner as far as a song is concerned. The overall mix is just about there. All the levels are right, all the instruments are balanced the way they are desired, and the song is basically done. Is it time to save that mix and move on to the next song? Not if you want to get the most out of your work. As discussed in the "Industry Pro Sheet" section of Chapter 6, there are all different profit routes to take with your music. Investing time in the songs now, while you're still in the studio, has the potential to reap big rewards in the future.

Artists and bands need to take the time to create the most opportunities and avenues for success and profit for each song. Analyze every conceivable scenario for promoting and soliciting a song for potential profits and then plan for it. Though these will occur out of the studio and after the songs or album is completed, you must plan for them before you even set foot in the studio.

How many mixes should a group have for each song? I like to have at least five different cuts and a consolidated version of the track as a whole.

While a song is being mixed down, the concentration and bulk of time should go to the song as a whole. Make sure all the levels are balanced, everything is equalized, all volumes are right, and the tune sounds the right way as a whole. Once you get to that point, though, take a few steps back and get the extra mixes too.

Mix 1 – The Full Song

The track that will go on the album. This is the full version of the song. This is the mix that everyone always gets.

Mix 2 and 3 – Two 15- to 25-Second Samples of the Song

Find two segments of the song that you want to showcase. While you're in the studio, you'll be able to cut or fade in and fade out of the sample you want to have. These can easily go on demos that you will send out for the album or put up online.

Many artists pull samples off a CD or an MP3 that has already been compressed. Compressed tracks are not as high quality as getting them right out of the track in the studio. These uncompressed samples will be at a higher quality, and you can very quickly set a place to fade in and fade out that sounds top notch and much more professional than most.

Having a second disc of just the samples of your album can be a great marketing move. If you send out a disc to industry people that has twelve tracks that are each twenty seconds or so, there is a much greater chance someone will take the time to listen. Remember, time is expensive. An industry professional is more likely to invest four minutes in a sample demo disc than an hour or more in a full album.

Tease with the samples. Fade in at a strong point and fade out right before a chorus or a hook. Leave them wanting more, and maybe they will go to listen to the full song or album.

Mix 4 – No Lead Vocal Tracks with Backing Vocals Still In

Have a mix with everything except the lead vocals. This track can be used for potential television or live radio shows. This can also be used when you perform but do not have a backup band or the ability to support a full group.

Having this track ready can open other opportunities for performances that may not be able to occur otherwise. If you make the industry aware that you have these tracks available, it will in turn make you available for more performance opportunities than most other artists.

Mix 5 – The No-Vocal Track

When you're mixing, create a version of the song without vocals or backing vocals but with all of the instrumentation. This can be used in certain TV shows, movies, commercials, and other media outlets. Having a version ready to go with no vocals will not only showcase your professionalism but also prove that you're prepared to meet the needs of the industry. Many times, artists are unprepared when asked if they have a version of a song with no vocals. They scurry around to get the files and find someone to mix it down without the vocals. Remove the stress and replace it with opportunity by having that no-vocal mix ready to go for anyone who might request it.

A no-vocal track that is well recorded can also be used by another artist in another country to sing over the performance tracks. You also allow for the opportunity to sell or license the song to a label or an artist to perform or record his or her vocals over your music. There are many ways you can use a no-vocal track to your benefit and profit, so make certain you have a mix of it done.

Other Mixes?

If they don't have a band, some people will go a step further and do a few minus-one mixes. These are mixes that are mixed down without a certain instrument, like the guitar or the drums. These can be given to potential touring players or new players you may have in the group. This is more for single artists who don't have a consistent band. Minus-one mixes can also be sold to fans who might want to play along with your songs. You could even hold a contest and have people record themselves and send it into your Web site. Call it the Guest Guitarist Contest or something along those lines. As always, do something a little different that might drum up some media attention and excitement by doing something most aren't.

The Backups

So you have all of the mixes and you're ready to take these songs to the industry in as many ways possible. Take the final step to make sure you have your backups organized. Make copies and save them in different locations. Make hard copies and keep them in a different physical location, like your parents' house or your Aunt Dorothy's guest room closet. That way, if anything were to happen to your hardware and your copies, you still have a backup somewhere else. I also recommend having downloads available on private pages or password-protected pages of your Web site so that if something is requested, it can immediately be sent.

Having backups of the album as a whole and backups of each song can make things much faster if you receive requests for the studio tracks. That means having a separate backup for each song so you can send the discs for just that song. If you really want to be prepared and have a good amount of Web space on your Web site, have a compressed file of the song so that someone could download it after an agreement is made for licensing. At the very least, have the tracks ready for FTP. When you show how professional and prepared you are with all these different mixes and then can top that off by delivering immediately, you're standing a few steps above most.

Song Titles

Oftentimes it comes down to all the little things that make the big things work better. Many of the details that are often ignored can add up to a heavy weight that will hold you back from going as far as you want to go.

One of those small things is the song title. As you finish and release your album, EP, or song, it's crucial to make sure the name of the song is always the same. This will help with optimization around the Web, uniformity of the song names, and better recognition both from a fan point and a marketing point. It will also keep things clear around copyrights and publishing.

A common mistake is to list songs in abbreviated ways, such as only the first two words of the title or some kind of acronym. These songs may have been written years ago and have been with you for what feels like forever, but for most they're brand new, and just as you need to brand your music and your band, you also need to brand the songs.

If you have a song called "Stuck in a Moment," make sure it's written out correctly everywhere it's listed. From the CD to the Web site to the posters, make sure it's always complete and full. Don't abbreviate in blogs or anywhere else you're writing about the song. Even if you're posting samples in places, make sure to use the full name. Don't use "Stuck," "Moment," "In a Moment," or any other alteration.

The more the song is seen correctly and written out fully, the more it will optimize online as well as become more recognized by fans and potential licensing groups and other profitable avenues. It will also keep things clear around copyright and publishing issues that might arise. If the name is the same across the board, the lower the chance of issues arising around legal matters, royalties, or even plagiarism. It's a small thing, but it's one more task that can help you in the long run. Decide the names of the songs and stick to them.

Track Order

Have you ever listened to a song on the radio and as soon as it's done, you can't help but hear the next track in your head? Do you ever have to play an album all the way through because anything short just wouldn't be right? Can you hear that beginning or ending of those songs and know, almost to the second, the space between the songs? That's the sign not only of a great band and great songs but also of a great compilation and formation of the songs on an album.

In our world of digital downloads, EPs, single releases, and demos, we've lost a lot of the beauty and structure of an album. It's more than just the songs; it's how they're laid out, and it's that last step before you master the record down.

When you choose and go to record your songs for an album, even after all the basic song preparation and pre-production, there's still a world of things to go over and review before, during, and after the recording. You need to address the marketing and promotion of the recording and the songs themselves. This is what I call internal music marketing, the layout of the album, which includes the actual order of the songs and how each song ends and leads into the beginning of the next one. The strongest songs can still be hurt by the order of a recording.

The goal is to keep the listener, which is harder than ever these days with attention spans being shorter than ever. Drawing in the listener to hear the album all the way through, and in so doing bringing them closer to the body of work as a whole, is something of a rarity these days. The best approach is to create a blueprint before recording. Make sure that you have a variety of keys, motion in tempos, and feels as well as a number of different intros and outros to make sure that everything does not sound the same.

Intros and Outros

Make sure that each of the intros has its own touch and originality. While some intros may sound close to each other, make sure there is something about each of them that distinguishes the intro to each particular song. The body of the song will speak for itself, but it's about making those decisions on how to lead the ear in and out of them. If you are in the pre-production stages and are still making decisions on intros, remember, you'll have tons of options that can take your current intro and spice it up.

A couple of options include fade-ins, drum fills, hook lines, selective instruments playing before the rest of the band joins, accent patterns, samples, and loops. These are just a handful of ideas to try. The same goes for outros. You can do the fade-outs, ending accents, whatever you want.

The Order

Jump a couple of steps forward: You have your album recorded; you're in final mix and getting to the decisions about the actual order of the songs. This is where it gets fun. Don't shortcut this part or just toss out a list. As I mentioned before, the order and the layout can help keep the ear listening throughout.

First, think of the creative element. Is there a storyline inside the album? Is there a method or motion that you started with or developed through the recording? Look at those songs and how they move.

Second, think technically. Make a list on a white board of each song. List the following ...

- Song Name
- Intro
- Outro
- Key
- Tempo
- Feel/Groove/Style

Seeing this list in front of you can put things in a different perspective and help you make decisions.

Also in final mix, get the producer or engineer to make you a recording of the first fifteen seconds in and the last fifteen seconds out of each song. Take that disc home and load it on your computer or your iPod and move the order around to see what drives you and the band best. This way you can spend a lot more time on playing, and with added options outside of the studio, you'll be able to take time and make decisions without spending studio time and money.

There are many approaches for deciding where the strongest song should go in a record. Some say track two, some say track three, and some say track one. There are a lot of ideas on how you should kick out the recording and how you should close it. You can research online about how people take the different approaches. In the end, in my opinion, it will change according to the style and the group.

The obvious bullet points are to bring the ear in and draw it in fast, so I don't think the first song should be a long one. It should be a grabber, something that will make people want to hear more. In the same way, with the last song, sometimes a long fade or a long song that carries the ear away can be effective. It all comes down to making the decisions give the album motion.

While I prefer back-to-back songs to have different keys, some tunes work well moving from one song to another in the same key. Take the time to set up the recording in the order you want it, play around with it to see what flows the best.

Lastly, have fun with the ordering. Have some friends who are completely outside of the recording come in and listen and give their thoughts on the order. Take some time and treat it like a puzzle. See what kind of picture the different orders can create for you; then choose the order and head to mastering.

Patience

One of the hardest points in any recording is the post-production and release phase. How do you actually choose the release date? When is everything ready and how will you release? Do you have a plan to make the release work for you and your group in order to gain quickly the highest amount of visibility? Oftentimes none of these questions is answered or even considered, and that failure can drastically hurt the potential of the release, the effect of initial sales, and the spike in marketing.

Most commonly, I see bands get the discs back from the duplicators, and whatever day that is, it becomes the release day. CDs start going out, maybe a CD release party occurs, but it's not much more than a normal show, and the only additional element is that it's called a CD release party.

The most effective releases are the ones that have a plan behind them. Just as you prepared to record your album and worked on the tracking and mixing with a great attention to detail to get everything right, you have to finish the project with the same level of focus and commitment. I see the great work ethic of an artist through the pre-production and recording process dissolve as soon as the recording is completed. Laziness sets in, and sometimes an ego builds with expectations that the recording is so good it will get out there and sell.

In all actuality, the post-production, release, and continued push of marketing, branding, and promotion is the most intense and the longest phase of doing an FSRP album with me or any producer, record label, manager, or agent. This is where you have to balance out normal life, playing, practicing, touring, relationships, and everything else while keeping a consistent level on marketing.

Is your promotional package ready to go? Do you have a press release that can go out nationally for the day of the nationwide release? Do you have digital and online sales systems ready to launch on the day of your release? Do you have a localized flyering campaign set up for the release? Do you have a special or discount for the release day or a sale for the first X number of copies or downloads sold? Do you have a basic advertising plan to hit markets around the country, even if it's just a couple of ads? If you have money to buy small ads or basic insertions to Web sites around the country, great; but have you set up an ad plan? Do you have a daily plan set in place for postings and updates on Web sites, chat rooms, bulletin boards, and online groups? Are they organized to different cities, colleges, and music genres? Do you have secondary merchandise, such as hats, shirts, and stickers, ready for sale?

If you have not answered yes to all these questions, take a step back. Of course there's a certain amount of money that's required, but the ad plan does not have to be over the top. The press release should be national if you want a realistic amount of respect and attention from the media. You should have all your ducks in a row for the most effective release.

Over twenty-seven thousand albums were released last year alone. This does not include all the independent releases put out under the radar. So how are you going to stand out? How can you be seen in the sea of music?

The answer is actually simpler than you think.

First … Patience. Think of the post-production and release with the same mindset that you thought about the recordings. Have you laid all the right tracks for everything to mix together well to create the song you want to make? If not, then fix that and hold off on releasing.

Second … Pull together everything for promotional and marketing support to give the release a fighting chance. Find a way to stand out and be seen and, even more important, be purchased.

In a way, releasing a disc that doesn't have the support in marketing, branding, and promotion is like releasing a song that's not fully tracked or is unmixed and un-mastered. You wouldn't rush through one of your songs to just to get it out, would you? So why rush the process that will get the same song out to the most people, the most reviewers, and the most media possible.

Be patient—get it all in order and then release. People are used to seeing another band releasing another disc. It happens every day. Take the steps to make yours memorable and recognizable on a scale that will help build and grow your popularity and your sales while helping to create a long-term buzz that will reach more and more people over time.

Complacency

You have created a recording as well as the support materials to promote, market, brand, and advertise the release and the group. You have taken the right steps to set up all the supplemental contracts and distribution. Your solicitation materials are organized and prepared to push your music to international markets, television, advertising, video game and potential movie licensing and placement. Let's also say you're now ready to solicit to higher level distributors, touring agents, managers, and labels that could help push you forward. This is a great place to be, and a lot of hard work has been done to get to that place. Unfortunately this is where so many artists begin to make the mistakes that can jeopardize and ruin a career.

When artists do something the right way or create the right product, music, or anything, an unfortunate trend occurs: A laziness, complacency, and arrogance starts to set in. Once the CD comes back from pressing and the release date nears, even as early as basic post-production, things can end up changing for the worst.

In the early stages of pre-production and fundraising, through production and recording, artists I've worked with will follow their plan and their approach to the tee. Once the album is completed, the artists are happy and they should be. They worked to design a plan, created a recording, considered every element that needed to be addressed, and executed what had to be done.

The problem is that the post-production phase needs to be treated with the same effort, the same attention to detail and the same kind of problem solving that made the earlier phases work so well. I've discussed different methods of promoting, booking, advertising, and marketing. These are all elements that have to take place and have to be given the same attention and effort as the recording and the music. This unfortunately is where many artists decide to short cut. They decide where money should be spent according to them and not according to the budget set in place when a plan for them was built. Some of these artists become a little arrogant, figuring that "It will happen" or "This is going to break through." These are the worst things to think, and this complacency is the key to the artist's project failure in the long run. This is also why labels and managers drop artists even when they're handling a great deal of the media and marketing.

Just as you need to practice to learn and maintain your abilities, you'll need to see post-production and the release phase as practicing and performing. You have to practice, and you have to continue to work on growing, or you will lose your proficiency in it. Don't put together the best package you can and then just relax. That's actually where the most work begins. It's true that having a product of industry caliber will give you an exponentially greater chance of success in today's industry, but it takes that last step of making sure you're doing every single thing you can do.

Just think of that amazing band that pops out of nowhere and you get into them and pick up all their older materials. You wonder how they could have become such an overnight success and yet have been around for so long. It really is simple. The best bands, the best packages, and the best look can't be seen if it's not being brought out to the public in all the proper ways. The industry is in a shift toward independent favor. There's less money being put into artists, and there are excessive numbers of artists who are out there doing it the wrong way, but doors open for artists who are showcasing themselves in the best way possible. It's your responsibility to apply the professionalism, work ethic, and intensity that you used to get the recording and project made to the post-production and ongoing efforts after the release. Even though you've created and acquired all the parts you need to create the career you've dreamed up, you still have to finish building it.

Be prepared, be patient, and be ready financially, technically, creatively, and emotionally and you will make the most out of every studio session.

FUNDRAISING/ INVESTORS

A central focus in the Freedom Solution Recording Plan or any recording is the budget. Whether you work with our layout, have a business plan for your recording, or are planning a full-scale release, it does add up to a lot of money.

Gone are the days when you could put out a demo, get signed, and then have someone else do everything for you. To be in control, to maintain your own work and your rights, is a much smarter way to go. However, this does require you to set up quite a budget, one you're going to need somehow to put together, to achieve effectively the release at its fullest capacity with the best chance for success.

This comes down to fundraising and finding investors for your project. The first step is having the business plan and the organization to explain, in detail, the execution of each step and why and how it will work. The next step is finding the actual funding.

If you're doing a project such as the FSRP, it's very possible to acquire the full capital through fundraising and investors. This is not about just looking for donations to record your album. That's one element of it, but you need to look at the larger picture, just as the FSRP business plan allows you to, by justifying the core ideas of why someone should donate to your project.

Below are some of the FSRP bullet points used to help artists fundraise as well as find investors.

243

1. Set up a business plan to outline every step of the recording and marketing process clearly and concisely.

2. Show the artist how to find funding through investors or fundraising.

3. Make sure an artist is in sole control of his or her music, image, and likeness.

4. Help the artist sustain success by introducing him or her to the full spectrum of sales, licensing, and performance options in the industry.

5. Empower an artist with the solid industry knowledge and problem-solving skills necessary to make responsible career decisions.

6. Create a recording and all related marketing, branding, and promotional materials at a level of quality that meets or exceeds industry standards.

7. Create a cost saving production package that saves an average of 75 percent over what artists spend on a major label production in Los Angeles or New York.

8. Position the artist favorably by donating a percentage of the recording's profits to a charity he or she believes in.

9. Allow artists to go forward as musicians, philanthropists, and role models while achieving self-sustainable success.

Now, each of these points is a good reason to produce a project this way, but they're also sound talking points when asking for donations or investors to help fund your project.

Look at them again from the point of view of making a pitch for a donation …

1. Set up a business plan to outline every step of the recording and marketing process clearly and concisely.

This artist is organized, professional, and paying attention to detail with a plan that shows the project can be executed correctly and come to fruition.

2. **Show the artist how to find funding through investors or fundraising.**

   The artist is being shown how to take a different approach to obtain capital and not lose the percentages that are normally associated with recordings.

3. **Make sure an artist is in sole control of his or her music, image, and likeness.**

   The artist is being empowered to stay in control and not be abused by the industry, as so many have been in the past.

4. **Help the artist sustain success by introducing him or her to the full spectrum of sales, licensing, and performance options in the industry.**

   This is a good sales or donation point. It shows that many avenues and options are being offered with opportunities to make profits in more ways that just the record itself.

5. **Empower an artist with the solid industry knowledge and problem-solving skills necessary to make responsible career decisions.**

   This shows donors and investors that they are giving to a project that teaches the artist how to approach the industry properly and gives the widest spectrum of choices and ideas to create success.

6. **Create a recording and all related marketing, branding, and promotional materials at a level of quality that meets or exceeds industry standards.**

   A recording being made with all materials prepared gives a potential donor the faith that the right steps are being taken to allot for the best chance at success.

7. **Create a cost saving production package that saves an average of 75 percent over what artists spend on a major label production in Los Angeles or New York.**

    This shows that the budget is well organized.

8. **Position the artist favorably by donating a percentage of the recording's profits to a charity he or she believes in.**

    This is a key part: By donating to the artist, donors are, in many ways, setting themselves up to be an integral part in giving to the charity the artist has chosen since their seed money assisted in creating the product that will give a percentage of each sale to the chosen charity.

9. **Allow artists to go forward as musicians, philanthropists, and role models while achieving self-sustainable success.**

    This shows the donors they are giving to a project that is attempting to make change in the industry. This represents more than just a simple recording.

This does not even scratch the surface of justifications as to why someone should donate to your project. The starting point is to read through your plan and pull out the points that strike you the most. It's up to the artist to raise the funds. It's about the artist finding the right way to address and explain the concept to each person, business, or contact he or she reaches.

Each potential donor or investor should be approached in a personal way that addresses him or her specifically. Don't try to create a cookie-cutter template of a letter, a pitch, or approach. Customize it to the specific contact. Remember it's not about money with every contact.

Below is a basic template for a fundraising press release. This is just one of the ways you can approach people to achieve your goal budget. Later on in the book, you will see another release more focused on a release for a show.

::::Press Release::::

#######

For Immediate Release

The Acme Band with their "out of control rock and soul" sound from Seattle, Washington, prepares to launch their career to the next level while protecting their music and giving an unprecedented 25 percent of the profits to charity.

Seattle, WA – March 9, 2010/MMM – Brain Grenade Entertainment LLC is working with the Acme Band to record and release a new CD as well as a basic distribution, marketing, and promotional plan with the required assisting materials to help them reach the next step of their career. BGE, the Acme Band, as well as their friends, fans, and family are working toward completing this project by fundraising and finding investors to cover the basic budget costs, starting the Acme Band out with no percentage or contractual obligations to anyone, as they pursue taking their career to the next level.

The Acme Band, based out of Seattle, Washington, has blasted off for a musical journey through the universe of soul, funk, rock, and blues. As likely to be inspired by Weezer or N. E. R. D. as they are by Otis Redding or Led Zeppelin, the Acme band will surely move your head, your heart, and your ass. The Acme Band is out of control rock and soul.

The Acme Band is also bringing the presence of the group's creativity and versatility beyond their music to charity: 25 percent of the profits from this album will be donated to a music education foundation for children. The Acme Band is showing their commitment to their music and their career while also showing a commitment to a cause they believe in.

The Acme Band has covered all the bases, another thing not happening in music today. The group has worked with their producer to set up a strict budget to take the project all the way from pre-production to the press release to the launch of the album. BGE's founder and the Acme Band's producer for this recording, Loren Weisman, explains his firm's interest in the Acme Band and this project by saying, "This group has the attention to detail and drive to bring this project from start to completion with the best, most professional results as well as the best chance to find long term self-sufficient success."

The Acme Band is fundraising and finding investors for all the capital that will be needed to bring this project from the pre-production stages all the way through the release by implementing the Freedom Solutions Recording Plan from BGE. The Acme Band is putting out this album free of debt, of obligations, and from any third parties to take percentages.

Visit www.braingrenadeentertainment.com or www.theacme-band.com for more information on the Acme Band and their upcoming album as well as sound samples and information about how to donate to this revolutionary project.

Contact:
The Acme Band
C/O Music Maids Management
2212 Queen Anne Avenue North #347
Seattle, Washington, 98109
PH: 206.376.9798
Em: info@musicmaids.com
WB: www.musicmaids.com

#######

I won't lie and tell you that it's easy to obtain the funds. It's a great challenge. However, if you have the attention to detail, the drive, and the ability to problem solve, adapt, and try things that are not always the most comfortable, you will succeed.

Actually, all those traits are needed to succeed in music anyway, so isn't this a great steppingstone towards creating the product you need as it prepares you for an industry in which you will have to apply all the above traits over and over again.

Why not start now?

Nourishing the Arts

It takes a creative approach to fundraise. Ask any professional fundraiser or non-profit organization. You have to have the drive, creativity, and the stamina to take a lot of noes before even a single yes. Fortunately, there are avenues to find funding besides going directly to individuals. This is key since most people will not achieve their full budget with personal donations.

Nourishing the arts is a conceptual program that has been implemented by a number of different organizations and charities. It's been called different things by different people, but the concept is the same.

The first step is finding a restaurant, café, pizza place, or any food establishment that has a history of supporting arts and charities. Having some kind of personal attachment can often help, whether you know the owner, you know someone who works there, or you used to work there yourself. The idea is that on a planned night, the restaurant will donate an agreed-upon percentage of its profits to the artist and his or her project. With this, the restaurant helps the artist, and the artist, in turn, helps the restaurant with the marketing and free advertising. The restaurant will also make stronger profits since the event will be planned on a normally slow night.

Discuss with the establishment what you're doing and how you intend to do it. Talk about the professional approach you're taking toward your album, your materials, and your marketing. Let them know that you'll be donating a percentage from every sale of your recording to your chosen charity. (This is specifically for FSRP clients or musicians who are giving a percentage of their sales and profits to charity.) This showcases you as a solid investment on behalf of the establishment.

Pick a night that is usually a slow business night for the establishment and remember to give yourself at least six weeks to advertise it properly.

Find an agreed-upon percentage of profit that the establishment is willing to donate.

Discuss and add additional marketing elements. Some places will do a special dish or a dinner named after your band. Certain establishments might raise the price of a specific item for one night to assist in the donations. For example, the scampi dish could be raised to twenty-five dollars from its usual fifteen dollars. The extra ten dollars from each scampi sold would be donated to the artist in addition to the discussed percentage of whole night. You can even work with some establishments to set up a dinner package that includes some kind of merchandise from the band.

For example, if someone orders the dinner special for Artist X, the customer gets four courses, a bottle of wine, and a band tee shirt.

If the restaurant is willing, donation jars can also be located around the restaurant, and information on the group can go out with the menus.

It's up to the band to advertise. The goal is to get the word out and get people in there that night. You don't need to get everybody to have dinner, but if people have a couple of beers or an appetizer, it can help. Putting together a press release can help as well. You may be able to get a higher amount of media attention since it's not an everyday occurrence.

When the night arrives, be there. This is a great opportunity to network with people, talk to strangers about your project, and have some good eats as well.

In the last three of these Nourishing the Arts nights I have been a part of, the artist has brought in more business for the establishment. Even after they gave the agreed percentage to the artist, these places still pulled in more revenue than they would have on a normal evening.

What places do you know? Who could you approach to set up an evening? Go through the list of people you know and who they know. This will add another layer to your fundraising while bringing more attention to your band and your project. It's like a win-win and then win again situation.

Bartering

In this hurting economy, many people are finding their bank accounts, wallets, and savings a lot leaner. Though fundraising is a necessity, why not also think about what you have as skills or services that you could potentially barter with someone else who may have resources or abilities that you need? Bartering is an excellent way to work directly with other individuals, build community and networking ties, while still accomplishing the things you need to get done.

Sit down and think about supply and demand. What can you do, and what is it worth? Many people have a lot more abilities than they know. Take the time to write down what you can do, and think about people who may have a need for those services. Make sure those people who may have a need for your services, have a service that you need yourself. Do you know a band that has a member who designs Web sites and you need a Web site? Maybe someone in your group is a plumber by day, and you know the band house he or she lives in is having plumbing problems. This is a perfect fit where both parties can help each other and save money at the same time.

Reach out to other bands, fans, and friends. Talk about what you need, from Web work to flyers, recording to mastering, car repair to editing. It doesn't have to be a trade for two entertainment or music services; it can be anything, just as long as both parties feel there is a fair and well-defined understanding of what is being traded for what.

Talk to people and ask them if they would be willing to barter. Find out what they have to offer and what you have to give. Think about how trading service for service could benefit both parties. Sit down with the band and brainstorm a list of what you can do and send it to friends, other bands, and people who you feel might have services you could use in return. Added bonus: this can lead to extensive networking that can potentially help you long after the economy has stabilized again.

Be considerate and careful about how you ask and how you offer. Some people just don't barter or may be offended at the offer. Just because it makes sense to you doesn't mean it's going to make sense to everybody. Ask first if they would consider an exchange or trade for services. Would they be open to having a discussion about bartering? Is there something they need or are looking for? Be assertive but not aggressive when it comes to asking, and make sure that what you're offering is truly worth what you are looking for in return.

If you're a beginner Web designer and you're asking a professional mastering engineer to do a barter for services, show some class and offer a lot of extra design time to make it balance fairly. Consider the experience and reputation of the person you are hoping to barter with, and make sure if you don't match that record that you're supplementing it fairly. This can be by doing a little more work or even paying a very small fee to make it feel like a fair and even trade.

At this point, let's say you reach an agreement with someone to barter services that both of you need. Make sure to put it in clear and concise writing. Many relationships, personal and professional, have ended due to lack of communication, clarification, and understanding of the other's expectations. Consider your actions, the service, and your agreement in the invoice. While no money is being exchanged, you are still being paid. Make sure to identify clearly what services are being exchanged as well as the extent of those services. Clarify the circumstances of potential "overtime." Clearly describe and make sure you know the expected outcomes. Make absolutely certain to get all of this in writing in order to avoid conflict and maintain the relationship.

Just because the economy is in the hole doesn't mean you have to slow down your career and skimp on the things you need. Network; communicate both with people you know as well as people and businesses unknown to you. Be prepared for the rejections because there will be many, but those rejections may also open the doors for the acceptances. Don't be offended and don't try to sell or push people. If someone says he or she doesn't barter or need any of your services, ask for a reference for someone who does.

Get and stay out there. Keep moving your career forward and use what you have to fulfill the requirements you have. Reach out to find those you can help while they help you. You'll save money, network, and open new doors to people, businesses, and opportunities you may not have seen before.

Raffles

Many different types of organizations and individuals who are in the fundraising process use raffles. Collecting items to raffle is often a very good start to a fundraising campaign since it can be easier to obtain physical items at first than directly asking for a cash donation. It can also be easier to ask people to purchase raffle tickets, which gives them the potential to win prizes, whereas a straight donation does not give a direct return.

Many artists that use the FSRP program find the raffle concept a good place to begin. Throughout a fundraising campaign, you can conduct a number of different raffles. The raffles can build confidence in the fundraising process.

Raffles work especially well with people or businesses that want to know "What's in it for me?" or "What do I get out of this?" Some people you approach will see value in the record you're making and the ideals that you're going to set forth; however, there are people who want to get something in return, even if it's only a chance of return. These are the people who will buy raffle tickets.

Think of someone who you might want to ask for a hundred-dollar donation. This person might easily have the money to give but may not be one simply to donate it. When you present your plan, that person might purchase one hundred dollars worth of raffle tickets with the hope of winning something, when he or she might have otherwise said no to a straight-up donation.

Basically, raffles are an effective way to achieve your money goals without directly asking for money for the project. It's part of the passive/submissive approach to your funding.

So how do you get the prizes for a raffle?

You ask. Ask anyone who has done raffles in the past; it's a lot easier and a great learning experience to ask for items instead of cash. It can also help you build your approach and hone your skills for when you get to asking for cash donations.

When you deliver a plan like the FSRP or a well laid-out business plan for your album and explain that there are numerous elements that make it a sound investment for any type of business, person, or company, you have a solid chance of receiving a service, item, or a gift certificate.

This does not cost anything for them in cash, and many businesses are already set up to give away certain products and/or services to charities, raffles, and benefits.

When looking for items for the raffle, make sure you make a quick pitch. Call ahead or e-mail and ask if you can speak with the manger or owner. Make sure you are talking to someone who handles donations or has the right to offer them. Make sure you're talking to the person at a time that's respectful. If you're looking for a gift certificate from a restaurant, walking in on a Friday evening and asking for the chef/owner … well … let's just say, that would not be smart.

Schedule a time, be brief, and cover what you're doing, why you're doing it, how you're doing it, and how a donation of a service or product could help you out. Sell yourself and sell the concept. With a donation to the raffle, this organization is helping independent music, helping the charity you have chosen, and also helping your group to serve as a role model for others.

Bring a copy of the fundraising letter or fundraising press release with you (note: you should have both of these either way if you are raising funds to help you), a copy of current music, a one sheet on the band, and maybe a shirt or some other kind of merchandise to give them as a thank you for their consideration. Also, point out the cross marketing that the company will get. Tell your contact about how you will advertise and market his or her company. Explain how the business will be mentioned on your Web site, on posters for the drawing show, if you have one, and in press releases. When an organization sees that you're thinking about how you can bring attention to it in return for its gift to you, you will see a greater response and a better chance at a larger donation or gift.

Look for services and products in numerous arenas. Restaurant gift certificates are always very popular. Oil changes, even a couple if you can get them, are great. Gas cards are also becoming popular. Items where people can choose their prize are also effective, as are gift cards from any store you like. Paintings, trinkets, toys, CDs, tool sets from a hardware store, coffee cards from a local coffee shop … just think of anything you'd like and go with it.

Services are a great approach, too. Cleaning service, a maid service for a day or a month, car detailing are other good ones. Go to one of those personal assistant companies and see if it will donate a personal assistant for a day. Just brainstorm and the ideas will come. Be creative and you'll find success with it.

Lastly, what are some services that the band or you as the artist could raffle off?

I've seen bands offer maid service for a day. This is a great idea, and it's good cross marketing for the band. Imagine the band cleaning someone's house in maid outfits, calling the local media to talk about the raffle, and the winner and a local newspaper coming down to take pictures of the band cleaning the house.

Raffle off dates with each of the members. My favorite raffle of all time was one where the guitarist of a San Francisco band raffled himself off as the soundtrack guy for the winner for a day. He followed around the winner for an entire day with one of those backpacker guitars and was the theme/soundtrack music for a lawyer, who bought fifty dollars worth of tickets. It was hilarious, it got media attention, and the band was featured in the arts and lifestyles section of the local music rag the following week.

Approach it with different themes. You can easily do a series of raffles. One can be restaurant themed, another could be seasonally based, and another could have a music theme or any another topic of your choice. For example, do a raffle that's all about clothing. Raffle off some gift certificates to a number of different clothing stores. The first prize would be the largest gift to a given store.

The same idea goes for restaurants. Grab a number of different restaurants; see if you can get more than one gift certificate. I have a raffle item I tell artists to try called "Eat out for the week." This entails a single raffle gift, usually first prize or the solo prize, where the winner receives seven gift certificates to seven different restaurants in town.

Organize the prizes you get and put them together into different raffles and different levels. This way you can ask for more from the raffle that has much more expensive prizes than what you would ask for in the raffle that has less expensive gifts and prizes.

Before you start, decide when the drawing is going to be. Do you want to make it at a show where people will have a final chance to buy tickets and you'll be able to announce the winners there? Do you want just to make an announcement, or do you want to hold it at one of the stores or establishments that has donated? Again, think marketing, think of how you will bring the most awareness to your raffles and at the same time get the most tickets purchased.

Get help selling the tickets. Get your friends to help. You can even give them a percentage of the tickets they sell. For example, if someone sells ten tickets at five dollars, maybe give him or her 10 percent. This can help with getting other people involved in helping you sell the most tickets.

Some of the businesses involved in the raffles may also help and sell tickets at their establishment. Take advantage of every avenue you can find.

Very Important - Check with the local and state rules regarding raffles. Some states will require that you call it something else. Certain states even consider raffles gambling.

Lastly, make sure that when you draw, anyone who purchased has a chance to win. Do not require the winner to be present. It will turn people away, and you'll sell fewer tickets. Just make sure you get contact information on each ticket.

Raffles are just one more approach to help you raise the money for your budget. They'll also help you get more comfortable with the ideas surrounding fundraising and how you present your pitch and your project to others. Remember, the more avenues and angles you take during the fundraising period of the FSRP, the faster you'll be able to achieve the budget for your project.

Garage and Online Sales

Some states don't allow raffles or make them difficult to execute, in which case sales of donated items through eBay or in a backyard garage sale can help you raise cash for your recording budget. This leans toward the more passive approach and is often very effective in the early stages while you're getting up the confidence to ask for money.

Going to friends, family, and various stores to get donated items for these sales is not unlike the raffle-fundraising concept and can help you get the items you need to make the cash you need. Start with your own stuff. What could you get rid of? Then talk to friends. Some may not be able to give you money, but they may have old items or things that they were going to get rid of or sell that they might donate to you. Remember the old saying, "One person's trash is another's treasure." It all comes down to how you spin it and how you market the sale of the items.

A musical garage sale, where your band plays while you sell, is one idea. Try to think up creative concepts that will make your tag sale stand out. The more you use creative marketing, the more people will come by to check it out. Oh, and by the way, postering telephone poles in a four-block radius is not exactly what one would call creative. Be different, be original, be you!!!

The same goes for online. Post items for sale on your Web site or on social networks. Talk about the project and about how the proceeds are going to your recording project. See if you can get some fans to bid for something like an old action figure or toy on eBay. It might even be something that's not worth all that much, but perhaps you can offer the winner something crazy or something involving the album credits. Imagine having a thanks to Jimmy Walters for buying my younger brother's old Lego set. It's a little obscure, but in the end it might be something that brings a little more media interest your way, which could, in turn, draw in potential investors or donors who were unaware of you before.

What item do you have that you could put a sticker of your band on?

Again, think of the different ways to approach the sale and bidding of an item. The more original it is, the more attention the items may get and the higher the price they may then sell for. Don't get lost in the basics of any idea, whether it's a garage sale, a tag sale, online bidding, or however else you try to achieve a portion of your funding. Give it your own touch, and you will find the results will be better.

Head to the basement and see what you can get rid of. Ask around to those people who might be getting rid of things or are willing to donate items to you, because in the end, one person's trash could turn into cash for your recording budget.

The Passive/Submissive Approach

The passive/submissive approach can be an excellent place to start with the initial contacts when asking for donations or money. Many artists who take the route of fundraising or finding investors have no prior fundraising experience or knowledge on how to ask for money. In the passive or submissive approach, you learn how to talk about the project and how to talk to people about donations by asking them who they think might like to donate to the project.

The idea is to learn how to approach others and refine yourself. You need to create the most effective personal approach to discuss the project, and at the point where you would ask for the donation, you take the passive/submissive approach and ask the person you're talking to if he or she knows anyone who would be interested in getting involved.

This is the last step before taking the direct, or assertive, approach. If your pitch is refined and ready, you'll find that some of the people you approach in this format may want to get involved or donate to the project themselves.

You can also ask opinions on what they think of your pitch and your delivery. This empowers the person you're speaking with. Many times people who are being asked for money feel backed into a corner and uncomfortable. By asking them what they think of how you delivered your pitch and how they think you could improve it, it can give them a more empowered, dominant feeling. This allows them to give their two cents and feel that they have helped you make your pitch better. Regardless of whether you disagree or agree, be respectful and attentive to every idea that they share with you and thank them for their feedback.

After all is said and done, some of these people, now in the power position, may donate to the project since they now have a sense of being a part of it and making it better. Involvement is a powerful thing. Certain people and certain personalities need this, while others do not.

Try to get the best sense of a person so you can individualize and plan the best approach to asking for donations. At the same time, take notes and ideas from those who offer feedback. You can use this style to learn, refine, and prepare your pitch for when you're asking in a more direct and assertive way.

Test your approach. Think about when you feel strongest and when you feel weakest. What reactions give you an extra boost of confidence, and what were you talking about? On the other hand, when you felt that they were losing interest, what were you saying, and how were you saying it? It's just like music: Every part has to fit together. It has to flow, transition well, and keep the listener's attention. Though it's possible that some of these listeners may give to the project, don't count on it, and don't look for it. Take the approach that you're simply asking for their opinions and for suggestions of people who they think might want to be involved.

Remember, you're testing the waters. It's a step above going after physical items for the raffles. You're talking directly to people about what you're doing and expressing that you're looking for money to do it.

Think about the marketing points, and don't drag it out. Review your plan and work the pitch.

Think about how to address the individual. Each person will be different, and therefore each approach should be a little different.

This is a great step to build your confidence as you effectively use your time to be proactive and search out potential donors. Make up a list of people you could talk to who would take the time to hear your pitch and see your materials. Again, it's all good training and preparation for the direct, more assertive approaches.

Just as you practice and prepare your music for the studio and for shows, you need to practice and prepare your pitch for the donors you're going to approach. You wouldn't go on stage and play a brand new song without rehearsing it; look at the fundraising in the same way. Tighten up the loose sections and make sure it's ready.

It's a challenging thing to ask for money, but it's also challenging to get up on stage and play music. You didn't master the craft after only one show. The more you practiced, the more you became comfortable playing with others and playing for the audience. Now when you go to ask for donations directly, you will deliver a stronger, more confident, and more assertive pitch, which is exactly what it's going to take to get people to believe in you and believe in donating to your project.

The Assertive/Confident Approach

The assertive/confident approach is the best, but also the hardest, approach to use when going after money. This is also known as the direct sale. It requires you to be direct, assertive, and confident.

As much as people talk about having confidence, security, assertiveness, and overall fortitude, when it comes to asking for money, many find out exactly how little they have. The best approach for direct sale is the practiced approach.

Remember, if you're a part of the FSRP plan or some kind of plan that is helping a charity with a percentage of its profits, you're not just asking for money to make your album. That is the worst approach you can take. For starters, remember the major selling points of the FSRP for your pitch. You are doing more than asking for money to make an album. You are asking for money to help set a new standard and benchmark in the approach to music. You are bringing new ideas to the table with a charitable approach to something you believe in, and you are taking the most organized and concise steps with a solid plan of action to see it through to completion.

Read through your FSRP blueprint package or your business plan. Gain an understanding of what you're doing from a number of different approaches. This will help you to refine and create your pitches. As you practice and individualize them, you'll gain the confidence you need to come off assertive and strong.

Believe in yourself, your career path, and the plan you are taking part in. Use strong body language when you're talking to people. Speak in a tone that shows you care about what you're doing without being overbearing.

Don't yell or be too loud. That can display a cockiness that will push people away. Conversely, don't speak too softly or stumble on your words. This will make you seem more nervous and less confident.

Individualize your pitch to the person with whom you're speaking. If you're speaking with someone who used to be in the music industry and got screwed over, bring up the elements about you having total control of your music and all your rights. If you're speaking with someone who feels strongly about the charity you're donating to, then address the element of the percentage that you're giving to that charity. Mention it early and often in the pitch.

You want to go with a quick pitch delivered in a confident, assertive tone and tempo. Remember to take the attitude that you're doing this and would love to have the person's help, but it will be done with or without that individual. Confidence brings security to the listener or potential donor or investor.

Try to give an overview of your plan that hits on the marketing points of the music, what you're doing, and how you're doing it. Give your pitch as a brief presentation. Allow for questions, and remember to write these questions down to have those answers prepared in advance for the next person who may ask them. If people give you a look of doubt and don't know what to say, offer the confidence to them. Ask them what they have questions about or what they feel is not clear or well addressed.

Regardless of a no or a yes, treat them both like yeses. If people says no, thank them for their time, never losing the confidence in yourself or your ability to achieve the budget for the project. Many times these "noes" will watch you from a distance and donate later.

Go to the numerous fundraising Web sites that are out there, even if once a day. Find out the tips, quotes, and approaches that are shared by the professional fundraisers who do this for a living everyday. Simply search "fundraising" and you'll see hundreds come up that may be helpful.

After each pitch, think about how it went well and how it didn't go as you hoped. By treating each pitch as a potential donor or investor, but also an opportunity to learn, you'll find more people feel confidence in you.

Eye contact is a big plus as well. Look directly into the eyes of the person with whom you are speaking. If you're sitting down with a number of people, casually address points to each person. Don't try to scan the group or focus on only one person.

Wear clothes that are clean. Dress well, but don't go over the top. If you're more a casual type than a suit-and-tie guy, you don't have to go suit and tie but wear something that shows you care about yourself and your appearance.

Review the business plan with a prospective investor or donor. Don't stop or spend too long on any given section: Run the person through it and allow him or her to stop or ask about sections.

Most of all, deliver your pitch as if you're talking to people who are helping to make your dreams come true because, in a sense, they are! You're looking for people to help fund your recording, the release, and the necessary materials to give you the best shot at reaching that goal. Think of what you're going to be able to make, as well as the spectrum of opportunities that will be allowed that most never get. This can help you build your confidence and your assertiveness.

You've played on stage to people who didn't like your music, but that didn't stop you. You kept playing because you knew you could reach new fans, and the more you played the better the band and the songs got. This is the same thing. Some people might not give or might not like the plan, but if you view it as a chance to make your pitch that much better, to be able to deliver it in a stronger fashion to someone else who will donate or invest, then you win whether it's a no or a yes.

Be assertive and confident. If you're not, learn and practice the skills to gain those traits. It will not only help you in the fundraising, but it will also give you the tools to handle many other facets of the industry that you will be faced with down the road.

The Line Item or Sectional Fundraising Approach

Line item and sectional fundraising can be a smart and more centralized approach for some people to reach the budget goals for their projects. It can also depend on the type of person you're approaching for help. The basic idea is, instead of looking for a number or monetary amount, you approach a potential donor or investor on more of a sponsorship level, asking for the person to take care of a section or line item that is laid out in the budget, pinpointing a direct need instead of the larger picture.

For instance, if you had a record that was being recorded in eleven sessions at a studio that costs five hundred dollars a day; you could ask someone to cover one day or a couple of days. You could even go a little further in detail and ask him or her to donate for the tracking sessions or the vocal sessions. This specified and detailed approach can bring more confidence to potential donors or investors because, not only do you have the big plan and all the large-scale information together, but you also have a solid grasp on the costs and an understanding of the small stuff.

Smaller donations could apply to gas and tolls or food costs for the session. Perhaps you have someone who might pay the session bass player because he's a big fan of the bass. It's about taking a different view of your budget; looking at everything as an individual item whose cost needs to be met financially. In this you can also offer credit on the recording. For example, I had one artist who had a donor pay my entire fee as the producer for the project. In turn, he became the executive producer to the producer. He ended up getting listed as one of the executive producers on the recording. He was thrilled and even has the album hanging on his wall. The band was thrilled—it was a chunk of the cost that was out of their way, and hey, I was thrilled. I got paid.

This approach can also get people more involved in your project and allow friends to team up together to help you. If a group of three people decided to donate the food budget, they could be given the list that is planned for the sessions and either pick up the food and deliver it or even cook certain meals for different days or nights and bring it down to the session.

This way it allows those donors to give financially and also to feel a part of the project and be more involved.

Another strong point for this approach is to breach the trust issues some people might have with the band members. The FSRP bank accounts are handled solely by the artists instead of the label or a manager. I like putting the responsibility and control into the artists' hands. However, some people may be weary about donating a large amount to be put in a bank account maintained by the artist or band. This has been an issue in the past. It's the concern that the money will be spent prior to the session on items not in the budget. In this situation, by going after a specific donation and having the donor pay that exact amount to the person supplying the given service, it can make each feel more secure about what the donation is going to.

For example, let's say you have a session player budget of four thousand dollars. You are a solo artist and are bringing in a truckload of people to record. Let's go even more detailed and say you are bringing in eight players at five hundred dollars a piece, totaling four thousand dollars. After booking the players in advance, you can explain who they are, what they're playing, and that they are confirmed for the date. The donor can then write eight checks out to these players for you to give to them when they do the session. It can bring up the trust level and make the donor feel more confident that the donation is being used in the specified manner for the given costs and not just putting a large cash sum in your bank account.

Look at the budget through a different set of eyes. What parts of it might appeal more to certain people you know? Who could you go to and ask for help on specific items? What kind of fundraisers could you set up that would be directly affecting specific parts of the budget?

Stay creative; take a look at the people or businesses you are approaching for money. Create a pitch just for them. While some people will respond better to raffles, some will respond better to the more assertive approach of just asking for whatever donation they can give. Others might respond well to the line item or sectional fundraising approach. Find the right approach for each person and complete the budget that you have set in place so you can get down to making that recording and all the elements that go with it.

Rallying the Troops

When you create an album, you're not doing it alone. It takes a number of people and pieces to help you bring a project to fruition. The same is true for fundraising. You don't have to do it alone, and when you don't, it can be worlds easier. Whether you're in a band and have a group of people to fundraise, or you're a solo artist raising funds on your own, bringing in a team of people can help you reach your budget faster. Friends, family members, and even fans can all play a part in what we call rallying the troops.

What's in it for them?

Close friends and family will always be supportive, especially if you are organized and have the details in place. Those closest to you will do what they can to help; that's what makes them friends and family. However, getting the help of others may require some kind of incentive. It doesn't necessarily make them selfish; it just means that time and resources are often hard to come by and they have to be driven to work on things that have something in it for them.

I advise people to offer a percentage to those assisting with fund-raisers. Talk to friends, talk to family about the project and about what you're trying to do. Then tell them that you will give them a particular percentage (of your choosing) for whatever they help raise. Most give 10 percent to friends and occasionally will give larger percentages to individuals who may have access to potential donors who could bring in a large sum.

Ten percent is not a lot to give away considering you are, in a sense, hiring a fundraiser. If a friend were able to take some of your materials and bring it to even two people that both donated $250 dollars, you would end up with $500. Then after giving $50 to the person who found those two donors, you walk away with $450 for your recording budget.

Bringing in a team of people who you know can speak and com-municate well, people who believe in you and understand your goals, can give you a wider spectrum of options and ideas. Just as they can help get out to donors, they can also give you ideas on who to talk to. This larger circle can help make a "cold contact," or someone you don't know at all, into a "warm contact," or someone with whom you have a connection based on common acquaintance.

Sometimes fundraisers who are working for a percentage can get you a sit-down with them and a potential donor in order to get you in the door to make your pitch. Remember, even though you end up making the pitch, the contact was made through your friend and that person should still receive the 10 percent or whatever your chosen percentage.

All of this allows your friends to be involved in the recording. You can set goals to inspire them. If they raise a certain amount, then the percentage they receive can go up after that. For example, if someone goes out and finds a thousand dollars total for you over a period of time, you can up his or her percentage as a sign of both gratitude and an inspiration to find more money and contacts since he or she stands to make more by doing so.

Certain goals can be laid out as benchmarks to hit for fundraisers, which could give them certain album credits. For instance, if someone were to raise a sixth or more of your budget, you could list that person as an assistant executive producer on the CD itself. Some people love the credit. Some people want to be involved, get the bragging rights, and be part of something. These people can be a great asset to you as you can help them live out some of their secret dreams.

Remember, the more people you involve, the more resources, names, and contacts created for you to achieve the budget. The more people who become involved, the easier it will be not only to find funding opportunities but also to spread the word about benefits, raffles, and fundraising shows. The more the word gets out, the more press and marketing will come your way. The more people you have spreading your info to their friends, the more those friends may in turn tell others. It's about building a major network to gain the most contacts to find the donors and investors you need.

When you think about it, it's really good practice since these are the exact same concepts and methods that you'll need to implement when marketing and promoting your recording once it's completed. Reaching out to people to raise money is much harder than reaching out to people to sell and promote your group and product. Thus, this stage of funding will create the foundational stages of grassroots marketing, which is the final and ongoing step after you complete the project.

Small Cash and PayPal/Online Donations

Small donations in cash and through PayPal can amount to much more than you realize and help you out more in the long term. Yes, it's amazing when someone comes at you with a thousand dollars or even five hundred or, for that matter, even one hundred. Still, barring that you have some very rich friends and relatives, a great deal of your budget will more than likely be raised in very small amounts.

Having a PayPal donation link on your site as well as on your other social networking sites is a great step to getting those small amounts to come in easily. While five dollars might not seem like much, fifty donations of $5 amount to $250. In a lot of budgets, that could cover half a day in the studio or a percentage of the food budget or even a session player to do some tracking or overdubs.

It's all about thinking with the broadest spectrum and not locking into the concept of trying to raise only large amounts. At the same time, don't concentrate on only the small amounts. The most effective fundraising occurs when you're looking at every angle across the board, both small and large.

Be creative in your approach for small donations. Think about percentages of your budget or parts of it. For example, if the engineer and studio costs total five thousand dollars, think about asking people to play a role in studio-time donations of five dollars. The donors in turn can feel as if they're being involved in a direct part of the project. True, it's only one-thousandth of the time, but it adds up. You can also cut it down to closer numbers, for instance if a studio costs five hundred dollars for the day, go after a fundraising campaign for "1 percenters" to be involved in a single day of the recording. It's a small amount, but for many people it can be a lot easier to go after very small amounts from a lot of people than it would be going after only a few people for very large amounts.

Many have heard about the ad campaigns launched a couple of years back where some Web designers sold a pixel for a dollar and filled up a site with one million little ads and made a million dollars. This really happened. It was a wild marketing idea and people bought from one dollar to one hundred dollars in pixels to do their ads. In the span of a year, a number of these sites were filled, and the creators became millionaires.

What could you sell online for small prices? What can you come up with to do something a little different to capture the donating audience out there?

There was a woman in Colorado who wanted to get out of debt and go back to school. She figured she needed one hundred thousand dollars. With a truckload of work going through chat groups, forums, and anything and everything online, she raised all the money, got out of debt, and went back to school.

It comes back to the creative marketing approach and looking at things from different angles. The small amounts you raise are just like the small steps you take on the pre-production, production, and post-production that you have to do everyday. These smaller amounts will add up and help to supplement the funding of your budget, so you can achieve the goal you have set. Every dollar truly counts and since it's easier to get a dollar than it is to get a thousand dollars, you should pay good attention and put good amounts of time into raising the small amounts to achieve your budget and your goal.

Fundraising Shows

Another way to raise the money for your recording budget is to put on fundraising shows. Whether you're doing the FSRP program or just raising funds for recordings, fundraising shows can truly show people what they are donating to.

Setting up a show that's the most effective and lucrative is where the effort on the part of the group or the artist has to take place. Marketing the show as an event and not just another band playing out one night will help lure people in and hopefully inspire them to donate.

Finding the help to put on the show the right way is part of the initial donation that you can get from the club and local media. Remember this is not just a normal show. If you're doing the FSRP, you're doing a performance to raise money for a project that will serve as a benchmark for independent musicians, and a percentage of the product you're fundraising for will be donations to a charity you believe in.

Discussing the different elements of your project with the venue and local papers may get you help early on in the form of a club donated for free or reduced, or getting a larger amount of the door profits. Contacting liquor sponsors to donate kegs is an effective approach as well.

Putting out a press release at the right time to bring awareness to the project, even if some don't come to the show, can help with the search for new donors and make other donors aware of what you're doing.

A group that's fundraising to give a percentage of their recording profits to charity, as well as giving a percentage of the event night to charity, can bring a great deal of media attention and show your commitment to the concept and the project. It can also help to get others to market and promote the show.

Give a dollar away per seat or per head that night. In doing this, you can approach other local businesses, including the venue, and ask for matching donations. All those businesses will aid in the marketing because it's a good cause *and* it's strong marketing for them. It's all about widening the scope of marketing.

How many ways can you …

Bring people through the door?

Get more donations at the show?

Bring awareness about your project to people who won't even be at the show?

Bring more exposure to your project and your plan in general?

All these elements need to be addressed to create the most effective show. It's not just about filling the room; it's also about filling the minds inside the club, outside the club, and all around. You are raising awareness. A fundraising show should serve a number of purposes beyond raising money. Create a show that's a performance, an event, something to stand out, and something where the marketing will make people aware of your project. That will make the event something that begins weeks before the actual show and has residual effects for weeks after.

The Post-Production Blast

Many of the artists who fundraise their budgets find it easiest and most manageable to break it down into four segments.

Segment One: Pre-production – This includes all the costs to get the Freedom Solution Recording Plan or your specific recording plan under way, which includes the costs for the business plan, the fundraising setup, and the beginning of pre-production.

Segment Two: The Recording – This includes all the costs around the recording, from the very start to mastering.

Segment Three: The Post-Production – This includes the preparation and creation of all marketing and promotional materials.

Segment Four: The Duplication, Press Release, Advertising, and Launch – This includes the duplication phase through releasing the recording to the media and the masses.

For the groups that have completed the first two segments, they now have a great album on hand. Oftentimes, they have raised the money to get them to the point of finishing segment two. The masters are in hand, and now the post-production needs to happen. The problem at this point is patience. Many make the wrong decision and don't properly find investors for their post-production needs. Shortcuts happen all too often at this point. Artists get excited to release quickly, they don't release in the right way, and the chances of success are cut down exponentially.

Just as much effort needs to be applied to the post-production segments, and the money you have set into the plan needs to be raised to make it happen the right way. Many people get confused at this point and don't approach fundraising in the best way possible. The artist took the right steps with the plan before, talking about what they were going to do and how they were going to do it, as well as showing a detailed plan to find initial funds to cover the first two phases, which really are the longest and most expensive elements. In the post-production side, not only do you still have the plan, you also have the product. You have the album you made; you have proof that you were able to stay within budget. You have shown that you're well past the 75-percentage point of doing exactly what you set out to do.

This fact alone can be a major help in finding the final financing you require. Take the approaches you used before and add the element of an actual recording that a potential investor or donor can hear.

Proof of concept is almost reached.

With the business plan and the recording, you can show what you've done and how you've reached the mark the right way. This will bring a higher level of confidence than earlier in fundraising because you've already executed a majority of the plan.

Some investors and donors feel safer about being involved in a project that's almost done, as opposed to giving in the early phases. When you show that you're looking for the exact funds to put out the release in the right way, including marketing, promoting, and advertising, you show that your ducks aren't only in a row, but they're already quacking.

The money you're asking for is to put out the album that you've already completed in the best way possible with the most chance for success. Investors and donors who might've turned you down earlier may give at this point, and people who wanted to see progress first now can see that you're almost there. You still have to apply the different elements of the various fundraising approaches mentioned earlier, and it's still going to be a challenge, but now you have a great deal of extra ammunition, information, and an actual product to go after the final capital that will bring the whole project to fruition.

The Investors/Loans for Your Project

Sometimes, to fast track a project, getting loans is a possibility, but you have to be careful. Finding the right person to loan you money or invest in your project is important. If you just go out and try to get someone to loan you money without looking at the stipulations, it may get you into trouble. The idea of getting a loan or investment for your project, while still being a donation of sorts, works by finding someone to give you a loan where you would only have to pay back that amount over an extended period of time with little or no interest.

These investors/donors make a donation by giving you a loan for an extended period of time without the normal stipulations of interest rates, percentages of profits, or for that matter, a piece of the pie. You still control the music, you still control your career, and you still control your percentages.

Unfortunately, there are a great number of scam loans out there, especially for the arts and music, so you need to look at what you might get along with the cash. What kind of agreements are they asking for? Remember, the goal is to look for funding that's either donated or lent in a way that allows the donor or investor no ownership of you or your music. If you get a loan that takes a high interest rate or in which the lender becomes involved in sales percentages, publishing, or royalties, then you're basically going against this concept.

These kinds of loans and investments are best from people you know or who have a strong and direct contact or second contact. They should be people who have faith in you and would invest upon knowing they will receive a return. Asking for a donation with no or low interest, as well as an extended pay-off time, is the best approach.

Fast tracking can help bring a project to fruition faster. Funding the studio elements as well as some of the promotional materials can give you the additional ammunition to go after donors to cover the remaining costs and pay back the investors. It's not about going into debt. It's more about speeding up the recording process while having more in place in order to approach donors later on. It's important not to lose sight of the loans you receive and remember to keep the same push and attitude that you'll need to raise the money you don't have yet. Continue with that approach and you will succeed.

Most of the time, though, I recommend that you stay with the fundraising and trying not to accrue debts that have high interest rates and small print attachments that will affect you later on. Be smart, pay attention to the details, read the fine print, and you'll be fine with this method or any. The more you understand it, the better you'll know how to approach it.

Monthly Installments

Whether the economy is in a strong state or not, your specific recording business plan may go a little slower or faster than usual or may be more challenging. But don't give up! And don't think that you have to wait until the air clears. First off, there are a number of ways you can continue to get funds, but also, the air is not going to clear for a while. If you want to wait this out, you won't get to record your album for a very long time.

It comes down to your efforts and how you're able to work. Anyone can work and do things when everything around is easy. It shows the true tenacity and character of someone when he or she can not only work hard on a challenging task but also do that challenging task in a challenging time.

Continue to use all the aspects of fundraising already discussed, but also see how you can alter and apply things to the economy and where it stands. Watch the news. Listen to how other companies large and small are dealing with the crisis and how they are overcoming these challenges to continue to sell and survive.

You're selling to people when you ask for a donation or an investment. You're selling them on the concepts of you, the organized and detailed plan you have put together, the spectrum of what you're creating, and all the avenues of both profit and sustainable success you're going after.

The second approach that I see right now in stores such as Wal-Mart and Target is the layaway and monthly installment plan. Unless you don't have a television, I'm sure you've seen that Kmart commercial in which the husband is raking leaves and asks his wife why she's going Christmas shopping since it isn't even Halloween. She answers back with a little whisper, "Layaway," and he responds with, "Genius!"

It is genius. People don't have the money right now to go out the day after Thanksgiving and spend a fortune on gifts galore. So these companies are looking to continue to get your business by letting you go out to shop for what you want, pay for it over three months, and pick it up right before the holidays. This also will help give the economy a little time to bounce back, and maybe by the time it comes to pick up the items, people will have a little less worry and thus spend a little more or put the remaining balance on their credit cards.

It's consumerism at its best, and there's a dirty side to it, but still, it's something that can be viewed in a positive way for you and other people raising funds. Right now, if you are looking to people to donate $250 to your project, most will probably say no and pretty fast. Even if you show them the blueprint and explain what's being done, as much as they may want to support it, there's more of a chance now that it will not happen since the economy has gone the direction it has.

Now switch gears with these particular people and approach the monthly installment angle. Then, instead of asking for a check then and there, ask for it over five months—a monthly installment plan for your recording plan from your donor. Explain where each payment will go. For example, the first payment will go to the pre-production invoice, the following month's payment will go to the logo design, the next month will go to the studio time, and so on.

This way you've not only created an easier way to raise large funds over a longer period, but you'll also give the donor confidence and remove the stress of cutting a large check on the spot. You're also keeping this donor or investor in the loop, explaining the progress you're making and the steps and benchmarks you're reaching each month. Doing this while the economy is bouncing back might make them feel more secure in you and the project, and they might even donate more.

Problems will arise when you least suspect them. In the end it's all about how you choose to deal with them. Take the assertive problem-solving approach, research and see how others are handling similar issues, then take the actions, make the changes, and revamp your approach to find the success you're looking for. This goes for everything in and around your career.

You are going to have to learn it sometime, why not now?

Learn these techniques and then be able to execute, act, and react better once your project goes to the public. In a sense, a good deal of your career will be similar to fundraising and finding investors, just in different forms. The skills you acquire from fundraising can be used to become distributed, get booked, find representation, dabble into the media, and so forth.

For everything that you don't want to do, there are others out there willing to do it. Only they are going to make sure they not only get paid for it but also have a percentage of anything you make off of it. So suck it up and learn these skills now while you maintain control of the recording.

YOUR BAND IS THE BRAND

So let's just say you're deaf and all you have to work on is imagery. Think of how many bands come off the same way: same look, same vibe on stage, same instrument setup, and same performance moves. It wouldn't give you a lot to remember since you can't hear the music. Think about your band that way when you begin to create the brand. Imagine what it would be like if you couldn't be heard. Think about how important your logo, your images, and your branding would be in such a situation.

When it comes down to it, many people are going to see you before they hear you, and some, including industry professionals, may make decisions based on your appearance before they hear you—if they hear you at all. These days, the package has to shine, and the band has to display itself professionally before anything else.

With so many artists out there and so many looking the same or working off a similar lack of professional appearance, don't you want to come across as professional and polished as possible? Don't you want them to go right for your disc or your link of music on a computer? The band is the brand, and you need to present yourself with professionalism, consistency, and uniformity to be seen and stand out. Of course it's about the music, but the band has to be the brand to bring the people and the professionals to your music, or you chance never even being heard.

Uniform Marketing and Promoting

Uniform ... it's not just what you wear to work anymore. Uniform is the idea of having consistency across all your marketing, branding, and promoting. While the music you make and the elements of your performance and appearance can be nuanced, it's important to stay uniform in your marketing, branding, and promoting.

This will not only help people recognize the brand and the concept that is you; it will also give a solid view of the elements in your music, which may be more versed and ever changing.

In a way, you can see the marketing, promoting, and branding of the group as the uniform base that will make people recognize you in the best and the most repetitive way possible. Then you can leave the change and improvisation for the music and the group on a performance level.

It is key to decide on and lock in on the following for your...

- **Logo**
- **Font (for your name)**
- **Tagline**
- **One-liner**
- **Full Bio**
- **Basic Color Scheme**

These are the basics of branding that will apply across all of the following elements to make you a defined brand. As much as you may not want to stay in a locked-in box, if you don't properly define the identity and basic images of what you are, you will find it much harder to grab onto the extended audience.

It's a proven fact: The majority of people are affected by branding, whether they are aware of it or not. When they see a font, a color, a logo, an image, and content that is constant or uniform, it draws them to a product or artist.

Here are the basic examples of where the above elements should apply to your...

- **Posters and Flyers**
- **Web site**
- **Networking Sites**
- **Entire Promo Package**
- **Merchandise**

It's not about being boring or redundant. Don't confuse uniformity with boring. You can still have wild and creative designs for your flyers; just make sure your name is always in the font that you use on all your other items. You can have creativity with your Web site design, but allow the basic theme to cross over to your networking sites in order to bring the new viewer as well as the regular viewer a sense of constant and uniform recognition. This will bring people back more often.

Think about groups like the Beatles. They have that Beatles font that was on everything. Think of The Who—same thing. It's just like Coca Cola or Frosted Flakes. It's how people make their products memorable. You're an artist and you're creating all types of different songs as well as improvisation and metamorphosis, but the most successful artists have the best and most constant branding.

And here we go back to "Well, so and so isn't doing it"

A lot of the bands of recent years have, to a point, stepped away from branding. The branding is still there; it just comes in the form of a marketing budget that allows the band to be played, seen, or advertised everywhere. When it comes down to it, if you don't have a half-million-dollar marketing budget, I highly recommend that you work on the uniform layouts and the branding. You're an artist, but to move your music and merchandise and to increase and strengthen your fan base, you need to be uniform in your branding, marketing, and promoting.

The same elements are applied to your tagline, one-liner, and bio as well. The more you use that same content, text, wording, or copy, as some call it, the more it will help to get stories and reviews written about you. It will also help industry professionals get a sense that you have a solid marketing base and a direct vision.

Have that uniform look and watch the results. Every poster can be a different color, but make sure the font of your name is always the same. In fact, it's as simple as this: Anywhere you have your name, if it's not in text as part of a sentence, it should be in the font you always use for your name. One single font. It doesn't matter what size you use, just keep it in that font!!!!!!

The uniform approach will help you brand your name, your product, and your sound. Leave the variances for the music and the true art. I'm not saying that you should make your songs or your sound uniform, just that the uniformity of your image, font, logo, and basic text will bring you to more people than switching it up ever will.

Logos

Creating a logo can be simple; however, creating an effective logo is a much larger challenge, and a lot of people have a lot of ideas on what a logo should be. Some feel it should be really artistic, others think it should be very simple, and still others feel a logo is unnecessary and switch up designs for every show and every album.

Your logo is one of the most important elements of your band outside of the music. It's the visual recognition device to show who you are. It's the visual balance for what people are hearing. A logo, many times, is even more important than the photo of the group. Now, you can disagree with me on this one, but a logo can fit in a lot more places than a photo and can play a large role in branding the band across all media.

Your logo has to be legible. Think of it this way, and this is a good check for your logo and yourself: If you put up a poster on a light pole on the side of the road, you should be able to drive by at a slow to regular speed and make out the logo and its assisting elements (we'll get to that in a few). If you can't make it out, it's not the most effective logo. Your logo should look good on the side of a pen as well as a seven-foot banner on the stage behind you.

So when you're creating a logo, ask yourself, Can it stand alone? Does it need assisting elements to make it clear? Are all the elements in place to be effective on a pen, a hat, a poster, an album cover, the Web, a newspaper, a bumper sticker, a cup, or any other type of merchandise? The logo that you create needs to work in all these mediums or it's not an effective logo.

The Full Logo Elements

In my opinion, a logo is made up of four elements:

1. The Logo Itself

This should be a design that can stand alone and has an artistic and pleasing quality to it, oftentimes some kind of image or graphic that's not necessarily the name of the artist and doesn't even have words.

2. The Name Font

This is the name of the artist or band in the font that will go with the logo. This font should always be used after it is decided upon. THAT IS BRANDING!!!! The font you choose should be on every poster, every album, every piece of promotional material … EVERYTHING.

3. The Tagline

The tagline is a definer of the band. Make sure you have the tagline in a uniform font that can be applied to the logo.

4. The Web Site Address

This is your Web site in a uniform font that, again, can be applied to the logo.

Below is an explanation of the different aspects of a logo set, using a fictional band called the Acme Band. To reference these explanations you can visit the Brain Grenade Entertainment Web site at www.braingrenademusic.com.

The Acme Band Logo Set

1. The Logo – The logo is the cat.

2. The Font – The font of the Acme Band had to be something that would be a constant and be everywhere. The font can often take the longest since it has the most applications in the most places and has to be able to work in the largest variety of sizes.

3. **The Tagline** – The band already had the tagline, but we needed to find a specific and uniform font for the tagline and how it would lay out into the full logo.

4. **The Web Site Address** – Same went for the Web site address and how it would sit into the different elements.

Once you have these items in place, you create your full logo set. Use your logo to create twelve different combinations of the above four elements.

Then you'll be able to apply across the board for any situation in which you'll need branding. Don't see it as stifling creativity. You can still create many images, posters, and photo ideas, but always apply the logo set that you've designed to brand your band.

Here are the twelve variations with the elements of each.

LOGO 1: LOGO – FONT – TAGLINE – WEB

LOGO 2: FONT – TAGLINE – WEB

LOGO 3: FONT – LOGO

LOGO 4: LOGO – FONT – TAGLINE

LOGO 5: FONT – TAGLINE

LOGO 6: FONT

LOGO 7: LOGO – WEB

LOGO 8: LOGO – FONT – INSIDE A BORDER (a line around the logo, giving it a solid border)

LOGO 9: FONT – LOGO – TAG – WEB – INSIDE A BORDER

LOGO 10: LOGO – TAGLINE

LOGO 11: FONT – WEB

LOGO 12: LOGO

Once these were in place for the Acme Band, they got high quality and low quality color and black-and-white versions of each.

1. Low quality grey scale

2. High quality grey scale

3. Low quality color

4. High quality color

So in the end you have forty-eight different images that can fly into anything and everything you need. It may seem like overkill, but having all these versions available on the Web for download will make life a lot easier. It will also allow people easily to access your images. Have you ever received a call saying, "We need an image to go to press with right now"? Or have you ever been asked if you have something with your font without the logo? If you haven't, you will, and this is a great solution.

Moving on, you'll need to understand the acronyms of the logo markers.

```
#   – The number of the logo
A   – First version of the logo
B   – Second version of the logo
C   – Alteration or additional logo to the set
L   – Log
F   – Font name
T   – Tagline
W   – Web site address

G   – Grey scale or black and white
C   – Color
B   – Border
BB  – Border with background
```

So for example …

1A THE ACME BAND LOGO – LFTW-G

In English: the Acme Band Logo #1A with the logo, font, tagline, and Web site in grey scale.

Get it?

All of these logos give you the most variety for the most placement and use for your band. Once you have the basic design, the font choice, tagline, and Web site in line, you can pretty much just shuffle things around with your designer and set these twelve in place. This will go a lot faster if you have the separate elements already designed and agreed on.

These sets will make it easier to make tee shirts, stickers, flyers, posters, Web designs, listings, and graphics for magazines, newspapers, and millions of other marketing and promotional elements. Placing the same logo sets on a promotional or download page on your Web site will also make it easier for people to access your logo as needed. Having both high- and low-resolution versions will allow people to place your logos on their Web sites or use your images to advertise you for a show. Of course you'll have a third version of these that are of the highest resolution for use on shirts, merchandise, and swag that you will control and not share.

When you brand and define the image, the name, and the group, you will bring a new level of recognition and potentially a new group of fans who would not have found you before. So many artists skip on the branding process, and yet it is one of the most crucial. Just as you define your music, define the images and the logo elements that will bring people to your music.

Taglines

Branding is a very important element of the business side of music. Just as the sound and the name have to be recognized, so do the artists' branding elements, of which a tagline is key. While the name represents the band and the creativity, the tagline should be a short quip that gives a solid overview and description of the artist. The tagline will help people see in what direction you lean stylistically and will give a little more information than the name and images provide. Taglines are a requirement today, hands down. With all the bands out there, the tagline will be one more element to allow the band to stand out.

What exactly is a tagline? The following are definitions from online. These can help you in deciding what's best for you when you begin working on yours.

- A simple, poignant phrase used to set off a logo/ad.

- A phrase or short sentence placed directly below a Web page's masthead. The tagline functions to quickly identify the purpose of the Web site. It may be a subtitle, an organizational motto, or a vision or purpose statement.

- Short statement describing a/your company's position or purpose.

- A phrase used repeatedly in communications and advertising that, through repetition, eventually comes to identify the brand.

Taglines are used by everything from food products to cars, companies to computers, and everything in between. From simple broad promo types like "Fly the friendly skies" to ego types like Frosted Flakes—"They're great!"—taglines add another marketing element to help draw in fans and venues.

If you're saying to yourself, "I don't hear about bands I know having taglines, so why do I need one?" Please know: All bands have taglines; many just aren't released. The larger scale groups that have money behind them start with taglines in their business plans for the labels. A business plan is designed to sell the group in order to acquire the funds to back them. When the plan is presented and funded, the marketing money comes into play, and taglines are not required as much because now cash plays the branding role.

Take your time coming up with a tagline and make sure it best represents you in the simple form. Add that line to your logo at times, and have it present on all promotional materials as well as on your Web site and anywhere else.

To help give a basic sense of how some taglines are created, I want to share the taglines of a few of the artists I have worked with and how we came up with them.

First off, Jeremiah: His tagline is "A gentleman of soul." We took awhile to get this honed in. We started off knowing Jeremiah is an R&B and soul artist. We wanted to find something that would help define him but not get him lost in the shuffle. Many R&B artists just list themselves as that: R&B. We knew we had to use the word soul or R&B. As we brainstormed, we thought about the king of pop, the godfather of soul, and other lines that had been used by others. As we presented Jeremiah in a clean cut, smooth, and clear image, we thought of the word gentleman. From there, we decided to stay away from ego, and instead of "The Gentleman of Soul," we thought something more gentleman like and less arrogant would be "*A Gentleman of Soul.*" That ended up being his tagline and an effective one at that.

Remember a tagline is not intended for the audience who knows you and has heard you; the tagline is intended to draw in those who know nothing of you or your music.

Das Vibenbass is an amazing jazz group. However jazz is a terrible word as a description alone and way too vague. Das Vibenbass crosses the spectrums of jazz, fusion, Latin, bebop, swing, cool, big band, stomp, rock, and blues to name just a few. The borders of jazz have been falling for some time. They've widened, thereby creating opportunities for different sounds and approaches. The group took some time with the idea and came back with, "Crushing the Borders of Jazz." I loved it. To me, it was a great way to come at the jazz idiom while showing the depth and diversity of the group in a nice tight little tagline.

A couple of thoughts on creating a tagline …

Take the time to create the right one.

Make sure it can represent you across the board.

Stay away from the ego and avoid the arrogant words like … innovative, revolutionary, and new. These take away from the tagline and the group as a whole. In the age of everyone trying to say how much better he or she is than everyone else, be original!!! Stand on your sound and your professionalism, not a cheesy arrogance that will end up hurting you in the end.

Ask friends; put out a mailing list bulletin saying you're looking for a short sentence to describe the group to someone who's never heard you before.

Each step in creating your brand will bring more people to the music. It's not about getting lost in the business aspects; it's about balancing the business with the music so you can bring people to your sound. Create the brand that is you and your music. Each small step will bring a new fan and a new awareness to your art.

The Bio

Creating an effective biography for a band or an artist can be as challenging as the tagline. To sum up your group and sound in a way that will draw people to your band is sometimes harder than making the music itself. The problem with bios is that all too often they are either poorly constructed or too saturated with ego. Your biography has to shine and envelop your group, your sound, and your marketing.

Not only that, but the bio needs to be formatted in a way that makes it easy for reviewers to site for potential stories, interview information, and reviews. In a lot of ways, it's like the press release: When you deliver a bio that's easy for the media to access, they will use it.

Also, like the tagline, logo, and images, stay uniform with your bio. It should be consistent across all your materials. You can, of course, use different sections of your bio and alter the length, but stay consistent. Keep people aware of what you're about, and as they recognize the words, images, and sounds more and more, they'll be more compelled to follow you—even the toughest crowds.

Below is an example of an effective bio for a band in the industry today. I am not by any means saying this is the template to follow, nor is it the only way to do a bio. However, from experiences I've had, this is a successful format that gets solid results.

The Acme Band Bio

The Acme Band, based out of Seattle, Washington, has blasted off for a musical journey through the universe of soul, funk, rock, and blues. As likely to be inspired by Weezer or N. E. R. D. as they are by Otis Redding or Led Zeppelin, the Acme Band will surely move your head, your heart, and your ass. The Acme Band is out of control rock and soul.

Bred on a steady diet of the roots of rock and blues, the Acme Band was schooled on the legends of Motown soul, funk, and rock & roll. Musical sponges to this day and

embracing all the technology that modern music has to offer, the Acme Band is just as exciting to see live as they are to hear through your speakers. The Acme Band brings you party music for the 21st century with the power to stir your mind and shake your behind.

Combining versatile technical ability with solid craftsmanship and a deep well of emotion, the Acme Band has emerged as a formidable musical force. The band's approach to music is enriched by over thirty years of combined experience, which gives the Acme Band the ability to express and enhance any possible influence through each member's unique sensibility.

The Acme Band will keep you dancing all night, and their songs will stay in your head so infectiously that you will be compelled to seek them out to listen again. In no time flat, once the groove starts pulsing and their melodies fill the air, the Acme Band will turn you from a casual listener to a fan.

This bio can be cut up into four classifications as shown below.

It contains the…

1. One-Liner

    The Acme Band, based out of Seattle Washington, has blasted off for a musical journey through the universe of soul, funk, rock, and blues.

    This is the first sentence of the bio. It's the first thing that the reader sees, and it can stand on its own without needing anything else. It's like a full sentence version of the tagline. This can also be used to describe the band if someone wants a little more information than just the tagline. It covers the basic information, like the name of the band, the location of the band, and the genre of the music.

2. **Short Bio**

The Acme Band, based out of Seattle Washington, has blasted off for a musical journey through the universe of soul, funk, rock, and blues. As likely to be inspired by Weezer or N. E. R. D. as they are by Otis Redding or Led Zeppelin, the Acme Band will surely move your head, your heart, and your ass. The Acme Band is out of control rock and soul.

This is the first paragraph of the full bio. Notice how the One-Liner is the lead of the Short Bio. Each part of the bio should start with the previous section. This is how you can maintain uniformity while still adding elements. Each element should stack evenly for the sake of continuity.

In the Short Bio, you continue off of the One-Liner's information about the styles by adding some of the influences. Adding four or five influences can help you give a ballpark definition of your sound to those who don't know you. In most cases, you can close the Short Bio strongly by ending it with your band's tagline. The Acme Band's tagline is "Out of control rock and soul." This is the bio that will often get used in shorter stories and reviews.

NOTE: If you follow this piggyback format in your biographies, writers and reviewers will not have to search around to pull elements to use; they can follow your format very easily.

3. **Medium Bio**

The Acme Band, based out of Seattle Washington, has blasted off for a musical journey through the universe of soul, funk, rock, and blues. As likely to be inspired by Weezer or N. E. R. D. as they are by Otis Redding or Led Zeppelin, the Acme Band will surely move your head, your heart, and your ass. The Acme Band is out of control rock and soul.

Bred on a steady diet of the roots of rock and blues, the Acme Band was schooled on the legends of Motown soul,

funk, and rock & roll. Musical sponges to this day and embracing all the technology that modern music has to offer, the Acme Band is just as exciting to see live as they are to hear through your speakers. The Acme Band brings you party music for the 21st century with the power to stir your mind and shake your behind.

This bio, following the piggyback format, starts with the One-Liner, adds the Short Bio, and then it adds another paragraph to become the Medium Bio. This paragraph adds even more detail to the sound of the band, from a deeper description of the influences to some basic plugs, delivered with confidence and assertiveness, without being too cocky. It also closes with something sharp that can be pulled by writers to be used in reviews.

For Example:

> **The Acme Band brings you party music for the 21st century with the power to stir your mind and shake your behind.**

This has an air of confidence without being over the top. They're not saying they're the best party music or that they don't sound like anyone else, but it's confident, fun, assertive, and gives a more detailed description of the group.

Finally …

4. **The Long Bio**

   The Acme Band, based out of Seattle Washington, has blasted off for a musical journey through the universe of soul, funk, rock, and blues. As likely to be inspired by Weezer or N. E. R. D. as they are by Otis Redding or Led Zeppelin, the Acme band will surely move your head, your heart, and your ass. The Acme Band is out of control rock and soul.

   Bred on a steady diet of the roots of rock and blues, the Acme Band was schooled on the legends of Motown soul,

funk, and rock & roll. Musical sponges to this day and embracing all the technology that modern music has to offer, the Acme Band is just as exciting to see live as they are to hear through your speakers. The Acme Band brings you party music for the 21st century, with the power to stir your mind and shake your behind.

Combining versatile technical ability with solid crafts-manship and a deep well of emotion, the Acme Band has emerged as a formidable musical force. The band's approach to music is enriched by over thirty years of combined experience, which gives the Acme Band the ability to express and enhance any possible influence through each member's unique sensibility.

The Acme Band will keep you dancing all night, and their songs will stay in your head so infectiously that you will be compelled to seek them out to listen again. In no time flat, once the groove starts pulsing and their melodies fill the air, the Acme Band will turn you from a casual listener to a fan.

The full bio piggybacks the One-Liner, the Short Bio, the Medium Bio, and then finishes out with the last two paragraphs. More details are added; the element of experience, the direction, and the vision of the band should be added in this section. Lastly, add a couple of sentences at the end that can be extracted and used by writers on their own.

Below are some bullet points pulled out of the last section. They can all be used by writers, reviewers, and media pros. Make their job easier, and you will read about your band in more places.

The band's approach to music is enriched by over thirty years of combined experience.

The Acme Band will keep you dancing all night.

The groove starts pulsing and their melodies fill the air.

The Acme Band will turn you from a casual listener to a fan.

An effective bio will help bring more people to your music while making it easier to write about. In a lot of ways, you want your bio to be geared towards the industry professionals because it's those people and groups that will bring the information about you to others. Watch out for an excessive level of ego and remember: A lot of the people you are trying to get to notice your band are used to seeing horribly formatted, terribly written, and vague biographies. Give them something different. Let your bio stand out, just like you.

Reach the people with your words and vision in a well-constructed and well-organized format. We all want the music to stand on its own and speak for itself, of course, so put together a strong bio to guide the fans, the writers, the reviewers, and the industry professionals to your music so that it has the opportunity to speak for itself and stand out in an industry that is so saturated today.

Letterhead

Sometimes it's the little things that can bring people to the larger things you want them to see. When you're trying to get a booking agent, a club, a promoter, a manager, a label, or anyone to listen to your music, every step and every piece counts. It's crucial to consider to whom you're sending your music or promotional package. Think about how many packages they've already looked at today. Think about how much they had to weed through to find what they were looking for. Remember the envelope, the package, and the basic presentation are what they see first, before they slip the CD into a player or go to the link to hear your music.

In such a scenario, it's the little elements of professionalism that will bring that person to your music faster and create a greater focus on your package and music.

A letterhead for your band is a very easy and professional touch. When someone opens a package and sees a cover letter with a letterhead showing the band's name, logo, Web site, and contact information, you start off on the right foot. Many bands send packages that don't even have a cover letter. Others send blank pieces of paper that are hand-written or terribly typed. Using a solid letterhead in all your mailings to booking agents, radio stations, labels, or managers will show that you understand the important of details and give solid attention to the small stuff.

This blank letterhead can now be used for anything formal that the band or artist might need it for. It can also be used as the template for a number of your core documents, to make them look as professional and effective as possible. Of the full, twenty-five part promotional package that I advise artists to create in different forms for sending out and solicitation, fourteen of the pages are built from the letterhead page.

These are the pages listed below.

- **Letterhead Page**
- **One Pager**
- **Review Page**
- **Press Release Page**
- **Album Information Page**
- **Industry Pro Page**
- **Artist Stat Sheet**
- **Show/Performance Sheet**
- **Stage Plot**
- **Input List**
- **Sound and Light Requirement Sheet**
- **Artist Contract**
- **Full Rider**
- **Backline Sheet**

Taking the letterhead to your promotional package and booking materials can help other people keep your information straight as well. Artists often have documents that they assume are being seen with their package as a whole and so leave out key information, but anyone who reviews your materials might fail to keep your package in one piece. This happens more often that people think. Taking that fact into consideration, every page of a promo pack—performance contracts, stage plots, input lists, and anything else—should be traceable to you.

Not only should they know it's you, but all of your information should be on every page—your name, your logo, your Web site, your contact info ... all of it!

Again, it's the little things that can make the biggest differences in someone getting to your music and looking over your materials. Take the most organized steps to prepare everything you send out. A letterhead may seem simple and foolish to you, but many in the industry will see it as highly professional. Applying that template to a number of your documents and showing the consistency of the promotional, professional, and soliciting sides of your group will help you immensely.

You've put so much effort into the music, the performance, and the recording ... You want the career? You want the success? You want the sustainability? Then you better put that same energy and attention to detail into all the elements of your presentation. It will help give your music and your performances the best chance at long-term success. Otherwise—well, you figure it out.

Stage Banners

The band banner is your opportunity for additional advertising *while* you're on stage. It's a beautiful thing. I'm a big advocate of bands putting a banner on the stage while they're playing. This provides another level of branding, marketing, and promotion that can help you find and keep fans.

A banner that's placed behind a band during a show, with the font of their name and the logo of the band, can help get that name and image into people's minds. Then when they visit any one of your networking pages or your Web site and see that logo again, it will remind them of your show. That, in essence, is branding.

Many bands make the mistake of saying that on stage they want their music to define them and bring the fans to them. On one side of the coin, it's true. In the end, it's all about the music, but if you're band number two in an eight-band night at some club, your name might get mistaken, forgotten, or just lost in the mix. Your bass player can begin to look like the bass player in the band before you, or your guitarist might remind someone of the guitarist in the group after you. Thus, when you deliver a great show that showcases your music as well as the image of you live, you're actually only halfway there from a marketing standpoint. Add a banner with your name and logo, and you deliver the full picture. You give the audience member—your potential new fan—a linear way to remember you.

There are even studies of name recognition and cognitive comparisons. When viewers are hearing music and seeing the band while also being able to see the name or have an item that ties the performance of the song to the performance of the group, there's a better chance of triggering a memory of that band's name the next day, or even a few days later. With proper branding and logo uniformity, you, again, raise the chances that if they find your page on any of the networking sites out there or see your Web site or any kind of promotional material about you, they'll automatically be drawn to you by memory much more quickly than if they had no visual trigger other than the venue's normal back drop.

Some places may give you trouble about putting up banners. Work with them. Don't just throw one up if they say no, but don't give up on it either. Sometimes you might need to drape it over an amp or hang it off the drum riser and have it side stage in a less visible place. Still, it's up, and you can reference it.

Bring along the things to make it easier as well. One group that I played with had a banner, and they had a really nice case for it, so it could roll up very easily and very professionally, which in turn kept it looking nice. In this case, they had scissors, a roll of clothesline, roll of paper towels, small bottle of Windex, and duct tape. This allowed for the group to be able to put it up in any situation that might arise and still have it look professional. The paper towels and Windex were included to keep it clean and looking sharp.

As previously stated, making mention of the band name during the show a good number of times can also help. Remember, branding the name is core to encouraging people to find out more about you. Every couple of songs, mention your name; then every couple of songs mention the Web site or a social networking site. In other words, reference yourself. Often. Kid Rock, for example, was a master at branding his name into all of his songs, in between the songs, and in the hooks of his songs.

There are other ways to stay in the memories of those new fans. Some people have their own guitar picks to toss into the crowd; others have stickers on stage that they toss to people who look really excited or into the performance. Having the occasional item or two, even a disc, to give away on stage can be a great way to market and push.

It's up to each artist to figure out how he or she will take advantage of the time on stage. Make the most out of the performance. Give the audience a great show, give them great music, and make sure they know who you are and how to find you. That, in my mind, is a successful gig no matter how many or how few people are there.

Of course it's about the music, but don't forget that every time you play, every time you're seen or heard, you want to make as many of those people as possible fans who will come see you again, buy your music, and buy your merchandise. See each show as an opportunity to increase your fan base and to brand your name, sound, logo, and image into the minds of the people watching so even if they don't become fans, they'll tell a friend or two about you. Market to them in the most powerful way you can: the live performance. It's the best way to create and keep a solid fan base and to get word of mouth moving.

Tell them what they need to know, tell them who you are, and tell them how they can find out even more. It's up to you to create a true fan out of someone who may need the extra little push.

Physical Appearance

In addition to all the branding items we've discussed thus far, it's also very important to focus on your actual appearance. How do you physically present yourself? This goes for the pictures you take, the way you appear on stage, and the way you look and sound in interviews, promotional segments, and talking to industry professionals and fans.

This is an area where people get way too stupid. There are those who show up in whatever clothing they have on, without any thought given to their appearance or presentation, and there are those on the opposite side of the spectrum who go way overboard with the looks and the vibe of how they appear. Fortunately there's a happy medium and one I recommend you visit when it comes to your presentation. Look good, smell good, and hold yourself well. From the standpoint of the stage and photos as well as merchandise, think along the lines of branding yourself by defining a basic look. It doesn't mean you can't switch it up, but think of the effectiveness of Slash's top hat, Alicia Keyes' bandana, Michael Jackson's glove, and a thousand other defined and refined elements that help brand the band with a physical appearance. Now it's true that larger artists will switch things up and change styles, but while you're growing to that level, have a consistency in your appearance and dress. This will help people remember you as well as brand you and promote you beyond the music. Define your look, and if you need help, ask someone. Ask someone you know who has a sense or might have an idea of what you do and don't look good in.

Small apparel consistencies can be remembered. Think of the Mighty Mighty Bosstones with their converse shoes. There are dozens of artists you can think of yourself who have that one consistent accessory or piece of clothing. On the same note, watch for copying a worn-out fad, like big jewelry or bling. It's been overdone. Too many have used it, and you'll just pigeonhole your look as a copycat. Also, chill out with the gang signs and the usual trying-to-look-tough look. Take the sunglasses off, too. And if you wear makeup, go light. If you go heavy on makeup for a certain look, fans and people in the industry might not even know who you are when you take it off. At the same time, look interesting when they photograph you for pictures and promotional shots.

This is also good advice to follow when it comes to talking to industry people, booking agents, and venues in which you're playing. Yes, you want to dress to impress and deliver your image, but you also want to make the right impression for the people working with you inside the industry.

When you're meeting potential managers, agents, reps, or people in the industry, give them an idea of what they're getting. They have your promotional package; now show them what you're like in person. Make sure you can deliver when you're handling business just as you do on stage. Wear clean clothes, brush your teeth, wash your face, and look out for body odor when you present yourself. These may sound like Captain Obvious kinds of things, but they're not followed often. Take off the sunglasses when you're meeting inside with someone. Look attentive and let one person be the spokesman or leader, speaking on behalf of everyone.

These steps will help you give industry people a sense of your image even with the music off and the instruments put away. This level of professionalism can also make the person you're meeting with want to see you on stage even more. It's about the music, but the image is important both to the fans and the industry people. Deliver with a strength, a professionalism, and a consistency, and you'll become easier to brand, market, and promote. Remember, the look can have a dirty feel to it, but keep the clothes clean and the personas professional. That way, the "dirty look" can be one of the elements that helps you clean up.

Perceptions

How are you perceived or viewed by people? How do your fans see you? How do new listeners or potential fans see you? How does a booking agent, a venue, a label, or just the general public and media see you?

How you present yourself is often how you're perceived, but that's not always the case. For example, if you have your music together and a strong promotional package and your marketing in order, you have the foundation to be viewed in the best light possible. In my opinion, the optimum view would be great artists who sound wonderful, have all their stuff together—from the promotional to the legal—and look like they're on their way up. This creates a gravitational pull. It almost silently says, "Get on board and know these guys/girls because they're going places."

Regardless of the genre, the sound, and the artist, appearances are important. Now that you have in place the different promotional items, marketing approaches, and branding methods with which to lay the groundwork for your image, you need to consider how you present yourself.

To garner the best estimations, most would agree that putting on a great show is always a good idea. Being well rehearsed, being on time, having a good connection with your audience, talking with fans, and being professional and respectful to those around you, including bands performing before you and after you, is a requirement if you want to come away with a strong and positive reputation as an artist or part of a group.

If you're upset one night and don't talk to some people waiting to speak with you, it might upset a fan, but hopefully it's a one-time event, and as such, it won't leave a mark. However, if you make your presence known in a negative way on a blog, a harsh social networking comment, or something where many people can see it, you're doing very bad things for the way in which you and your music are perceived.

Success begets success, even when it isn't there yet. If you show yourself in a successful and positive manner, you'll be perceived that way. This doesn't mean you should brag or go over the top. Once again, you shouldn't be using crazy "ego" words. These are often found in the harder rock and hip-hop Web sites, where groups talk about how they're the best, they're going worldwide, they're taking over, they're about to drop, and so on. Don't do it.

If someone e-mails me with a song or songs that they want me to listen to, the quickest way to get me to delete the message and move on is to tell me that that I have never heard anything so good or that nothing compares to this sound. I even received a threatening e-mail that said I had to listen to the song, and if I didn't think it was going to go to the top or if I didn't help bring it to the top, I would feel the pain. I listened to that tune and it's not going to the top. I have yet to feel the pain, but I still think it's funny that I got that note. Talk about the wrong approach!

As for online comments, think about what you're saying when you leave a remark that the world can view. Do you really want anyone and everyone to see those words? I hate, I repeat, *hate* when friends on whatever social network site have a conversation in the comments section or main part of the page; that makes either or both of the parties look bad. E-mail your thoughts. Don't leave it out in the open to be seen by the world.

Leave strong comments that give people a good perception of you, something that will make them want to click on your link or find out more about you. People should see you as an artist on the way up, someone they want to find out more about, and someone they'll want to listen to. While it's one thing to discuss certain difficulties publicly, as a way to connect with your fans, don't whine and don't complain.

Don't talk about how you wish you had an agent or a manager or how it feels like you will never find a label. Don't go into trash talking another group or blaming someone else for your lack of success. In the end this only makes you look weak and like someone who's going nowhere.

Think about all the musicians on all the music Web sites, all the different social networking sites, and all the music that's out there now, just a click away. There is endless competition to get fans to take the time to visit or listen for even a minute. Present yourself in the strongest way possible. Be assertive and not arrogant, be clear and not confusing, and give yourself a strong and positive base so that others will see you as someone they should want to listen to and learn more about. Anytime you leave a comment on the World Wide Web, make sure it's one that leaves the intended reader, and anyone else who comes across it, interested in finding out more about you.

It's about your delivery in the end, before people hear you, before they even see you, you have to create a perception of yourself to draw them in. Make it the right one.

Honor in the Music Business: A Contradiction in Terms?

All industries have liars, and the music industry is definitely no exception. Many people don't follow through on their word; many lack honor, consideration, and professionalism. It's unfortunate that those who do lack honor—who lie or skip out on promises—grow defensive about their lack of honor when called out on it. Instead of righting wrongs or taking steps to modify their actions, they offer excuses for why it's okay for them to be dishonorable.

In the arts, as in any other profession, you must have professional abilities and skills, but today, with so many artists going after the same jobs, the same tours, the same records, it takes ability, professionalism, *and* honor for people to call on you and continue to call on you again and again.

Your word, it is that simple

This is not rocket science. In fact, it shouldn't even need to be mentioned. But honor is an issue. False promises, outright lies, back stabbing, and just plain absence is a problem in the industry, but the industry is getting more and more fed up with it. While many superstar names have been troublesome in the past and put up with, these days, with the economy, time restraints, and other issues, more people are leaning towards working with those who can not only play but also have the honor to show up, perform, follow through, and deliver. Attitudes, egos, and lack of professionalism are not tolerated like they used to be.

When you give your word, follow through with it. Honor it. This will lead to more work than you know.

Your Actions

When you're booked for a session, a show, *anything*, be there and be there on time. If you are going to be late, call. If there are things that are going to keep you from fulfilling your obligation or your promise, then do everything in your power to remedy the situation with a replacement or some kind of fix.

I'm amazed at how people give up with no consideration of the person who has booked them or whatever the agreement or contract situation is. I, for one—and I speak for many—don't call people back who flake out, blow off, or bail at the last minute. This adolescent behavior is unprofessional, dishonorable, and disrespectful. I don't care how good a musician is. When he or she shows a lack of respect or consideration for me, an artist with whom I'm working, or the promise they've made, then I'm done with that person.

Things Happen

Now I'm not saying things don't happen that you can't control. Car problems, accidents, emergencies, etc. can prevent anyone from being able to honor his or her word. When it comes to professionalism, honor, and respect, it really isn't as much about how you behave when everything is perfect. It's about how you behave when problems occur.

When anything, or *everything*, goes wrong, how do you problem solve? What kind of effort do you put into rectifying the issue? If you get into a car accident and you're okay but stuck waiting for a tow truck, are you the type to call and say you can't make it and leave it at that? Or are you the type who either tries to find another way to get to the session or makes calls to the studio or producer asking if they can call anyone else while you, yourself, are working to find a way to get that session covered?

It comes down to the follow-through, and while a solution will not be reached every time, if something has to change or a commitment has to be broken, I know that the person I hired did everything he or she possibly could to make it right. That is honor. That is professionalism. That is follow-through.

You say you're going to be somewhere. Show.

You say you're going to do something. Do it.

You say you're going to pay someone. Pay.

Honor your commitments, your promises, and your own goals. If something goes wrong, do all you can to make it right. Regardless of the booking, the gig, the contract, the promise, as long as you do what you say you're going to do or make every effort to resolve an emergency situation, then you truly are a professional with honor in every sense of the word. You want to have a reputation of a skilled, competent professional whose playing matches his or her honor and dependability.

It can make all the difference in the world. When people know they can count on you through thick and thin, your reputation will spread like wildfire, but don't forget that the same thing goes for the opposite as well.

The band is the brand. The elements that you bring to the brand will help get you out to more media and more of the public. Remember, once they are captivated, they will be drawn to the music. Unfortunately, you can't always draw people in with the music first.

MARKETING AND PROMOTIONS

There are so many aspects that need to be taken care of when it comes to finding the right and responsible way to achieve success in the music industry. You have the music itself, with all the creative and artistic issues that surround it. Then you can talk about the legal elements, the promotional elements, performance elements, branding issues and sales. And while each of these elements is individually important, there is one common issue that surrounds all of them: marketing.

Marketing is the biggest part of your career outside the music itself, and as much as you might hate the fact, marketing can sometimes overshadow the music. Have you ever seen that band and you had no idea how they could get that particular gig or how they could be selling so many CDs? Maybe you wonder why they're doing half as good as they are when you see yourself as better. Perhaps you know of other bands that are just as good and have gone nowhere. The answer is marketing.

A good deal of this book is about marketing because this book is about sustaining and surviving in the music industry. Of course the music is first, but the marketing has to come second or else no one will ever hear your music. Too many artists get into the mindset of saying that they are all about the music, and the music will be heard by the right people, but how will the music be heard? How will the right people find it? It has to be marketed to the ears that need to hear it.

All the different elements—the design of your logo, the consistency of your font and name, your promotional package, and the way you use the Internet—will affect your outcome. The work that you put into your promotion, your fan retention, your shows, your booking, sales, soliciting, and everything else will decide how well you do. Disagree if you want, but when it comes to success, from the smallest independent to the biggest major label act, it all revolves around marketing. The better your marketing, the better shape your group will be in, and the more shows and opportunities you will have.

I believe it comes down to three steps:

1. **Pre-production** – The pre-production step of your marketing approach involves the careful consideration of the materials you prepare to market and how you put together the foundation and the blueprint of your band, your sound, and your image. This is where you lock in the bio, make sure the logo works, and define certain aspects that will be uniform across the board. Do you have the right posters in place? Are your Web site, networking sites, CD, press pack, merchandise, and everything else created to be as effective as they can be?

2. **Production** – The production step is all about making sure you have all the items in place, as well as a plan to do the smallest marketing task to the largest stunt. The organization of a solid multi-tiered approach is essential, including the flyers you're putting up, the contacts you're going to reach out to, the ads you're going to buy, the hands you're going to shake, and a database of addresses and e-mails you're going to maintain. If you don't have a plan as to how you're reaching out to people and with what frequency, you can risk spamming or bothering people who will then throw your things away or delete your e-mails, two things you want to avoid. You need to make sure you're doing the most effective things on a daily, weekly, monthly, and yearly basis.

3. **Execution** - Let's not forget the execution of the production plan you build for your marketing strategy. Just as you write songs or work a tune until it sounds the way you want it to, you

should hone your marketing until it achieves the same level of perfectionism. You've created all the pieces and you've made a plan. Now you're headed to the deep end of the pool. This is a non-stop effort and has to be done relentlessly, diligently, and consistently.

Don't imagine that you'll magically have a team of marketing people who will do all this for you. You'll be the one to stand at the CD table instead of drinking after a gig. You'll be the one who gets up a little early to add a few friends on this or that social network before you head to your day job. Even if you do make it big and have a marketing department behind you, you'll still spend time on phone calls, in interviews, attending events you don't want to attend, and working on things far from music.

Even the biggest names in the industry spend more of their day on marketing than they do on music. It sounds crazy, but it's true. The artist of today, especially an independent, must market and market in the strongest, most effective way possible. You must market better and harder than musicians before you because of how easy it is to market these days.

There are millions of bands with MySpace sites, millions buying up the latest directory and spamming everyone they can, millions trying to sell themselves and their music to new fans, millions trying to be seen by the media. So when you market, your marketing has to stand out. If it doesn't, you're just one in the mix of millions.

So You Think You Have a Background in Marketing

I always find it interesting how many artists just think about the recording and only when it's completed face the scary world of what it's going to take after they release, at which point they have to take a series of steps backward to clean things up before they can move forward effectively. Even when this happens and the artists realize the elements that have to be taken care of—the ones that they missed the first time around—they still cut corners.

If you did the recording right, you didn't cut corners, at least I hope you didn't. So why cut corners on getting the music marketed and solicited the right way? It's essential to find the right plan for marketing. Many artists actually have a sense of what it's going to take. We've all grown up with marketing and branding; it's the same marketing and branding that made us want Cocoa Puffs and Trix. The box was cool or the cartoon was neat.

It worked for us even if we didn't eat that cereal, and those rules apply to music ... mostly. The concept is correct; the execution can be very different. So, back to our artists who decide that the marketing plan they've read about is just too challenging, and when they talk to someone in marketing, they're told, "Oh no, you don't have to do this" or "In marketing, you can easily do that." This is not saying these people who are in marketing are wrong; they're just wrong about marketing musicians, especially independent musicians.

Think about it: A product, whether it's a car, a coffee, or a TV show, is a lot different than an up–and-coming band. I've even seen marketing firms crafted by ex-major-label employees who end up doing more damage than good when it comes to creating a new marketing firm or group.

First off, you need to look at the dollar amount. Some marketing people have a great deal of experience and great ideas when they have a lot of money to spend, but most independent bands are not going to have a budget to throw around like those used for marketing the major-label acts. The whole idea of what you create for marketing items and approaches has to be adjusted to the budget you actually have, as opposed to the budget of the bands you love. Let's say you love a group that has a very detailed logo. You need to understand how much that logo is being put out there and the cash needed for such visibility. That group can afford to have a logo with a little more detail and even a font that might be a little harder to read because the exposure of it allows for it. As an independent artist with a much smaller budget would be advised to go with a logo that's a little easier to read, whether it's on a pen or on a poster, a logo that produces a stronger sense of branding and recognition since he or she doesn't have the money to put it everywhere.

Now this single example can relate to a ton of other elements that answer the question, "Well so and so does it this way so why shouldn't I?" The answer will usually be money and exposure.

Just because some claim to be great marketers doesn't mean they're right for you. You need to find out if they know how to market a product with a minimal to non-existent marketing budget. These people aren't lying when they tell you they know how to market, but lo-fi marketing is an approach that's still being created.

Let's make a sports comparison. Think of a baseball player who is 5'9" and weighs next to nothing but calls himself an athlete. It's true; he's an athlete, but imagine him trying to play on the defensive line of the New England Patriots football team. He would get killed. A football player is an athlete, and a baseball player is an athlete, and some can play both, but more often these are two different worlds of athletics.

Think of marketing the same way, and pay attention to the person who's giving you the advice. Just because someone can sell a car doesn't mean he or she can sell a band. Make the right decisions on the advice you choose to follow. Just because someone tells you to do something and has experience in the field doesn't mean it's the experience that fits your situation. Make sure you move forward with the people who can help you move forward with plans that apply to you, your budget, and your career.

Marketing Essentials

Press and Promo Kits

I push very hard for artists to create the right promo pack. So many people have their view on exactly what a kit should be, and most of them are missing something or adding too much. The package I recommend is a complete and full inventory of what you should have at the ready, though it's not the package you will send to everyone. Think of it as a set of necessary components that you can pull from for any given situation. The press pack for certain venues will differ from others, and the one you send to a label will differ from what you send to a talent buyer or agent. This is also the most cost-effective approach. You can store this package in its separate forms online and on your Web site and then download the pieces needed to fulfill whatever pack you're making. This will reduce print costs as well and will also make it easier to send your components to online package places like Sonic

Bids. This gives you the option to send your promo pack electronically, circumventing print costs altogether. By adding your basic information on Sonic Bids and then including Web links to each of the pages in the pack, you allow the potential persons of interest to pick and choose what they want to see without overwhelming them with too much or leaving them with too little.

Below are the twenty-one pieces you should have in your pack, each one described in detail. Every component should be in its own document with your logo, font, tagline, Web site, and all contact information. Imagine pages being separated or parts lost; each page should be well defined so that it's obvious it belongs to your band. By making every page able to stand on its own, you'll help to brand your band and allow people to find you easily.

Full Press/Promotional Kit

1. Press Kit Folder

2. Compact Disc

3. 8 x 10 Promo Shot

4. Letterhead Page

5. One Pager

6. Review Page

7. Press Release Page

8. Album Information Page

9. Show/Performance Sheet

10. Industry Pro Page

11. Artist Stat Sheet

12. Business Card

13. Postcard

14. ¼ Pager

15. Show Poster

16. Album Poster

17. Return Address Label

18. Artist Sticker or Bumper Sticker

19. DVD of Live Performance/Press Video

20. Stage Plot

21. Input List

1. **Press Kit Folder** – This is the folder that will hold everything. A simple two-fold works, but you want to make sure on the front you have the FONT, TYPE, LOGO, and TAGLINE for the group. To have an insert for a business card inside the folder is a good idea. Some set up a CD insert as well, which has shown to be effective. Then have the Press Package listed. On the backside, either attach a return address label or have the contact information on the center of the back of the folder, either on the bottom or top.

2. **Compact Disc** – Either the album or a demo disc, with the proper graphics and information on the disc to showcase and highlight the group.

3. **8 x 10 Promo Shot** – The 8 x 10 glossy shot of the band. Make sure the picture is formatted with the information below including all contact info.

4. **Letterhead Page** – The letterhead will be used to type or write your cover letter to whomever you're sending the package. Make sure to include on the bottom of every letter that additional information is available upon request. Most of the time you will not be sending all of the twenty-one items, but listing in the letter that those elements are available is a good idea.

5. **One Pager** – This is the basic outline of the group. This includes your extended basic bio, which covers who you are and what you're about. A small photo of the group on this page can be helpful, as well. This page can be constructed off a template of your Letterhead Page by adding the header ONE PAGER, the photo, and the bio. This shows the continuity of graphics and the package as a whole. People want this 90 percent of the time.

6. **Review Page** – This page is for reviews. A common mistake made by artists is to include clipping after clipping of reviews. Keep this to one page. You can use a smaller font to make room for more, but keep it to one page of reviews. Then, mention at the bottom that other reviews are available upon request. This can also use the Letterhead Page template.

7. **Press Release Page** – This is a formatted press release page that can be built off the Letterhead Page template. A press release is an easy way for anyone to grab the news format and copy it into a story that could be written about you. Most of the time, the press release in the package would describe your album release, but it could also be about a special upcoming show or other event of which your group is a part.

8. **Album Information Page** – This page includes the album cover graphic as well as most of the key information about the recording. It includes a short album bio, who worked on it, anything special or different about the recording, the songs, and some comparisons. This will provide reviewers and media people accurate information about your music. This sheet is again based off the Letterhead Page template.

9. **Show/Performance Sheet** – This sheet is a highlight of shows, festivals, openers, showcases, and key events the group has played. This sheet is not required or asked for as much as it used to be, but it is still something some agents and venues want. Emphasize versatility when you can, and if you have mainly done small local venues, you may want to hold off on this sheet until you have more experience under your belt

10. **Industry Pro Page** – This page explains the recordings you have as a whole, and those that are available. This sheet shows you have samples ready, no-vocal versions of songs available for international use, and depending on your style, loops or versions without backups. This is used when the album you created was mastered and produced for various industry outlets.

11. **Artist Stat Sheet** – This is a bullet-point list of that which makes you as a group stand out. The artist stat sheet should contain single-sentence blurbs that explain marketing elements about the group, the album, or other information on the band. This is a sheet that is well received by management and labels.

12. **Business Card** – Having a card that you can slide into the package is very effective. Make sure it has your complete information, as listed above. People often hand off personal or management cards that don't even have the band name on them. Having a card with the contact information, the name of the group, the logo, and the tagline makes for a more professional pack, and makes you more easily recognized. This card will go out with every single pack.

13. **Postcard** – The postcard serves as a small advertisement about the band and the album. This can be used as a mailer and can also have printing on the back for upcoming gigs. Also, the graphic can be used to buy ads in music papers or magazines. This is a great promotional item that can serve numerous purposes.

14. **¼ Pager** – The ¼ pager is just like the postcard, but printed so it breaks out evenly to four small sheets from a piece of 8.5x11 paper. These can be printed on nice stock like the postcard but can also be printed on regular paper.

15. **Show Poster** – Sending a show poster to a venue can be helpful for the venue to do up quickly a poster that has the best information about you. Having this and other items downloadable can mean a venue that's far away has the chance to print up your details and fill in its location for the show. You can make all sorts of different

posters of course, but having a template poster that is available in your pack as well as online is a smart thing to do.

16. **Album Poster** – this is a basic album poster that can be downloaded and placed in stores carrying your recording. It can also be used as a graphic for some online stores. This can also be printed out and used at merchandise tables at shows.

17. **Return Address Label** – Have a strong return label to put on the envelopes you put your packages in. This shows professionalism from the moment someone receives your package. A simple return address label can show the person reviewing the pack that you mean business and that you are covering all bases.

18. **Artist Sticker or Bumper Sticker** – This can be placed somewhere around the venue if being sent to a venue, or just used as some free swag for the receiver. Always put a sticker in the kit – you never know where it will end up.

19. **DVD of Live Performance/Press Video** – This is a bit of an extra, but for some venues, festivals, and labels, showing what you look like and how you do live can be very helpful. Make sure it's clearly marked and distinguished from the CD you send.

20. **Stage Plot** – Sending a stage plot, or a link to a downloadable stage plot is a great idea. Have a well-constructed accurate plot of your stage setup and needs. It can help the venue, will make your shows better, and will make you look very prepared and professional.

21. **Input List** – Some venues want the input list straight out. They can figure it out from the stage plot, but having an input list ready as well is a good idea.

I know. It's a lot of stuff. But there's no denying that the BGE full press/promotional kit covers all the bases and showcases the artist in the most professional and polished way with the materials being organized, concise, and clear. Yes, it's true, most bands don't have this pack together, but do you want to be like most bands? Organizing a packet like this will allow for many more opportunities and make booking and solicitation much easier. Don't cut the corners that you see others cut; set a new mark and then watch the returns on your efforts. When you cover all the bases, you will find a lot more doors open for you.

Promotional Photos

Promotional photos are the physical images that represent you as an artist or band. It's important to send the right message through with photos, showcasing the artist in a professional and original format.

Try to get five key shots:

1. Show the artist or band in front of clear a background. Go for simple poses—not contrived—while looking toward the camera.

2. Same as shot number one, but look away from the camera. The group can be looking at each other or looking in one general direction.

3. A fun shot—have a shot that shows a sense of humor or at least has the artist smiling.

4. A serious shot. Don't look tough, but think serious. Think about the music, the craft, and the respect you want to achieve.

5. A live shot. Show the band playing. See if you can get into a venue early and get a shot of the band on a **nice stage, with microphones up and lights on, insinuating a performance.**

This set of shots will cover you for your press kit 8 x 10 and other promo shots. Don't hesitate to touch them up in Photoshop if you need to. If you have the budget, definitely hire a photographer. This can't be stated enough: These pictures are an important part of your package so it's worth it to take them seriously.

Original photos that are simple images are the best. Stay away from busy backgrounds. They can pull the eye away from the artist and create a confusing visual experience. Go with solid colors that work well in both color and black-and-white pictures.

The artist should not wear clothes with labels or logos. Steer clear of items that have any kind of writing or distinguishing marks.

Since marketing and merchandise opportunities can arise from these pictures, you want to make sure a potential client sees you as a blank canvas. Stay away from things that look too contrived, like wearing sunglasses or creating shots with the drum-kit setup in places where it would not normally be. Avoid stereotypes in these pictures—don't make the gang signs, don't try for the tough-guy or tough-girl look, don't overly slut it out in your wardrobe, don't try to be so different in a picture that it just comes off stupid. It's always best to be as natural and relatable as possible.

You can still be creative. Think about setting up a shot with a theme in your wardrobe or with a theme that relates to one of your songs or the name of the album. Make sure the background is clean and simple, or at least organized. Check out your pictures for lighting, and make sure you don't have excessive shadows on your face and body.

Wear clothes that fit you or fit the sound you're playing. Deliver the image in the same professional manner as you deliver your music, your marketing, and your promotion. Promotional pictures are just another key element. Give them the attention they deserve and you will see better results across the board.

Marketing Your Shows

I receive a lot of questions about the right way to market and promo an upcoming show. One problem I find with some artists is that they market a single show and don't think past that. Each time you promote a show, it's wise to think of how you can promote your group for future appearances, acquiring information that may be helpful later on while getting your name out there even more.

Press Releases

The first step in promoting your show is the construction of a proper press release. Putting up flyers is not enough, and you can't simply count on your networking sites or mailing lists either. This is especially important if you're playing a show in a new area: Announce it to the media at least four weeks before the show. The four-week window allows papers and radio stations to have an opportunity to list you and possibly do a story on you. Sending out releases and information on gigs only a couple of weeks before the gig often misses the deadlines of these papers and won't help you with any additional press. E-mail or fax the release to the venue, the booking agent, and the local media for that city.

If you have the money, or if it's a larger show, use a press release distribution company. I stand behind Chris Simmons and www.Send-2press.com. I have known Chris Simmons for a number of years and love how he handles his business. He's also a musician, which made a difference to me early on. Send2Press can help you write the release as well. They have different options for different locations and a plan of attack for where releases can go. Take a peek at the options. It's a solid choice if you have some money that you can invest into a release. Going with a larger scale release when you're putting out a recording is also a smart choice; it will reach a much larger audience.

If you're sending the release out yourself, research the locations that you're sending it to. For each venue or city you're playing, find a number of places to which you can send it. Keep this list for the next time you're returning to that city or location, and you'll have less to research.

If you're playing a number of shows in your hometown or somewhere in a twenty-five-mile radius, pick the show that should be the best one and forego the rest. It's best not to play more than one show in a twenty-five-mile radius in a six-week period. Again, this gives crowds the sense that they need to see you. Don't give them the option of seeing you this week or next week or the week after that.

As for where to send your press releases, research the cities you'll be playing in. Find the local TV stations, radio stations, newspapers, weekly entertainment papers, college media papers, and Web sites. Find out about local networking/promotional sites for that town. You can dig in and find a good number of places to send this release. Find out who the music writers and entertainment writers are. With the Internet today, it's easy to do these things yourself. Doing this kind of research will also create a very useful database for you to use and also to trade with other bands that might be coming to that city. In turn, those bands may have information on another city that you can use. Work the collective and communal aspect as it will allow you to get more information more quickly.

The Body

Make sure you fill in all the pertinent information. You need to be fast and precise, bringing a basic marketing element to your release. Every piece of information regarding the show and all its elements should be in there. Remember the old who, what, when, where, why, and how. The "why" is your marketing angle. Don't portray it as just another show. Bring something special to each night and find an angle that would make a newspaper, radio station, TV station, or Web site look and want to do an article. Think about it: The media receives dozens of releases, so just as you should make your band stand out, you need to make your release stand out.

The Parts

A release can be formatted in a number of different ways. I've found this format to be the most conducive to getting stories and interviews.

The biggest rule, and Chris taught me this, is DON'T USE CAPS ANY MORE!!!! Don't lead the headlines with capital letters.

Here is the breakdown of the parts and a sample release that I wrote with a band for a show.

1. "For immediate release" – This differentiates the releases that are set for a later date.

2. Fill in the Event, Date, Time, Location, and Tickets lines. Start right out with what this is, for the media.

3. Headline – Bring your solid headline about the show and the band.

4. Lead – Where is it coming from, what is the date of the release, and who is putting it out?

5. Lead Paragraph – Sum up the show, the location, and the band. If there is a special element about the show or some kind of marketing touch, add it here.

6. Band Biography – Do the brief bio of the band.

7.   Venue Biography – Do a brief bio of the location. You can usually grab it from the venue's Web site. Give the start time for the band.

8.   For more info – Give the Web site and number for the venue, and give the Web site for your band. These days you can add your most popular social networking site as well.

9.   Contact Info – Close with the contact info for the release. Specify who the contact point is and how he or she can be reached for a potential interview.

10.   Note to editors – Adding this note for potential reviews of the album you're pushing can help get requests for stories or reviews of the album.

Here's an example:

For Immediate Release

Event: The Acme Band

Date: Friday, February 12, 2010

Time: 9:00 p.m. show

Location: The Counterbalance, 1424 Queen Anne Ave N., Seattle, WA 98109

Tickets: $10.00 Cover

The Acme Band hosts a fun and live musical journey through the universe of soul, funk, rock, and blues at the Counterbalance.

Seattle, WA – January 19, 2010 / Music Maids Management/ MMM/ The Acme Band will take the stage at the Counterbalance in Seattle, Washington, on Friday, February 12, 2010 for a fun evening of live music aimed to stir your mind and shake your behind. This show is part of the group's winter 2010 tour called the "We Sent You Tour." This tour is supporting their latest release, *Muzicke*. Twenty-five percent of every copy sold is donated to a non-profit music organization in the Pacific Northwest that helps children's music programs.

The Acme Band, based out of Seattle, Washington, has blasted off for a musical journey through the universe of soul, funk, rock, and blues. As likely to be inspired by Weezer or N. E. R. D. as they are by Otis Redding or Led Zeppelin, the Acme band will surely move your head, your heart, and your ass. The Acme Band is out of control rock and soul.

Bred on a steady diet of the roots of rock and blues, the Acme Band was schooled on the legends of Motown soul, funk, and rock & roll. Musical sponges to this day and embracing all the technology that modern music has to offer, the Acme Band is just as exciting to see live as they are to hear through your speakers. The Acme Band brings you party music for the 21st century, with the power to stir your mind and shake your behind.

The Counterbalance is located in the Queen Anne section of Seattle, Washington, with a stage, bar, and a barbershop. Formerly Christine's Rock Room, the Counterbalance opened in 2006 with a commitment to great food, spirits, and haircuts, a welcoming staff and environment, and continued support of quality live music.

The show starts at 9:00 p.m. Come see the Acme Band at the Counterbalance, Friday, February 12, 2010 and try one of ten beers they have on tap or a haircut. This show is 21+. For more information on the Counterbalance, please visit www.counterbalancemusicandhair.com or give them a call at 206-494-0827. For more information on the Acme Band, please visit www.theacmeband.com.

Contact:
Marian Li-Pino

Music Maids Management
2212 Queen Anne Avenue North #347, Seattle, WA 98109
Ph: 206.376.9798
Em: info@musicmaids.com
Wb: www.musicmaids.com

Note to editors: Review copies of the *Muzicke* CD available
to media pros on request.

-END-

There are other ways to format releases, but this is an effective
one and it gets attention. Don't drag on in a release, and remember that
the person receiving your release is also receiving a great many more.
The more people you reach, the more people you tell and the better the
chance you'll be heard and your music will be passed along.

After the Press Release

The press release is essential, but it's only the beginning. For any show,
especially for any new area you're playing in, do some Internet research
to find out some key information that will help your promotions:

3 major newspapers

3 major radio stations

3 local music or entertainment papers/magazines

3 TV networks

3 colleges or schools in the area and their arts and entertainment
sections

10 networking sites/entertainment groups for that city

10 online communities for that city

You can dig deeper and find even more avenues if you wish. As
you find these e-mails, fax numbers, and addresses, SAVE THEM.
Create a new database that will allow you to go right to it the next
time you're playing that venue or city. You'll be able to send out your
information much faster.

About three weeks before the show, start posting on message boards, craigslist, and social networking sites. Two weeks out, do it again. Don't over spam, but as you strategically send information multiple times, it will be recognized and remembered, more each time, and will more likely be taken seriously.

If you have friends in the city where you're playing, try and get them to do a couple of series of posterings. Doing a huge blitz right before the show is actually not as effective as putting up fewer posters more often. Do this over a few weeks before the show, and you'll get a better turn out. If you have the funds to hire a postering service, make sure it does a couple of different hits. Upon arrival, if you have time before or after the sound check, toss a few more posters up as well. Make sure the poster has the right information on it. Mention where you're from and make sure the information, location, date, and price are clear and easy to read. Make sure your Web site is also on the poster.

Contact the venues or booking agents and tell them you're doing all you can to market the show. They will be thrilled and might be able to supply you with a list of media contacts. You're helping to fill a venue and make them money as well, so in turn you'll find most venues will be more than happy to help you help them.

If you've already created merchandise, send some free discs, a couple of shirts or whatever you have to some of the media contacts along with a press release. Free swag is always welcome.

Being different is a key element as well. What's different about your band or the show? Is there some kind of giveaway, special anniversary, or something that you can tie in to the city? Add an additional marketing element to the show, and it may bring more people out than those just those looking to go to a show.

Any day in which you can take a few minutes doing a few small steps can bring back big returns. Add a few new friends or connections on your social networking sites, find out about a college radio station in a town you're playing next month, or research some bands that pack the house and see if you can get a double bill with them.

Every step you take toward promoting on a wider scale will not only help the show that you're promoting but will also help you for the next time you come back and allow you more exposure as a whole.

What's So Special about This Show?

It's funny to see some of the flyers and posters bands create to market their shows. I've seen more shows listed online or posters on telephone poles that say, "MUST SEE SHOW" or "CAN'T MISS SHOW" or "HAVE TO BE THERE." Then there was, "THIS SHOW WILL BE AMAZING" and my favorite: "YOU WOULD BE A FOOL TO NOT BE THERE."

OK, now the unfortunate part, for starters, is that 90 percent of the time there's nothing backing up these claims. The attempt at strong marketing is there, but nothing is brought into focus, which translates to all talk. When you want to promote a show and make a claim that's a little grander, then back it up.

Here's an example: When stores say you can't miss a particular sale, if it's solid marketing, it's backed up with a reason. For example, "CAN'T MISS SALE 4-15-09!!!! Only once a year, 50 percent off all shoes and boots!!!!!" So what has been created is the hype, which is in big block lettering, followed by some reasons why the date is pertinent—the whole "only happens once a year" part. That creates a sense of urgency by saying if you miss it, it won't be happening again for a long time. Lastly, there's the key marketing point telling you why you should go and why it's only once a year: the 50 percent off. That's a pretty steep reduction and something that will probably be the hook point for people to get down there and stock up on shoes and boots.

Get it? You've got the hard statement and the date. The reason why the date is so special. Then the reason why being there is so special. This is an example of effective marketing, which will capture an audience and capture sales.

In the exact same way, as a performing musician or band, you should want to capture the audience and the sales of your music and your merchandise. However, if you call your show a "can't miss" or "must see," and it's just another show, then you're basically crying wolf, or fire in a packed theatre. After a while, people are going to catch on and your "can't miss" shows will be missed by more and more people.

In the same way, if you really have more of a must-see kind of experience, maybe some big name sitting in with you or some wild element that makes this particular show above the others, but have been claiming "must see" about everything, it may be ignored and not attended. So don't cry wolf, and don't tell people the theatre is on fire, unless, of course, it is. Make sure that if you call it a "must see" show, you define the elements of why it's a "must see." Remember, it has to go well beyond just you performing. Those are normal shows, just like a store operates every day when it doesn't have sales. You have to curb the ego enough to realize that not every show is a "must see" or a "can't miss"; otherwise you'll turn away your audience and any potential new fans.

With that being said, how do you create a show that can carry the elements of a "must see" or "can't miss" performance?

Let's review the three signage points.

1. **You've got the hard statement and the date.**

   This is where you have the "can't miss," "must see," "have to be there," or however you want to phrase it. This is the part where you capture the attention. This is also where most artists stop, and that's why they lose the momentum and the crowds. So at this point, take it to the second and third steps.

2. **The reason why the date is so special**

and

3. **The reason why attending and being there is so special for this night over others**

   Do you have a famous person sitting in with you? Have you not performed in nine to twelve weeks and will you not be appearing again for at least a couple of months? This brings greater truth to it being a "can't miss" kind of show since, if people do miss it, they won't get to see you again for a long time. Are you applying some kind of marketing element to make the show special? Are you giving away a percentage of the night's proceeds to charity? Are there going to be any prizes? Is there a special anniversary, something to mark the date that makes it different from others? Are you filming a video? Can you think of some kind of creative marketing approach or stunt to draw more attention than usual?

If you can't answer yes to any of the above, it's not a "must see." Sorry, but it just isn't. If you're playing a club or venue and doing your set with some other bands doing their sets, it isn't a "must see." It's a show, which is what musicians do every night. This doesn't take away from the music or the band being special, but it *is* business as usual.

Create and plan for some "must see's," but make them worth the description. The more you secure your marketing and the truth in your advertising, the more you will be able to grow a fan base that will not only like your music, but trust your word and your marketing. In the end this will make your announcements and your promotions more respected and believed. Then, if you say they can't miss it, they will actually believe you and show up. Isn't that exactly what you're trying to get out of them anyway?

The Yin and Yang of Band to Fan

Not long ago I spoke to a band that was complaining that the people coming to their shows were bothering them too much afterwards when they were tired and didn't want to socialize. I tried not to laugh as we sat in a coffee shop and just looked at them and said, "You are either in the wrong business, or you need to become songwriters or members of a backup band. It comes down to a simple fact: Your fans are your lifeline to the continuity and sustainability of your career. There are no two ways about it."

If you've chosen the route of being performing and touring artists, you have a responsibility to your fans, not only to perform for them but also to solidify them into your fan base and continue to cultivate and grow that base. In a way, you can look at it like this: your fans are your bosses. If you grow a fan base that's solid enough, you'll be able to survive on the sales of your music, your merchandise, and your performances. The fans are the ones who are fronting that cash. It's easy for musicians to lose sight of that.

It's true that larger scale artists are more private. They're not as approachable and easily seen before or after a show. Some of these artists do connect, but they have such a large fan base and such a solid following that it allows them a little more privacy yet exposes them to a higher level of publicity with enough frequency to maintain that status. While they might not shake every hand at a show, they were most likely up at the crack of dawn doing morning radio spots, TV appearances, and numerous newspaper and magazine interviews.

So that emulation of trying to be elusive after a show is only going to hurt you when you're still a new act, trying to solidify your fan base. Just as you give your fans a piece of you as you share the music in recordings, they are giving you their attention and their enthusiasm. This is not a one-on-one relationship. You are going to try to capture as many fans as possible, and at the same time, those fans probably have a thousand other bands that they like as well.

There is a yin and yang to the foundation that can be built between you and your fans. Every action has a reaction: As you solidify your base, they purchase your tickets and downloads and become walking billboards for your merchandise. Think of every act committed by a fan. Have you ever received a letter? A friend request on a networking site? An e-mail? Respond to all these things with a letter back or thank them for the request, and do it in an honorable way. If someone added you and mentioned how much they think you're cool and like your music, respond with a "thank you" and something personal. Don't just advertise yourself on their page to try to capture more fans. By making this kind of response, you connect on a more personal level and increase the possibility of those people sharing you with others.

Take time before and after the shows. Say hello to everyone. If some look like they want to say hi but seem shy, approach them. That goes for guys and girls. Make sure you're not just flirting. Talk to everyone. Remember they paid money for your show and took time from their day to support you. Talk to people. Many fans want a sense of connection with a band that they like, so give it to them. Think of ways where you can personalize your approach to fans as they have personalized an approach to you.

You will better understand what to do when you step back and see that there are two sides working together. Too many musicians get caught up in the "holier than thou" vibe, and that is not what it's about. These people—these fans, these purchasers at shows, and online—are giving you the ability to have a lifestyle of self-sufficiency in music. You have to recognize this. Once you do, you will connect more with your audience and your fans and promote a strong reciprocal connection. It's all a balancing act, and once you accept that angle, you can take the necessary steps to solidify your fan base and ensure its constant growth.

Conventional Marketing Avenues

Merchandise

Marketing your secondary products can be just as crucial as pushing the music itself. When people wear your shirt, your hat, or any piece of clothing that you have your stamp on, they're marketing and promoting you. People can't wear your music. I mean, no one is walking around with boom boxes on their shoulders anymore. So *you* have to create product and merchandise that is going to draw people to want to wear it, display it, or share it.

This comes back to the logo and font uniformity that you should already be using. I can't stress it enough. The font and logo you're using on the Web site, the CD, your promotional materials, and your branding should carry over to merchandise. Your merchandise is another level of promoting, marketing, and branding your image, your music, and your product. The continuity will define and make people remember you, your name, and your likeness. Then when they are drawn to the music, they will want the secondary products and support you in ways you can't even pay for.

I recommend artists start with Web sites like CafePress. Cafe-Press is a print by order site that will create a single item with your image and upload. The upside is that you can have a number of different items created that people can choose from. The downside is that they are a little more expensive, you will not make as much profit, and sometimes the quality is a little less. I believe having a site like this in conjunction with selling merchandise you've bought in bulk is a good idea. The more people who are wearing your shirts, displaying you on coffee cups, stickers, notebooks, towels, or whatever else, the more people will see you.

Think about creating items that can get to the most people possible. Are you friends with a number of bars and restaurants? Then do a run of coasters with your logo, your font, tagline, and Web site on it. Who knows? This can be incredibly effective. You may also send these items—posters, flyers—to clubs and bars you're playing a few weeks out to push the promotional campaign for that show. Remember, branding is the staple. The more people who see you, recognize you, and remember you, the better the chances that they will come to see you.

Setting aside a merchandise account and having certain monies brought from each member as well as a percentage taken off the top of gigs and profits will help you create more and more merchandise, which you will be able to put out to more and more people.

Think outside the box. Create items people aren't used to. Why not try a small line of towels or even sheets? Get creative; the worst-case scenario is that you might have to give away a product for free. But remember, even if you're giving it away, it's adding to your marketing. DO NOT view merchandise as profit. It can be nice to make some profit off merchandise, but the artists that look to use the revenue from merchandise sales to make more merchandise get their brand out much more. Make the stickers, create the clothes, have the hats, and hell, even make the pens. Get that merchandise out there.

Create contests that will inspire people to both buy and showcase your merchandise. When you create the stickers, offer a contest on your Web site once a month: the coolest place where one of your stickers shows up in a picture wins a CD or another merchandise item like a tee shirt. Think about it, somebody might be going to France, sticks one of your stickers on a pole by the Eiffel Tower, and takes a picture of it. This is now a cool picture to add to your site *and* you're being promoted in Paris. Or, maybe a couple of girls take pictures of themselves in Las Vegas with your shirts on. These are all great merchandise marketing elements.

Be creative: Every single piece of merchandise you sell or give away is one more way you can be seen and remembered. On some of it, make sure you have a Web site or a way to find you. For example, a tee shirt with a logo and a font is great and can be artistic and cool to wear, but a coffee cup with that logo, that font, and the Web site on the other side, might get someone to find you a little easier. Just as you set up your logos with the different formations of logo, font, tag, and Web, you can create merchandise in the same way.

Get your name out, get your image out, and get your Web site out. Allow people to find you through merchandise—both apparel and novelty items—that is well made. Go for the tee shirts, but don't forget the pens, the cups, the napkins. Hell, I even know people who have done urinal cakes with their logo on them. Anything memorable that will make someone take a second look is one more effective way to reach an audience and fan base that has not been able to see you yet.

Reviews

Reviews of the band for live performances, recordings, and individual songs are very helpful for marketing and promoting your group. They also fill up that review sheet you should have with your press package, which in turn can help you get reviews. A common problem with reviews in promo packages is that there are either too many or too few. I've seen band posters and promo packs in which artists list numerous reviews from the same paper, even the same article. I've also seen artists list reviews from only a single area. For example, if you're in Seattle and you have a review from the *Stranger*, the *Seattle Weekly*, and the *Seattle Times*, it reads that you are possibly too concentrated or localized. Some bands stack their packets with reviews, full of cutout copies and sheet after sheet of text. I received a promo pack from an artist that had twenty pages of reviews. This is too much. It's a waste of money to make those copies and a waste of a packet to put them in.

So how do you get reviews to put onto the review page and the Web site and posters? It's actually easier than you think.

First, go after a review every day. I'm not talking about contacting the *New York Times* or *Rolling Stone*. Start with the Internet. There are thousands of review sites out there where you don't even have to send full albums; you can actually send them digital samples or MP3s. (Of course, make sure your copyright and publishing is in order before you start sending the music out.)

Look past the Web sites, though. Most major cities have local arts papers. These folks will want a physical copy, and I believe that if you're sending out one copy a week to a reviewer or paper that has some credentials and has been reviewing for some time, you're setting yourself up for more recognition and a better chance of receiving reviews.

Next, do some research. How do certain magazines review artists? Find out about their credentials and requirements for reviewing music.

Make sure you're following the instructions; otherwise you chance being tossed in the trash. At the same time, make sure the reviewer is not someone just looking for a free disc; there's a lot of that out there as well.

When you're looking to get better reviews, you want to show a review sheet that will make someone give you better reviews. Many see this as kind of a lose-lose situation. If you don't have any reviews, how are you going to get someone interested in giving you reviews? Then again if you only have reviews locally, how do you get someone to review you and see you as a national act and not just an artist that only has local reviews?

The answer is actually kind of simple, but it still seems to evade people. Go to the smaller local reviewers, but not just in your market. If you're from Boston, then e-mail or contact the Los Angeles, Seattle, Chicago, Houston, Atlanta, San Diego, and Miami markets.

Think about it—how much cooler and more professional does it look to have reviews from all across the country, even if they're from smaller papers or Web sites, instead of a whole bunch of reviews from just your hometown? Giving the sense that your music reaches further than county lines can make a big impression.

Showing people who may either hire you or review you that you have reached outside of your backyard will not only show your drive; it will also show that you are pushing beyond comfortable boundaries, and that can mean more to you than just the review.

What about people you know? Ask your producer, your engineer, local clubs, or places you have played for reviews as well. The options are endless. You can fill those review pages and the reviews on your Web site very easily.

Make sure that you're grabbing legitimate reviews too. Don't add reviews from places where you can make it up yourself. For example, reviews from CD Baby, and most social networking sites are not reviews to have in your package. Yes, these are fans, and you don't want to take that away, but using them gives the appearance that you're really trying to get any review you can. The other thing is that anyone can write a review on CD Baby or any of these other sites. Make sure that your reviews are coming from professionals or writers. They hold more water.

One last note on reviews—it never hurts to have a sense of humor. One of my personal reviews on my producer and drummer promo sheets is "What a jerk, I never want to see him again." – Loren's Ex Girlfriend. Now, whether there is truth to it, and in some cases there is, it's still funny. It also adds an element of humor and shows that you don't take yourself too seriously. In the world of huge music egos, this can fall in your favor.

A solid review sheet can have small fonts with the logo or name of the given paper or reviewer as well as either the date it was posted or the importance of who reviewed you. Cut out one-liners and short paragraphs from these reviews. Give the person seeing your review sheet a lot to see very fast and over a very broad region. Keep it down to a sheet or two sheets if you really feel the need. You can also supplement the review sheet by adding links on the bottom to a review page on your Web site, to a blog on your networking or blog sites with even more reviews, or to the locations of the articles written about you. This is much better and is a much more professional way to streamline your reviews and get the people reading them to check out as much as they can.

As you get better reviews from larger scale papers or higher echelon people, remove some that might be a little less recognizable instead of filling up too many pages with every review. On the Web site, categorize the reviews from where they are. Provide a table of contents so readers can sift through the reviews at their leisure and not have to scroll down twenty pages, which I have seen. Big no-no, don't do it.

A solid review sheet or couple of review pages can be very refreshing to those who are used to seeing poorly put-together packets. Capture their attention with the streamlining and ease of scanning your reviews. It will lead you to better and more reviews, as well as more opportunities.

The review page makes a difference. You should treat it as one of the most important parts of your package. Make your review page draw people in so they'll take the time to read each entry and make it apparent that they're from all over. Make reviewers of your review page see that they need to book you, sign you, or for that matter, review you.

Interviews

Reviews, interviews, and stories are a must in the entertainment industry. They help to give exposure to your group and your music, as well as support the press and media packages that you need to build online and in your physical press kits. Many artists don't like interviews, while other artists might like them a little too much.

The more packages you get out, the more you play. The more you promote, the more opportunities you will come across, on all different levels, to be interviewed. It's important to be prepared and to present yourself in a way that will make it easy to convey what you're all about while at the same time making it difficult for the interviewing party to get information wrong or misquote you. Not every writer is perfect; many are far from it at times. Going into every interview as prepared as possible to help the person doing the interviewing will, in turn, help get the best potential story out about you and your music.

First, treat the interviewer with respect, regardless of how small the paper, the radio station, or the Web site. When people feel respected, it makes them more interested. Don't pull a rock star attitude; these people have seen it more than enough times. Be different, be respectful, and be ready.

Whether you're meeting at a show, your rehearsal space, a coffee shop, or anywhere, make sure to be on time. It doesn't matter if they're late, but if they are, then just be better and more professional. These things will stand out and last in the mind of your interviewer. Remember, some of these people do this all day long. When you make their life easier, they will want to make your story or review better.

Send along an artist stat sheet in advance of the interview, or bring one with you to the interview. An artist stat sheet is basically a bullet pointed sheet with key marketing and promotional points about the band. Short, one- to two-sentence bullet points that would be easy for the interviewer to insert into the story or review will help the chances of the article coming out a lot better. Many upper echelon acts and labels will send out a basic version of the stat sheet before appointments with high profile interviewers. In some cases, this is even where it is listed what questions can and can't be asked. Don't even go there ... just giving an example.

Be ready for the questions. You may not know every question you're going to be asked, but for questions that are directed toward the band, the more uniform and consistent you are on the key elements of the group, the better. Make sure to promote and repeat things throughout the interview, whether they're writing notes down or taping you. Your tagline, your Web site, your album name, and the single you are promoting can all be brought up. Brand it into their minds so it will get into the story.

Talk slowly and clearly. Be heard. Again, whether the interviewer has a recorder or is taking notes, try to speak so your words are easy to take down or easy to understand when being played back.

Now, I'm not suggesting that you be all business. Please don't take that from these ideas. It can be an enjoyable experience, so have fun with it. But at the same time, behave. If you feel something is off the record, don't bring it up, and if you want to avoid a question, be smooth as you move your interviewer away from the subject. Anything is better than "No comment" or "Next question."

Keep your delivery fresh and new while keeping it consistent and accurate. You may be asked the same question by fifty different people. It is tedious. You might get into a situation where you do a series of interviews in the same day and are asked almost the same questions over and over again. Keep in mind that these are separate interviewers and they are there for separate stories, so it's your responsibility to answer each question with the same fresh approach that you gave the first person. A tired physical response or a sigh in response to a question can put off an interviewer, and you may get things written about you that you don't want to see.

Turn off the phone, or if there is a crucial call that may be coming in, let the interviewer know at the beginning of the session. Don't be one of those people who plays diva and picks up every call, going on and on. This is their time too, and it's time that has the potential to help you from a promotional and marketing standpoint. Never forget that.

The reason you want to try to answer the same questions in the same way is to show a consistency across the stories and reviews written about you. When industry professionals see consistency, it builds trust in you and your product. You want to have fun, and you can word things in different ways, but your answers related to the basic topics, like how the group formed, info on the album, future plans, your shows, and so on, should have a similar ring to them.

It can be a strength to have a spokesperson for the band who handles the interviews. The person who is most patient might be the guy or girl for the job. Another note: Make sure that you don't go on and on when you're asked a question; try to stay brief. Don't give a dissertation on each question.

Lastly, regardless of how tired you are, how spent you are, how many times you have heard the same question over and over and over again, be happy to be there. If you're at a café, offer to buy the interviewer a coffee. If you're at a bar, offer a beer. These people deal with so many egocentric, over-the–top, and rude people; give them a break from that. Look at it from the standpoint that, though they're doing a job for someone else, they're likely helping you out in the end.

It doesn't matter whether it's a big media group or a small local radio station that's doing the interview. Your answers should hit home the quick bullet points, your core message. Don't come off arrogant or cocky. Make sure to give thanks to those who are seeing the shows, buying your music, and supporting you. With every interview, you have another piece of media for your press kit, your Web site, and possibly other links where you can be read about or searched for online. So make every one count, be respectful, and watch the results.

Magazine and Advertising Runs

So, you've got a little bit of money, and you want to do an ad campaign that goes a little farther than just stickering or having people post things about you online. Don't get me wrong, I'm not undermining the importance of those elements in the least; they're absolutely necessary, but if you can begin to build a budget that allows you to take advertising to another level, it's a very all-sorts-of-good thing. (One of my favorite lines in the studio …"That was very all sorts of good.")

Research is a core element of advertising. Finding out the best places to advertise and the prices for placing your ad is important. Even if you don't advertise in a magazine or newspaper or trade paper that you research, keep that information and build an advertising database for yourself. For that matter, you should be building databases for everything. If you found out about it or researched it, keep that info. It might not apply right now, but it could be useful down the line.

Back to the ads ... Create and have available for download on your Web site a number of different ads in different dimensions. The basic dimensions for advertising are listed in most advertising sections of magazines, Web sites, newspapers, and other media formats. Find out what they require, what the options are, and the pricing. Trust me, *Spin* magazine might not call you back if you want a story done about your band, but send a letter, make a call, or send an e-mail saying you're interested in ad space and you will get information back, pronto!

There are many options in advertising from print to Web. Spend some time to find out about how long an ad can run. If it's on the Web, find out about click-throughs, impressions, and different page locations. While some places will be crazy expensive and might not be something you can afford, others will have great options and rates.

It's best not to spend your entire advertising budget all at once in a whole bunch of locations. Spread it out!!!!!

When bands get an insurgence of funds and bring it to advertising, they often buy ads that are way too expensive and way too small. You don't need to advertise in the back page of *Rolling Stone* for a single month. For the same amount of money you spent purchasing an ad that no one will look at in a major national magazine, you can buy six larger and more eye-catching ads over six months in the smaller city magazines.

Again, think when you advertise. Buy just a single ad a month and see how it works for you. Does it bring in more fans? Do sales go up? Do you get more people added to your e-mail list when you post in the *New England Performer*, or is it better when you buy an ad in the *Seattle Stranger*? Either way, separate so you can clearly tell the difference.

Also, long-term advertising keeps your presence and awareness more consistent. Many artists and even management groups will buy a flurry of ads all at once. This can help with a spike but does not give bands long-term exposure.

Figure out what you want to advertise as well. Do you want to promo a tour? Are you just getting the word out on the band and its Web site, or do you want to advertise a new album or release? Plan your ad accordingly and figure out what audience you're going after.

Think about what different places might be most effective. Every ad doesn't have to be placed in a music magazine or an entertainment-based publication or site. Why not buy an ad in a magazine or Web site that is not focused on music yet somehow ties into you or your fan base? For example, one Goth band that I knew had a great deal of success advertising their Web site and new album in a clothing magazine. In fact, the sales went so well, they renewed the ad for another month.

Also figure out what is not effective. If an ad doesn't work well for you in a certain publication or on a certain Web site, make note of which one and keep that information. Track and study the results. This will help you know where the best places are to advertise and market yourself.

Try small ads in obscure locations. See if there's a college newspaper that's either daily or weekly and try a week run for the album in that publication. You never know. There's not a set marketing plan that will guarantee success, but the more you can experiment, the better chance you'll have at a different type of exposure.

Start off small. Buy a couple of Web ads; see how they work. Research advertising in all kinds of mediums and markets. Move around the country; if you place an ad in Seattle one month, try Atlanta the next. If you advertise in the UCLA student paper one week, try NYU the next. Bounce around, find your market, and reach people that might never have heard of you otherwise. This approach can really help you connect with audiences on a much more effective and widespread level.

Soliciting

So you have the recording, the press package, the Web site, the social network sites set up and all your materials in order, and you're ready to solicit. Whether it's for shows, management, labels, talent buyers, agencies, booking agents, tours, festivals, or anything else, you want to make it complete and professional. It is a REALLY good idea to have all your materials in order and ready. Having the package ready and all your materials, inside and out, in the shape it should be is extremely important and will allow for the most opportunities and callbacks.

The package that was discussed in the press pack section is everything you should have available, but it's not always what you want to send. Make sure you set up a specific packet for each individual to whom you send something. In the intro letter, you can always mention that you have additional materials available for download. This allows immediate and instant access to whoever wants it.

For example, on the bottom of your cover letter or as a last page in the package you can list …

More information available upon request. Needed documents can be mailed, faxed, or downloaded at the following locations.

Stage Plot – located at www.theacmeband.com/stageplot

Input List – located at www.theacmeband.com/inputlist

By having these links listed on your cover letter or back page, it offers everything that people might need or request without overwhelming them.

Fast-forward a couple of steps: You have the materials, music, professional layout, and a package that is specifically designed for the person to whom you are sending it. Now, how do you send it?

Having a strong cover letter is the primary element. This is where you make your case and where you will either stand out from the rest or blend in with everyone else. This is also where too many bands and artists make many mistakes. Arrogance, ego, and attitude are not what you want to portray here. Doing so will bring you down in most cases.

Below are the top five worst things you can put in the cover letter. This list was made up with help from friends in the industry. We had a good chuckle e-mailing our favorites back and forth. The funniest part was that all of us, in all different parts of the industry, have heard all of them at one time or another.

Top Five Worst Things to Put in a Cover Letter

1. We are totally new and different.
2. We are on the verge of blowing up big time.
3. We are the next big thing.
4. We will deliver the best show you have ever seen.
5. We don't sound like anyone else.

Of course you want to be confident and being assertive is good, but **always avoid the above phrases!!!!!** They are red flags for all industry pros. It's just unprofessional. Address your audience as if they were your heroes. Would you tell a person who booked one of your favorite shows of all time, some legendary act, that you are going to blow him or her away?

Below are some very professional opening ideas that are used in the industry.

Offer yourself or your band as a service. Highlight in a brief outline how you can be a strong entity to book, sign, or hire.

Show that you are easy to work with, professional, and business-minded. You want to display that it would be a good business move for the person, company, or venue to bring you in. You have to look at it from the other's side.

Soliciting is not a linear process. It is a parallel one. Just as you want a gig, a manager, a label, or a tour, you have to show, in turn, that you have the strongest potential to make it a good arrangement for the person with whom you're dealing.

Explain your marketing; use your artist stat sheet to define your marketing and promotional abilities.

Ask nicely! Even when presented with rider and contract options, don't be selfish. Take what you need and don't be the rock star with over-the-top requests. When people are offered the world, honor and respect goes to those who take only what they truly need. You will be asked back sooner, you will be taken more seriously, and you will be considered more professional.

Soliciting can be a scary thing, but it doesn't have to be. Remember: Come off strong, assertive, confident, and professional. Edit your work. Make sure the cover letter and package are correctly put together for the person to whom you are sending it. This is the step where you reach out and pull the industry to you. Make sure everyone you reach sees the best picture possible.

The Art of the E-mail Contact

The ignorance, the arrogance, and the unprofessional nature of the solicitous e-mails I receive on a daily basis from artists or their management never ceases to amaze me. I'm told this goes for overall basic e-mail etiquette in any and every profession. Still, the lack of effort is jaw dropping.

I'm a music producer and run a small music production and consulting company. On any given day, I receive an average of twenty e-mails that are completely out of left field. We're talking the "wheel is turning, but the hamster is dead" kind of e-mails. That totals about one hundred of those a week. Again, I'm a solo music producer running a small organization, so just imagine for a moment how many e-mails the big boys must receive.

If you're soliciting an individual, think about what you're sending out and to whom you're sending it. Your lack of preparation, consideration, or professionalism can destroy that contact and get your e-mail deleted. Worse yet, the person will never get to your music, which was the main point.

I compiled a number of e-mails that I usually just trash and sent out an e-mail to friends at all levels of the industry and asked them for their top five worst e-mails, cover letters, or first-contact communications. Without further adieu, let's dive into my favorites.

1. **Yo, I have the hottest thing ever. You gotta check this out. This is gonna blow and I wil take you wit me. (a crappy social networking site address) (a name).**

   When you address someone as "yo" it appears that you are mass e-mailing or spamming everyone and anyone who will listen to you. Second, when you state you are the hottest thing ever, you've set the bar pretty high for yourself. You're also using certain keywords that will automatically turn off most people getting that communication.

   The spelling and style are atrocious. The assumption that this person is going to be larger than life and deigns to carry me along is just flat out rude.

   Result: Trash the e-mail. Skip the Web site. Move on. That was what I did when I received a similar e-mail, and that is what all others I spoke to did when they received that type of e-mail.

   Action: Tone it down. Spell check. Pick up an English style guide. Everyone needs one! It's not just for grammar nerds! Use confidence, but use it carefully. An e-mail saturated with confidence comes off as arrogant. Also, supply a little more information.

2. **My name is John Smith, I am the manager for John Doe. (Facebook link) Thanks, John Smith.**

REALLY??? The first time I got an e-mail like this, I was floored. I actually closed my e-mail application and reloaded it thinking the message was truncated or cut off some how. When I asked my friends if they had ever received anything like this, they responded with, "All. The. Time."

This is the, um, *less than bright* individual who has given you very limited information and seems to have these wild expectations that you will immediately race to the Web site, listen to the music, and make the magic happen overnight.

Result: Trash the e-mail. Skip the page. Wonder at just how foolish people can be.

Action: Formulate a letter! Introduce an act if you are the management. Make it snappy; summarize in a strong, professional tone. Then ask or request an action. Are you looking for guidance? Are you looking for a producer? Are you looking for a contact? What is it that you want? Then sign that e-mail with your name, your company if you have one, an e-mail address, and a phone number. Maybe add a Web site or social networking site link to your organization as well.

3. **Hello, I am the president and CEO of blah blah blah Entertainment. (You know, that would actually be a pretty cool name for an entertainment company.) We represent x artist and are ready to sit down and discuss a plan to bring him over to your organization with us so we all can get rich. We have been waiting for the right moment, and the time is now. Call us so we can begin to negotiate ...**

Okay, these are viewed as fun e-mails to many in the industry. They are very common. On the plus side, the writer does bring up the "we" element. This person is thinking a little more towards the reality that profit has to be seen by the artist and the companies or people who take that artist to another level. However, this is also a writer who comes off as someone who knows nothing about business yet tries to be the Donald Trump of the music industry. The arrogance of bringing an artist to the company or individual, instead of the confidence of submitting an artist for review or a signing inquiry, is a bad idea.

Result: E-mail is usually trashed. Sometimes there's a quick check to see if this CEO/president is real, but most of the time no one is going to ever hear that song.

Action: Strongly present yourself, but don't lie. Overconfidence reads as weakness. Also remember that all anyone has to do to confirm your validity is search for your company's name in the Secretary of State online database. If you're looking to work with a producer, an agent, a label, or whomever, you need to illustrate your business sense and your drive to learn instead of lying about your credentials.

4. Attachments in e-mails.

These are the e-mails where people send a song or even six. I've had massive e-mails come in with zip files of songs from artists to whom I have never even spoken. They'll also attach many large picture files, which is unprofessional and rude.

Result: Not only trashing the e-mail, but now you have really annoyed me and everyone else I talked to. You are flagged, if not blocked, at this point.

Action: Do not send music files, pictures, posters, or any kind of attachment unless the file has been specifically requested. While some of the other annoying aspects of artists' e-mails may catch a person on a good day so they let them fly, this is one that upsets people. You're slowing up an e-mail download or a computer and taking up space and time that is not yours to take up! Time is damn expensive!

Placing direct links to song files that are streaming is a good idea. Let someone be able to click on a link and get right to the song, not having to look through a page or find a button. Links that are directly set to streaming songs are very professional and get strong, positive attention. The same goes for pictures. Place a link to a picture or two. Lastly, title the links; tell the person what it clicks to. For example:

The Acme Band's 8 x 10 Promotional Picture - http://www.theacmeband.com/promophoto.htm

That is sharp and professional. I know exactly what the link is and where it is taking me. Try to rename the link as well so people know what they're clicking on instead of www.theacmeband. com/473thecouchlooksbetteronfire74893-9383

You may also combine the two above so that the text "The Acme Band's 8 x 10 Promotional Picture" *is* the link to the picture. Keep in mind that old rule: (Professional) actions speak louder than (arrogant) words (and sale tactics).

Oh and last point. Check your damn links to make sure they actually work or for that matter go where you want them to. Captain Obvious takes off again, but many screw this up.

5. **Failure to follow instructions, of which there are too many e-mail examples even to list.**

Many companies, producers, and agents have specific rules on what information to e-mail as well as what information not to e-mail. Some people ask you to fill out a form or ask for specific information. Unfortunately, all too often, artists mass e-mail to the point of spamming, using static and template e-mails that do not follow instructions and, at the same time, display that they're not personalizing their e-mails.

Result: Again, trashed e-mail and another contact lost.

Action: Individualize every e-mail. Make sure, if you are asked to supply a certain piece of information or present things in a certain way, you do it and do it right. Some of these professionals are actually testing you. They want to see if you can follow instructions. So follow them and have a better shot at producers or agents not only reading your e-mail but actually listening to your music.

Take the time to craft an e-mail. If you're sending out an e-mail to find a producer, book a gig, solicit a label, or find a manager, you can craft a basic template letter. But take the time to individualize it and format it so that it complies with the requests of the particular person or company receiving it.

Follow the instructions if there are instructions. If there aren't any, do your best to construct a precise, brief, and to-the-point e-mail. I really recommend sending the basic e-mail to friends of yours who aren't in the music business. Let them help you edit and put together the best letters. They can help with editing too.

Have a solid subject line. If you are looking for a review, then have that clear in the subject.

RE: Review Inquiry for the Acme Band from Seattle, WA.

This is nice and clear and to the point. I know someone is looking for a review, the name of the band, and where they're from.

Tread very carefully on follow-up e-mails. Many times if you don't get a response, the person is flat-out not interested. Do not open up with, "Why didn't you answer me?" My latest personal favorite is one that said: "You will be so sorry you didn't contact me, you are an idiot and I will show you." On one hand, I hope you do "show me." I genuinely want to see everyone succeed in the music business. On the other hand, when you tell me I'm an idiot, I absolutely do not want to talk or work with you. Also, if our paths were to cross down the line, you have now left a bad impression.

Lastly, avoid words in all capital letters. Don't send headers or bodies of e-mails with all caps. It's annoying and makes you look stupid.

Every contact you make, every solicitation you send, every review you pursue is important. Display your level of professionalism in that first e-mail to get the best results, and hopefully, the reader will follow the link and hear your music to find out more about you. Remember that these people are already being contacted by tens of thousands of others. If you avoid the common mistakes, you will bring positive attention to your e-mail.

When people put effort into their communications with me, I want to return that effort and read the whole e-mail, visit the links, and listen to the music. They pay attention to the details, so I will return the favor. Many people inside the industry feel this same way.

Take the time to craft the e-mails. Show your professionalism, show why your e-mail should be read, and show why the person should go on to listen to your music and consider you for whatever you're requesting. Stand out and stand strong in your communication, and your e-mail will be read and considered, unlike those thousands of others who make common and foolish mistakes and end up on a straight path to the trash.

The Elevator Pitch

People tend to want plenty of time to explain themselves, their sound, their vision, their goals, and anything else that has to do with them. People like to share as much information as possible. They feel they need to explain everything when it comes to getting a fan or finding a label, a manager, an agent, etc. However, the fast pitch, the one-liner, the quick explanation is the most effective way to present yourself. It shows consideration for the person to whom you're pitching, and it proves your overall organization and professionalism.

It's understandable that you want to use as much time and as many words as possible to describe yourself, your goals, and your abilities, but when it comes down to it, you need to remember a lot of others are doing the same exact thing. The more professional your presentation, the better you will be heard and the better impression you will leave.

Your Fast Pitch

What is your fast pitch? It's a quick and descriptive summary. It's an elevator pitch: the pitch that you make in the elevator when you only have a few seconds to present yourself or your idea. The same pitch should be in your soliciting materials as well. Make sure the one-liner of your bio or that first sentence of your bio is a grabber. Make sure it's strong, detailed, and quick.

The same goes for your tagline. Think of it as a shorter version of the first sentence of your bio. How can you sum up your band and sound in a brief, unique phrase? Stay away from the "We are indescribable," "We don't sound like anyone else," "We are totally original," "You have never heard anything like us," or any of those stupid lines that will immediately cast you in an unoriginal light.

For both the written word and the spoken one, think highlights, think memorable, think precision. Remember that other people are doing pitches along the same lines, so the faster, the more precise, and the more detail provided over the least amount of time, the more you will stand out. Make sure to figure out what you want to convey, what you want to share, and how to answer questions with simple, quick responses that cover the crux of the question but compel the person asking to dig deeper.

Let them dig deeper. Make them ask for more. It's a much better situation than disclosing too much and either making them bored or turning them off from what you're trying to share. Prepare yourself to present just like you would prepare a song in performance. Go over the basics:

Who are you? What do you want? What do you bring to the table?

Make sure that your answers are quick and to the point. Don't drag on and don't waste time. Get straight to the point. You have no idea how many people will appreciate that. At the same time, when you are to the point, you will find an audience that will want to know more and ask you for it.

Sports Center

Imagine it like a sports center. You have two reporters who are giving the highlights and details of a one-hour game in two minutes. Don't go into the longwinded story of how you were formed—it's not an interesting marketing point. Instead, tighten it up! Summarize your marketing points, your strengths, and any exciting elements to draw people's interest. Be quick, informative, and if you can, add some humor. Many salesmen and saleswomen will tell you it's all in the fast sell or the fast ask. The longer you go, the more chance you will lose them—both their attention and their interest.

Know the Pitch and the Different Parts of It

Just as you need a strong tagline for your band and a strong one-liner to describe your band, you need to know what parts to say next and what a particular person might want to hear.

1. **The Who**

   For example, if you are presenting yourself to a label, a club manager, a booking agent, or a talent buyer, he or she is going to want to know the fast summary of who you are. So what's the one-liner? What's your tagline or fast description of your sound? Who do you sound like and who has influenced you? Be quick, punchy, and informative. Cover it quickly, give the liner notes, and your listener will come back and ask for more if interested.

2. The What

Now if you're looking for some kind of deal, an agent or manager, a distributor, or some kind of opportunity, you're going to add on to the who you are with what you want.

Note: Do the best you can to avoid the "uhs" and "umms" as well as the you knows" and the "likes." These, along with other noises or extra verbiage that people use when they're uncomfortable or insecure, are called filler words. They make people look ridiculously unprofessional. Work to avoid them.

After you have presented who you are, go to what you want and what you are looking for. Be precise. I cannot count how many e-mails I've received with plenty of "the who" but none of "the what." I couldn't tell if they were looking for a producer because all I got from them was a long-winded explanation about the band and nothing else.

Above all, get right to the point; make the person want to know more.

3. The Why and the How

These are best used at your discretion. Explain why your listeners want to give you what you're asking for and how it would benefit them. Always remember that whatever you're asking for, in some ways, is a donation to or investment in your band. Why would others want to invest or donate their time, skill set, product, people, or efforts in you? What will you bring them in return? Answer that quickly, and you will be light years beyond most.

At the same time, you might not even get to the why and the how. It might be for a later conversation. Be a good judge of character. Let go when you're losing someone; ride with it when you have the persons attention.

Of course you and your sound are more detailed and complex than what fits in the time-span of an elevator pitch, but on that first impression, get the information out in the fastest, strongest, and most organized manner that you can. Leave the extra information for the next conversation or follow-up questions. Whether you're looking for money, a label, distribution, investors, donors, management, or anything else, it's going to come down to that first pitch and first impression.

The Tone of Your Voice

The tone of voice you use in writing and speech can have a huge effect. The inflections, tempo, dynamic, phrasings, and embellishments can really make a difference in how what you're saying is perceived by others. It's not unlike music: Sometimes it isn't the lyrics or the notes that are used but the nuances, embellishments, and dynamic ways to deliver them that can make a song a hit. Whether you're speaking with a booking agent, a venue, a label, someone from the media, or anyone else in the industry, it's important to think about your tone of voice, the tempo of your delivery, and the sensitivity needed to communicate with specific individuals.

There are a couple of key elements that can help you when you're talking to an individual or a group of people. Think of things from their angle and what they are used to hearing. Be different by being respectful and having an understanding that you're not the only person who's made this call or contact. If you're making contact with a booking agent for the first time, think of all the calls and e-mails that this person probably receives, as well as the common or overly used phrases that have probably been said to them, and avoid those phrases.

A Few Simple Rules

Simple things like "Thank you for your time" and "Let me get to the point" can really show a great deal of respect to the person with whom you are talking by demonstrating an awareness of the fact that you're speaking with someone who is busy. It also shows an understanding that the world does not revolve around you.

It sounds crazy and stupid obvious, but make sure you're calling from a place that either has good reception for a cell phone or from a landline. Call from a place where you will not be disturbed or where there are not a lot of noises in the background. Turn off the music; make sure extra noises such as the hum of a dishwasher, washing machine, dryer, or extra people in the background are quiet. Speak clearly, and don't be too far away or too close to the mouthpiece.

I Sound Like That?

All too often we don't think about how we might sound with someone on the phone, and that can hurt the professionalism as a whole. When you're asking for something, whether you're looking to be considered for a manager, a label, a booking, or an interview with the media, make sure you come across as clear and concise as possible.

I also don't recommend doing first-time contact calls while you're walking where the street noise is bad, or walking up a hill where you might begin breathing heavily. It comes to the elements that may be small but can make a big difference.

Ok, so at this point, you have a clear signal, distractions and extra sounds are muted, and you are in a location where you can be heard and understood.

Now for the Call ...

Think about what you're saying. Prepare your approach and your words. Talk at a solid pace but not too fast. People who speak too fast or too slow can often come off as annoying. In addition, speed can be associated with nervousness. You want confidence and assertiveness without a sense of arrogance or weakness conveyed to whomever you're speaking with.

Breathe and Listen

Give room at the end of your sentences for questions, in the same way a comedian may insert a light pause for audience laughter. If you're not interrupted, keep going, but if you are interrupted, address whatever is said. This allows the person with whom you're speaking to address concerns or questions as they come up.

Red Flags

Don't overshoot. Confidence is key, both in your voice and delivery. Don't use all those awful clichés and never-say lines that have been overheard, overused, and overdone. These can turn people off very quickly.

Give and Take

Whether you're discussing being booked for a certain show, signed to a label, picked up by an agent, or having a review or story done on you, make sure that you discuss the benefits of why it's good for the person or organization with whom you're speaking. Many artists reach out in a linear way, thinking only of what they want, how they want it, and what it's going to do for them. By going after what you want, but explaining the benefits to the particular person you're speaking with, you will draw greater attention from him or her and be seen as a potentially safer and smarter investment, as well as not being seen as selfish and self-centered.

If you're talking to a club about a booking you want, discuss how you will help to draw people and the efforts and methods you will take to fill the venue so that the venue can make money. If you're talking to a management group or manager, talk about the efforts you take and will continue to work on to make promoting, marketing, branding, and booking your group easier for anyone involved. If you're talking to a newspaper, magazine, or media group, go over the extra marketing points about your group and how you have prepared materials or information to make the story stand out and allow you to be a little different from other stories.

The point is to show that by getting what you're looking for, it will be mutually beneficial to whomever you're getting it from, as well as giving the appearance that you're fully and completely aware of the other party and the fact that he or she needs to benefit from the situation as well.

Speak Clearly

Speak with a full voice; don't mumble and try to avoid the "uhs" and "umms." Don't change your voice if you're hit with a question for which you don't know the answer. Many people get quieter or their voice trembles if they feel they're backed into a corner. If you don't know an answer, say with confidence that you will either find it out or you do not know.

The better you can present yourself when you're on the phone, from the tone to the delivery and tempo to the confidence in your voice, the better you can sell yourself and your group or product. Take that extra minute to prepare and collect yourself to be as professional and confident as you can be before the call. Just as you warm up, stretch out, and make sure you're ready to play your music, take those same tools and bring them to the phone calls. The confidence and professionalism in the voice, mixed with all your physical materials being well prepared and organized, can set you up for a solid one-two punch for whatever you're going after.

Giveaways

What kind of core product should you have and give away for free? How much should you charge for product? When should you discount or hold sales, and when should you not? I'm never so amazed as when I hear how many different opinions people have on these topics and, to be honest, how selfish people can get, staying way inside the box when thinking of free things and pricing.

First, do not look at the basic product as money you should make back.

THAT IS THE WRONG APPROACH!! Notice the caps, notice the volume … WRONG APPROACH.

Thinking that you should make all of your money back on the initial disc pressings or products is an awful idea. Yes, you should make some cash on it, but the right mindset is that giving away a great deal of product is going to equal a greater marketing beginning.

The more people who see your shirts or play the music for friends, the more you will get of new fans, new interest, and most of all, MORE SALES!!!

Set up a ratio of sales to a ratio of giveaways. Remember, on this first batch you may not make as much as you'd like to, but the marketing elements will draw more sales down the road.

Another idea is to set up a giveaway plan and set aside, by the month or the week, what you are going to give away and how you are going to do it.

Here is an example of a weekly plan that I set up for a band a few years ago but we are going to use the Acme Band since they seem to be the happy little example group throughout.

The Acme Band Giveaway Plan

Weekly/Shows

- 3 free (gifted) album downloads sent to people on your mailing list

- 2 discs sent to independent music magazines with consolidated press pack
- 4 discs given away at every show
- 10 stickers given away at every show
- 1 tee shirt per show to viewpoint pop person (I will explain this in a sec.)
- 1 glassware item to online store purchases as a gift to an existing sale

These guys were not selling or moving a lot of merchandise. They had the recording finished, and I came in to consult mostly on their launch and the tour they had begun. Their sales were in the hole, and they were charging an arm and leg for product. When they finally grasped the idea that you had to spend money to make money, they started moving a lot more merchandise. They saw the most recent order of merch as a 60 percent to 40 percent loss to gain. They were giving away 60 percent and making 40 percent. The calculations worked out well as the next order swapped percentages and they made 60 percent profit and gave away 40 percent. On the next order, by the end of a seven-month tour, they were making 75 percent to a 25 percent give away or loss. Those rates, by the way, are much better than the deals you would get with the labels.

Oh yeah, before going any further, **make sure you have full ownership and rights to your logo and the branding on your merchandise!!**

Make sure you do not have to pay a percentage to the person who did the design. That can hurt you in the giveaway, as the designers will sometimes ask for a flat percentage of the products created in some deals.

You should really have your own online store as well. Set up a store that has your entire product catalog, from music to merchandise, available on your site, which you as the artist or band has to ship. You can make a great deal more this way.

Of course it can be good to use CD Baby, Amazon, iTunes, Cafe-Press, Borders Online, and many of the other online stores and distribution methods. This will help people be able to find you. However, push them to your own store, and you will make a higher profit without percentages being taken, and you will also be able to have a better idea of where the sales are happening, who is buying and when.

OK, so back to the weekly plan. Just as putting up flyers and ads, working the Internet, making phone calls, and sending out press kits and packages to people is marketing—so is **giving stuff away!!!** Every time someone gets something for free, you are working the marketing angle hopefully to get more people to become aware of you, and find more people to buy those exact items that you give away.

Here is the justification for each thing:

The Acme Band Giveaway Plan
Weekly/Shows

3 free (gifted) album downloads sent to people on your mailing list

Gifting free downloads does not cost you anything. You can send a code or a gift certificate-type item to a fan as part of a drawing or a random choice. This is great marketing and will also get the word out that you can get FREE STUFF if you are on this band's mailing list. This is great advertising.

Constantly bringing content to the people on the Web is a great way to keep people returning to your site to check in and check for updates and shows.

2 discs sent to independent music magazines with consolidated press pack

Once a week, pop out two discs in the mail to indie or major music magazines that ACCEPT SUBMISSIONS!!! Don't just send along to *Rolling Stone*. There is a difference between giving something away for free and getting your package tossed in the trash and wasted. Look up magazines, physical or online, that have a large database of readers or subscribers and send out a basic pack and a disc to them. Slow and steady wins the race, or at least will get you more recognition. Instead of some massive marketing campaign, send out a couple of discs a week to various places for review and for promo. You will find more articles written about you in the long run. You will find more fans as well as increase your reviews, your database, and your network.

4 discs given away at every show

Sales, sales, sales at shows. You know the basic budgeting of major tours is not actually for the performance. Money and sales are mainly budgeted around merchandise. It's sad, but true. You want to do all you can to sell at a show. Original marketing tricks can bump up the sales you might get with only a salesperson and a merch table.

A couple of good tricks …

- Start selling all your merch a few bucks down and then up it a dollar each hour. This way, if people buy the merch when they first walk in, even before they see you play, they get a reduced rate since they are "taking a chance."

- If someone buys a smaller item, announce that he or she is one of the winners who get a free disc. This will give people the idea that there may be FREE stuff. It may get people to buy some of the other merch, to see if they can "win" and get "free stuff" too.

- If your merch person or someone in the band overhears someone who seems to be more popular or a more dominant person, the type that seems to have others hovering around—the leader of the followers if you get my meaning—give that person a free disc. Thank him or her for coming to the show, and in so doing highlight this person's "coolness." It can draw others to purchase, to be like him or her.

- This is kind of a rude one, but it's true. Giving a disc or a shirt to one of the really good-looking or sexy patrons, if she will wear it or hold it up, can also … well, increase revenue.

10 stickers given away at every show

Stickers rock!!!!! They can be good to sell, but also to give a lot away!!! Have contests with them!!!!! Post on your Web site and mention at shows that once a month you will have the coolest (insert your band name here) sticker location contest. Have people e-mail you pictures of the coolest place that they put up your sticker, and each month, the person with the coolest location will win some kind of merchandise or prize.

Note: This could increase sticker sales as well as get fans to put your stickers around the world, trying to best someone else's location. You can also put up the photos that are sent in on your Web site and show how far and wide you reach. Now you will have marketing and stickers all over. This has been effective with a lot of groups.

1 tee shirt per show to viewpoint pop person

Viewpoint pop people are those in the audience that I was talking about above. Popular people, people who are well seen, whether they are attractive, sexy, just kind of wild looking or whatever … these are good people to have market your tees. If they are already drawing attention to themselves for whatever reason, having your shirt on can only help your marketing cause.

1 glassware item to online store purchase as a gift to an existing sale

Again, giving away things when people are buying is a strong marketing technique that will make other people take notice. When someone gets something free in addition to what he or she already bought, it can influence others to purchase.

This is just the basic overview. You can go into many more marketing techniques using free giveaways to increase your sales.

Price Tags

Last but not least … how much to charge????

I've heard many people say—and I've said it myself – "I really will not pay fifteen dollars for some new band's CD that I don't really know." Even for those new bands that I have seen live, I don't want to pay an arm and leg for a CD or a crazy price for a sweatshirt.

So charge less. I know you all want to make money, but add it up … 3 CDs sold at $15 at a show only comes out to $45. Ten CDs sold at a show for $10 is going to come out to $100. People are willing to take chances on easier numbers. I find that a lot of the artists who go for even and lower pricing tend to sell more. Remember even through Disc Makers, the average cost of a basic thousand-press package is somewhere around $1.75 a disc, after tax and shipping. Then figure based on the 60/40 loss ratio.

We'll take ten CDs for example: four are sold at $10 for $40 total, and six are given away. Subtract the CD costs for all ten, or $17.50, and you still walk away with a profit of $22.50. That includes giving away six CDs and you still show profit.

Don't be selfish. These numbers will alter as more people hear you, review you, and find out about you, because you are being smart and … giving product away now! Find a price set that will inspire people to purchase. Have sales and discounts on certain days online and test the waters. Follow and track your sales to see who is buying, when they are buying, and what they are buying. This is what any good retail business would do, and now that you have CDs, shirts and other merchandise, that is exactly what you are … a retail business!

Think about it.

Endorsements

Free stuff! Everybody wants it. Getting free gear and being able to say "I endorse so and so" is a very interesting topic, and one that is often approached from the wrong angle.

First of all, a lot of people talk the talk but don't walk the walk. These people claim to endorse companies and have no idea what they are. There is a fine line and a keen difference between a musician who exclusively uses a product and one who does not. The former actually endorses a company. I find it completely foolish when people lie about their endorsements or overly advertise that they are endorsed but don't mention any of the elements involved in endorsing a product.

Simply put, whether we speak of your endorsing a product or a product/company endorsing you, we are talking about you as a marketing avenue connected to that product/company, an avenue from which it can gain exposure and revenue. It's the endorser's responsibility to use a given product exclusively, of course, but also to use it in a way that showcases the quality of that product and the quality of the player (i.e., you!) that is now associated with the product. An ideal endorsement is more than the sum of its parts; both sides gain.

Endorsements are not about giving free or discounted items to nobodies. As harsh as that sounds, if you are not signed, not touring, not teaching on a high level, or not in a media spotlight that could influence others around you, then you do not make an attractive candidate for endorsements. It's crucial to think about what you can do for the product and its company, not the exposure and "street cred" you get in return for having an endorsement. It's also a good idea—no, make that an excellent idea—to make sure you have a solid definition of your endorsement.

Artists who come to Brain Grenade Entertainment claiming to have endorsements often raise immediate red flags. We wonder if they're just talking trash, if they bought something directly from the company, or if they are under consideration for the endorsement. One of the first things we do when artists claim to have an endorsement is to check that product's artist roster. Nine times out of ten they are not listed. Often, the people who we might know from that company have never heard of these artists or their bands.

That's why it is important to put out a strong, defined, and honest image. We don't check to be jerks; we check because a lot can be said in a bio or a one-sheet of a band that might be untrue but is not easy to verify. This is. When someone claims to have an endorsement, it's something that can be easily confirmed. If it doesn't check out, all the other information the artist supplied and all aspects of his or her presentation is called into question.

Therefore, even if you are in the process of getting an endorsement but are "not quite there yet," don't advertise it. If you do mention it informally, give your contact point in the company, demonstrating that you know such things will be checked, and talk frankly about how it's coming to fruition.

How do I get an endorsement???!!

Endorsements can help; that's no lie. It's additional marketing for you, and it can open up opportunities with that company. As an endorsed/endorsing artist, you or your group may be approached to attend or perform at trade shows, conferences, and other corporate functions. An individual artist who has an endorsement may also lay the groundwork for other members of their band/group to gain endorsement status as well. Many larger companies want you to have a major label deal to be considered for endorsements of any kind. These companies are not the place to start. Do not hound them with full promotional packages that discuss why you are going to be the next big thing. That is wasted time, wasted packs, wasted stamps, and in the end, wasted money.

Also realize that most companies have different levels of endorsements. This can help in your cause. If you were to ask for a free amplifier, chances are you are not going to be taken as seriously as the artist who wants to develop a relationship with a company and asks for a very small discount on the same amplifier in a detailed letter which explains how he or she would like to start a relationship with the company.

Below are the top five things that you should never say or list when looking for an endorsement. I've asked reps from companies that I've endorsed in the past what their favorite lines were. These were the winners and a few of the retorts.

1. **"You need to endorse me; I am the next big thing and a lot better than a ton of people you already give free stuff to."**

   Most of these companies don't "need" to endorse anybody. You are coming out of the gate with an oversized ego and giving the impression that you might be difficult to work with.

2. **"Your stuff is pretty good, but if you custom made it my way, it would sell so much better."**

   Opening up with how they need to change their products to your specifications and your design is an insult. Such rights are reserved for artists who have been with these companies for a long time or top-echelon artists with extremely high visibility.

3. **"My gear is from your company, but it's in really crappy shape, and it needs to be upgraded so I can sound the best I can, and it will help your image as well."**

   So, you are already representing their product in a poor light and focusing on your needs while not defining how the company might benefit from developing a relationship with you. This gives the impression you're looking for a handout, which does *not* position yourself as a desirable endorser.

4. **"You need to put my name on some stuff. It will really sell."**

First off, if you want your name on stuff, there are numerous companies that will, for a fee, put your name on sticks, picks, and whatever else you might want. Named products are—and should be—reserved for the highest profile endorsers and clients of the company.

5. **"I don't use your gear right now, but if you give me a rig, I will use you exclusively."**

This is my favorite and this is one I, myself, have heard bands talk about. Now, for a high profile artist who may not be using the company's gear, switching over may bring that company desirable attention from some of his or her fans. As a local artist, regional, or up-and-coming, however, it really is over the top to ask and again appears as though you're just requesting a handout.

But getting away from the negative side of it, ask yourself a few of the questions companies would surely want answers to if they were going to consider you for an endorsement.

- **Why should they endorse you?**
- **What do you bring to the table?**
- **What market would you be able to reach that they are not already reaching? Or what market could you supplement and how?**
- **Do you deliver the image that the company would want to portray?**
- **Would your endorsement bring additional sales and more attention to their product? If so, how?**
- **How will you be a continually effective endorser?**

When you can answer these questions in detail, you'll improve your chances of receiving an endorsement.

Developing a relationship with a company and proving that your endorsement will help them is another good approach. So many artists are out there for themselves. Be different: Show the company that you understand it's a business, and that developing this relationship would be a smart business move for both parties. Taking a professional approach will assure the company that you are worth being involved with.

Start small. Don't ask for a full rig or free stuff. Inquire about the different levels that are offered by the company and ask if you can start at the bottom. Explain how you can prove that you are a quality endorser. Again, this will show you're not selfish and that you truly are trying to develop a relationship with a company and product you believe in.

This brings us to the crucial point: **Believe in the product**. Do not endorse something just because you can get the endorsement. It doesn't help the company or you. Artists who have a history with a product or company, especially in pictures that clearly display the product and its label, show continuity and a long-standing relationship.

When I was first drumming, I played on Pro-Mark drumsticks. I played a model called the Simon Phillips 707. I am a big fan of Simon and loved the ball tips of those sticks. I tried a couple of different brands as a teen, but always came back to Pro-Mark and specifically to those sticks. Most drumming shots of me from the time I was thirteen on, have me holding a pair of Pro-Mark sticks. So, when I state that I have been playing Pro-Mark for eighteen years, it rings true and the proof is in the pictures.

It's also a lot easier to talk about why you like a product when you really actually like it. To tell a company its product is great or "I don't play anything else" is not really much of a line unless you are a top-level client. When it came to Pro-Mark, for me, I told them honestly, "I found that the sticks have a great center balance, are well crafted, and have a touch that I can't find in other sticks."

I have used Pro-Mark on the bulk of the recordings I have been on as a drummer. I always have a couple of sets of the 5As, 5Bs, Elvin Jones Signature set, Hotrods, 3ALs, and my old favorite 707s on hand for the drummers I produce in the studio to try to get different sounds and feels, as well as turning other drummers on to the sticks. This comes off a lot stronger than "They are good," and it also ties in the marketing element.

Figure out why you like a stick, a guitar, an effect, or any other product. What has it done for your sound, your writing, and your performance? See what you can add in a marketing sense that other endorsers may not have already.

- **Are you a solid player?**

- **What's your experience?**

- **Do you teach?**

Covering a basic résumé about your playing and your career to date, as well as projects you're involved in, can help with endorsements as well.

- **What makes your band stand out? (BESIDES YOUR MUSIC!!!!)**

- **What makes you stand out?**

- **Are you involved in charity work?**

- **Do you tour frequently?**

Then tell what you would do for the company. Talk about how you will do additional marketing for the business and then show that it's being done. Explain that you will have the company's logo or mention on recordings that you endorse its product. You can also mention in early stages that you would be happy to put on the next release that you exclusively use the given product.

- **If you're the drummer, will you place the logo on the bass drum for shows?**

- **Will you wear a shirt or other item at least once a week, advertising the product?**

- **Will you reference it in your promo materials?**

What other ideas can you come up with to justify the company standing behind you as you show how you will stand behind the company?

Lastly, when connecting with the company, be respectful! Try to find out exactly who you are supposed to contact. Do not send e-mails to every address at the company. I have heard too many stories about this happening.

Bad idea. Bad. DON'T DO IT!

Inquire respectfully, ask nicely. See if the company is currently looking to sign endorsers, and if not, ask if there is a good time of year or better time than now to submit a letter or package. If it has a form, fill it out and send it to the appropriate contact. Just because you've heard that your favorite star works with Mr. X. from your favorite company doesn't mean you should inundate this guy with your e-mails or calls.

If you don't hear back, don't continue to hound. Think! Is it during a convention or trade show period? This is not a good time to go after endorsements, and most likely, these guys and girls are not at their desks. Doing a ten-day follow-up by e-mail is professional. If you don't hear back after that, leave them be. It's not that these companies are being disrespectful, but they are receiving thousands of e-mails with the same requests as yours. They can't possibly get back to each person. It would take days to do that. Also, if you continue to hound, you will be flagged and possibly ignored. In making contact, as I listed above, stand out in a good way: explain why you want the endorsement and especially give the company a reason why it should want you.

Take these steps in a respectful and professional manner. Look at the idea of endorsement from all angles. If you can honestly answer all the questions and present in a professional manner, then you may be ready to apply for an endorsement. If you are not, wait a while; get some more experience or marketing elements under your belt before you make contact. Your responsibility, originality, creativity, and patience will help you and also portray you in the best possible light to a potential endorser.

Friends, Holidays, Families, and When NOT to Market

With all the marketing that has to be done, with all the promotion and all the information that you need to constantly talk about and work on, is there ever a time to cease and desist?

The answer is yes, and it can often be forgotten.

Just as it's crucial to promote, promote, and promote, there are times when it's best *not* to talk about your music, band, and career. Many people work jobs that they don't discuss in depth when they're off work. The hard thing about music is that in many cases social scenes are work scenes. While someone who works behind a desk from nine to five can turn off the computer and go home, leaving work at work, musicians can't really do that. But there are times when we have to.

I talk about music, I talk about the book I'm writing, I talk about the artists I'm producing, I talk to people who come up to me and want to talk about music or the business. I talk music, music product, and music business, and I talk a lot. On the upside, at least in the past, I was always in work mode, even having fun doing so, but there's a point at which you need to take a break from work and music and give those around you a break from it as well.

Ask friends of yours, significant others, and casual acquaintances who know you outside of music if you talk too much business. Ask them if they seem to find conversations drifting back to the topic of music or your career. This was pointed out to me recently, and it's something I'm guilty of, too. It doesn't mean you can't fill your friends in on what you're up to, but designate times that are not about your career or your music. Leave the CDs at home, don't talk about the shows, maybe even designate nights or times when you're going to be all about other things and nothing about music.

It's good to take a break, to get reenergized and to have time when you can shut it off for yourself and for those around you. It's exciting and oftentimes a different type of career than many may have, but listen to conversations and notice if other people talk about nothing but their jobs. You might be surprised what you hear. I know I was when I stepped back and realized when I spoke it was mostly about work. Now, I love my work, and my work has been my life for a long time, but it's important to step away from your job, regardless of how much you love it or hate it, for your sake and the sake of everyone else.

Online Marketing

E-mail and Posting Campaigns

E-mailing has made elements of marketing much easier than it's ever been before. I kind of feel old when I explain to younger bands that a mailing list used to mean we actually printed out postcards, letters, or flyers and then addressed them as well as stamped them and put them in actual mailboxes.

With the Internet, mailing lists have become much more green as well as much easier to do. It doesn't cost anything to send out an e-mail, but artists need to think about the costs of too much e-mailing or posting and how it can have a negative effect on your fan base. For starters, plan an e-mail newsletter that has consistency and regularity. This way it becomes something that people will want to read. You do not need to send out e-mails every single day, and if you do, you're going to lose the effect of your e-mail newsletter as well as people's desire to read it.

I recommend a newsletter that has:

- **A show section** – talking about the upcoming shows.

- **A fan section** – something about people at the shows.

- **A contest section** – some kind of contest or game just for people subscribed to the newsletter.

- **A story or article that the band writes** - maybe a bio of one of the players or something different and original.

- **A news section** – the latest updates on the band and happenings.

- **A picture section** – a couple of pictures from recent shows meant specifically for the newsletter.

- **Something just for the newsletter people** – most of the above only for the newsletter people.

Make the people receiving the newsletter or that are on the mailing list get something special that can't be seen on one of your social networking sites or your primary Web site. Give people a reason to be on the list. If you're just putting up the basics from your site and your social network sites, then they can get it there and don't need to be on a list.

If you do a giveaway or a contest once a month, maybe a CD, a tee shirt, or some kind of merchandise or prize, it can also make your newsletter more popular and get people to sign up for it.

Make sure!!!

Make sure every newsletter has a link or information on how to unsubscribe. Sometimes people will either want to get off a list because they're receiving too many e-mails or maybe they just aren't interested in your band anymore. That is their right, and you should respect it. If someone asks to be unsubscribed, then do it and leave it at that. Don't get sensitive and don't e-mail back asking why.

I've been on various lists that I did not even sign up for, and most of the time when I click unsubscribe or ask to be taken off, it's not a problem. I had one person, though, e-mail me and ask why I would want to be taken off, as well as telling me I don't know good music. I simply get too many e-mails and did not want to get the constant battery I was receiving from this artist, but after that e-mail, he lost a fan.

Take the right steps and do not just add people to your lists or steal information from other lists and cold e-mail. **Do not buy e-mail lists, either!!!** Very unprofessional and very annoying.

Now when you send these out, make sure to hide the e-mail addresses in the BCC section or "sent to a band e-mail" that distributes to everyone. When I sign up for any kind of e-mail list, I do not want everyone on that list to get my e-mail. Many others feel the same. Respect the privacy of the e-mail list that you grow and the people on it. It can make a big difference.

Send monthly, or every other month as well. People have ways to check in with your networking pages, your Web site, and other places online to find out the most immediate information. The regularity, mixed with the space, can make people really want to read your newsletter and check it out more thoroughly than those received day after day.

Keep copies of your own newsletter and use it as a template for the next one. Use the format and change out the information, the pictures, and the contest, and have a solid look and uniformity to it. This can keep things very sharp and professional looking.

On the same note, when you are posting bulletins on your site, on craigslist, on your social networks or anywhere else online, use common freaking sense! Yes, you have to advertise. Yes, you have to post. Yes, you need to market. But, avoid the spamming and avoid the ego posts. Reach out to your audience without looking down on them or talking an excess of trash. I'm tired of reading bulletins or posts from artists who say they are taking over the world and have ten thousand friends on some social network site. I really don't get the people who call themselves the most original and best thing to come out of this city or that city, or people who leave comments on famous people's networking sites, not only asking the particular star to check out their song but also spamming all about themselves.

I read one post on MySpace in which the artist said he was going through the massive numbers of MySpace e-mails, and he promised he would get back to everyone. He had nineteen friends. Even if they all e-mailed him ... **well, doesn't that make you feel a little stupid?**

If you're posting, read over your post. Edit it correctly. Figure out a strong—but not arrogant—headline that will draw someone to read it. Get over the ego trip. Yes, you want to look good, but when you talk crap, you look like a fool. Be confident and assertive but don't go over the top.

And, as with the newsletter, don't post a bulletin too often; put up information as it's interesting. I mean, if you're posting bulletins too often and with too little information, you're basically becoming the boy who cried wolf and will be ignored.

Whenever people ask me how to set up a headline or an ad that makes them look good, I ask them to tell me what they would say about themselves in front of their idols or favorite musicians. What would sum you up, but in language respectful of those you look up to? This is a good way to think, since you never know who might be reading your bulletin, post, or headline.

Use discretion, use patience, and use professionalism when you're sending newsletters, posting bulletins, or doing any other kind of advertising. Make sure you have your information well organized and edited. Make sure you're giving a headline that's worth reading and not over the top or arrogant. Take the steps to use this form of marketing to its most effective and productive ends. The more respect you show, the more interest you will gain.

But It Makes Sense to Me

There are a lot of musicians and groups that artistically want to stretch people's minds and make them think—make them really dive deep into the meanings of their songs, their name, their image, their marketing, or any other underlining elements that artists think will add that hip or cool edge to them. The problem that can occur, though, is flat out confusion or actually deterring more people from listening to your music than bringing them in to find out more about you.

Don't get me wrong—adding elements of depth and extreme creativity is a great thing, but think about it as a later step or being placed deeper in your marketing instead of it being a first impression. Make it something that fans will have to dig for as opposed to overly confusing the new listener or first-time visitor to one of your social networking sites.

Wild stories, confusing bios, songs that make no sense or tie into the more experimental side of you can be red lights for many people. For example, if you're a grunge/industrial type band with fast loops, dirty guitars and in-your-face samples with brash harmonies and powerful hooks, having song sample number one on your site be one of the tunes that is least like your sound or one of your more experimental and, say, softer and trance-esque, you may lose the interest right off the bat of the listener who happens to pop onto your Web site for a minute.

Get over yourself.

The reality is that when new people are visiting your Web site or one of your song sample sites, most are only going to be there for a few seconds unless they're drawn in. There are forty million MySpace music pages and that number continues to grow even as MySpace goes down in the rankings of the social networking world. People are being tossed links from spam e-mails, from friends, from strangers, and from third parties everyday.

While every musician wants to think that people are spending a number of minutes listening to every sample, looking at every picture, and reading every piece of text, the truth is the majority are only spending seconds and moving on very quickly. We are a nation of ADD, ADHD, and every other acronym that points to the bulk of us having less and less of an attention span everyday. People have endless options, so it's up to you to grab them, wow them, and thus pull them in to want more. It's crucial, just like having a fast pitch for industry professionals, also to have a fast pitch to grab fans from the masses.

It's fine to go deep and to challenge your fans, but first get those fans through the door, interested in you, and wanting to be challenged. Make sure you have created a crystal clear image that will demonstrate you, sell you, and entice them to want more. It's a hard thing to separate how you see something from how the bulk of the public will see it. Remember, just because it makes sense to you doesn't mean it will to most people. You're the artist. You're right smack in the middle of it all, and a big part of building the fan base is creating the right appearance and marketing to pull in the people who are sifting through thousands of sites and turn them into interested fans.

Too Much Information

With the creation of updating micro-blogs such as Twitter, as well as the status updates featured on sites like MySpace, Facebook, and Imeem, getting a quick message out to the masses is easier than ever. But when is it too much? Where is the line between marketing and sharing too much information? Does too much information end up hurting more than helping?

Every nugget of personal information—from what you had at dinner to the crappy day you had—may be too much information, especially when you have fans following your updates. Separating your personal life from your professional life is a good idea that will keep the bulk of people who subscribe to your updates interested and actually reading.

Maybe you have a Facebook site or something that is strictly limited to you personally. This should be the place where you can share personal information with people who know you and care. Your other Internet sites—MySpace, Twitter, Last FM, etc.— bear the weight of your profession. These are what the rest of the world will read. Mix these two, and suddenly everyone subscribed to your feed knows that you're about to go to the gym or going for a walk at this specific park. What if you or your band has crazy stalker fans? What if, by sharing personal information, you put yourself in danger? Another good reason to separate the two, don't you think?

Let your band sites, your music networking sites, and your micro-blog sites all reflect things that are pertinent and related to you musically.

An effective and productive example feed may read:

- **Link to pictures from our show in NYC last week**
- **New blog on the latest recording sessions**
- **Update from the road—Austin, TX**
- **Show cancellation info for 3-10-09**
- **New song available today on iTunes**
- **We are on the line-up for this festival**
- **New video link from our Saturday show**
- **Link to a new article about us in the** *Boston Globe*
- **We are appearing on this TV show on this night**
- **Anyone know of good restaurants in Atlanta? We are playing there Friday**
- **Check out the band we opened for the other night**
- **We are launching our new Web site tomorrow**

These links pique interest, and I might follow them to find out more information. There aren't excessive or irrelevant posts, so I'd probably stay subscribed to this feed. Don't be one of one the people or bands that flood their feeds with superficial and stupid updates. If you're only putting up interesting, informative, and solid updates, then you will maintain the fans and followers you already have and potentially draw others to you.

It's true that some of the heavy-hitting celebrities have thousands of people flock to their updates just to hear that they're out for a jog. But it's doubtful that a new fan—or even an established fan who actually has a life—is going to want to hear all of your personal thoughts on life, politics, and the universe in general.

What not to do.

These are a couple of examples of pointless updates that I found on three different sites in less than five minutes.

- **I hate you Jim. No, well maybe a little.**
- **I'm Hungry.**
- **Katie Thompkins is kinda bored and cant wait till tomorrow.**
- **Sitting at my computer and never going to make it in music.**
- **A beer.**
- **Watching Seinfeld and don't feel like practicing.**

And this one that inspired me to write this excerpt:

- **I'm going to the (band x) show alone tonight since my friends are standing me up. They suck, why doesn't someone meet me there.**

This was listed on one of the sites where anyone can see anyone else's post. Upon following the link, I found this person's music profile, link, and location. For the reasons I've already highlighted, this was not a smart move. Astoundingly, this is very real and happening everyday. Not only can too much information be damaging to your marketing and promotions, but it can be downright dangerous. So separate your personal life from your profession. I know that music is a passion, but I don't care what you had for lunch today. I want to be interested in what you post. I want to discover things that would make me want to buy your music and your products. I want to receive updates that are professional, but fun, as well as intriguing.

With people supplying an excess of information that might only apply to a very select few, limiting your posts can be one of the key elements that will keep people reading. Your goal is to organize your pertinent information in a manner that will optimize your marketability and bring you positive promotion and exposure. Write in order to hook new fans and to maintain the existing ones. It's the best approach to get the most out of these sites.

If you still want to post about your personal life, be my guest, but do it on a site that you keep strictly personal and limit it to your friends and family. You will appear much more professional, much more interesting, and you will be much more likely to have fans who will subscribe to and read your professional posts.

Blogging

Blogging has become an obsession as of late. Many people are out there complaining, commenting, and documenting more than ever. It's amazing that there are so many blogs out there and yet it's mostly page after page of dribble. I'm not saying that bands and artists should write a book's worth of blogs or try to adapt to a specific formula, but I do think that now more than ever, bands and artists should be blogging as part of promoting, marketing, and exposing themselves to the world.

First of all, blogging is a great way to optimize the network of your information. Second, whether it's a band diary or updates on time in the studio, blogging is a great way to provide fans with a better sense of who you are and what you like. For example, a link to a YouTube video you love or a fellow musician you admire will give your fans and friends a larger overview of what you're about.

Don't forget to switch it up between members (if you're a band) and that the blogs don't have to be long and complicated. Just keep updating your site and make sure new things are being posted on a regular basis. If something exciting is always happening, people will keep coming back for more—and folks, consistent traffic is great promotion!

Think about it: Even as a solo artist you could break up the week into a series of different blogs, entertaining various subjects that will bring you more attention online, all the while connecting to fans outside the music realm. The greater sense of connection you build with your audience the greater the intrigue and dedication. Give new fans a reason to come to your site and the ability to learn old and new things about you with ease.

Tracking your experiences could eventually lead to a band diary, or maybe even a book, if fame treats you well. Stories about recording, touring, or anything interesting could also be used as a promotion tool. On a personal level, it could also document your progress and provide valuable perspective in the years to come.

It all comes down to the simple things that can make the biggest difference for you, your fans, and your career. Start blogging. It's cake! Say what you're thinking and share a little more of yourself with your audience. Of course, stay positive and don't fall victim to all that "woe is me" crap. There is enough of that out there. Give people something to read, something to click through that's fun or enjoyable, something that ties you to readers and will make them come back for more. Just as you share your music with your fans, share your thoughts and ideas outside of music, and maybe you will draw people in through other means.

The Wider Web

I see certain artists with only MySpace or Facebook sites. Some of these artists even buy domain names and point these domain names to their MySpace with no Web site happening. Others buy a site and put up a "coming soon" that goes well past soon and reaches a really long time. MySpace is a standard right now for musicians, but it's not the be-all and end-all. As a musician who's doing all that you can, you need a Web site. You need to have the ability to host your own e-mails, host music, and host and store marketing documents, samples, and downloads. You need to be able to track sales and have access to business and personal documents for bands that are on the road. A Web site these days can be like an online file cabinet for all your information, your stats, and your content. In many ways, it's the backside of the site that's more important. These are the things that the public cannot see, but that you can access and get to the people who need such information.

It's a standard of professionalism, too. I'm more impressed when I see an e-mail with a domain name at the end of it. It shows that the artist is looking to be organized and professional across the board. milo@theacmeband.com is a lot sharper than milo438lovesturkey@yahoo.com.

I recommend keeping the theme and colors the same on your Web site and MySpace or other social networking sites where you can implement your colors and themes. Your Web site can be simple and down to earth from a viewing standpoint, but social networks need to supplement your main site and if you can add the colors and the themes, they should be there.

Beyond that, what about all the other social networks? I recommend you sign up, track, and be on all of them: iTunes, CD Baby, Facebook, Twitter, Blogger, Community Musician, LinkedIn, Mog, Hi5, YouTube, Last.FM, Vimeo, ReverbNation, Kudzu, Flickr, OurStage, and the countless other picture, sales, blog, networking, updating, and video sites.

Think about it: If you just put up a few posters in one section of town, only so many people will see you. The more places you poster, the more chances people will see you. Just as a guy who never goes to one section of town would never see a poster there, but if you have one right outside where he works, he'll see it, the same goes for people who might just be on Facebook or some other site. Get on all the sites you can to get the most visibility. Just a single social networking site is nowhere near enough, and just a Web site isn't either. You can use a certain site as a primary, but you want to be everywhere.

Keep a spreadsheet with the login, password, site address and other pertinent information. Then keep a basic document with the content you will use, and use it across the board. The same bio, the same tag line, the same pictures, the same songs, the same booking information. The more you show up in a uniform way across the Web, the more attention you will get, and the more each site will help to optimize the other and bring you up in searches. This way, you can track everywhere you are and have the ability to make updates that are correct across the spectrum. On the other side of things, if you get signed and need to take down certain songs or change information, having this sheet will make your life easier when the label, manager, or agent asks for a list of everywhere you have put yourself up on the net.

Have a Web site; it could be a simple one that primarily points to your social networking site of choice and contains your logo, font, tagline, bio, maybe a few pictures and samples with contact information, as well as links to buy your music and merchandise. A news or update section could be included as well. You can still use one of your social networking sites as the primary, but make sure the Web site is correct and up to a professional standard, even if it's simple. This covers the front side of things and, by having the e-mails, shows the professionalism of the group.

Then, having the different sites, such as the ones listed above, will help broaden your Web presence. Then comes the other side of the Web site and, in some ways, the more important part—the storage, organization, and coding section that can create an online office that's available to you wherever there's an Internet connection.

Think about this aspect of the Web site as a backstage. It's a place where you can store a great deal of your information which can then be made available to venues, newspapers, magazines, and other people in the media or in the industry. You can store downloads of your entire promotional kit, your music, your contracts, and your logos. You can maintain your e-mail lists, newsletters, and any other key information. By sending links, you're not blasting people with massive downloads. You give them the option to grab the information as needed as opposed to stuffing their e-mail with a mucho megabyte file.

This "backstage" can make life easier on tour as well. By having both password-protected and direct links to key marketing documents, you can easily send links or even texts to places where you're playing so they can access your basic posters or contracts. You can send links or access to certain media people who will then be able to print or download your logo for stories and articles as well as press releases, sound samples, and anything else. You can keep private lists for just the band; core information that is safely protected online, and always accessible to the group or management. This is not something you can do on many of the social networks.

So, yes: of course you want a specific social networking site, and it can even be your primary site if you like, but you need to have the Web site for its virtual office. Having a Web site with the hosting options and a backstage of information is a key part of making things much more organized, accessible, and professional.

Domain Names

The question is, how many do you own? With the inexpensive price of domain names these days and the same for pointing a domain name at a Web site, I recommend buying a new domain name every month. Now hear me out before you laugh it off. You have your primary site and primary domain name, but how many people are going to know the name of your site? Buying that as a .com, a .us, a .net, and whatever else can potentially drive more people to find you. In turn, as the search engine spiders run over the different Web sites and domain names, you will become more searchable.

Next, how do you spell it? Do you have a name or a band name that could be confusing or misspelled? As a drummer and producer, I have almost as many misspellings of my name on records as I do correct spellings. For example…my name is Loren Weisman but I have been credited as …

1. Lauren
2. Lorne
3. Lorin
4. Loran
5. Lorrin
6. Wiseman
7. Weiztman
8. Weismann
9. Wiesman
10. Wesman
11. Weismin
12. Weismen

That's five different misspellings of my first name and seven of my last. Combine the two names and you have even more mess ups. Now I only own the Web site domain of www.lorenweisman.com. It's all I need at this point, and I don't really even use that site anymore. If I were a solo artist however, trying to attract fans and sell my music, each month I would purchase a different misspelling. This would work two-fold. It would connect people who were misspelling my domain with the right domain site, and it would also optimize responses on the search engines – for instance "Did you mean this?" or "We can search this spelling of the name as well."

Grabbing the right Web site name can be just as important as what you put on the sites you're on. In the end it's about how easy you are to find. If you have a really long Web site name or MySpace extension, it can make it harder for you to be found, harder for you to advertise the site, and easier for someone to screw up when looking for you. If you have a site and your name is Gerald Worthington Jackson, it's a good idea to purchase the domain name www.geraldworthingtonjackson.com, which is your full name and can help people who are searching for you. At the same time, seeing if you can buy a shorter name, such as www.geraldjw.com or www.gwjackson.com or www.gwjmusic.com, can make a positive difference.

For one, those are shorter and less likely to be screwed up. Second, they're easier to use in advertising on flyers, postcards, and business cards. They can be a little larger in font and a little easier to remember. Finally, when it comes to e-mail, it will be both easier (to remember the extension) and shorter (so it fits on promotional or marketing materials). A shorter e-mail will get messages to you easier. For example Geraldwjackson@Geraldworthingtonjackson.com is a damn long damn e-mail and would suck to fit on a card or even remember, while Gwj@gwjmusic.com is worlds better and much easier to remember or add to a business card.

The same goes for Twitter or the other social networking sites, and it's almost more important there. If you're advertising your Web site and Twitter or WordPress together, like www.braingrenademusic.com and www.twitter.com/bgellc, having them be close in size can make things more uniform and easier to read. At the same time, again, it makes it easier to find and harder to screw up on. Remember, Twitter and many of the other social networks are going to optimize off keywords so you don't have to worry about the name being perfect. Put more emphasis on the name being strong because it's easy to find and remember. BGELLC is just the initials of Brain Grenade Entertainment LLC or (Limited Liability Corporation). The two sites also fit very easily on our letterhead, our sites, our cards, and our promotional items and look a lot stronger and shorter than www.braingrenadeentertainment.com or www.twitter.com/braingrenadeentertainment.

We do own the domain name www.braingrenadeentertainment.com and point it at the Web site—as well as www.braingrenademusic.com—but BGELLC is shorter and easier for people to remember. The easier the site is to remember, the better it is for fitting onto promotional and marketing items and the simpler it will be for people to get to you, which is exactly what you want. If you can't find it in .com, go for .net. There are a lot of new extensions and ones that you can buy, and you can buy a number of different Web names and point them at the same site, but right now, people know .com and .net most, so go with those as the priority.

Sometimes a name you want is already taken and is being used and may have high traffic. More than likely, getting that name is not going to happen, and it's time to move on. Other names that offer buy-outs from domain sites can cost a great deal. I wanted to buy a short domain name that was only three letters long and when I filled out the request form for the price, they quoted me ten thousand dollars. There are people and companies out there that just buy up domains and hope to turn them around and sell to people who want them for profit, so that can be an issue.

Always be thinking about the small elements, and you may find that they can help the big elements in a big way. Something as simple as a domain name or a social networking site might lead people to you online, and these are the names that are on your promotional materials, your product, and your marketing items. Take the small steps early on in every area that will make the leaps even larger down the line. It's a few dollars a month, and it's a small step toward closing the gap between people trying to find you and people coming upon you by accident who then become long-term fans. On top of that, you will have more words, sites, and tags pointing to you, your music, and your images. This is a good thing.

Next, do you have a single? Do you have a tagline that could also work as a domain name? These are domains you can purchase as well. Sometimes people might only know you by a song, so let that song direct them to you. You don't have to renew these names unless you want to, but you can benefit from having a constant flow of different avenues to be discovered by new fans and strangers alike.

Learn about other avenues of optimization as well. Are you tagging your photos the right way? Do you have the proper tags on your Web site and your networking sites? You can even start showing up in other searches that might not have been for you. It's key to be as detailed as possible in anything you do online. Learn about optimization. There are tricks and tools out there that you don't have to spend money on. There are optimization companies out there that can do it for you, but you can take the basic steps to get things working before paying money to others. More people are finding out about new music and new groups on the Web. Make sure that you have the tools in place and the extra work done to have them find you, whether they're looking for you or not.

Optimization

This is a simple concept and not too hard to grasp. With networking sites on which you have a very large and busy page, it's going to take longer to load. The more images a page has, or things that take up memory or bandwidth to load even on a small level, the more it's going to slow down the load of the given page. This applies for your Web site as well.

Now it's true, most people are broadband these days, but sometimes signals waver and reception is not so hot. Think about how fast your page loads and the images on it. I don't like waiting. I'm not the most patient guy, and if it takes too long, I might just move on. Many are like me, so make sure your page loads fast. This doesn't mean you have to lose the quality of the images you put up. You can still post and design very good-looking sites, but the key is to optimize the images and the graphics you use. Make sure you have someone who not only understands design but also understands how to compress the images correctly so they will load faster. At the same time, optimize and tag the images so they can be found by Web crawlers and make you easier to search on.

You can add titles to images so they identify your band name as well as other keywords to make the most of every picture. Then as the optimization kicks in, these very images will become something people find through different search options and keywords.

So make sure those images are optimized and compressed. This will mean you have new methods to be searched under and the pages will load faster. The right compression of images does not take away from the quality and the appearance, but again, it will load faster and for those who have slower connections; it can make all the difference. Also, even with the faster connection, when a page shoots right up and looks sharp, that shows a strong level of professionalism.

Once you've dealt with the optimization and compression of your images, you can start thinking about networking and showcasing sites where people can leave comments. It's then that you have to deal with the issue of OPI or other people's images. When people leave comments and messages, oftentimes the bands will leave large scaled images. They're doing their little version of promoting on your site, which I think is kind of cheap.

What's even worse is the images that people leave, the "thanks for the ad" or excessive posters and advertisements that people put up on other people's networking sites. First, they take up a lot of real estate, and second, with all those images, you now have a much slower-loading page. On something like MySpace where you want the player to load so you can have people hear your music, this can be a big problem.

My recommendation is to disable html comments and let people leave just text for you. This will guarantee a faster load of your site and keep away the larger images that can both offset the look and slow down the load of your page.

Classified Ads

I find it funny that when it comes to placing ads in classifieds, people are very detailed about what they want, but when they're looking for people, they don't use much detail. Some of the most popular musician classified ads are ridden with awful, non-descriptive listings that make finding what you're looking for much harder. Add to that the usual complainers or the people who are ripping on other people's ads, and you've got a mess of a place that should be just for networking and connecting. Places like craigslist, a great number of networking sites, and city weekly online magazines have free postings, so anyone can write or say anything.

In the end, you're not going to fix the classifieds system, but you can take steps to get the most effective responses for the ads that you place. You'll also be able to identify some of the pros and cons of the ads that you may want to answer yourself.

I don't need to tell you, or even show examples, of how many bad ads there are out there, especially those looking for musicians. I saw one ad that said, "looking for guitarist that wants to rock." That was the bulk of it. There were no influence listings, no goal, no styles, no vision of a band, no samples, nothing. Whether you're sixteen or sixty, use detail. A good ad can potentially capture the eye of just the guy or girl you're looking for. A bad one can turn away that strong potential person and leave you with few options or terrible ones.

If you're looking for a player, just as you would with your band, start off with a strong headline or tagline. Draw someone in to open your ad and read more. Then in the body, give the basics: who, what, when, where, how, and why. Some questions you should answer in your ads:

- **Who are you?**
- **Is it an existing band?**
- **Are you established?**
- **Are you just getting started?**
- **Who are your influences?**
- **What are looking for in a player?**
- **What are you looking for in a person?**
- **What is the vision of the group and of the music?**
- **What is the background of the group?**
- **Why are you looking?**
- **Are you trying to stay semi-pro?**
- **Do you want to take it all the way?**
- **Is it a hobby or weekend thing?**
- **When are you looking to get together and get moving?**
- **When are you looking to practice and how often?**
- **When are you thinking about recording?**
- **Where is the base of the band?**
- **Where do you want to play or tour?**
- **How do want the band to be?**
- **Are you open to changing the name or the concept?**
- **Are you set in your ways or vision?**
- **How do you want to approach the marketing, the recording, and the ownership?**

Yes, it's a truckload of details; but a strong ad that includes all these elements is going to bring you a better chance of better responses with the types of players that you're looking for. The same goes for any other services as well, from distributors to producers to studio players to selling or buying equipment. The details should be there, and they should appear professional.

Write it and edit it. Don't come off cocky. That can turn away potential players you might want to contact you. And anyway, you're not going to take over the world or change the music industry. Hell, you're writing an ad to find a missing piece, so don't come off over the top.

Include links to Web sites, samples, or social networks so that someone can see and hear you.

Leaving holes leaves questions. When I read about a renowned producer who is so busy you have to book him right away or he won't be able to fit you in, it makes me wonder: Why does he need to post on craigslist? When I see ads that are run too often, it makes me question: Why do they need to run so many ads?

If producers or labels are as hot as they claim to be or they talk about what they can do for you, you would think in the ad there should at least be a couple of links to a real Web site, a social networking site, or something to reference the person or organization. I'm especially wary when there's no name or contact listed in an ad. I understand that people have a right to privacy, but if you're advertising, you need to put yourself out there.

In placing and answering an ad, make sure all the details are in place. Don't get caught up in the world of classified bashing or ranting in the classifieds. It's a waste of time and a waste of space, and it should be in a rant or opinion section. Go there for the reason you're there, whether it's posting or searching, and find what you need. Don't over post if you're supplying a service, and make the ad as effective as it can be so you can find or get what you're going after.

Templates and Effective Repetition

"If it ain't broke, don't fix it" is a saying that can be very effective when it comes to work already completed, yet I notice so many artists who don't apply the concepts or templates that they worked so hard to create in the first place. Oftentimes the work that artists do is repeated in a way that's not needed. The examples range from booking contacts to promotion, pre-production sheets to press releases, and just about everything in between. Let's take a gig press release for example. If you were working with Brain Grenade Entertainment on a consultation for shows, you would get help setting up the press release for a show you have coming up. You would also get a link to the press release blog that shows the format and reasoning for why it's set up the way it is as well, as a review of what you've written.

This is where you have to think beyond the linear. The release and the blog were not to help you get one press release for a single show. That would be pointless and a serious waste of time and money on your part. But if you take what you've learned, the formatting, the reasoning, and you see the gig press release as a template, then you have an effective document format for all your future shows. Save the press release as a separate document labeled Press Release Gig Template. Then everywhere there is wording that refers to a city, a date, a room, the bands you're playing with, and anything else that is show specific, color it red or blue so you can update the document as needed. Then when you're getting ready to submit a new release for a new show, save the document again as a Press Release for that specific show, replace the colored letters from the template with the pertinent information, and double check to see if there are any added specifics needed for that particular release.

Now you're being more effective with a document that can be used over and over. You also won't have to rewrite a release every time you need one. This is a big time saver and it will supply you with a basic, professional, and effective template to work from.

Along the same lines, the Freedom Solutions Recording Plan blueprint layout is made not just for a single business plan for the artist. It's a plan that's set up for the specific recording and project, but it also has all the supplemental elements and documents that can be used by the artist for future projects. These projects will be easier for the artist to produce and prepare alone without the need of Brain Grenade Entertainment or myself, since they've gone through it before.

It's all about making things as effective as possible for that moment and the next and the next after that. The entire pre-production business plan phase is not about just creating a single plan. It's about …

- Teaching the artist, as the plan is created for the specific project, how the different elements are created and formatted and why.

- Empowering the artists to be able to do it themselves for future projects so they don't have to spend the money that they spent the first time since now they know how to do it for themselves.

- Showing the artist how to set up a basic template system that runs the gamut of budgeting, production, post-production, and release.

These elements of setting up templates and their effective use can come from your own experiences, both positive and negative. For instance, if you set up a show and go through a certain marketing template that you as the artist created, based on ideas, suggestions, and things you've learned from your own experiences and the show has an amazing turnout, then track it and template it.

How did you advertise? What was effective? Where did you post? Were there any stories about the show that helped pump it up?

On the other side, when something goes really badly, analyze that as well. What went wrong, and why did it go bad?

All the concepts I've written about don't contain anything groundbreaking or genius. They all come from documented experiences, both good and bad. I began keeping notes and creating template concepts from every tour, gig, and session in the past sixteen years. I wasn't writing down pages and pages of stuff; it was more of a diary with bullet points from each experience. This is just the collective data from big successes and miserable failures, all put together to help other musicians help themselves.

The main point is to use the experiences and the tools given you, or those you've learned about, and apply them again and again. Laying the blueprint and taking notes on ideas and results will help you decide how to handle the information in a way that you can apply to make the next experience or task easier. Keep learning from your own and others' experiences, the good and the bad ones. ook at every idea, every sheet and every approach to simplify and apply yourself. When you learn something, whether it was shown to you or it came from personal experience, look at how it can help you and create templates for the best results, for you and for every facet of your career.

Marketing in Any Economy

Whether you're an indie artist or a major artist, the state of the economy can have a direct impact on your success. It can be scary, watching the market numbers go up and down, and having to deal with all the fear-mongering stories in the news claiming we're heading toward another great depression, or total economic collapse. Economic woes and the nervousness that comes with them can make things more frustrating than they need to be.

Even in the toughest markets you have to remember that the economy will recover. That doesn't mean things will not be hard—or sometimes even very hard—during an economic downturn. But while you're waiting for the market to recover, it's important to look at the strengths of the situation—and there are strengths—and figure out what needs to be done. Analysis and creative thinking will help you in times of a bad economy as well as times of a saturated market or any other time where money problems come up. Also, if you can become a problem-solver and can find creative approaches to reach your goals, you can show the industry that you're proactive and assertive, as opposed to one of the countless whiners or blamers who has a list of reasons for why they aren't where they should be.

During the economic downturn of 2008, an unnamed news-caster on a top news network delivered a news report that described how alcohol and cigarette sales continue to be strong during a down economy because of their use to reduce stress. Makeup and cosmetics are said to thrive because they give the feeling of some level of control and pampering when everything else feels like it's going to hell. Then there's music. People still seek out music because they can get lost in it, use it as a release and a way to relax and get inspired. Music still thrives through crazy economic times, but just as economists and politicians plan changes in investments and government, musicians, too, must plan and adapt so they can continue to flourish, or even build a fan base.

There are plenty of simple things you can do to help inspire sales and support during bad economic times. Price reductions on CDs, downloads, and merchandise can help some. Knock those prices back a bit. Make that price something people know they can handle and are willing to take a chance on. Try some clever marketing tricks. There's a restaurant in Seattle that had a special discount day where it sold everything on its menu to match the Dow Jones' closing number. When it opened at 5 p.m., everything on the menu was $8.75. It was a great promotional gag that kept the place jam-packed and had people eating out on a day where things were scary, sharing in a sense of camaraderie about the state of the market.

There are many approaches you can take to reach an audience that is collectively tightening its belt. Why not try a drawing, where everyone who buys a download on a certain week is eligible to win some promo item or gift card? Hell, maybe even a gas card. Think of it: A few more people come to your site and buy a few extra downloads. One of their names is chosen, and the person gets a $25 or $50 gas card. The marketing behind that can be great because there's a press release you can send and potentially get a story from a local or even national publication. That marketing might, in turn, bring even more people to your group and your music.

What are your strong marketing points?

Do you own all your music? Have you been able to record using a smart budget? In times when people are particularly cost-conscious, a well-budgeted recording and release can not only be about the music, but also set you up as a role model to other musicians. You become the group that knows how to tighten the belt, budget correctly, save money, and still deliver. That can be a major selling point.

Use your head. You have more ideas than you realize. There are other things you adjust in life to keep you on track without putting yourself in a financial hole. Surely, some of those ideas can apply to music and the business of music as you create the revenue you want to survive today.

YOUR CAREER

Most musicians, when asked what they want out of a career in music, will give the same answer: SUCCESS!! They want to sell records and they want to tour, they want to be rich and they want to be able to buy all the toys. It's not very often, however, that these musicians think about what exactly such a career entails.

Musicians need to think about how long they want to tour. They need to think about what kind of lifestyle they want to live on a realistic level, which includes insurance for medical, dental, life, and so on. They need to think about the ways to manage money in the short term and long term. It's fine to go after the big dreams, but as you look to the stars, make sure you're also looking at your feet and where you'll be tomorrow, next week, next month, next year, and five years after that.

It also comes down to how you will improve as a musician and an artist, down to whom you will study with and the time you will commit to practice. Beyond that, how will you organize your music, and who will you share it with when it comes to copyrights and publishing. What happens and what do you plan for and when should you change the plan?

Just as many people meet with career counselors and financial advisors, you need to work with a very realistic and detailed plan to make sure you're not only preparing your career to attempt to go to the big time but also preparing and organizing your career for the long run.

If you want to have the most chances for success and create the most avenues for profit and long-term sustainability, you must bring the same attention to detail to your career planning that you bring to your music. Go beyond dreams of riches to the dreams of a house, a family, retirement, and fiscal responsibility. Then take it back to ground level and the smaller goals of furthered education of your craft, the legal organization of your music, and your promotions, and from there the long-term investments and planning for the future.

That approach will serve you well. It's planning for the best-case scenario—being rich and famous—as well as the realistic scenarios of being sustainable and having long-term income to allot you the things you want and need. It also takes into account the worst-case scenario, the time when you may have to decide that music will just have to be a hobby or a part-time thing and you set your mind to getting and keeping that day job.

When you approach your career from the responsible and mature standpoint, lay out all the details on the table, and organize them effectively, you can truly create the blueprint for a real career.

Educate Yourself

If you're a musician or in the music industry, do you know who Michael Rapino is? Do you know what Live Nation is? Do you know who the remaining four major labels are? Do you know what the RIAA is and how it affects you? Do you know what the difference is between a record label and record company groups?

You should.

Whether you're an independent musician trying to stay independent or you're aiming for the majors or you're going after a smaller career in the music industry, you need to be educated and updated regularly. Just as lawyers review laws that change and doctors review new methods of performing surgeries and helping patients, musicians need to keep up to date with the industry they're in.

So what's happening in the industry? What changes are coming? What releases are doing well? What new artists are on their way up? What older artists are on their way down? All this information is important and greatly pertains to you and your career. Whether you're marketing yourself or another group, whether you're trying to get funding for a record or trying to get more dates for a tour, when you know what's going on, who's being effective and who isn't, you have much more information to work with to move yourself and your music forward.

Take an hour a week, or even fifteen minutes a day for four days, and do some research. Spend time getting a better sense about something—anything—in the industry that you might not know that much about. Take some of that time to find out what's happening with touring, with labels, distribution, management groups, and publishing. The more you learn about the industry around you, the more you can plan the best approaches with the music and promotional materials you already have.

Look to real publications and real sites and references from industry people. Don't just read the angry industry blogs and the fan magazines. They can be supplemental information, but make sure you find the best information from the best resources. Know the difference between the opinions and the facts. People get into a lot of trouble when they take opinions and make them facts.

The music industry is an ever-changing-world, and the basic foundation gets rocked frequently. You cannot study something from years ago and expect it all to apply to today, especially in music.

As you look at different bands that are like you, look at different bands that are not like you. The more you can learn and apply from those like you and those that are different, the greater overview you can have of the industry. Take the elements that you've learned that are correct and don't copy the elements that may be missing from others; instead look more to find out where they're playing, who's giving them reviews, how they're gaining a larger fan base.

Look at the larger companies as well. Find out what they're doing. This will give you some helpful hints and may also demonstrate some things you might want to avoid. You need to educate and empower yourself with a spectrum of knowledge and a full overview of the industry you're in. The music world, especially now, is ever changing. Educating yourself about the industry around you is a requirement, not an option, if you expect to succeed and maintain that success.

Oh, and by the way, start with researching and answering the questions at the top if you don't already know the answers.

What Did You Do for Your Career Today?

When I first meet with artists, I often ask this simple question: What did you do for your career today? Because I'm well aware that by the time they talk to me, many feel overwhelmed and have already retreated into a mindset of excuses—I only have so much time so it's not worth it, or it's already late, or I'm burnt out. But excuses don't help you at all.

That's not to say feeling overwhelmed is unreasonable. The music business is intimidating once you begin to look at the business aspects and everything that you need to do to become self-sufficient as well as effective and productive, but there's a little secret people don't know: The little stuff can be just as important as the big stuff. It's about forward motion, and forward motion can take place in the smallest snatches of free time. Whether you're waiting for someone else to do vocals on a recording before you mix or you're waiting on a tech guy or girl to set up your Web site, there's always stuff that can be done.

A simple checklist can include:

> **Updating a networking site.**
>
> **Adding friends to a networking site.**
>
> **Researching new venues or contacting a new venue.**
>
> **Researching new review sites or magazines and/or sending to them.**
>
> **Researching booking agents and/or contacting them.**
>
> **Researching new management companies and/or contacting them.**
>
> **Researching hotels or places to stay for tours and adding them to your database.**
>
> **Reviewing your set lists against shows and figuring out what song should go where.**
>
> **Writing a blog and putting it up on your networking sites.**

Flyering for a local show or putting up stickers and other promo materials.

Contacting a new radio station and sending out information to it.

Sending out a press package to someone in the industry for anything from reviews to production, record deals to a licensing deal to a booking.

E-mailing back fans or people who leave messages for you.

Putting up a new video on a video site.

Signing up for a new network site for exposure.

Finding a new place where you can sell your music online.

Contacting a new record store and asking about consignment for a few recordings.

Following up with a venue you just played.

Making contact with a new band that is in your genre and with which you might be able to perform.

Posting pictures on a picture site.

Researching licensing opportunities for your music or sending to a licensing site.

Giving away a free disc or free merchandise to someone.

This is just the start of a list of small things that don't take up much time but can help you to be incredibly effective and move forward in the right direction. These are the quickies that add up. For example, putting up a picture on a photo site might not seem like much, but if you're consistently signing up for new photo sites and putting up your pictures, even if you only sign up for one free photo site a week and only put up one picture a day, you're creating activity and continuity. After a month you'll have four photo sites and twenty new photos up that are being optimized and seen by people who may not have seen you in other places.

In the same way, that one little venue you research can be added to a database of venues you research each day, so by the time you're either self-booking or working with a booking agent, you have a solid and extensive list from which to work, complete with all the information you may need.

Like I said: It's not always about the big things. Of course those things matter, but small things can be built into larger things. Yes, it's wonderful when you have five straight hours to dedicate to the business of music, but even if you're only dedicating five minutes a day—especially on those days when excuses creep in—you're moving further than many others who simply do nothing at all. Just make sure when you crawl into bed you can respond to the question "What did you do for your career today?" with an answer that shows effective productivity, regardless of how little or how much.

These small steps go the distance in the long run; make sure you take one or two each day. If it's truly your dream to make it in music, then it's going to come down to the continuity and the commitment of the big and the small on a regular basis. Hey—it's how you learned and continue to know the instrument you play. Just apply the same "practice concept" to the business side of your career.

Notes on Productivity

When are you at your best and when are you at your worst? When do you get the most business done? When does your practicing seem most inspiring and self-fueling? On the other hand, when do you seem to be accomplishing less? When do you feel uninspired? When is rehearsal a drag? We all wish we could be operating at 110 percent all the time, but often it just doesn't happen that way. So instead of comparing your phenomenal productivity of yesterday to your lackluster today, why not take a closer look at the patterns and factors that allow you to be your best and, alternately, bring out your worst?

The first thing to consider is your physical well-being. Are you getting too little sleep, the right amount or too much? What about the food you eat? Those sayings about brain food—they apply to you personally. What does eating heavy foods do to your creativity? Eating light foods? How does this nourishment affect your business sense, even your attention span? Maybe eating junk food helps you practice better while eating healthily allows you more concentration when you're working on the business side of things.

Another factor to consider is your emotional well-being. How does the stability of your relationships affect your productivity and creative output? How does a fight affect these things? Loneliness?

Some people are more effective with certain tasks at certain times of the day. On a similar note, doing certain tasks before others can affect your productivity. For instance, if you're stressed out by accounting and then go to a less stressful task that still manages to upset you, it could be that the stress is being carried over from the previous task. Reorganizing the order of odd jobs may help.

There are a million more factors that can be personalized and specified. The point is to think about why particular activities were so good or so bad. Look for the patterns and maybe track them in a diary. What elements could be attributed to the greater success of whatever you were trying to accomplish? This will help you know how to mimic these factors for success in other areas or for the same thing at another time.

For me, I write better in the early afternoon. I can do it in the morning or in the evening, but I've found, after looking at my patterns, that I'm much more productive and effective when I write in the afternoon, shortly after having lunch. When I'm doing music pre-production or brainstorming, I tend to do better earlier in the morning than later in the afternoon and often come up with my best ideas on an empty stomach.

Take the steps to know yourself and how you work, and you may be surprised at what you can easily change for optimum results. With limited hours in a day and incredible workloads, doesn't it make sense to take a couple of minutes to analyze and figure out the details of our effectiveness and productivity so that every minute is well spent?

Who Owns What?

So when it comes to your music, your songs and your demos ... Who owns what?

Very often people don't think about who owns or has rights to songs, or their work on certain songs, when an artist or group is recording them. Then if a tune starts making money, collaborative contributions or samples from other songs can become a big issue.

Let's give a best-case scenario. A friend of yours gets a song of yours licensed to a movie or a commercial, and it begins airing at a great rate. The song is now a profitable item. Now let's add a worst-case scenario to this best-case scenario. You used two other people to help write it and asked a number of people to do a favor by recording instruments for it. Perhaps you even used a sample from a song you didn't write.

Now a few people hear the song, and you start getting calls and e-mails. "I played on this" or "I helped write that." Words like "Favors should be rewarded" and "How much is my cut?" begin to get thrown around. You will also get the "I got you the deal, so I want a cut" line too. Then someone recognizes the sample you used and reports it. This is a very common thing. There are musical hall monitors out there just looking to bust people for doing wrong. These are the tattletales who are going to get you sued by a label, publisher, or the copyright holder from whom you've stolen. Welcome to a world of crap, but know that you opened up the front door by not addressing all the issues that could occur.

So what's the best way to understand and deal with all these potential issues? It's actually easy; one of the few things in the music industry that is.

First, clarify all aspects of your music. Make sure you have a clear understanding from everyone you're working with related to the ownership of every sample you use. Create a clear understanding of who's shopping it and what the expectations are. Then get it all in writing.

Think from an optimistic but prepared level. If you have anyone else involved with a song or your album, make sure everything is clear and in writing in advance of anything happening. When someone says they're doing a favor, clarify it. Ask the question, "Hey if this song takes off, are you expecting a certain cut"?

If you're paying a musician to play on your music, make sure it's clear he or she is being paid for the performance and the session and will make no additional percentages on that song. On the other hand, if the person plays a major role in that song, make sure that's all worked out in advance. It will make your life worlds easier.

Don't steal samples. I personally prefer artists to create their own samples, but if you're going to use someone else's work, make sure you take care of all the logistics around the licensing of it and do it the right way: legally!!!

Tend to these issues on the front side, and the backside will be much more comfortable. Yes, it may seem like overkill, but it will save you the hell of lawsuits, arguments, and serious problems if something should happen with one of your songs.

Take the prepared approach. Clarify, communicate, and create written documents that state everything that should be stated for every possible profit outcome of that song or body of work. Ask any musician who's been involved with any type of copyright dispute or royalty lawsuit: Each can only wish he or she went this route. Take this path from the start, and you will be much happier in the end.

Handing over Responsibility

When is the right time to get a manager? When is the right time to go after an agent? When do you go after the labels? What kind of labels? Should you work with a booking agent? Should you work with a promoter? If and when you do, you need to be prepared to understand the responsibility that's going to come with handing over certain aspects of your band, your music, and your business to someone else.

You need to think along the lines of what is being done for you, what is being said about you, and the professionalism in how you're being delivered and presented to others. You want to make sure you're getting the reports from these people about what's being booked, what's being sold, what's happening, and basically what you're paying for. All too often, bands get excited at the idea of signing with a manager, a publisher, an agent, a label, or whomever. Many feel as if a weight is lifted off them and they're free to be more of the "rock stars" that they see themselves as. In turn, there are a great deal of people and companies out there that know this fact and work to take full advantage of it by taking more money, larger percentages, and doing less work than they say.

Plan regular meetings. If someone is being paid or taking a percentage of everything from sales to bookings, along with time and hours logged, you should know what those hours are and what's happening during them. It's the foolish musician, whether a local artist or major-label millionaire, who just lets the business take care of itself.

Look at Billy Joel and what happened to him a number of years back. His ex-wife's brother was handling his career, and Billy just let him run with it. Well he ran with it until Billy realized he was almost broke and had to go back out on the road just to make money to support his lifestyle.

A warning sign for a potential agent or manager who's taking the reins on many of the business aspects is hesitation if you ask this person to report hours and activities or to meet with you to talk about what he or she is doing. This is information you have a right to know about, and an honorable organization or person would be willing to share with no issue whatsoever.

It's your responsibility to review things and look for discrepancies. Why would people who are trying to put one over on you or trick you out of money or opportunities come out and share what they aren't doing for you or the illegal things they're doing behind your back? Ask for references of these people; talk to other bands that have been involved with them. Research for yourself and not just from the press materials you're handed or their Web site.

Even if everything checks out and you begin to work with someone who may be taking over booking, marketing, promoting, distributing, or anything else, it doesn't excuse you from being involved in the business side of it. Just because you now have someone booking the gigs and promoting doesn't mean you shouldn't be helping in any way that you can. Talk to the booking agent or the manager and find out what efforts he or she is taking and what you can do. Yes, having someone involved and someone who's being paid can take work off your plate, but it doesn't mean you shouldn't help with making that booking as effective as possible. What can you do to help hit a few places online that are not being hit by the other person? What can you do to supplement what's being done for you? Together things can be even more effective.

As you hand over responsibility, it's not all about not trusting a person or a label. It's also about knowing what this industry is and has done in addition to being as well informed as possible about everything having to do with your career. It's your responsibility to make those who are working for you accountable, and if you're not holding them accountable for their actions, then you're screwing yourself over. In some ways, once you hand over responsibility for the business aspects of your music and your band, you're the one who has to become just that much more responsible.

Music Banking

The goal for most musicians, or should I say, most aspiring musicians, is to be able to depend on their music career. It's the idea of being able to work only as a musician and not have anything to distract them from practicing, performing, recording, promoting, and marketing their music.

You should think about your career and your finances just as you think about pre-production, production, and recording. Even if you don't have the money, plan for your needs and what you want before you quit your day job. If you set up a goal and a system of knowing what you're going to need in the short term and the long term, as well as on a monthly, quarterly, and yearly basis, you can not only get financially organized, but you can also make a much more professional and well-prepared decision as to when to quit the day job and go full time with your music.

Also think about your future. This doesn't mean you have to have a partner at the time, but do you think you're going to want to be married? Do you think you're going to want to have children? Do you have a goal to live somewhere? To own certain things? Take all these long-term ideas into consideration and set in place a functional, financially sound template for your future *while* organizing the present.

I'm not a financial advisor by any means, but what I found most effective was to open up a series of different bank accounts to maintain money in separate places. There are five key accounts I recommend you open for the music business and four for your personal business. Now, some think this is crazy, but the level of organization it brings will simplify things drastically and make you more aware of the money you're earning and the money you're spending.

The Business Accounts

The first account is your income account, which is specifically for the album, the downloads, and the merchandise as well as the performance payments. This would be the income account or the first account. Use it for tracking and tax purposes and it will make things easier because it's mostly inbound or internally circulated money.

The second account is your artist or band logistical account. This is the account to which you transfer money from the income account, and from it only pay out to logistical items such as gas, hotels, food for the road or the gigs, tolls, parking for shows, band purchases, and other necessary items. Having this as a separate account gives you an easier tracking system for the money being spent on your band as a business, thus making bookkeeping a breeze.

The third account is the recording budget account. I advise artists not only to have an account specifically for their recording when they're doing the FSRP but also to have that same account used down the line for other recordings. You'll be able to track every dollar that goes into the recording process. Regardless of the demo, the album, the EP, or the single day in the studio, you can track expenses as well as decide what money will be shifted to this account.

The fourth account is your promotional, marketing, and branding account. This account is strictly for all things promotional. This is different from the first account because this is all outbound money. It's money that will be shifted to this account from your first account and used only for posters, flyers, advertising, duplication, Web work, and anything and everything promotional. This, just like the other accounts, will give you a full picture of how much is being spent and on what. Also, as you access this account and the others, you will know exactly what's there and not make the common mistakes of using allocated money on the wrong things.

The fifth account is the tax account. This is one of those accounts you don't get a card for, you don't get a checkbook for, and you set it up strictly for deposits and zero withdrawals. For safety's sake, everything that you bring in from sales on anything, automatically deduct 20 percent and deposit it into this account. Do this and you will never have tax problems. At the end of the year, after taxes are done, more often than not, you will find that you will not have to pay any extra if you're diligent and constantly putting that 20 percent of everything away. On some occasions you may even have money left over that you can use. Trust me, if you don't open up any of the other accounts I've mentioned, go to the bank, open up an account, call it tax account, and drop 20 percent of everything into it. It will be one of the smartest decisions you make.

That, in my opinion, is the best way to handle band finances. You can set up budgets and designate what goes to where every time money comes in. Just as you designate the percentage for taxes, you can have a percentage going to promotions or a percentage going to the next recording. Then you can decide what everyone can get paid. This process will streamline and simplify things radically.

The Personal Side Accounts:

The first account is your personal account. This is where your basic banking and living happens. This is the account where you deposit the checks you would write yourself from the business account as well as wherever else money is coming from. This account is where you get your spending money, however you spend it, from rent to food to coffee or whatever else your little heart desires.

The second account is like the business account, a tax account—yes, you're going to get taxed both as a business and as an individual. There are accountants who can help you with this process and make things easier, but I would advise that for everything you deposit, you put that same 20 percent away for taxes and don't touch it.

Now remember, if you're tracking receipts both as a business entity and individual, a great many write-offs can occur, but let those write-offs be a wonderful surprise at the end of the tax season.

The third account is what I call the "far future account." This is money you slowly put away. Think of this account as the money you will retire on, the money that you will live on after you don't want to work anymore. This could also be the money you invest into CDs, stocks, mutual funds, and other items that will help you accrue money slowly. Don't maintain a card for this account and don't touch it. Also, when you invest into certain long-term, high-interest-bearing things, make sure you can't touch them. Let it be viewed as money that's not yet yours but will be years down the road.

The fourth account is for short-term goals. This is the money you might be putting away for a house or to help you stay afloat and live as a full-time musician during the rough times when money is a little tighter.

Every musician wants to bank on his or her career, but in order to have a career, a lifestyle, and long-term sustainable success, one must organize. Even if you open the accounts with only a couple of bucks, you can get into the necessary habits of saving. You can build a vision of where you are right now but also see clearly into the future.

Many musicians just look to the stars and think they will be millionaires; they don't plan and don't prepare. Given all the opportunities from performing to licensing and from sales to insertions, it's now more possible than ever to maintain a realistic salary level. By preparing not only for the most avenues of success and sustainability but also for your financial needs both now and in the future, you can achieve a long, successful, sustainable career with secure finances in place.

Effective Information Collection

Organization is the central component to most businesses and companies. This same organization needs to take place with bands as well. It takes a lot of work to set up Web sites, book shows, plan tours, work advertising and marketing plans, and increase sales and fan numbers. It can be tedious and incredibly time consuming, and it will require an attention to detail that you might not be used to.

Still, it has to be done if you want to make things effective and productive for your group. The most common problem I come across is that most artists don't look past the given project or task they're working on. As I mentioned previously, any task you're working on should have an effect on the goal at hand, but it should also serve a long-term purposes as well to make your time and your work as productive as possible.

For example, let's say you're a Boston-based band and you're playing a festival just outside Atlanta, Georgia, this coming summer. Taking the opportunity to find shows on your way down and on your way back up might give you the opportunity for a small tour if the band has the time. This would allow you to reach new audiences in places you may not have played in or haven't yet marketed to.

Now this is simple and obvious. Most bands will search for venues and try to book shows that take them down to this festival and then take them back. Most bands will find accommodations, whether they're staying in hotels or trying to find a house they can stay at. That's often where it stops. A lot of bands will get the club names and the club contacts and that's it. That is an ineffective use of travel time, work time, and band promotion time. Think of every place you play and every town you go to as a place you will return to. You may not return to that venue specifically, but each stop should be viewed as a research collection mission.

Let's say this Boston group goes west first and books its first night in Springfield, Massachusetts, on its way down to Georgia. Bands need to understand that, the first time you play in a city you've never been to, it might not be the best show. All the more reason to collect information on bands that are in that area and have a great draw. It also brings us to another database you may want to keep in your records in an Excel type document.

High Drawing Bands in Cities – This is something you can collect from research online as well as when you visit new cities. What bands always draw a great crowd? Who is their contact point that you can network with to find out their schedule? How far out do they book?

The idea is to collect information that you can maintain in databases that you can easily access for any city you hit.

When I was on tour with one group, the road manager—Jack Dorin (kick ass RM, FYI)—kept a ten-page Excel sheet.

The databases he kept were as follows:

> **Venues** – This had all the pertinent information on venues—contact points, addresses, phone numbers, fax numbers, capacities, the style of venue, and more.
>
> **Hotels** – All the places to stay in a given town and the best prices.
>
> **Restaurants** – A basic layout of the best food places.

Radio Stations – Every core radio station and type of format for that given location.

TV Stations – Every network in the area.

Newspapers and Entertainment Rags – All the papers in that area. This was the easiest one. Every city Jack went into when he was a roadie, he would pick up all the local papers in the mornings, copy out the core information, and then toss the papers so he was not dragging along a small tree in the tour bus.

Major Points of Interest – This was a database of all the schools, colleges, major companies, etc. in a given city.

Local Band Database – As listed above, the database on the bands that are a really strong pull in each city.

Sales – Tracking the sales of the band in each city, not just the sales as a whole, but what was sold and where it was sold.

Overall Sales Records – A sheet showing all physical sales, downloads, and show payments. Who was paid out and what was paid out to whom.

Each city and each show was a research project, and if we had time, the backup band was sent out to find information about the town. We would dig up information that would help make the next trip there twice as successful.

Collecting information can be tedious, but the attention to detail and time spent on the front side can save hours and days on the backside. Everything you search out will make things effective for that first stop, but it will make things even more effective for the next time. You can even purchase databases that have been collected online, like college booking databases and press databases.

Format and template things for yourself so that each show and each piece of information you find is easy to add right in and then later reference. You don't have to create a massive database structure of information overnight. Taking small steps each day, adding information as you go, is just as effective, if not more so.

Whatever information is most important to you, keep that in a database as well. Keep the records for all your expenses, all your shows, all your Web materials, everything, easily accessible ... **and of course:** Back it up and make sure there are updated backup copies on disc somewhere safe. The more information you have collected and the easier it is to reference, the easier it will be to be more productive, more effective, and more efficient.

Secret Info Stash

When you're organizing all the elements of your music and business, do you have it as organized as it should be? As you build up your stash of information and begin to collect Web sites, logins, passwords, usernames, and access codes, it's absolutely necessary that you track, maintain, and protect this information. In these days of people hacking accounts and stealing passwords, it's not only important to protect and keep track of this information; it's also important constantly to update and change passwords to keep security at the best and highest level possible.

I recommend to every band that they create a secret stash, or a safe document, that is password protected on their computer but also printed out and stored with your most sensitive documents in a safety deposit box, a safe, or somewhere that is not easily accessible. The document will represent all your core information in different sections. This also can be updated and easily accessed every time you need information. I advise the following breakdown:

Personal information

- Phone numbers

- E-mails

- Emergency contacts

- Addresses

- Medical information

This should include all of the medical information for every member of the band. It can also include the most essential band contacts and their role.

Financial/business information (the most important)

- Bank account info
- PayPal
- iTunes account
- CD Baby
- Cafe Press (merchandise account)
- Vistaprint
- Duplicator account

This should include your bank login, PayPal, or however you're being paid through different distribution centers. It can also include your merchandising company, booking contacts, and all companies working on promotional and distribution materials.

Basic bills

- Phone
- Internet
- Electric/water
- Rent or mortgage
- Car payment
- Credit cards
- Etc.

Does the band have a phone plan? Does the band have Internet? Having all these things together will make life easier whenever things change. It can also help you budget as money comes in to what needs to be taken care and when.

Basic Web and networking information:

- Web hosting
- Domain name information
- E-mails

- Social networking sites, logins, and passwords

What is the login to your Web hosting and domain name information? What if you need to make changes or hand off the information to a designer? All the more reason why you should have this well organized. Also with all the different network sites, you should have different passwords and tracking of what you've got up and where you are.

I know so many people (including myself) who have forgotten a password, a login, or even a membership to a particular site. Maintaining a backup sheet where you can track all your key information is a great solution for that problem, and it can make searching for information a piece of cake. Secure this information in a document that is password protected and store that password somewhere else!!!!! Also, have a printout available and accessible by someone you trust in case something goes wrong with the computer and/or you're out on tour and not around.

The more you problem solve, organize, and prepare for worst-case scenarios, the less problems are likely to occur, and when they do, they'll be solved a lot quicker. Remember that in these times of hackers, spammers, and phishers, the more you secure your information, change up passwords, and continue to secure your private information, the better the chances that it will stay private. Start your secret stash sheet today. Collect all your information, and store it safely and securely. It will make a difference down the line.

... But THEY aren't doing it!

"But they don't do it that way." This is something I hear way too often in response to the attention to detail my approach to the music industry requires, especially when it means a band has to do something differently from what they're currently doing.

They're half-right. It's true; many don't put in the effort that I look for and believe is best. They're half–wrong, however, in that there are a lot of behind-the-scenes details that you never see, which allow the artist or bands to look as solid as they do. Part of marketing is to make the act look larger than life and make it appear effortless.

About half the time I start with a consulting client or an artist I'm producing, I hear … "They don't do it that way" or "This is the way I've seen it done, and it's not the way you're talking about at all."

The Majors, the Indies, the Newbies, and the Luckies.

In the major labels, they *do* set in place the type of budgets and layouts I've been discussing. The majors are corporations that set up business plans, prospectuses, and marketing layouts on any project in which they're going to invest. They also set up these layouts to acquire investors and backings for projects. This is the same format as the independent labels.

When you think of even a basic independent budget, you don't think a label owner can go to a group of people and say, "Hey, give me some money so I can make a record and see how it does." It's going to take a plan, justifications, basic goals, and expectations to gain the capital to make the recording.

Setting up a business plan like the Freedom Solutions Recording Plan (FSRP) gives an artist a complete layout, from pre-production to post-production to the release and initial marketing. This sets up a blueprint that can guide the artist and justify the investment for potential donors, investors, or angel capitalists.

I create many FSRP blueprint business plans for artists who are part of other labels and management groups. These are not albums I produce myself, but rather I help to justify the investment in artists for labels, managers, and agencies with which they may already be involved in.

Of course your favorite artists are not going to have the business plan from their label up on their Web site. A lot of the details around the creation and funding for some of the upper-echelon artists are kept private, just like many of the other elements. The industry isn't necessarily trying to hide them; they're just looking to give the best appearance without going into the intricacies of business.

The image of some alt rockers should be the shows, the band, the vibe, the tour bus, the merchandise. That is what they want presented. Not the marketing encapsulations, budgets, layouts, and tax sheets. I mean, hey, taxes aren't very rock and roll.

Now, occasionally you will run into a band that actually came out of nowhere, had none of their stuff together, and just broke through.

This is the Cinderella story. This story comes to fruition less than .001 percent of the time. Trying to follow the lucky ones is not much of a recipe for success. At the same time, imitating your favorite big label acts is not the smartest approach either. While it's a strength to be musically inspired by them, copying their marketing tactics can be foolish.

Think of it this way. Take one of your favorite bands, one whose logo might not be at the level at which I advise independent artists to have their logos—perhaps it's a little extra artsy and hard to read. That logo is effective not because of its layout; it's effective because of the marketing campaign behind it.

When a marketing and promotional campaign is launched for a major label or high-level, independent label band, a great deal of money is put out for advertising, branding, promoting, and any other kind of public exposure. These groups have large sums of cash that allow, not so much for corners to be cut, but for images and elements to be different since the balance of effective materials to cash on hand is shifted more toward the money.

Now most groups are not millionaires and thus are going to put the bulk of the money into the recording. Still, money has to be budgeted for promotions, marketing, and branding. If this doesn't happen, how will you get the word out about the recording on which you're spending all your money?

Taking the steps to have a logo that's effective and materials that go above and beyond, with the proper content, bios, and professional layouts, is crucial. From the appearance of your disc to your social networking sites to your Web site and everything in between, it has to stand out, be easy to recognize, and have uniformity and continuity so that you can reach not only the new fans who will gravitate to you when they first see you but also the fans who will take a little more encouragement. These are the ones that continue to see your logo and your tagline around and see your music and your bio showing up more and more. These are the type of fans you might call the late bloomers, and when you have a constant and steady stream of good marketing, the more they'll see of you and the more they will be drawn to you.

A band, artist, or group is still, in a way, a product. It takes the right marketing to find the sales, recognition, fan base, and continuity to survive in the industry. It's no longer about waiting for that big deal to happen and letting some big label come in, sweep you up, and take care of all the little intricacies. It's now up to you. Creating the most detailed package that encompasses everything from the music to the assisting materials is absolutely required to survive today. Making those items stand out in the best and most effective way possible may mean pulling back some on the artistic marketing elements. **(I am not talking about pulling back on the artistic elements of the music!!!)** You may have to make the logo a little bulkier, you might have to choose a tagline that you always use, and you might have to make your package as a whole more top notch than those you see around you, but it will produce results.

With the mixture of the strongest elements from your pre-production, post-production, and release, combined with the efforts of the artist to push through to new channels everyday by collecting contacts and resources, by researching new venues and avenues through which to distribute these materials, you will have a fighting chance for success. It takes all of these elements working together, and the minute you cut corners is the minute you diminish the opportunities you might otherwise have had.

When you say to yourself, "Well they aren't doing it that way," take a careful look to see why they don't do it that way. Ninety-nine percent of the time it's because they have the supplement of large money or a marketing push allowing them to do it differently. The industry is dramatically changing. What was the way even five years ago is not the best path now. Arm yourself with an excess of preparation, details, and a well put-together package, with the music, the marketing, the promo, and the branding in order, and you will thrive.

When It's Time to Change the Plan

A major problem that arises in many careers is deciding the right time to change what's being done and find a more effective approach. Musicians and artists as a whole often have a very hard time shifting mindsets or accepting change when it comes to their careers. This can be detrimental and only perpetuate the problems or lack of success.

Here's an old-time quote to apply to the situation: "Don't change horses in mid stream." In my opinion, if the horse isn't going anywhere and you're sitting in a puddle of water, it's time to get down, get your feet wet, and get moving on a better horse. Wow, think I took that one a little too far!

The point is you need to look at your goals and figure out where you are at every step of the way. Don't look too far into the future, or you won't be able to see the path right at your feet. Yes, becoming a multi-million dollar superstar is a great dream, but the dream itself can put you on a path that can keep you from achieving that goal and worse, keep you from achieving basic self-sufficiency in music.

Some bands use the same formula for booking, promoting, recording, marketing, and soliciting with this very dangerous and ill-thought-out notion that it will just happen. I hear too often, "If we keep doing what we have been doing, we will get _____ (fill in the blank here: noticed, seen, signed, rich, famous, successful, picked up, and every other word that would equate to the dream of success)."

Take for example people who go on diets to lose weight. If they don't see any results after a month, then isn't it time to take stock of what's wrong? What's happening and why are things not working?

When you track and analyze what you're doing, how it turned out, and what positives and negatives occurred, you'll be in the best frame of mind to move forward effectively. Which brings up the fun stuff—MORE WORK!!! To be able to track and analyze, you're going to have to keep and organize information so you can decide if what you're doing is the best thing possible.

- How many shows did you play in a month?

- How many people were at the shows?

- How much merchandise did you sell at the shows?

- How much merchandise did you sell online?

- How many downloads did you sell?

- How much did it cost for gas, advertising, equipment repair, etc.?

- How much money came in?

- How was that money distributed?

- Where did you market and how much did you market for shows, for product, etc.?
- How many Web site hits?
- How many social networking hits and plays?
- How many friends added in any of the social networking sites?

When you have all the information, you can run it against ... yes, you guessed it ... more information!

Where and when did you advertise and market? Answering this question can give you clues to surges in sales or profit. How much promoting did you do for the shows? If the biggest turnouts had a different amount of postering or marketing, then maybe apply that level for all shows.

You can then also ask yourselves a series of questions that can allow you to see what's happening and what is and is not working. This can also help you see if your manager or agent is doing his or her job correctly. If he or she doesn't have the information to the above questions, then that person's not being an organized or effective manager.

At the same time, if you're doing something that's only producing limited success, you need to bring it to the next level. If you're not moving forward, you're moving backwards. It's crucial to take an educated, intelligent, and humble look around at what's happening. Creating time frames and setting goals is also a very good idea. Whether it's a certain number of shows a month, a certain amount of sales a month, a certain amount of solicitations, or a certain number of bookings a month—set a goal and hit it. If you don't make it in the first month, then aim for the next. If you don't make the next, then it's time to get some help or readjust the plan and the approach.

Many artists use the consulting services I offer as a daily check up as well as a reminder to take a different approach or see things from a different perspective. These are not artists I am producing; these are artists who schedule one to two consults a month in order to go over where they are and organize ideas to get to the next level.

Having someone look over what you're doing with a fresh set of ideas and a fresh view can really make the difference. Make sure whoever you talk to is someone that has an understanding of the industry as it is and not as it was or as it reads in a book. It is key to find someone who has a true knowledge of the industry.

There are stories out there about bands doing it one way and then just being found or discovered, but those stories are right up there with the chances of winning the lottery. You need to give the same attention to the business of your music as you do to the music itself. This attention is what allows a song to start in one place and grow into a full arrangement with all the pieces that developed from the ground up. The business side of music is the same way. If you're not clearly tracking what's happening around you and how it's happening, you won't gain the full understanding of what you're doing right and what you're doing wrong. Take the steps to make sure the work you're doing for your art and your career is as smart, effective, and productive as possible to get the best results.

Back That Thing Up!

Backups are always important. This is not a news flash. The horror stories about a crashed computer or a lost disc are everywhere. We've all had that freak out—or at least most of the people I know have. Are you taking all the steps to make sure that you've backed up everything you need to? Is it properly marked? Are your old backups discarded safely?

I recently had my PC crash. The motherboard went bad. I'm not the biggest tech guy, but I knew I was in trouble. Fortunately I had most everything backed up, and have a friend who was able to get the last few things off and taken care of. I'm now on a MacBook Pro and have been taking some time to reorganize everything from music files to documents to plans. I went through discs and discs of crap as well as files that were backed up with different dates and different names. I have a lot of things well organized, but I don't think I was organized to the point I should've been until this minor catastrophe struck. Minor only because I'd backed up. For artists, musicians, and everyone really, it's incredibly important not only to backup your information but also to know where your information is.

Get rid of old demos or at least catalog them as you burn them. Don't let music sit around unmarked or unnamed. Make sure to mark them clearly. I spent hours going over old discs and figuring out what was what and making sure to mark it correctly. Even if you have a truckload of discs or tapes, try to review one every day. It will feel less overwhelming, and it can get you moving toward your goal of organization.

Make sure you're tracking your backups. I've begun naming folders with the date at the end of each name. Then as things change, I update or backup again. Make sure you're discarding or replacing older backups or that they're marked with the date so you aren't going back to outdated information.

Remember, a lot of the music or backup information that you might be throwing away is still key information that you don't want anyone to hear or see. Make sure your music, your information, and your personal information is not getting in the wrong hands. Make sure to destroy discs you're getting rid of the right way. Don't just toss them in the trash. Break them in half. Scratch across the disc a number of times to make sure the information cannot be read. Or my new favorite … **nuke em!** Put a CD in a microwave for two seconds, maybe three max, and watch the light show. It's pretty cool and completely destroys the disc. I was going nuts with this the other day and fried twenty old discs. It's entertaining and safe … I think.

This is pretty obvious stuff, but make sure to have your ducks in a row. Organize your backups; have a couple of copies of your information in different places. Keep the information, music, and work you have done, protected and secure. Don't let a terrible loss be the catalyst to start. Start today.

Looking for Management or Representation

If you have completed the CD and the promotional materials and set your branding and marketing in place but feel that you want to concentrate more on the music and less on the business, or you feel it's time to turn over the booking, promoting, and marketing to another person, this might be the time to think about management or representation.

Finding a manager is easy—they're everywhere—but finding a good manager is a challenge. I've seen all kinds. It comes down to how the manager or management group is going to work for you and what they're actually going to do. Talk is cheap and actions are truly what matter. The same goes for Indie labels, talent buyers, and rep agents.

You have to decide who you're going to go with, what you're going to get, and what you're going to have to give.

You need to find someone who's organized, has a game plan, and has the experience to bring you forward towards your goal. This manager, label, agent, or whomever needs to be able to keep you in the loop and explain every step along the way, as well as what he or she is doing and when.

Interview managers as they interview you. Find out what they've done and what they believe. What's their approach, and is it something that you believe in? How often do you meet? Will this person or group show you time logs and work charts? It's your right to know what's going on as well as what's getting done and when.

Also, clearly define who's responsible for doing what. Managers have many different fees and percentage plans with the different bands that they work with, and they're based on the work that has to be done.

If you have completed the entire FSRP process or something similar to it, you'll be able to go to a manager with not just a recording but an entire promotional package that will have many different elements to help with the marketing, branding, and promotion. The more complete the package you give someone to work with, the more effective and efficient he or she can be for you. Since the person won't have to create an entire package and, instead, will be able to implement and import your information into his or her formats, your manager will be able to book faster, promote quicker, and market you with greater ease.

See if you can sign a preliminary deal or begin with a trial period with a manager. Set down some basic ideas around booking and promotion and see if it goes down the way it was discussed.

Again, always read the fine print. What do managers want in return besides percentages?

- **Do they have exclusive rights to you?**
- **Can they profit or get in the way of bigger deals?**
- **Will they have a percentage of profit if you achieve a certain profit level, even if you're no longer working with them?**
- **How will they market you?**

- What tools will they use?

- What kind of money will they spend?

- Do they have effective and proven techniques?

- What physical media will they use? How will they market online?

- What plans do they have for booking shows and properly promoting them?

- What plans do they have for booking tours?

There are dozens of other questions you can and should ask to find out what's going on and how it goes on with these potential suitors. A manager can make life easier for a band if he or she is working well with the band and presenting you in the best possible way. At the same time, managers have ruined deals, lost bookings, and ripped off bands due to poor planning, unprofessional execution, and an all around lack of knowledge. A good manager or management group has to have a clear understanding of the market and the music industry today. They have to be up on information that, in this industry, is ever changing. I've seen management groups still using ten-year-old models, and you can guess the results; they just won't cut it anymore.

And in those ten years, things have changed dramatically. Managers and management groups need to be on top of all of it; it's their job. Make sure that every question you have is answered, and make sure you have a very clear and solid agreement on paper.

Lastly, make sure you have an out clause in the contract. This is the biggest safety if something's not working or the relationship is not benefiting your band. It should be stated somewhere in the contract that if the manager is not doing the things he or she agreed to do, with no explanation for the lack of execution, you have the right to terminate your agreement, and the manager will have no rights to your band or your work anymore.

Remember it's all about the details, and finding the right manager involves a truckload of details.

Organizations

Many musicians shy away from joining groups and unions mostly because they fear exorbitant costs or don't want to bother with the tracking and organization that's required. It's foolish not to connect in this way, just as it would be foolish to avoid networking sites, resource groups, and mailing lists that deliver top-notch information about events, contacts, and opportunities you might not find out about from other sources.

Even some of the organizations that have an annual cost can be well worth it in the end. Explore different searches and keywords that might pertain to you and not just music groups or band organizations. Look deeper. Use the noggin. Join statewide band directories. Sign up for mailing lists that are going to give you information on how to insert your music into different media. Look up vocalist organizations for your singer, drumming groups for your drummer, and bass associations for your bass player.

The idea is simple. Joining these organizations can network you with people you wouldn't otherwise reach and can potentially open up opportunities that you wouldn't normally hear about. Not every single group you join will be the most productive or effective, but they put your information out.

It's a crucial part of your career actually to grow. The more networking you do, both for fans and for other music industry people, the more you'll learn and be able to see what's happening out there. What are you seeing people do that's working, and what are you seeing people doing that's not working?

The organizations out there can talk about everything from publishing to press releases, new venues to new managers to new labels. It's important not only to study the information you get but also to make sure the information is coming from a reputable source. There's a lot of information out there, and while it's great to be involved and get your name to as many different groups and organizations as possible, it's even better to question and double check the information you receive for its truth and validity.

These organizations can come and go quickly, which is part of the reason I'm not listing any here, but it's simple to research them online and sign up as it seems appropriate. One step you can also take to protect yourself from those that spam, or those that might start as a good organization and then go bad, is to sign up with a specific e-mail that's meant specifically for mailing lists and organizations. This is commonly done for networking sites as well. Brain Grenade Entertainment uses one specific e-mail for all its networking sites and one for all the organizations it's a part of. That way, it doesn't clog up the normal e-mails and makes things easier to track. Also, as you sign up for these organizations, make sure there's a clear way to unsubscribe and cancel. The more reputable organizations will always have these options.

The music industry is ever changing. Information that's true one day might be false the next. It's important to have your fingers on the pulse of what's happening. While attacking the networking sites and reaching new fans is a very important aspect of your marketing, promotion, and sustainability, it's just as crucial to have an understanding of what other colleagues and fellow musicians are doing and not doing. Take a part of your day to learn about others, about changes in the industry as well as changes or petitions in laws and regulations that involve everything from file sharing to publishing. It's key to success and, in the end, just the smart thing to do.

Students and Teachers

Everywhere you look in the classifieds, in the music stores, the clubs, on telephone poles, craigslist—anywhere relating to music—you'll find dozens of advertisements for teachers. The problem is in distinguishing who can actually teach and who's trying to make an extra dollar and has no teaching skills whatsoever.

In the day of YouTube, other social networks, and Web sites, it can take less than thirty minutes to set up an impressive Web site, advertisement, flyer, or marketing presence that says for so much an hour you can learn everything you'll ever need to know. I really can't stand these ads. As a drummer first and foremost, I like to scan YouTube for different drummers now and then. I've seen a good deal of drumming instructional videos online. Not long ago I watched a drummer, who could not have been more than twenty years old, talk about a topic and perform it at a, well, below sub par level.

This guy was well spoken; he had a good tone to his voice and a pretty decent camera presence. His drumming and the way he explained what he was doing, however, were very beginner, not remotely advanced enough to be teaching. Music instruction is one of areas where you don't have to be licensed as a teacher to instruct privately or tutor. In my opinion, it's unfortunate that anyone can call him- or herself a teacher. Now, in these video's comments, there were a great many rude and harsh comments blasting this kid, and as out of line as they were, they all had good points. However, in between the harsh comments were other drummers saying thanks and that they learned something new. It's a great thing to go out there and research, but if I was learning how to land a 747, a novice pilot who had landed a two-engine plane only once and was talking well above his knowledge and abilities might not be the one I'd listen to.

Now, if I watched and began to study a professional certified pilot video, where the teacher had years and years of experience as well as tons of training and tons of landings, I think I would feel a little more confident that I would be getting some of the best information I could. I'm not saying that there aren't young teachers who can help you get started on the right foot; however, with any instrument, having a solid foundation is key. It's important to learn the fundamentals from some- one who has them down and is able to explain and demonstrate them so that you don't start bad habits that could keep you from growing to your full potential.

I'm all about people learning in the most effective, specified, and individualized way, but if the foundation and the roots are not in place, unlearning might have to occur later on. I studied with a number of teachers early on who were either teaching overly advanced concepts, didn't know how to teach that well, or were just too young and inex- perienced. When I got to my next teacher, I had to relearn how to hold the sticks. It was awful and frustrating as hell. After months of retrain- ing my hands, I found I could do things I could never do before, and things were much easier when I was gripping the sticks in the best way to fit me and my playing. I moved much faster in my technique and my practice after unlearning and relearning.

Cut the corner on the unlearning. Take the time to search out the best teacher to fit you. Research the teachers you contact or find online.

- What is their experience?
- Who have they studied with?
- What do others say about them?
- What is their approach?

Watch out for teachers who are just looking for cash. The ones most concerned with the finances or a committed number of lessons, or even not letting you cancel on short notice, should raise red flags. Watch for these red flags. A teacher who talks too big or spends too much time playing during the time he's suppose to be teaching is another warning sign. Take stock after a series of lessons. Are you learning? Are things moving too slowly, and if so, is it you or is it the teacher?

Then, just as you should find a solid teacher, be a solid student. Realize you're going to have to learn basics that might not be a walk in the park, or even fun. To get to the best lessons and to be the best student, as well as build the potential foundation to become a teacher yourself, you have to have a mind that is open to learning different ideas and concepts.

Become your own teacher as you continue to study with others. Learn how you're best able to understand concepts. Track your progress and figure out how you learn and what makes learning work for you. Lastly, remember, you're never a master. Even the masters still study, and the truest master will never admit to being one. As you hone your craft and better yourself on your instrument, make sure you are taking the steps forward to allow you the most creativity, ability, consistency, and accuracy with your instrument.

Take lessons, even if you're no longer studying on a consistent basis. If you're on the road, see if you can meet up with certain teachers in different cities to add some different approaches to your playing. Find out who your favorite players studied with, and research the methods and approaches that they used. Always learn and always study, but make sure you're learning and studying effectively and make sure it's from a worthy teacher.

Advances

For a very long time, advances were the dream and aspiration of most struggling musicians, regardless of genre and style. The idea that someone appears and puts money in your lap, allowing you to quit your day job, record an album, and begin to tour, was the ultimate fantasy. The sad truth is it was actually occurring and *has* occurred in the industry for years.

The temptation is almost impossible to resist, which is part of the reason advances were so popular for so long. Wave cash in front of a band, give them a shortcut to quitting their jobs, getting into the studio and out on the road, and most would take it. However, 99 percent of advance scenarios are equivalent to a deal with the devil. An artist is approached, usually one with great potential and a spectrum of possibilities in the industry, and is handed an advance that's deliberately unstructured. An advance that doesn't designate every dollar sets the artist up for failure in that they won't stay within the initial money guidelines and will then need more.

It's not just the record labels—it's talent agents, management groups, and even investors claiming to be labels or management that just has money. The music business is a glamorous world, and many outside of music want in. These investors, sometimes referred to as angels or even venture capitalists, will look to invest into a band in the hopes of a wild rate of return. Some producers and studios will even drop a little upfront money into projects, which should not always be accepted. As soon as money is given, it's expected back, with interest as well as profit.

So here comes the reality of it …

An advance, by anyone, is a loan. You're going to need to pay it back with interest and percentages of what you make for profit. From the advancers' view, they're helping to fast track your career. In turn, they're going to want a high interest rate on the advance as well percentages of the songs, publishing, and potentially future works. It's a tease, and most musicians don't look at the fine print. The average musician thinks only about the fact that he or she will have money to pay the bills and get into the studio and doesn't look at things in a realistic or organized fashion. The real question when it comes to advances and the stipulations surrounding them is:

Are you willing to give up what's being asked of you for the immediate money?

Look closely at the fine print. I guarantee, and I'm not someone who makes guarantees, you will do better struggling a little longer, working that day job that you hate, and continuing to push on if you want to maintain control of your career and your music. The moment you take that money, you become an investment to that third party, which more than likely will have written into the advance contract that it can now make decisions and call shots on your project. Once you take that money, you're contractually in bed with someone else.

Most likely that group won't have your vision for the music. They want to see you get big, and they want to make money off of you. These makeshift labels or investors also may not know the first thing about the business or how to make it work, and they may end up hurting you in the end. If you get sent to an awful studio or are pushed to do things in a way that they shouldn't be done, it may hurt any chances you had of success.

A big thing to remember: Money doesn't make careers. Just because you have a budget doesn't mean you'll be a success. You can still fail with a budget, just as you can with no budget at all. The difference is, if you take an advance, you could be sued by the investor, label, manager, or parties who gave you the advance.

Labels, even the major labels, sue artists on a regular basis for the failure to bring profit or return on investment. Many artists go bankrupt in the process and lose everything.

Even with your failure, the advancer may have written in rights to your music and could potentially take your own songs out from under you and have them recorded by another band. You may say this can never happen, but it can and it has. Check the contract carefully.

As the old saying goes, if it's too good to be true, it probably is. I can't stress it enough to stay away from advances. Fast money and shortcuts are not the way to success, and even if you achieve a short-term success or a boost in the beginning, the losses over time can outweigh the initial gain.

There are many major label artists who took that front side cash and not only had to pay it back with a high interest rate and hand over a percentage of first recording profits but also were oftentimes locked into giving or "sharing" profits from future works that the advancer is not even involved in.

My advice is to stay clear of advances, but if you do get a loan from a private investor, make sure the guidelines are written out clearly and fairly. Never sign anything without having it looked over by a lawyer. Just because you don't see the wording about something you wouldn't agree with doesn't mean it's not hidden in the contract in legalese that you may not catch. Find a music lawyer or entertainment attorney who can review the contracts for you.

The more patient you can be, the more attention to detail with which you can approach your career, the better the results will be. Stay in control; don't bring in a third party who is going to deviate and change the vision you have. Read between the lines on all deals. Be on the lookout for bad contracts, and don't compromise your dreams. Advances in most cases are the worst option, with the worst results down the line.

Music Contests ... and the Small Print

I'm sure you've all seen the different music contests around, promising if you send your song in to play some battle of the bands you could win great prizes and even a major recording contract! Oh yes, because real major label recording contracts are up for bids every day on MySpace and craigslist. Wait ... no. Come on people, when you read about a "major" label seeking talent on some network site, think for a second.

For starters, there are only a couple of major labels left, and just because people say they're going to take over the world doesn't mean they have the ability to do so. The same fact goes for these people who call themselves "A-list" producers. An A-list producer is Timberland, Daniel Lanois, Rick Rubin, T Bone Burnett, DJ Flash, Quincy Jones. These are the guys who sit down and make hit records and have the money behind them to make it so. If you're a part-time producer, a full-time producer, or record company owner, it doesn't make you

A list. Hell, I have hundreds of albums, and I wouldn't even consider myself a D list producer.

The point is, pay attention to the details; read between the lines. When you are contacted by e-mail or if you find out about a song-submitting contest, a battle of the bands or any kind of event where you have to submit something and could potentially win gear, win studio time, get a recording deal, get a management deal, or get something else, check it out!!

Warning signs and red flags for these types of contests include your having to pay some kind of fee to submit your music or join a site. Now, don't get me wrong; there are some honest events where part of the point is to promote a site that they make you join. For instance, as much as I don't find it all that great, sonic bids is something every band should have. It's not the greatest by far, but they do have a corner on aspects of the market for applying and submitting to certain festivals.

Hidden things can include rights to the song that you submit after the contest is over or even rights to the band. Imagine this, "Contest X" (which really exists out there) asks you to submit a song to a contest. It's a five-dollar entry fee, and you have to sign up through a certain music site. If you win, it advertises that you get a truckload of free brand-new gear and a "potential recording deal," as well as some booked showcases in high profile cities.

So, on the side that people didn't see, or actually should see in the "click here to agree to terms and conditions" section, which most just breeze over; was the fact that after eight thousand bands submitted their songs for this contest, this particular crew of three people had just made over forty thousand dollars in registration fees. Ten thousand went towards purchasing the gear they were going to give to the winner, and another ten thousand compensated their advertising expenses, Web creation, and basic overhead for a week to put this thing up. So before the contest winner was announced, they were already looking at a twenty-thousand-dollar profit for three guys doing about a week of work.

These three geniuses now also had signed rights from all the groups that had submitted songs to take 50 percent of their publishing if the song that was submitted went anywhere at any point. Yes, this was right in the terms that were breezed over and signed by all these bands. Once the winner was announced, they got them the gear and told them that they couldn't get a deal, but would be shopping them to some labels, which they tried to do since these guys now had a percentage of anything that the song could do. As they shopped, they were also going to take a percentage of the band as a whole, for finding them a deal. By the way, the band never got a deal.

Then last, the high profile showcases ... These guys booked three shows, one in LA, one in New York, and one in Atlanta and asked interns—yes, interns—to show up to these events. Then the three guys contacted the bands and told them they had to book their own flights, hotels, and transportation to show up to these shows. A back line was going to be supplied for them. The truth of that was that the three guys set up the headlining band to allow the winner to use their gear to, well ...basically, open for them. Some showcase, huh?

Of course the bands couldn't get to the showcases, but technically the contest did what it said it would, and they did get a whole bunch of free gear. So that's the win side of it. The lose side is, if that particular band ever goes anywhere with the song they submitted, a percentage is owed to the three guys, which was written into the contest rules as an exposure clause, for up to five years after the contest. Think that's nuts? Well it is, but you know what? The band agreed to it in the small print.

So in the end, our wonder boys of "Contest X" walked away with twenty thousand dollars profit for doing about two weeks of work, as well as rights and percentages of the winning band's song. Some other contests will actually take percentages if they get you to a final round or even a semi-final round. Pretty slick and pretty sleazy.

Not all contests are sleazy, and they're not all bad. My point is, check the fine print, and make sure you have all the details straight before you offer up your music and your works. Make sure you know what you're getting involved with over the long term before you go for a short-term win. You might get some cash prize or some gear, but you could lose out big time in the long run.

All and all whether it is a contest, a contact, or some type of connection that puts up a red flag, then raise the flag high and check it out to make sure everything balances out. In the music business, one of the core mistakes that seems to go across the spectrum is when artists jump headfirst into situations, contracts, agreements, or deals that they don't fully comprehend or understand. The short-term solutions end up creating the long-term problems. Be detailed, do your research, and check people, contracts, companies, and offers out till you fully understand them and have the information in writing that is clear, concise, and—well, to be honest—something that could support you in case things go wrong and you have to go to lawyers or to court.

Success in the music business of today comes down to the patience, the attention to detail, the follow-through, and the research of any contest, any deal, any offer by the artist. In the end, it is your responsibility, and it is your job to find out what is going on in the small print whether it is for contests, gig contracts, or anything else. You can blame everyone else for your mistakes, but when you make them, you end up being the one that has to pay. In the end, it's your career.

Conclusion

We are going to stop here. Well at least for now.

    You now have an outline and a blueprint with a number of applicable ideas with which to guide your career and your plan for success, but this is only a guide. The music industry takes more than your best. It's going to take your utmost. You'll have to be very honest with yourself about every step you take, every choice you make, and every action you execute. It will require your complete attention, your total effort, and your nonstop drive and determination to reach the goal of a self-sufficient and self-sustaining career in the music business.

    As I mentioned before, this is a guide filled with reference points but not every single one. It is a little hard to claim or tell someone, "This is how you do this, and everyone should do it the same way." Every situation is different, and that is a primary reason why I touch on and go in to limited detail in many of the subjects and do not go into exact detail. It would take thousands and thousands of more pages to go in to every detail, every point, and every scenario. Every artist and every band comes from a different background, not only musically but emotionally, creatively, financially, networking wise, connection wise, approach wise, and work wise. Still, when you skim the surface and bring out some of the key elements that everyone can relate to and needs to apply in some way, that is a start. It is also why I am calling this volume one. There will be more to come, more points, ideas, and discussions of other issues with more details.

In the beginning of the book, I have the quote stating, "It is going to be a harder road than you thought and short cutting, half-assing, and second-guessing will only hurt your career in the end.

Step Out, Step Up, and Step Forward. If you can't take those three steps, you don't belong in today's music business."

It may seem harsh. It may seem mean. But it's true. In a world where so many have given up on their dreams and in an industry where people are shortcutting with excuses and blame, that quote stands true.

As a society, we have allowed ourselves and each other to settle for less than what we dream, desire, and truly want. We have allowed ourselves to accept that everything happening around us is way too much for any person to deal with. We have justified why things are hard and why we can't achieve the dream, and we have bought right into our own lies. The blame, the excuses, and the reasons have allowed us to feel that it is okay to shortcut ourselves and dismiss our dreams.

If you are not doing all you can in the hardest times just like you claim you would do when it is that "right time," then you're getting nowhere fast. If you are shortcutting and skipping steps you know you shouldn't skip, they will catch up to you down the road. Stop making bad excuses.

Doing it the right way and in the smallest steps doesn't mean it will not be hard, and it doesn't mean that success will show up fast either. Still, if you are doing your best and working through the rough times while taking the correct steps, you have a greater chance of achieving those dreams and goals. You will also stand out because it is a rare few that are actually following through the right way, right now. Be one of them.

Leave the blame behind; the industry is messed up. Get away from the complaining; it is not moving your career forward in music. I like listening to comedians like Patton Oswald and Greg Proops complain. Still, they complain with a purpose, to be funny and to make you laugh. It's their job, not yours. Your complaining about the music industry is not moving your music careers forward.

You are smart enough, you can commit, you can follow through. Even if it takes changing the habits that have hurt you in the past, you can do it. One step at a time. It takes time to become successful just as it takes time to change unsuccessful habits.

Be patient. Be willing to learn. And be picky about what you learn. Make sure the information you are getting is from a source that is not only reputable and one you can trust but also up to date and up on the times and what is happening now.

It comes down to the seconds and the small decisions to make the best moves and actions for the longest, self-sustaining career possible. So make those plans, kick in the attention to detail across the board, build the foundation and the blueprint to build on so that it is sturdy and strong enough to support you through the bad times as well as be there to help you flourish in the good times.

You've got this. The dream is yours if you want it. I do not care who says you can't. From what I have seen and experienced, I know there are so many different avenues and approaches, so many different ways to develop, reach fans, and get your music out there, so many ways to move your music into places to create revenue. You will have to shift your mindsets; you may have to alter your dreams from the Grammy and millions to a more sustaining, long–term, and realistic successful path that can occur. You are going to have to study, work harder than you ever have before, and really learn what it means to be a multi-tasker. Problem solve the problems, plan the workload, and keep the dream in sight while realizing it will take a great deal of the less than fun stuff to make the dream come to fruition.

If this career is truly your dream and you just can't imagine yourself doing anything else, if the music is what you need to live and breathe, if you are prepared to do anything and everything you can, and if you never short cut and never take failure for an answer, then you will and you can.

The dream is yours. Now make it real. Good luck and best wishes.

LW

ABOUT THE AUTHOR

Loren Weisman is an accomplished music producer and consultant based in Seattle, Washington. Having worked on hundreds of albums, studio productions, and tours as both a drummer and producer, he gained a spectrum of insight on the music industry as a whole. Loren is also the founder of Brain Grenade Entertainment LLC.

www.lorenweisman.com

www.artistsguide.net